CIVIL WAR CAMPAIGNS of the 10th NEW YORK CAVALRY

With One Soldier's Personal Correspondence

to Dan - Happy reading!
Ron Matteson
Sept. 14, 2007

CIVIL WAR CAMPAIGNS of the 10th NEW YORK CAVALRY

With One Soldier's Personal Correspondence

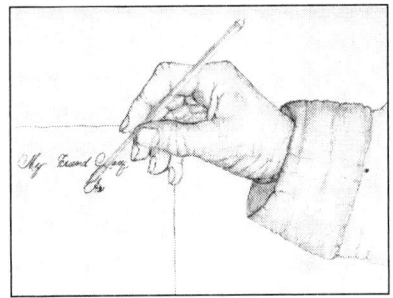

By Ron Matteson

Published by Lulu.com

Civil War Campaigns of the 10th New York Cavalry,
by Ron Matteson, ISBN 978-1-4303-2488-1

Published 2007 by Lulu.com

DEDICATION

This book is dedicated to all of the descendants of Justus and Mary Matteson in the hope that they will learn more about some of the sacrifices their ancestors have made in keeping our country safe, secure and functioning as the great nation that it is. The Civil War is a major example of individual dedication to duty, in that many extremely smart and dedicated individuals played key roles in military and civilian activities. In fact many military men went on to continue their public service in civilian roles - foreign representatives, elected congressmen at the state and national level etc. On the other hand many stayed in the military, serving in the Western United States as a stabilizing influence until civil authorities gained control.

ACKNOWLEDGEMENTS

Several people have contributed to the quality of this book. Kevin Crandall helped create the cover artwork. Suzanne Braselton and Peggy Gile contributed greatly to the quality of the book by proofreading and graphics arts suggestions.

DP Newton took us on a guided tour of the Belle Plain Landing area in Virginia, where the 10th New York Cavalry wintered in 1862-1863. He is the curator of the White Oak Civil War Museum in nearby Falmouth, where he also spent a considerable amount of time with us.

Much of the history of the Tenth New York Volunteer Cavalry that I have included in this book is taken from Preston's *History of the Tenth Regiment New York Volunteer Cavalry* [1]. Some of the sketches included in this book are also from Preston's book. I am deeply indebted to the Higginson Book Company for encouraging me to extract freely from this volume.

Finally, I would be remiss in my introductory comments if I didn't express my appreciation to my wife Juanita, for all the support, understanding and patience she has demonstrated as I spent the hours, days and weeks working on this project. This book has been accomplished only with her support, understanding and wonderful cooperation. I greatly appreciate all the help I always get from her, for whom all things seem possible.

PREFACE

This is what I call my "3rd Edition" of the two books on "Justus in the Civil War". I had access to letters between Justus Grant Matteson, my great-grandfather, and his future spouse Mary Louise Hatch, and transcribed them in the earlier editions for members of the family. In studying about some of the events in which he had been involved, I noted references to Noble Preston's *History of the Tenth Regiment New York Volunteer Cavalry* [1], published originally in 1892, and was able to get a reprint of his book from the Higginson Book Company in Salem, MA. My book is the result of reprinting the letters between Justus and Mary, with information added from Preston and other sources about the various activities in which he was engaged during the Civil War. The 10th New York Cavalry was engaged in many critical operations with the rest of the Army of the Potomac, fighting mostly in northern Virginia.

This project was very educational for me. History was not my best subject in high school, but I had some interest in the Civil War due to my great-grandfather's participation. In writing this book I learned a lot about the Civil War, especially the part of it that was carried out in Virginia, since my great-grandfather spent his entire time in the 10th New York Volunteer Cavalry in Virginia (excluding the expedition north in 1863 during the Gettysburg campaign and the momentous Battle of Gettysburg). I reviewed the battles of the Civil War in which Justus participated, and took trips to Virginia to see many of the areas in which he fought. I found this project to be extremely interesting and enjoyed it, but the joy was tempered greatly by the fact that almost one million fine young American men were casualties of this war.

Since Justus was in the cavalry he rode his horse during marches and some battles, giving him much more mobility than infantry soldiers. (He was raised on a farm, and hence was no stranger to the riding and caring of horses.) The infantry, on the other hand, walked everywhere they went and fought from fairly stagnant positions on the battlefields.

The activities of the armies of both sides were greatly constrained by geography and weather. They rarely did much during the two or three winter months of each of the years 1862-1865, except perhaps an occasional cavalry raid. There were railroads, but these were not often used for troop movements, and each side concentrated on destroying the railroads used by the opposite side.

The rivers of Virginia greatly dominated the movements of both the North and the South. The great Rappahannock River was the dividing line between Northern and Southern armies for much of the Civil War. Troop movements of any length involved crossing many small rivers (often called "runs", as in Bull Run, Mine Run etc.) and usually a few large ones. They used bridges if they existed and the enemy had not destroyed them; fords if these shallow zones existed and even resorted to swimming when required. On maps in this book will be found the Potomac, Rappahannock, Rapidan, Appomattox, Pamunkey, Po, Shenandoah, Occoquan, North and South Anna, James, Chickahominy, and Mattapony. These were just the largest ones. Countless other streams, creeks, and runs added to the difficulty of navigating through Virginia on horse or foot. The waterways had a tremendous part in planning the strategies of the various campaigns. Quite often plans were foiled due to flooding waterways, destroyed bridges, picketing forces on the opposite banks etc. There will be accounts in this book of cavaliers being stranded on the wrong side of a river, large campaigns being aborted due to rain, mud and overflowing rivers etc.

In creating this book I have included information from Preston's book. I have also included several official military reports written by military commanders after important battles and other events. There are tables near the beginning of each chapter giving a list of the events covered in the chapter, their dates, and a reference to their location on maps included in the chapter. There are also short reports on many of the engagements compiled by the National Park Service Civil War Sites Advisory Commission (CWSAC). This commission studied the battles of the Civil War, and selected 384 of the most significant, for each of which they wrote short reports included on the NPS Civil War web pages. I have included 25 of these reports in this book, these being the ones most pertinent to the 10th NY. There are many other web sites containing information about the 10th NY, which are referenced in the appropriate chapters and the Bibliography. Several other books and web sites were used to supplement the information, and are also included in the references at the end of each chapter and the Bibliography at the end of the book. The events, battles, campaigns and engagements involving the 10th New York Cavalry are well-known by Civil War buffs and are exciting to read.

Justus Grant Matteson was born on December 21, 1839, making him twenty-two years old when he enlisted with the unit from Solon, New York. His father and mother were Cyrus French Matteson and Sally Baker Matteson. They had one other child, Clarissa Adelia Matteson, called Adelia or Delia in the letters. His parents and sister remained in Solon during the war. Justus's father later married again, to Frances Gilles. They had a daughter Thenia, born on July 7, 1878, who of course would be a half-sister to Justus.

Mary (Mat, Mate, Matie, Molly as Justus called her in various letters) and Justus were married on July 4, 1868 and had three children - Frank Leroy Matteson (this author's grandfather), Maude Bell Matteson and Alta May Matteson.

In the Justus and Mary letters included in this book the original spelling was retained. Some poor spelling may be due to limited education, some may be due to the desire to get a fast letter off before the next move and some may be due to local colloquialisms. An occasional period or other punctuation has been added for clarity. Question marks, blanks etc. have been used where original writings are indecipherable. Apparently punctuation, like periods at the end of sentences and capitalizations of the first words of sentences, were not used as much in those days. Frequently it is not possible to determine the end of one sentence and the beginning of the next one, except by the context. Note that it is very likely that more than the 60 letters included in this book were exchanged among Justus, Mary and others, which did not survive the war period.

Justus was distantly related to Ulysses S. Grant, a fact which he ignores in his letters, and a fact of which he may not even have been aware.

In this book references are annotated in the text where appropriate by square brackets: [4], and listed at the end of each chapter. There are also occasional short insertions and explanatory notes in material from other sources and these are also enclosed in square brackets: [explanatory note included here]. Maps, tables and figures are referenced by two numbers, the chapter number and the sequential number of the item: Map 2.3 (the third map in Chapter 2), Figure 7.5 (the fifth figure in Chapter 7) etc.

Primary insertions from other works are indented about one-half inch. Secondary insertions (quotes from other sources included in the primary insertions) are indented an additional one-half inch.

Ronald Grant Matteson
Walworth, NY 14568
2007

Reference

[1] Preston, Noble D., *History of the Tenth Regiment New York Volunteer Cavalry*, New York, NY: D. Appleton and Company, 1892; reprinted by Higginson Book Company, Salem, MA in 1998 (710 pages).

CONTENTS

CHAPTER 1
Rounding Up the Boys in 1862

"See the rascals! Go for 'em, boys!" Judson Kilpatrick

Background of this Book

This book describes the operations of Company L of the 10th Regiment of New York Volunteer Cavalry in the Civil War. (In this book the Regiment may be referred to as the "10th New York" or "10th NY".) The narration features transcriptions of letters transmitted back and forth between Justus Grant Matteson, a private in Company L for over thirty-four months, and Mary Louise Hatch, a seamstress in a shop in Homer, New York. Justus and Mary were schoolmates in Solon, New York, a farming community near Cortland. Justus was in the U.S. Cavalry from September 7, 1862 until July 19, 1865. He spent most of this period in Virginia as part of the Army of the Potomac. His actions included the following major events, as well as many of the 150 other actions involving the 10th New York:

> Fredericksburg (Chapter 1)
> Stoneman's Raid on Richmond (Chapter 2)
> Brandy Station (Chapter 3)
> Gettysburg Campaign (Chapters 3, 4)
> Bristoe Campaign (Chapter 5)
> Mine Run Campaign (Chapter 5)
> Wilderness Campaign (Chapter 6)
> Sheridan's Raid on Richmond (Chapter 6)
> Cold Harbor (Chapter 7)
> Sheridan's Trevillian Raid (Chapter 7)
> Siege operations against Petersburg (Chapter 8)
> Appomattox Campaign and Lee's surrender (Chapter 9)

The book will describe many of the activities of the 10th NY as we look at the letters and activities of Justus Matteson. Descriptions of many of these activities come from the book *History of the Tenth*

Regiment New York Volunteer Cavalry, written by Noble D. Preston [1], one of the members of the regiment. Noble Preston was Regimental Commissary Officer, and was promoted through the enlisted ranks to become commissioned as a First Lieutenant before the war was over. At the engagement at Trevillian Station, VA on June 11, 1864 Preston "voluntarily led a charge in which he was severely wounded", and for which he was awarded the Congressional Medal of Honor. He also served as the *ad hoc* historian of the Regiment.

Preston's book is a detailed account of the 10th New York. After the war was over Preston spent a lot of time gathering first-hand accounts from many of the participants in the various engagements, battles, raids, pickets, etc. in which the 10th New York was involved. That is one reason that it took until 1892 to get the book published (Figure 1.1). This book also contains rosters, organizations, stories of prison life and escapes and a few official reports by cavalry commanders.

While this book will describe many of the activities of the 10th Regiment as a whole, the emphasis will be on Company L of the Regiment, and operations in which Justus Matteson was involved. The letters by Justus and Mary are exciting, in that they give first-hand accounts of several historic events, both military and civilian: floods in Homer and Cortland; diphtheria epidemics; battles of the Army of the Potomac; Lee's surrender to Grant on April 9, 1865; Lincoln's assassination on April 14, 1865; etc. In addition, this book adds descriptive information about some of the battles, engagements, and campaigns in which Company L and the rest of the 10th NY were involved, thanks to Colonel Preston and other sources. (Preston seems to have received an honorary promotion to Colonel after the war.)

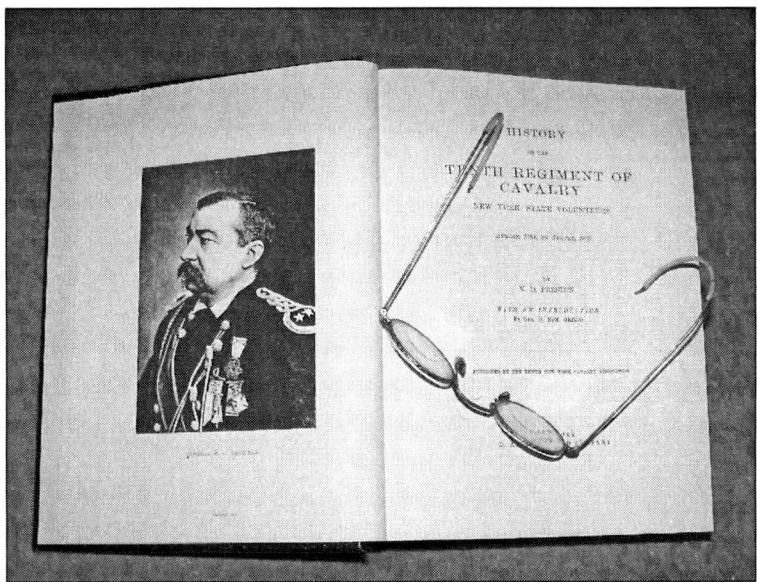

Figure 1.1 *History of the Tenth Regiment of Cavalry New York State Volunteers*, by Noble D. Preston

Missions of the Cavalry

During the first two years of the Civil War the Federal cavalry was subordinated in many ways to its potential roles. Sometimes cavalry units were assigned to a general officer to serve as messengers between the general and his staff ("gallopers", see sketch in Figure 1.4), to carry orders during battles, to help units keep track of adjacent units etc. Another of the common mistakes in those early days of the war was to use cavalry as infantry support, so that the latter used to shout derisively "There's going to be a fight, boys! The cavalry's coming back!" Eventually more definitive missions were developed exclusively for cavalry units [2]:

1. Reconnaissance and counter-reconnaissance screening: reconnaissance was the key to effective knowledge of the enemy by military commanders, and counter-reconnaissance was used to screen military movements from enemy commanders.

2. Defensive, delaying actions: used by the cavalry to screen retreating infantry, as in the critical retreat of the Confederate Army from Gettysburg.

3. Pursuit and harassment of defeated enemy forces: performed superbly by the Union Cavalry in the pursuit of Robert E. Lee during the Appomattox Campaign.

4. Offensive actions: most frequently employed against enemy cavalry, as in the battles of Brandy Station and Yellow Tavern.

5. Long-distance raiding against enemy lines of communications, supply depots, railroads etc.: Stoneman's Raid on Richmond, Sheridan's Raid on Richmond, Sheridan's Trevillian Raid, the Bristoe Campaign, the Mine Run Campaign, the Hick's Ford Raid, etc. Most of these raids, although irritating, had a relatively short-term effect on the overall war effort.

Recruiting the First Two Battalions

A regiment in the Army is a unit that is usually called upon to act as an entity and become a cohesive group of soldiers. They usually stay together and become very well bonded for a lengthy period of time. Higher levels come and go, through various organizations and reorganizations, but the regimental group sticks together. The regiment is usually called on to enter a large battle or campaign as a whole.

At the start of the Civil War, the U.S. had only 5 regiments of cavalry. Between 1861 and 1865, 272 regiments of cavalry were raised for the Union, and 137 regiments were raised in the South.

A company, for example Company L of the 10th New York, is one of the 12 companies that make up a regiment. The company is therefore a tightly bound group of soldiers, which is usually called upon in whole to perform missions not requiring the entire regiment. The regimental commander is usually a colonel (eagle insignia).

The structure of a regiment in the Civil War called for approximately 1200 men, consisting of 12 companies of 100 men each. Rarely did it actually have this many cavaliers ready for duty, however, due to expiration of enlistments, illness, battle casualties, capture, temporary duty assignments, etc. 35-50 men per company and 350-500 per regiment were more typical. The longer the campaign the smaller the unit became, due to the attrition factors mentioned above. In fact, Preston indicated that during the active campaigns of 1863 and 1864 the regiment's number for duty was frequently reduced to between 75 and 250 men (from the assigned value of 1200), even though more than 2100 men served in the 10th New York at various times during the four years of its existence.

A regiment was divided into three battalions of four companies each. A battalion, in turn, was often divided into two squadrons of two companies each. At the higher levels, a brigade normally consists of three or four regiments plus some artillery support ("horse artillery"), and was commanded by a brigadier general (one star).

The 10th Regiment was formed in 1861. Company A was formed in Syracuse and mustered in on September 27, 1861. Companies B, C, D, E, F, G and H were mustered in at Elmira in December 1861. These first eight companies formed the nucleus of the 10th NY and initiated their training at Gettysburg, PA. Little did they know that the pivotal battle of the Civil War would be fought on the outskirts of this very village in mid-1863. They would return for this battle, where they would provide key support for the Army of the Potomac.

After formation and training these first eight companies (two battalions) guarded railroads and the city of Washington, DC until the other four companies joined the regiment.

Preston describes the formation of the first two battalions as follows [3]:

> Major John C. Lemmon, of Buffalo, received authority from the War Department, under date of August 3, 1861, to raise a regiment of infantry in the State of New York, to be ready for service by the 2d of September - one month from the time authority was granted for recruiting it. ... [The "infantry"

designation was later changed to "cavalry" for some unknown reason; either the original designation of "infantry" was a mistake, or the original intent was later changed to cavalry, due to pressure from some part of the War Department organization. Another attempt to raise a cavalry regiment, the Morgan Cavalry, failed; and the recruits from this effort became part of the 10th; this may have helped the switch from infantry to cavalry.]

The early recruiting culminated as a two-battalion organization, recruiting was begun and zealously prosecuted in various places in western New York. The Porter Guard Cavalry was named in honor of General Peter B. Porter, of Niagara Falls, who had been a distinguished officer in the War of 1812, and who afterward served as Secretary of War under President John Quincy Adams.

Early in August recruiting offices were opened in Buffalo, Syracuse, and other points. Company A, Captain M. Henry Avery, of Syracuse, was the first to complete its rolls and present itself for muster into the United States service. ...

The recruits in these first two battalions were from Syracuse, Jordan, Jamesville, and Tully, in Onondaga County; McGrawville, Cortland, Cincinnatus, and Freetown, in Cortland County; Red Creek and Victory, in Wayne County; Fulton, in Oswego County; Chittenango, in Madison County; Buffalo, in Erie County; and Elmira, in Chemung County; Erie, Niagara, Chemung Counties; Buffalo, and Niagara Falls.

Preston continues describing the organization of the 10th New York [4]:

The numerical designation of the regiment as the "Tenth New York Cavalry" was announced by the Adjutant-General of the State on the 12th of December. ...

Companies B, C, D, E, F, G, and H were mustered into service on the 23d of December (Company A had been mustered on the 27th of September), and the regiment was in readiness to leave the rendezvous. On the 24th of December, they were marched to the depot and departed by train for Gettysburg, PA.

After training, the regiment left Gettysburg for Perryville, MD, on the 7th of March, 1862, where it arrived the next day. On the 26th they were transferred to Havre de Grace, on the opposite side of the Susquehanna River. The regiment was assigned to the guarding of the P.W. & B.R.R. for a while, and some shifted to Baltimore. Horses and equipments were issued to the regiment in Baltimore, and on the 15th of August it marched to Washington and encamped near Bladensburg, where it received its full complement of horses and arms.

Recruiting the Third Battalion

Company L, Justus Matteson's company, and Companies I and K were mustered in Elmira in October 1862 and joined the regiment in December 1862. Company M mustered in November 1862 through January 1863 and joined the regiment in February 1863.

Formation of Company L

Captain Alvah D. Waters' Company L was organized on October 24, 1862, and mustered into service on the 29th of the same month. Justus Matteson came from Solon in Cortland County. Other members of Company L came from Cortland, Taylor, Virgil, Freetown, Homer and Marathon in Cortland County; Lewiston and Wheatfield in Niagara County; Buffalo, Collins and Aurora in Erie County; Otto and Persia in Cattaraugus County; Watkins in Schuyler County; Lyons in Wayne County; Pitcher in Chenango County; Big Flats in Sullivan County; and Elmira in Chemung County. The original organization of the company was as follows:

COMPANY L:

Captain Alvah D. Waters

1st Lieutenant, George Vanderbilt
2d Lieutenant, Burton B. Porter

Sergeants:

Frederick A. Gee (First Sergeant)
Jason L. Reed (Quartermaster Sergeant)
Franklin L. King (Commissary Sergeant)
Joshua W. Davis, David H. Rines, Llewellyn P. Norton,
Andrew J. Lyman, Royal Miller

Corporals:

Orrin C. Dann, John R. Maybury, Thomas H. Doolittle,
Ballard Kinney, John W. Mathews, Thomas K. Ashton,
Charles E. Blauvelt, Walter H. Angel

Abram G. Van Hozen, Walter Green (Teamsters)
Levi D. Ruddock, William Law (Farriers)
Kirtland Herrick (Saddler)
John Traver (Wagoner)

See Appendix A for a list of privates in the original formation of Company L. The original number of men recruited was 100, but 50 others joined the company at various times during the war as replacements for members wounded, killed, captured, deserted, or those whose terms of enlistment had expired. The original number of men assigned to the entire 10th New York was 1,118, but a total of 2,101 served, for the reasons mentioned above.

Cavalry Corps Evolution and Commanders

The Cavalry Corps evolved through many changes in structure and leadership. An outline of these changes follows, especially as they affected the 10th New York Cavalry.

Bayard's Cavalry Brigade Composition October 1862

In October 1862 the following was the composition of the cavalry brigade commanded by Brigadier General George D. Bayard:

First Pennsylvania Cavalry, Colonel Owen Jones.
Tenth New York Cavalry, Lieutenant-Colonel William Irvine.
Second New York Cavalry, Major H.E. Davies, Jr.
First New Jersey Cavalry, Lieutenant-Colonel Joseph Karge.
Battery C, Third United States Artillery, Captain H.G. Gibson.

These regiments did not serve together in the same brigade for the entire war, but were closely allied and maintained a close feeling of friendship for one another.

Cavalry Division, Army of the Potomac

Organized July 1862
Commander:
George Stoneman, Brigadier General, July 1862-January 1863

Cavalry Corps

Created and organized February 1863, broken up May 1865

Corps Commanders:
Geo. Stoneman, Major General, February 1863-May 1863
A. Pleasonton, Brigadier General, June 1863-March 1864
P. H. Sheridan, Major General, April 1864-May 1865
William Wells, Brevet Brigadier General, June 1865

Division and Brigade Commanders of organizations in which the 10th NY Cavalry was placed:

March 1862 to October 1862
Middle Department, guarding railroads, defenses of Baltimore and Washington, DC; Col. J.M. Davies, commanding.

Civil War Campaigns of the 10th New York Cavalry

October 1862 to February 1863
Cavalry brigade, Army of the Potomac (AOP)- BG George D. Bayard
(until killed in action on December 13, 1862; then BG D.McM. Gregg).

February 1863 to June 14, 1863
3rd Division, Cavalry Corps: BG D.McM. Gregg
1st Brigade: Colonel Judson Kilpatrick
(The 10th New York was brigaded with the First Maine and Second
New York Harris Light cavalry regiments.)

June 14, 1863 to August 1863
2nd D;ivision, Cavalry Corps: BG D.McM. Gregg
3rd Brigade: Col. Judson Kilpatrick

August 1863 to May 17, 1864
2nd Division: BG D.McM. Gregg
2nd Brigade: Col. J. Irvin Gregg (cousin of D.McM. Gregg)

May 17, 1864 to February 1865
2nd Division: BG D.McM. Gregg (resigned Feb. 3, 1865)
1st Brigade: Col. J. Irvin Gregg

February 1865 to May 1865
2nd Division: Col. J. Irvin Gregg (acting)
1st Brigade: Col. H.E. Davies, Jr.

May 1865 to July 1865
2nd Division: Col. J. Irvin Gregg (acting)
1st Brigade: BG M.H. Avery

On July 10, 1865 the regiment was consolidated with the 24th NY
Volunteer Cavalry, and the consolidated force received the designation
"1st Provisional Regiment NY Volunteer Cavalry."
During its service the regiment lost by death a total of 537 men.
Killed in action: 5 officers and 54 enlisted men. Died from wounds in
action: 23 officers and 228 enlisted men. Died from disease and other

causes: 1 officer and 151 enlisted men. Lost by capture: 15 officers and 214 enlisted men, some of whom were paroled or exchanged.

(This book is mostly based on the chronology of the 10th Regiment; whenever there is a letter in existence between Justus Matteson and Mary Hatch or one of his other kin, that letter will be inserted in accordance with the current time frame. The first letter preserved, from Mary to Justus, follows.)

Friend Jut,

The toils of the day are past, and I set myself to answer the last letter I received from you the other day. But how different your thoughts must be from what they were when that letter was written. Then you were a scholar, now, but they tell me you are a soldier. It is right that you should go, I suppose but it seems hard to have our friend leave us and especially when they are in so much dainger.

But your school has been short but I hope that you will return to your friends and then you can finish your education.

I thought that you would call before you went but the time is short that you can stay with your friends. But oh, I cannot think that all of our friends are going never to return. We must not think so, we must look at the bright side and do all of the good we can. But if you come home you must call and see me if I am in town. But one word of advice, be careful of your health. you know that you are not very healthy, and above all do keep good company. there will be a great many of you together, some good and some bad. Mr. Ireland will hand you this. I think that you will find him a good mate if you make his acquaintance. Do not think that you will be forgotten in your southern home or if you fall on the battlefield, no never. the boys that leave their pleasant home and friends, to free their and our country can never be forgotten, no never. If the Cortland boys are sick we will come and take care of them if we are needed.

Your picture I shall keep and cherish as the face of a friend and one that I may never see again. you see that I am inclined to be sad tonight. I cannot help it. I should think that I was heartless if I could feel gay. The happy hours that I have spent in your society will be remembered, the hours that we spent in school, spelling schools and all will be remembered, and especially the evening that my sily tongue made me so much trouble, but that is all past and more trouble comes.

But some of these days when you have nothing to do take your pen and write, and write to Matie. she will be glad to hear from you. And oh if we never meet again remember that it is a better world above.

I see that I have made such poor work writing but I have had something else to do this summer besides writing; excuse all mistakes and accept this from your friend.

Matie L. H.

September 18

As I have not had a chance to send this to you and as you are in the place I will write a few more lines and tell you that I am well. Nell will give this to you, Mr. Ireland has concluded not to go. Be a good boy, and write as often as you have time.

Matie

Summary of 1862 Actions of the 10th New York

The 10th New York was engaged in several operations in 1862. These engagements are listed in Table 1.1. Company L, due to its late arrival, was only involved in two engagements in this list, the Battle of Fredericksburg and the skirmish at Kanky's Store, just south of Dumfries. Other engagements of the 10th New York in addition to the ones listed in Table 1.1 included Sulphur Springs, Frying Pan, Germantown and Centreville in late August and early September.

Map #	Events	Dates - 1862
	Chesapeake Bay, near Back River, MD	April 4
2	Leesburg	Sept. 17
3	Upton's Hill	Sept. 18
5	Centreville	Nov. 2
6	Aldie	Nov. 2
7	Thoroughfare Gap	Nov. 2
8	Salem	Nov. 2
9	Warrenton	Nov. 2
4	Rappahannock Station	Nov. 15
10	Morrisville	Nov. 15
16	United States Ford	Nov. 15
15	Brooks Station	Dec. 5
11	Fredericksburg	Dec. 10
12	Falmouth	Dec. 10
13	Belle Plain (Camp Bayard)	Dec. 11-15
14	Kanky's Store	Dec. 12

Table 1.1 1862 Engagements of the 10th New York Cavalry

A table like Table 1.1 is given near the front of each chapter in this book. It lists actions of the 10th NY described in the chapter and the date(s) of the action. It also shows a "Map #" which is the annotation of the place of the action on one of the maps in the chapter. All locations are in Virginia unless otherwise noted.

Capture of Schooner on Back River, Maryland

On the 4th of April, while Company A was guarding the bridge over Back River near Baltimore, the troopers made an important capture of a schooner laden with recruits and material for the Southern Confederacy. (The Back River runs east through the northern suburbs of Baltimore and into Chesapeake Bay.)

Regimental headquarters were transferred to Patterson Park, Baltimore on the 25th of June, where the regiment was quartered, except Companies A, C and G, which remained to guard the important bridges on the line of the P.W. & B.R.R. Horses and equipment were issued to the regiment while here, and on the 15th of August it marched to Washington, encamping near Bladensburg where it received its full complement of horses and arms. From this point a detail was sent to New York State to recruit the third battalion. Companies I, K and L of the new battalion joined the old organization in the field at Brooke's Station, VA [#15 on Map 1.2], December 5, 1862 and Company M joined at Camp Bayard, near Belle Plain, VA [#13 on Map 1.2] about a month later.

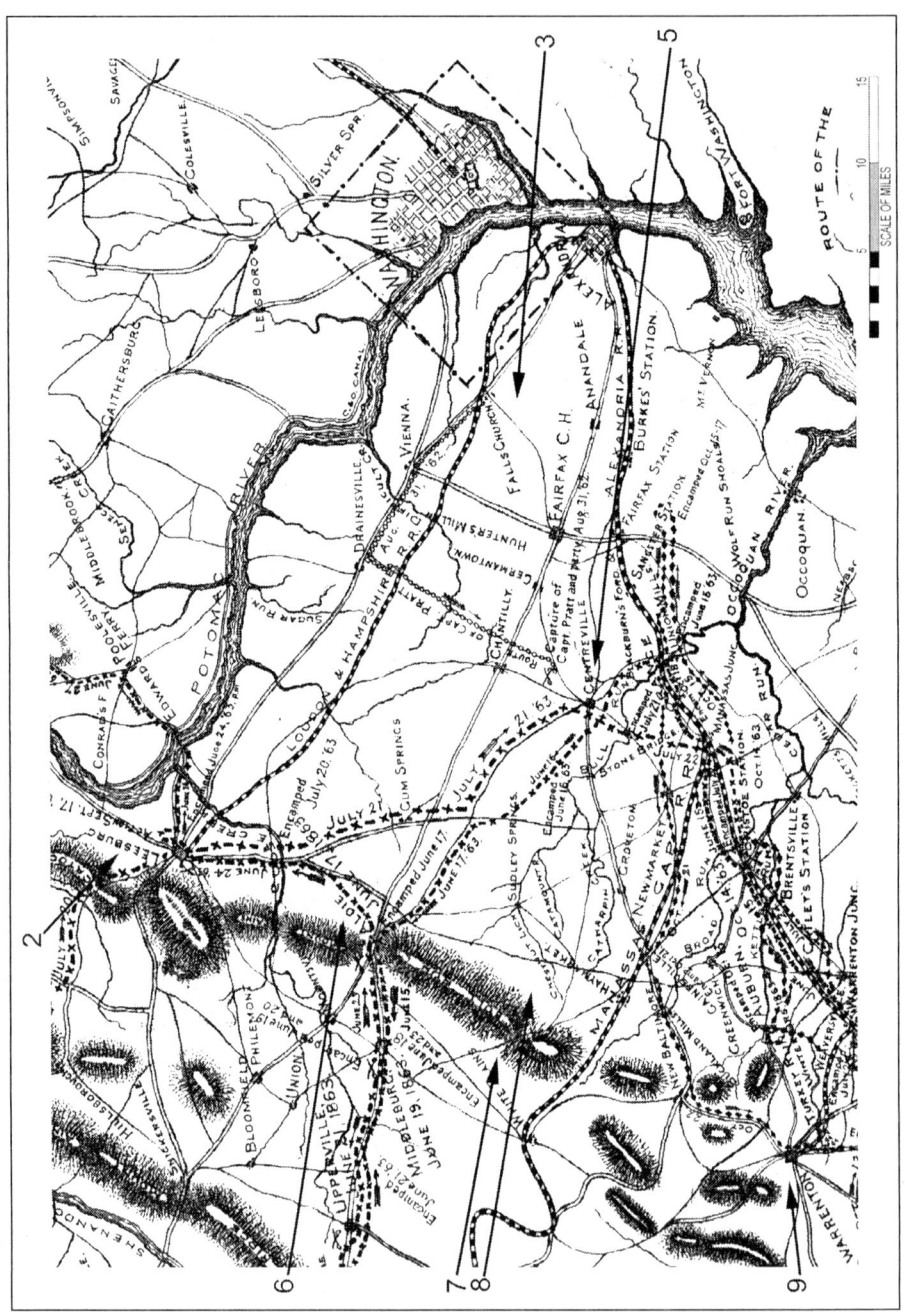

1.1 Tenth New York, Leesburg to Warrenton

Battle of Leesburg

Prior to the arrival of the third battalion some of the men went up towards Leesburg [#2 on Map 1.1] for reconnaissance. Preston tells how the Battle of Leesburg developed. This was the biggest contest in which the 10th New York was involved up to this time [5]:

> On the 14th of September, ten men under command of Sergeant Edson of Company D made a reconnaissance in the direction of Leesburg, going beyond Goose Creek without encountering the enemy.
>
> The first exchange of courtesies the Regiment had with the rebels was at Leesburg on the 17th of September 1862. Lieutenant-Colonel Kilpatrick, of the Harris Light Cavalry, with his own regiment and three companies of the Tenth under Major Avery, left Fort Buffalo, near Upton's Hill [#3 on Map 1.1], on the 16th day of September, for Leesburg. Lieutenant Weed, who had been ill in Washington, arrived in camp the day after the expedition left, and at once followed.
>
> Coming up with the Regiment, he took command of one squadron, Captain Bliss commanding the other. On reaching Leesburg, the latter officer with his squadron was sent forward into the town to ascertain whether or no there was any one at home to receive company, and if he was successful in finding them, to fall back and so induce them to come out. When Bliss deployed they seemed annoyed and came at him viciously. He retired before them until they came in range of our battery, when Bang! Bang! went the guns, and several shells were landed in their midst. Lieutenant Weed was ordered to charge and, as the boys went forward with a cheer, they saw the rebel cavalry massed in the streets. Kilpatrick, taking in the excitement of the occasion, had started forward when the charge was made.
>
> As the command reached a little knoll, giving the boys a good view of the enemy, Kilpatrick rose in his stirrups and

exclaimed "See the rascals! Go for 'em, boys!" and, with these words ringing in their ears, the boys went for 'em. The rebels fired a few shots and broke, followed closely by Weed and his men through and out of the town. As they drove the cavalry before them, a force of infantry from behind a fence on their flank opened fire, wounding seven and capturing one man. Lieutenant Weed seized a carriage which was just leaving town, containing "Massa and Missus," as the old darky said, and into this he had four of the wounded placed and taken back, the others being able to get away without help. A number of arms were destroyed and a quantity of ammunition and a fine large Confederate flag fell into our hands.

In addition to the captured and wounded from the Tenth, already mentioned, the charging party lost one horse killed and fifteen wounded. Among several close calls experienced, the poncho of Sergeant H.E. Hayes, of Company A, rolled and strapped to the front of his saddle, was pierced by a rebel bullet. There were a large number of the enemy's wounded and sick lying in extemporized hospitals about the town, but they were left undisturbed.

Of this engagement Corporal E.W. Stark writes as follows:

> When near Leesburg we were ordered to support a battery. I think there were but two companies, Company A being one. After a few shells had been thrown among the rebels we were ordered to charge through the town. I was in second rank. As we went through the town, my horse being a good runner, I in some manner became mixed up in the front rank; in fact, I got some ways ahead of the rest of the boys, and commenced firing. My horse acted so I was compelled to turn him about to prevent being carried into the midst of the rebels, who were strung across the road. The balance of our command had halted and were pouring in a rapid, well-

directed fire, which was being returned with spirit by the rebels. Lieutenant Weed, who was in command, ordered us to fall back. There was a good board fence on one side of the street and the rebels had taken position behind it, and, as they were perfectly protected, we were compelled to retire from the terrible fire we were subjected to. It was a miraculous thing that more of our men were not hit, as we were directly abreast and close to them, and they had but to take deliberate aim at us through the cracks in the fence. As we were falling back I received a flesh-wound in the arm, near the elbow. My horse was shot twice, but neither wound disabled him. I think William Wilbur was wounded in the shoulder. Joe Cook, our bugler, had his horse killed, and as the horse went down Cook was caught under him and fell into the hands of the rebels. Cook had a fine live turkey strapped to his saddle. Bugler and gobbler were both gathered in. I do not recollect who was wounded besides those mentioned. No attempt was made to follow us.

Sergeant W.W. Williams, of Company D, after paying a handsome tribute to Sergeant Truman C. White (afterward lieutenant), says that on the way to Leesburg the command halted at Drainesville (about 14 miles northwest of Upton's Hill) and sent out scouting parties, and while waiting there some one of the men found a beautiful blooded seal-brown stallion, silver mane and tail, which appeared to be much admired by Colonel Kilpatrick. He says when the detachment reached Leesburg, part of the command took one street and part another, and when they had got fairly into the town the rebels opened a brisk fire on them from the buildings, from behind fences, etc., and someone gave the order to left about wheel, which was done in good order, but very lively. Sergeant W.J. Robb came rushing back, brandishing a revolver, and threatened to shoot the men if they attempted further skeddaddling! On matters being explained, Robb joined in the falling back.

When returning to camp at Upton's Hill, an old lady made a piteous complaint to Colonel Kilpatrick that his men had taken everything she had for herself and daughter to live on. The boys were all pretty well encumbered with the "free-will offerings" of the citizens along the route, and Kilpatrick left an aide at the old lady's gate to solicit contributions from them. The result was the lady was presented with poultry and provisions sufficient to supply a good-sized division of hungry Yankees. "Freely ye have received, freely give." The Bible injunction was literally and liberally followed.

The following are the reports of Colonel Davies, of the Leesburg engagement:

UPTON HILL, VA, *September 18, 1862*

Lieutenant-Colonel McKEEVER:

I have a message from the expedition I sent out. Will be back tonight. They found at Leesburg one regiment of infantry and a battalion of cavalry, which they drove out of the town after a sharp action, in which the enemy's loss was considerable. One flag and a number of prisoners were taken. Our loss was but slight. The Tenth New York Cavalry behaved very gallantly.

J.M. Davies, *Colonel Commanding Brigade*

UPTON HILL, VA, *September 19, 1862*

Colonel Kilpatrick gives great credit to the admirable manner in which our guns were served, and the conduct of the Tenth New York Cavalry, which twice charged through the town.

J. M. DAVIES, *Colonel Commanding Brigade*

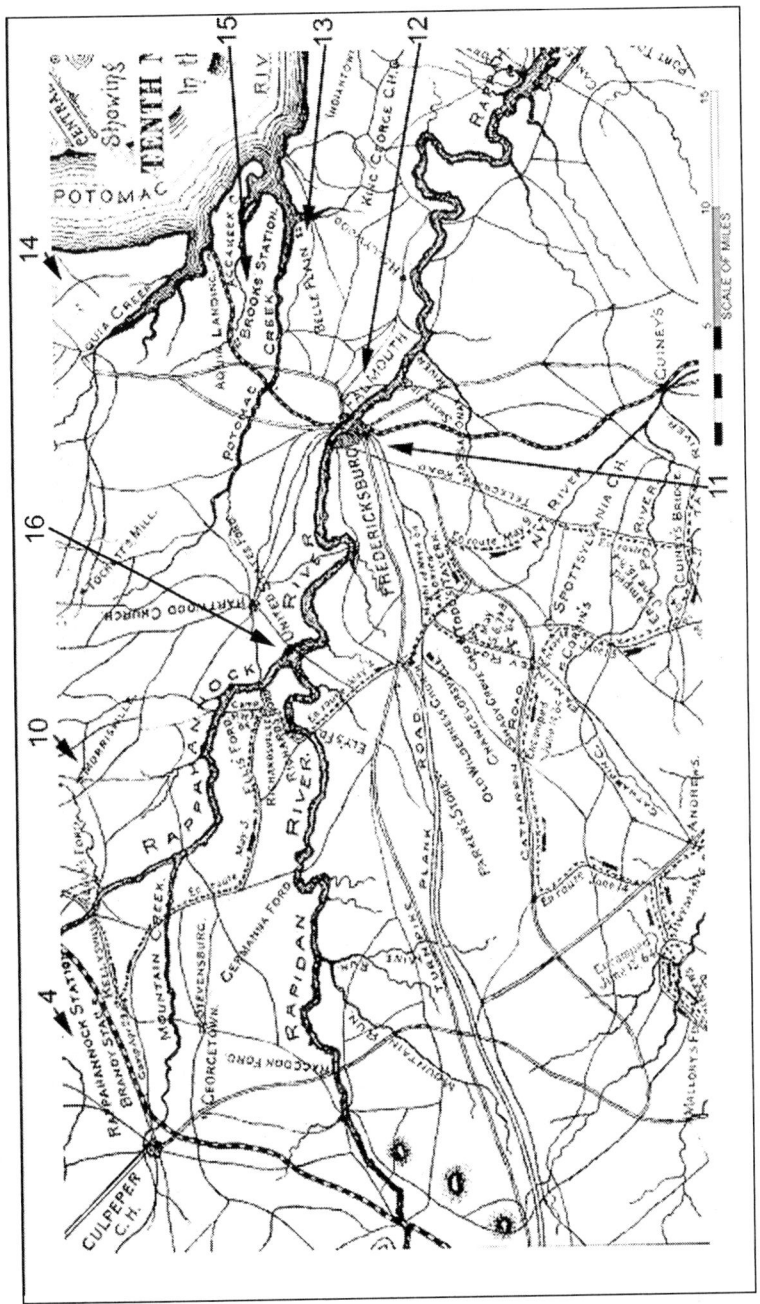

Map 1.2 Tenth New York, Rappahannock Station to Belle Plain

Battle of Rappahannock Station

A few weeks later the entire brigade went towards the Rappahannock River [#4 on Map 1.2], resulting in another battle with Confederate forces. Preston describes the action [6]:

> Bayard's brigade took the lead in the advance of the Army of the Potomac to the Rappahannock River. The 10th NY broke camp at Centreville [#5 on Map 1.1] on the 2nd of November 1862 and reached Rappahannock Station on the 7th, where it went into camp. The route was via Aldie [#6 on Map1.1], Thoroughfare Gap [#7 on Map 1.1], Salem [#8 on Map 1.1], and Warrenton [#9 on Map 1.1]. Skirmishing with the enemy's cavalry was continued nearly all the way. No large bodies of Confederates were encountered, however. ...
>
> The Regiment was encamped just east of Rappahannock Station the 15th of November 1862, when Captain Peck was ordered to report with his company, consisting of sixteen men, to Major Harhaus, of the Second New York Cavalry, at Morrisville [#10 on Map1.2], for picket duty. Upon arriving there he was sent to United States Ford [#16 on Map1.2] on the Rappahannock River, where he was directed to remain on picket. He reached the Gold Mines, a small settlement a short distance from the ford, just at sundown, and established his reserve about a half-mile from the little hamlet in the direction of the river, sending a sergeant and two or three men to the river, scouting. Sergeant W.N. Harrison and Private John Hicks were sent at the same time some distance in the opposite direction on picket. On the morning of the 16th Captain Peck stationed Sergeant Guy Wynkoop with a corporal and three men at United States Ford, leaving but nine men on the reserve, including Orderly Sergeant Bonnell and Sergeant John C. Reynolds. During the forenoon the Captain, with Sergeant Bonnell, started in the direction of Fredericksburg [#11 on Map 1.2] on a reconnaissance, taking Harrison and Hicks along as they came to the point where they were stationed. The party

returned about noon, Harrison and Hicks resuming their places on picket. From the time of the arrival of Captain Peck and his little party on the ground there had been a feeling of uneasiness, and although this reconnaissance developed nothing new, it did not in the least allay the anxiety of the men. They were about twelve miles from the main reserve at Morrisville, and their small numbers and the condition of the country invited a visit from the enemy, who were fully informed by the citizens of the exact condition of affairs. Every precaution was taken against surprise, but with so few men it was impossible to successfully resist any sudden attack of a superior force.

About noon a body of forty or fifty rebels came charging down upon Harrison and Hicks. As they were clothed in blue, Harrison at first sight supposed they were a party sent from Morrisville to relieve Captain Peck; but the "yell" admonished him of his error, and springing to his horse he mounted just as a Southern Goliath in stature rushed upon him with a demand to surrender. Harrison declined the invitation, tickled his horse in the ribs with his spurs, and started for the reserve. A scrub race followed between him and his would-be interviewer, but Harrison's nag came under the wire several lengths ahead. Hicks was unable to get to his horse, and was taken prisoner.

As soon as Captain Peck heard the firing, he ordered the men on reserve to fall back to an open field close by, taking a bridle path through the thicket. Reaching a gateway a stand was made, and as the rebels came charging down, closely pursuing Harrison, the Company H boys discharged their carbines into their ranks, causing a short halt. The little band contested the ground across the open; but soon another party of thirty or forty rebels opened fire from the opposite direction, forcing them to abandon their position around an old house. Captain Peck then called out to the men to take care of themselves as best they could, and he himself made an attempt to reach the woods, to accomplish which his horse would be compelled to leap a fence; this he obstinately refused to do, and the Captain slid from his back, over the fence, just in time to avoid capture.

In the scramble from the house six of our brave fellows were made prisoners, among the number being Lansing Bonnell, who received a frightful saber cut across the right side of his face and head, and Joe Brearley, who had a slight bullet wound. Chet Wilcox gained the woods in safety and hastened to the ford to warn Sergeant Wynkoop of his danger. Sergeants Bonnell and Reynolds, and Privates Lorenzo Allen and Lemuel Barker ran the gauntlet safely, passing through the gate where several rebels were stationed, while close behind them followed their pursuers "too numerous to mention", calling on them to surrender and applying to them vile names. Corporal Harrison's horse became unmanageable and carried him into a dense under-growth, where three or four rebels followed, demanding his surrender at the point of their fusees. He was marched to Fredericksburg that night, arriving just after dark, and was lodged in the guard-house with ten others of Company H. Next morning they were taken to Richmond and placed in Libby Prison, and three or four days later exchanged and sent to Annapolis.

After safely passing the rebels stationed at the gate, Sergeant Bonnell and his three companions went flying through the little settlement of the Gold Mines, the rebels "ki-yi-ing" close behind them. Reaching the junction of the roads where our picket had been posted, they encountered another force of the altogether too-numerous enemy, but the only course open to them was to "go through" or die trying. It was hot work, but through they went, the bullets flying fast, the boys doing their best to outrun them. About twenty of the numerous throng continued the pursuing business as the boys sped on, with Morrisville [#10 on Map 1.2] only ten miles away; but one by one the horses of their pursuers gave out and they abandoned the chase. Reaching Morrisville, Bonnell and his party found the place deserted. Continuing, they arrived at Rappahannock Station about dusk and reported to General Bayard. Captain

Peck, Sergeant Wynkoop, and others came in early the next morning just as camp was being broken preparatory to a move. Captain Peck was placed in arrest at once by order of the General, and was not released till about the 1st of January at Camp Bayard.

The following is the report of General Bayard:

HEADQUARTERS TENTH NEW YORK CAVALRY
RAPPAHANNOCK STATION, VA
November 16, 1862

The rebel cavalry from Falmouth surprised Captain Peck and his company, who were sent to picket Richards and United States Fords. A sergeant and four men have returned; the Captain also escaped. I will arrest him for gross carelessness when he comes in. Probably some eighteen or twenty men are captured with their arms and everything.

GEORGE D. BAYARD, *Brigadier-General*

Lieutenant-Colonel Irvine's report:

HEADQUARTERS TENTH NEW YORK CAVALRY
RAPPAHANNOCK, VA
November 16, 1862

GENERAL: Sergeant Reynolds, of Captain Peck's Company H, last night sent to Morrisville to report to Major Harhaus for picket duty, has just come into camp, and reports that Captain Peck, with fourteen men posted at the Gold Mines, was attacked about 1 P.M. today by about one hundred men in their rear. Captain Peck rallied his men after being fired on and made a stand, fired his carbines, then fell back a few rods. On the rebels advancing, emptied his revolvers. By that time the party were nearly surrounded, the Captain's horse shot under him, and they undertook to cut their way through to the rear. Five of the men succeeded in doing so and brought away seven horses. Captain Peck escaped into the woods, and, the Sergeant thinks, succeeded in escaping. The Sergeant and four men were chased and fired on for two miles toward Morrisville, when the rebels gave up the chase. Nine men are missing and seven horses. Two horses were shot, including the Captain's. Whether any men were killed the Sergeant can not tell. He has no idea where the rebs came from, but knows that they did not cross at the ford. Captain Peck's rear-guard was but a little way off and the attack was a surprise.

Your obedient servant,
WILLIAM IRVINE
Lieutenant-Colonel Commanding 10th New York Cavalry
GENERAL BAYARD

Prisoner Exchange and Parole

In the section describing the fighting at Rappahannock Station, it was mentioned that 11 troopers from the Tenth New York were captured while on picket duty. They were sent to Libby Prison in Richmond, but "paroled" three or four days later. Under agreements made between the USA and CSA, captured soldiers could be returned to their own governments by either parole or exchange. When "exchanged", a private was released on one side at the same time a private was released from the other side. They were immediately free to go back on duty, or back to civilian life if their enlistments had expired.

A prisoner who was "paroled" was turned over to the other side without a matching transfer in the other direction, but was not free to return to his unit. He must be kept in detention until a prisoner is transferred in the opposite direction, at which time he could rejoin his unit or go back to civilian life, depending on his enlistment requirements.

Non-coms and officers were exchanged on the basis of a certain number of privates who would also be exchanged. As examples, a colonel being exchanged would require 15 privates to be exchanged in the opposite direction, and a captain would require 6 privates.

The exchange and parole rules fell apart in the last couple of years of the war as the Union added more black soldiers to their ranks. The Confederacy refused to treat them as equals in the exchange process, and since the Union had a much larger manpower pool on which to draw, the exchanges and paroles were suspended.

(About this time Mary writes to Justus again, replying to a letter from him which apparently has been lost. He is still in the Camp of Recruits, and writes back to her in the letter following Mary's.)

November 11, 1862

Cortlandville

Friend Jut,

think not that you are forgotten because I have not answered your kind letter that I received a few weeks ago, far from it, you and the other boys that have left their homes to free their country can never be forgotten. I received your letter in due time and was glad to find in it a portrait. although it could not speak, it brought to mind more forcibly that you was far far away living in a camp life. I thank you many times for it and will send mine the next time I write, which will be as soon as I hear from you again. I left Mr. Pecks five weeks ago stayed at home two weeks. this is the third week that I have been in Cortland. am sewing with Mr. Kateline. like it very well. I room the first house below Mr. Hunter's. have got some acquainted with the girls. like them very well, and have not seen any of your people since you left. guess they are well. How I wish that you were here going to school. I think it would be far pleasanter for you and I know it would be for me. I have seen Nell a number of times. he seems to enjoy being in Cortland again. his father and mother have gone to Canada. I have not seen George. Yesterday was drafting day but no drafting was done and I do not think any will be done in York state.

Jut you have got a new cousin. Miss Clarissa was married three weeks ago today (Don't you believe that I have mourned these three long long weeks) but I am getting over it now. They did not make any wedding. you know they are poor people and could not afford it. she was married at home then they and Jerome and Minerva went to Groton, staid all night. it rained both days so they had a fine time. This school closes this week. Jerome White is agoing to Homer to school next term.

We have some snow here Sunday morn. the ground was white with snow and I thought very cold. I do not ere feel that you will see snow this winter. How do you like cooking and doing your work. I wish that I lived in fifty miles from Alexandria. I would come and cook for you some day, but by the time you get home I shall know how to sew, so you must fetch your clothes to me and I will make them for you. was in to Mr. Warfields last night. they had just received a letter from Dennis so I got the directions. I did not not write before for I thought you would not get it. It is rather dull times here, everything is so high, provisions and everything is raising every day. I do not know what poor people will do. You must excuse this poor writing and confusing, for I have written it at noon and on the cutting bench which is so high that I can hardly reach, so you see that I have not had a very good place to write on.

Take good care of your health and enjoy yourself the best you can and write often is the best advice that I can think of now.

Why did not you come home with Mel and Geo and go in their company or have you got better company. How I wish that I had wings. I would come and see you all (Is not that a funny wish)

Write soon and accept this from your cousin Matie H.
P. S. Direct to Cortlandville.

Camp of Recruits
Nov 15th '62

Friend Mary

I recieved your letter the thirteenth and was glad to hear from you. I put a letter into the post office for you the morning that I recieved your letter. I directed it to McGrawville for I did not know then that you had left Pecks.

You spoke of my being far away. I cannot make it seem so. it appears to me that we are not more than fifty or a hundred miles apart. and as for a camp life it is not quite as agreable as it is to be where where a person is free to go where they please. but I like it as well as I expected I should.

This war must be put down and I am one among the many who have left their homes for a while to fight for our countrys freedom, not as our fore Fathers fought to gain it, but to retain it. And when that is accomplished I am comming home to friends whom I presume will be glad to see me by that time.

You ask me how I liked cooking. I do not have it to do yet. we have three men in our company that voulenteered to do it in place of other duty. As for my work I think that I can do it about as well as any woman.

I would like to be up there this winter. it seems as though I mint enjoy myself better than ever but I shal have to wate untill others sees fit to giv me the oportunity.

I was on gard day before yesterday up to yesterday at ten Oclock and had to drill two or three hours yesterday so that I do not feel first-rate to day. We have the first best of officers to lead us.

I was surprised to hear of Clarrisas marriage. amost all the boys letters speaks of some ones wedding. Well I dont know but I presume the girls will all be married off before I get home and I shall have to live an old Bach all the days of my life. now would not that be a pitty.

This is the second letter that I have written to day and I am getting tired. write as soon as convenient. and except this from your friend J. G. Matteson.

P.S. please direct to
Co.L. 3rd. Bat, 10th N.Y.S. Vol
Camp of Recruits near Alexandria Va
In care of Lieut. Vanderbilt

**Figure 1.2 Captain George Vanderbilt,
who became the Company L Commander**

First Battle of Fredericksburg

The first real duty that Co. L was asked to do, was to provide escort duty for General Smith, of the "Left Grand Division" of the Infantry. He was on the "march to Richmond" via Fredericksburg (#11 on Map 1.2), and participating in the Battle of Fredericksburg, and needed cavalry support to provide courier and guard services during his advance. The following is a hilarious account by Captain Vanderbilt (Figure 1.2), commanding Company L troopers, of this first real duty of the Company, as included in Preston [7]:

The morning of the 10th [December 1862], Companies L and K were detached and ordered - the first named to General Smith, of the Left Grand Division, whose headquarters were near White Oak Church at the time; and the latter to General Reynolds, commanding the First Army Corps. Captain Vanderbilt describes in graphic terms his first experience in escort duty, which is here given in his own words from a letter to the historian some years ago.

Figure 1.3 White Oak Church

[The White Oak Church still exists at the same location in Falmouth, #12 on Map 1.2, as shown in Figure 1.3, a photo taken by the author in May, 2006. It was used as a hospital during the Battle of Fredericksburg and at other times during the war. Justus must have passed it several times on his travels to Camp Bayard near Belle Plain, #13 on Map 1.2.]

"I just want to say a word about our march to the river. Please remember that my company had been mustered into the service only about six weeks before, and had received horses less than a month prior to this march; and in the issue we drew everything on the list-watering-bridles, lariat ropes and pins - in fact there was nothing on the printed list of supplies that we did not get.

"Many men had extra blankets, nice large quilts presented by some fond mother or maiden aunt (dear souls!); sabers and belts together with the straps that pass over the shoulder; carbines and slings; pockets full of cartridges; nose-bags and extra little bags for carrying oats; haversacks, canteens, and spurs, some of them of the Mexican pattern, as large as small windmills, and more in the way than the spurs on a young rooster, catching in the grass when they walked, gathering up briers, vines, and weeds, and catching their pants, and in the way generally; curry-combs, brushes, ponchos, button-tents, overcoats, frying-pans, cups, coffeepots, etc. Now, the old companies had become used to these things and had got down to light marching condition gradually, had learned how to wear the uniform, saber, carbines, etc.; but my company had hardly time to get into proper shape when "the general" was sounded, "Boots and Saddles" blown, and Major Falls commanded:

'Shoun! Air T'- Ount! A-O-U-N-T!'

"Such a rattling, jingling, jerking, scrabbling, cursing, I never before heard. Green horses - some of them never had been ridden - turned round and round, backed against each other, jumped up or stood up like trained circus-horses. Some of the boys had a pile in front, on their saddles, and one in the rear, so high and heavy it took two men to saddle one horse and two men to help the fellow into his place. The horses sheered out, going sidewise, pushing the well-disposed animals out of position, etc. Some of the boys had never rode anything since they galloped on a hobby-horse, and clasped their legs close together, thus unconsciously sticking the spurs into their horses' sides.

"Well, this was the crowd I commanded to mount on the morning I was ordered by General Smith to follow him. We got in line near headquarters, and when he got ready to start he started all over. He left no doubt about his starting! He went like greased lightning! As soon as I could get my breath I shouted, 'BY FOURS, FOR-D, A-R-C-H!' then immediately, 'G-A-L-L-O-P, A-R-C-H!' and away we went over the hard-frozen ground toward Fredericksburg. In less than ten minutes Tenth New York Cavalrymen might have been seen on every hill for two miles rearward. Poor fellows! I wanted to help them, but the General was "On to Richmond!" and I hardly dare look back for fear of losing him. I didn't have the remotest idea where he was going, and didn't know but he was going to keep it up all day. It was my first Virginia ride as a warrior in the field. My uneasiness may be imagined. I was wondering what in the mischief I should say to the General when we halted and none of the company there but me. He was the first real live general I had seen who was going out to fight. Talk about the Flying Dutchman! Blankets slipped from under saddles and hung by one corner; saddles slid back until they were on the rumps of the horses; others turned and were on the under side of the animals; horses running and kicking; tin pans, mess-kettles, patent sheet-iron camp-stoves the boys had seen advertised in the illustrated papers and sold by the sutlers at Alexandria - about as useful as a piano or folding bed - flying through the air; and all I could do was to give a hasty glance to the rear and sing out at the top of my voice

'C-L-O-S-E U-P!'

"But they couldn't "close." Poor boys! Their eyes stuck out like those of maniacs. We went only a few miles, but the boys didn't all get up till noon. My company was used as orderlies to infantry generals. Pitt Morse was orderly for General Russell. One day the General was sitting on his horse with Morse just behind, when he (Morse) spied a nice round ball (percussion shell) lying on the ground. He jumped off and got it. Had no other place to put it, so laid it on his oats-bag in front, intending to take it home when he went! (Wasn't that innocence?) The General suddenly turned to give him an order, when his astonished gaze fell upon Morse's shell. 'What in the world have you got there?' shouted the General, laying his hand threateningly on his revolver. 'Get down off that horse and don't you drop that shell! Be careful, now. Go and lay it in that water, and then report to your commanding officer; I don't need you any longer.'

"Next morning," Captain Vanderbilt continues, "we saddled at break of day and started for Richmond via Fredericksburg. We went into camp some distance north of the [Rappahannock] river, crossing the lower pontoon bridge the following morning with the infantry and artillery."

Companies K and L were present with the army at the Battle of Fredericksburg, but neither company was seriously engaged.

On the 13th of December, the brigade commander, Brigadier General George D. Bayard, was killed in the battle. Bates's History of Pennsylvania Volunteers says "At three o'clock in the afternoon, when the storm of battle was raging fiercest, General Bayard, now in command of the whole cavalry force, was struck by a shell and instantly killed."

General Bayard was originally colonel of the First Pennsylvania Cavalry, of which David Gardner was afterward lieutenant-colonel. The latter officer was near the General at the time he was wounded and gives an account of it, substantially as follows: The brigade, after crossing on Franklin's pontoons, drove the rebels back and established a strong line of videttes. A dense fog prevailed, which late in the day had risen, thus fairly disclosing the positions of our troops, which were being vigorously shelled.

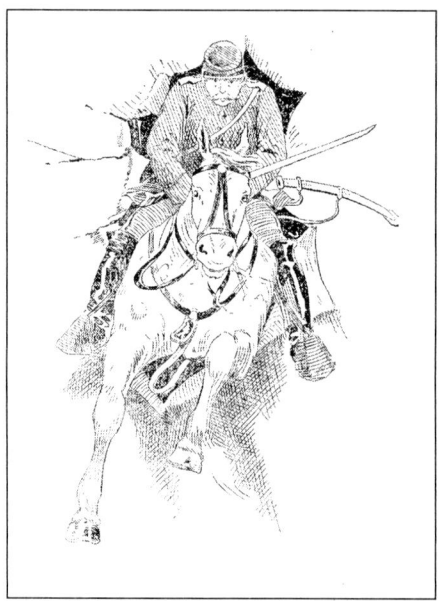

Figure 1.4 Galloper (from Preston's book)

An officer of a regular battery near by had invited the General to partake of lunch with him, and on arising from the ground where he had been reclining to accompany the officer, he was struck by a shell on the upper part of the thigh, shattering the leg. He was immediately removed in an unconscious condition to a house and laid upon a bed, and consciousness soon returned. To the question, "Doctor, what are the chances for life?" he received the answer, "There is a chance, General, if you survive the shock of the amputation." He instantly replied, "I don't want to live, sir, with the leg gone." He proceeded with deliberation to dispose of his property, making his will and dictating letters, which he signed with his own hand. One of these was to the lady to whom he was to have been married on the day he was buried. The preparations for the wedding had been made, and the young hero had his leave of absence in his pocket, but refused to avail himself of its privilege when he learned of the approaching battle. He was perfectly calm and collected up to the moment of his death, which he awaited with the courage of a true soldier.

The rest of the Regiment was only peripherally involved in the Battle of Fredericksburg, a disaster for the Union army. The Civil War Sites Advisory Commission of the National Parks Service (CWSAC) describes the battle as follows [8]:

On November 10, Burnside, now in command of the Army of the Potomac, sent a corps to occupy the vicinity of Falmouth near Fredericksburg. The rest of the army soon followed. Lee reacted by entrenching his army on the heights behind the town. On December 11, Union engineers laid five pontoon bridges across the Rappahannock under fire. On the 12th, the Federal army crossed over, and on December 13, Burnside mounted a series of futile frontal assaults on Prospect Hill and Marye's Heights that resulted in staggering casualties. Meade's division, on the Union left flank, briefly penetrated Jackson's line but was driven back by a counterattack. Union Generals C. Feger Jackson and George Bayard and Confederate generals Thomas R.R. Cobb and Maxey Gregg were killed. On December 15, Burnside called off the offensive and recrossed the river, ending the campaign. Burnside initiated a new offensive in January 1863, which quickly bogged down in the winter mud. The abortive "Mud March" and other failures led to Burnside's replacement by Maj. Gen. Joseph Hooker in January 1863.

Battle of Kanky's Store (also called Battle of Dumfries)

The 10th NY, sans Companies L and K, was involved in a battle near the area of Kanky's Store (#14 on Map 1.2) near Dumfries. The cavalry was attacked by Gen. Hampton's gray cavalry on December 12. According to Confederate reports, several prisoners were taken and several wagons of supplies were captured.

Preston describes some of the action in which the 10th New York was involved [9]:

> On the evening of the 10th of December the Regiment was ordered to the rear of the army for picket and scouting service. The location was dismal and forlorn - a more than usually hard-looking spot on the badly scratched and scarred face of "Ole Virginny." Sergeant Mortimer Spring, of Company D, gives his experience at this time as follows:
>
>> It was on the night of the 11th of December, 1862, when the Union army, under General Burnside, was preparing to cross the Rappahannock and give battle to the rebel army under General Lee. A part of the Tenth was doing duty on the right and rear of the army, on what was known, I think, as the Dumfries Road. The reserve was about a half-mile back from the picket-line, on a cross-road, which led to the Dumfries road. Midnight was the time for my relief to go on duty, and as there had been firing on the right of the line all the early part of the night, the Lieutenant and Sergeant took seven or eight men and went in that direction, sending me with the remainder of the relief to the left. I had posted all but two of my men, and was going with them down a hill, the road at that place being through a dug-out. The bank on either side was as high as my horse's back, and on each side was a rail fence. An open field was on the left and dense timber on the right, with a

heavy growth of underbrush. We were marching quail-fashion, single file, when all of a sudden, there came from the under-brush a gruff demand to "surrender."

I knew from the noise and rustling that we were outnumbered by at least two or three to one. I reached for my revolver, as each particular hair seemed to stand on end. Instantly came the command, "Hands off that, or I'll blow your d-d brains out!" They had the drop on me, and so, turning to the man nearest me I said, in a low tone, "Follow me." I drove the spurs into my horse's side, and I think he jumped fully twenty feet as he flew down the road. They fired a volley at us, but neither I nor my horse was hit, but the horse behind me was shot through the neck. That changed ends with him, and the other horse of course followed, leaving me alone. The boys on reaching camp reported me killed, while I, in turn, supposed they were killed. By the time I reached the outpost the boys were scrambling for their horses lively. At the outpost was a building which before the war had been used as a grocery store [Kanky's Store?].

In this building the Corporal and one man sat before the fire while the third watched, the trio relieving each other at stated times. We formed in the road and awaited the approach of the enemy, but they did not come. Supposing my comrades to have been killed, I proposed to the Corporal to let me take one of his men and go to camp for a relief party, but he objected to remaining, so I proposed that he should take one and go, and I would remain. To this he consented, as he could reach camp by going across the open fields. Posting my one man to prevent being cut off from the open field, I took position in the road, where it seemed to me I remained three or four hours, when I espied a man approaching from the direction where the rebels had fired on us. I got the drop on the fellow, and allowed him to approach within about ten paces, then it was my turn to make the cold chills creep over the other fellow, as I shouted, "Halt! who comes there?" A very complacent, almost meek, "Friend," was responded. "Advance, friend," I commanded, never losing my advantage, but having him constantly covered. Approaching almost to the muzzle of my gun, with all the assurance of an old acquaintance, he said, "Where are the other boys?" I said, "What other boys?" "Why, the Company B boys." "What do you know about the Company B boys?" I queried, still keeping him covered. "Why, weren't they on this post?" "Who are you, and what brought you here?" I continued. He replied that he came with some others, under Lieutenant Jones, from camp, supposing when they heard the firing that we were all captured and the Lieutenant had halted his command and sent him to reconnoiter; so that instead of a reb, as I supposed, he was one of the coolest Yanks I ever met.

The Regiment remained in this locality during the Battle of Fredericksburg, scouring the country for marauding and raiding parties, and picketing the roads in every direction.

Winter Quarters 1862-1863

Preston winds up the year 1862 with a description of picket duty and finally getting situated in winter quarters near Belle Plain Landing (#13 on Map 1.2) on Potomac Creek, near Falmouth, VA [10]. The Potomac Creek area no longer looks like the bustling place of 1862-1865. Figure 1.5 is a current photo taken by the author.

Figure 1.5 Belle Plain Landing (2006)

On the death of General Bayard, the brigade which he had so ably led was increased to a division, and Colonel D.McM. Gregg, of the Eighth Pennsylvania Cavalry (captain Sixth U.S. Cavalry), was promoted brigadier-general of volunteers, with rank from November 29, 1862, and assigned to its command.

The Regiment continued to picket the northern part of Stafford County until about the 20th of December. ...

Orders were received on the 22d of December to be ready to move the next day; and on the 23d the brigade, now composed of the First Maine, Second New York, and Tenth New York regiments of cavalry, commanded by Colonel Judson Kilpatrick, of the Second New York Cavalry, went into camp near Belle Plain Landing, where it was destined to spend the winter months in what came to be known as Camp Bayard [#13 on Map 1.2].

They remained here for the succeeding three months and more. ...

The boys swung the axe and used the spade with vigor and the wilderness was quickly transformed into a miniature city. As time rolled by, giving promise of permanency, the hastily-constructed mansions were improved in architectural appearance and home comforts. [A photo taken by the author of a model hut display in the White Oak Civil War Museum is shown in Figure 1.6.]

Figure 1.6 Model hut like those used by the cavalry near Belle Plain

The place was christened Camp Bayard in honor of their lost commander. Soon the cavaliers transformed the location into a place of comparative good looks. The log huts had been erected with little regard for alignment or regularity, but as time passed they were arranged and fixed up so as to present a decent appearance. Tents had been issued about the time the Regiment went into camp. These served for roofs. Even the detestable Virginia mud was brought into use to render the cabins comfortable, filling the chinks and cracks. [Some remnants of these camps are still visible. The author recently walked through the area with DP Newton, curator of the White Oak Civil War Museum, and he pointed out some of the depressions which were used to lower the floor of the huts below ground level, and smaller holes that were used for post holes.]

Major Avery had a large log house erected. The horses were carefully looked after, the camp rigidly policed, and every effort put forth by the officers to render the Regiment efficient.

Figure 1.7 Period photo of one of the Camp Bayard campsites

Weaponry

Some mounted forces used traditional infantry rifles. However, cavalrymen, particularly in the North, were frequently armed with other weapons [11]:

> Most Northern cavalry units were armed with Carbines, which had a shorter barrel than a rifle, but were less accurate. They were easier to handle on horseback, however. Most carbines were .52- or .56-caliber, single-shot breech-loading weapons. They were manufactured by a number of different companies, but the most common were the Sharps, the Burnside, and the Smith. Late in 1863, the seven-shot Spencer repeating carbine was introduced, but it saw relatively little deployment. (Confederate forces were able to use captured breechloaders, but were unable to duplicate the metallic cartridges needed by the Spencer.)

The northern cavalry was fortunate in having the carbines available to them. This weapon was light, small, easy to load and easy to handle on horseback. A picture of one carbine is shown in Figure 1.8. These were the rifles most commonly used by the cavaliers at Camp Bayard. Included in the photo is an enlarged picture of one of the bullets used in some of these weapons. Thousands of bullets were found around the former campsites of the 10th New York near Belle Plain, and piles of them are on display at the White Oak Civil War Museum. In fact the Museum brochure indicates that there are about 90,000 bullets displayed at the Museum.

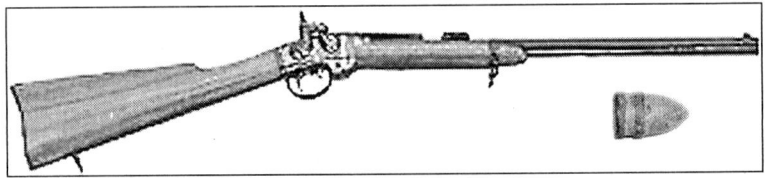

Figure 1.8 Smith 50-caliber carbine

Sabers were used by the cavalry, but more frequently by Northern cavalrymen. They were terror weapons, more useful for instilling fear in their opponents than as practical offensive weapons and Confederate cavalrymen often avoided them simply because they considered sabers to be outmoded, unsuitable for the "modern" battlefield. (There were instances in the war in which Union cavalrymen taunted their opponents to "Pick up your sabers and fight like gentlemen!") The American cavalry saber was lighter than the typical European saber, the latter being similar to the older U.S. Model 1840 "wrist breaker". The curved blade of the saber was generally sharpened only at the tip because it was used mostly for breaking arms and collarbones of opposing horsemen, and sometimes stabbing, rather than for slashing flesh.

The saber commonly carried by the cavalry is shown in Figure 1.9. The author has a similar sword over his mantle at home, which was carried by Justus G. Matteson of the 10th New York.

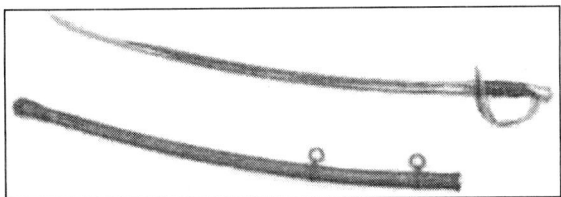

Figure 1.9 Cavalry saber

Pistols, which Southern cavalrymen generally preferred over sabers, were usually six-shot revolvers, in .36- or .44-caliber, from Colt or Remington. They were useful only in close fighting, having little accuracy. It was not uncommon for cavalrymen to carry two revolvers, for extra firepower, and John Mosby's troopers often carried four each. Figure 1.10 shows the Le Mat cavalry revolver.

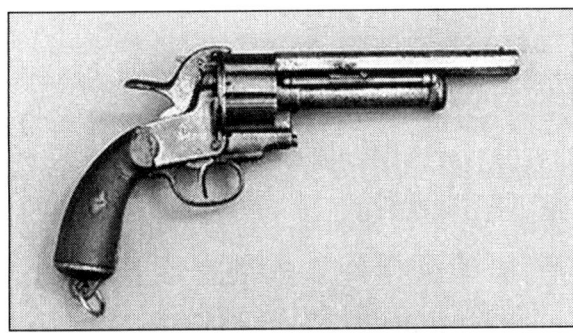

Figure 1.10 Le Mat cavalry revolver

The next chapter describes the action of spring 1863, including Burnside's Mud March, Battle of Kelly's Ford, and Stoneman's Raid on Richmond.

References

[1] Preston, Noble D., *History of the Tenth Regiment New York Volunteer Cavalry*, New York, NY: D. Appleton and Company, 1892; reprinted by Higginson Book Company, Salem, MA in 1998.

[2] Wikipedia, the free encyclopedia that anyone can edit: http://en.wikipedia.org/wiki/Cavalry_in_the_American_Civil_War.

[3] Preston, *History of the Tenth New York*, pp. 1-2.

[4] Ibid, 14-15.

[5] Ibid, 42-45.

[6] Ibid, 46-50.

[7] Ibid, 54-57.

[8] National Park Service, Civil War Sites Advisory commission (CWSAC), http://www.cr.nps.gov/hps/abpp/battles/va028.htm, Battle of Fredericksburg.

[9] Preston, *History of the Tenth New York*, pp. 53-54.

[10] Ibid, 57-59.

[11] Wikipedia, http://en.wikipedia.org/wiki/ Cavalry_in_the_American_Civil_War#Equipment.

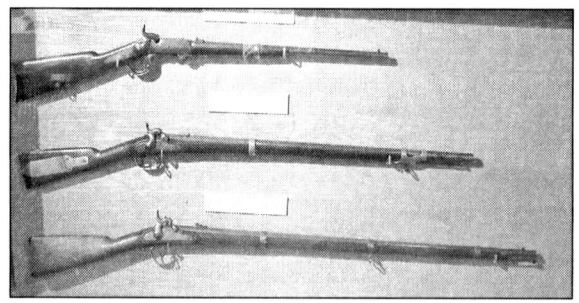

Figure 1.11 Rifles on display at New York State Military Museum

CHAPTER 2
Picketing, Mud March and Stoneman's Raid - January-June 1863

"More Virginia to the acre in Camp Bayard than could be found in any other part of the state." Noble Preston

Winter Camp

P reston describes the winter camp of 1862-1863 at Camp Bayard, near Belle Plain Landing, Virginia (#1 on Maps 2.1 and 2.2) as a place not too attractive [1]:

> A dreary, uninviting spot was that where Bayard's old troopers encamped on the 23d of December, 1862. They had become so accustomed to sudden changes, leaving quarters on which they had spent much labor, that few did more than make arrangements for present needs. It can hardly be believed that this place, where they remained for the succeeding three months and more, was the result of choice. It would rather appear to have been accidental that the command found itself fixed in the location where it dismounted amid scrub-oaks and bushes on the evening of the year 1862; but with assurances that they were to go into winter quarters the boys swung the axe and used the spade with a vigor that made a bad scar on the face of Dame Nature in a short time. The wilderness was quickly transformed into a miniature city, and as time rolled by, giving promise of permanency, the hastily-constructed mansions were improved in architectural appearance and home comforts. The place was christened Camp Bayard in honor of the youthful commander who had but recently lost his life in battle.

During the first half of 1863 the 10th New York engaged in several operations, many of which are described later in this chapter. The following table summarizes these actions, locations, and dates:

Map #	Events	Dates-1863
1	Camp Bayard/Belle Plain	Winter Quarters
	Picketing while in winter quarters	Jan. 16-20
2	Lambs Creek Church	
3	King George Court House	
4	Burnside's "Mud March"	Jan. 20-23
5	Battle of Kelly's Ford	Mar. 17
6	Army of the Potomac review by Gen. Hooker and Pres. Lincoln, Falmouth	Apr. 6
	March to Kelly's Ford	Apr. 13-28
1	Camp Bayard/Belle Plain	Apr. 13
7	Bealton	Apr. 14
8	Rappahannock Station	Apr. 14
9	Picketing Liberty, Waterloo, etc.	Apr. 14-21
10	Warrenton Junction - camp	Apr. 22-27
5	Kelly's ford	Apr. 28
	Stoneman's Raid to Richmond	Apr. 28-May 8
5	Kelly's Ford - crossed Rappahannock	Apr. 29
11	Rapidan River - crossed at Ely's Ford	Apr. 30
12	Louisa Court House	May 2
13	Thompson's Crossroads	May 3
14	Hanover Station	May 4
15	South Anna Bridge	May 5
16	Pamunkey River	May 5
11	Rapidan River crossed	May 7
5	Kelly's Ford	May 7
7	Bealton	May 8
	Picketing from Bealton	May-June
9	Liberty, Fayetteville, Sulphur Springs Road.	
10	Warrenton Junction	

Table 2.1 Early 1863 Actions

2 - Picketing, Mud March, and Stoneman's Raid

Picketing, Skirmishing and Foraging

The 10th New York did not just lay around all winter. They left Camp Bayard frequently during the first three months of 1863, as indicated in Table 2.1.

Some of this activity occurred in the Northern Neck, that peninsula of land between the Rappahannock and the Potomac rivers (See Map 2.1). They went to the Lamb's Creek Church area (#2 on Map 2.1) and towards King George Courthouse (#3 on Map 2.1), for the period January 16 to 20. They went beyond Lamb's Creek Church to Mathias Point from January 28 to 31. They went to the "Neck" again on February 8-12, 15-28, and March 9-19, as reported by Preston [2]. This was not good duty - living in the open in the windy, cold, wet weather; foraging off the land for food; and of course standing the risk of an encounter with rebel troops.

A Digression - Lamb's Creek Church

Lamb's Creek Church is shown in Figure 2.1.The church was originally built in 1710 on the King's Highway (Route 3), and was known as the Muddy Creek Church. In 1790 it was moved a few miles to the east, and rebuilt on its present location in King George County. It has not been used as a church in recent years, but has been kept in good condition.

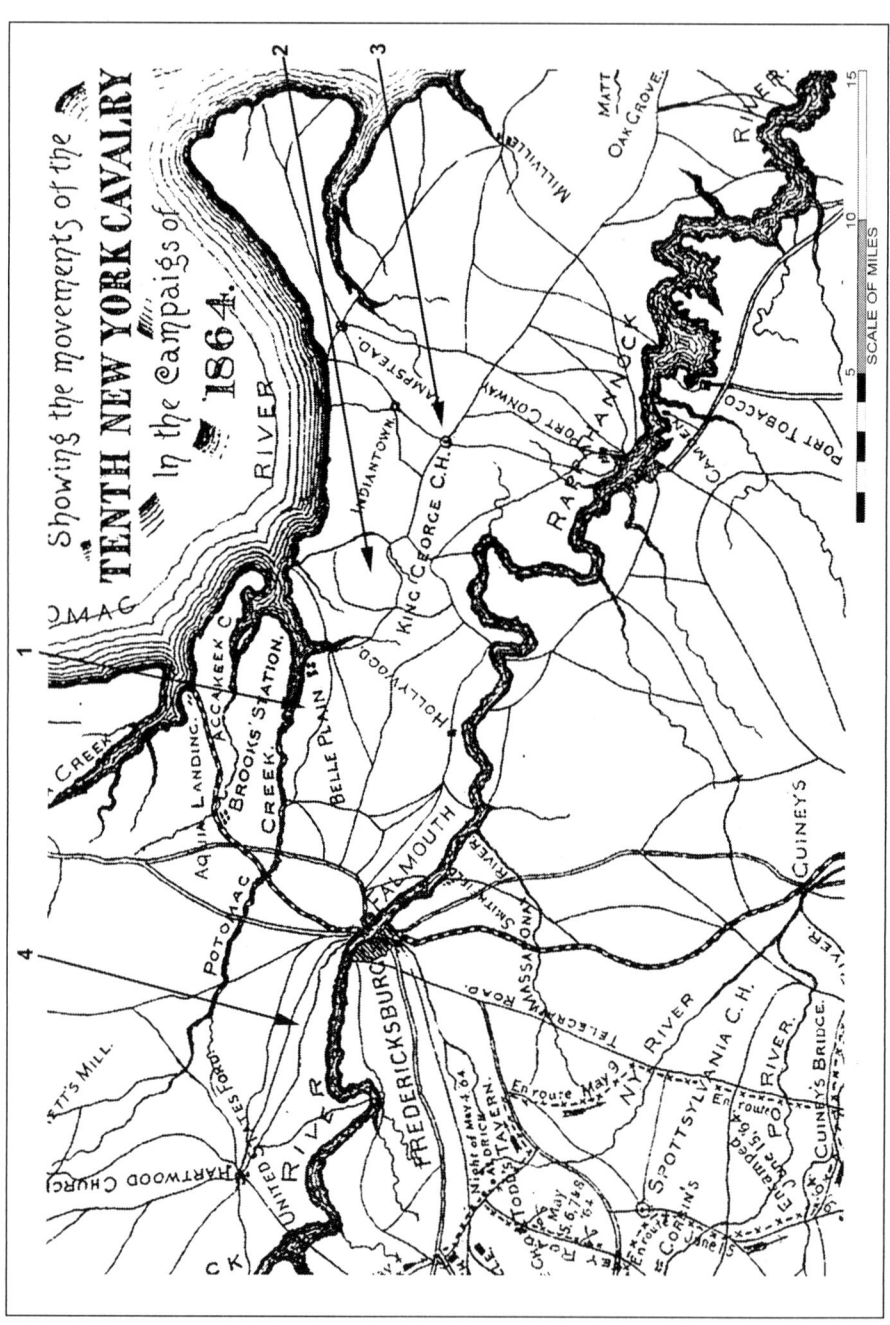

**Map 2.1 Area around Belle Plain, King George
Courthouse and Lamb's Creek Church**

Figure 2.1 Lamb's Creek Church (2006 photo by author)

A monument giving its history is on the grounds, and is shown in Figure 2.2.

Figure 2.2 Lamb's Creek Church monument (2006)

The monument reads "Lambs Creek Church, reerected 1769-1770; removed from Muddy Creek site, in use in 1710."

There is also a sign in front of the church giving its denomination and age, as shown in Figure 2.3. Several soldiers killed during the Civil War are buried on the grounds and a few tombstones can be found there.

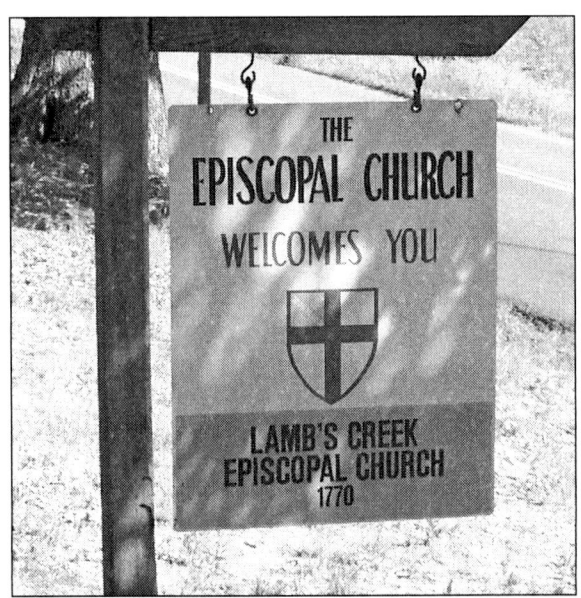

Figure 2.3 Current Lamb's Creek Church sign (2006)

The Mud March

Early in this period, General Burnside decided to move the entire Army of the Potomac around Fredericksburg, planning a surprise flanking movement on Lee's army. Instead of surprising anyone, the entire Army of the Potomac became mired in the mud (the infamous "Mud March" of 1863). The following is a partial description of the Mud March from the book *Washington Weather* [3].

During late January [January 20-23] of 1863, General Burnside's Union Army was in camp across the Rappahannock River from General Lee's Confederate troops, who were camped around Fredericksburg, Virginia. Burnside had been feeling increasing pressure to move against the Confederate Army after his defeat at the Battle of Fredericksburg a month earlier on December 13, 1862.

Burnside's plan was to march his army several miles to the northwest of the Confederates and cross the Rappahannock, circling around the left flank of Lee's army. He would then attack the Confederate Army near Fredericksburg. The weather had been fairly dry and mild for most of January and the prospects for a winter campaign seemed good.

On the morning of January 20, 1863, the Army of the Potomac formed columns and began the march up the Rappahannock River [#4 on Map 2.1]. Unknown to the soldiers, a massive storm was developing near the southeast coast and had started to move northward. Rain began falling during the evening of January 20 and continued to fall heavily on January 21. Burnside's army quickly got bogged down in the mud. Temperatures hovered in the upper 30's, adding a chill to the drenched soldiers. Wagons sank to their wheel hubs in mud and artillery became hopelessly stuck. A team of 12 horses and 150 men could not pull one cannon out of the mud. Also, the soldiers slipped and fell repeatedly, while others lost their shoes in the thick mud.

The Mud March (see sketch in Figure 2.4) therefore resulted in nothing but misery for the troops, and the cavalry retired back to Camp Bayard. The 10th New York did not participate in the Mud March; the entire regiment was on picket duty near Lamb's Creek Church while the Mud March was going on.

Figure 2.4 The Mud March - a miserable affair

The following letters were exchanged between Mary and Justus around this time. Figure 2.5 shows an example of the handwriting style used by Justus during this period.

January 11th, 1863

Absent though remembered friend,

I must say that I have neglected your letter too long, but you have moved about so much that I have not known where to direct. So you will excuse me this time if I try to do better next time <u>will you not</u> . we are having a very cold winter, no snow. I have not had but one cutter ride and that was a short one on New Years day. How did you spend your holly days in camp. I am living in Cortland yet. like it very well. I have been home one week. I did not see any of your people, but learned that they were all well. there has been one wedding in town since I wrote to you last. Jeanette Greenman was married to Mr. Roby Christmas day. Also one death. Mr. Reeces child died a few days ago. Mr. Reece has sold his place to George Townsend and Jason Rawley. Mr Green teaches our school this winter. I guess that he does not give as good satisfaction as Mr. Reece did last winter. Mr. Reece is married to a lady in Truxton. he is in the place, I have not seen him. the new company left Cortland about a week ago. I guess that it was rather hard for the boys to leave their homes this time. I have heard that S. Robertson has run away. is it so? I hope it is not. How does the Freetown boys get along? most everyone that is left in Freetown was married New Years day. I wish that you was here to go to church to day instead of being way down there. why do not you come home? pretend to be sick or hurt yourself.

when you see Denis Warfield tell him that I send him my best wishes and that I would like to have him write. tell him that his people are all well.

Jut I send my picture in this. is one that was taken for me but I do not think that it is a good one. I suppose that I wanted that it should look better than I do. but I am shure that it does not. will you please write me soon?

You have my best wishes for your future happiness and health, Jut. You must be careful of your health. be a good boy and come home to your friends again.

Matie L. Hatch

55

Camp Bayard,

Sunday, Jan. 18th, 1863

Dear Cousin,

Although distance seperates us, and I'm in a reble land among those who are traitors to our country, I will try and look forth from behind the cloud that is now before us to the future, which I hope may return with peace and liberty to the land.

But let us look at the present and past for a while. I recieved your kind and welcomed letter barring date the eleventh yesterday.

I suppose that you would enquire after my health first. As for that, I am well at present and hope that this will find you the same. It was with pleasure that I beheld your picture when I unfolded the letter. I thank you vary much for it. I shal carry it as long as I am in the south (unless I loose it by misfortune) to look upon as a tokon of one whom I shall long remember as a schoolmate and friend in other days.

It has been vary pleasant weather here this winter, but for a few days it has been quite cold. no snow yet this month.

Well, well, I've made quite a mistake by writing on the wrong page. but I presume that you will excuse me when I say that my hand is numb with the cold and I am in a hurry for I have to write one or two more letters this afternoon. for I may not have a chance to write again in some time if ever, for we have to be packed and ready for a start at six O'clock tomorrow morning, with three or four days rations cooked. I should not be surprised if we heard the whir of the mini before long. We wen out on picket yesterday and the day before, saw aplenty of Rebbs.

to day we have had a general inspection. the whole regiment wen out togather for the first time. Solomon Robertson did not run a way. Clif Wiles is writing by my side. He is well. He an G. W. Elwood is all the Freetown boys there is now in the company. Warfield is well. As for getting a furlow, it is out of the question. And to play sick is not so easy so I shall stay, untill Uncle Sam sees fit to send me home. I am surprised at the number of marriages that has taken place up there this winter. Pleas answer this, and give my love to all enquiring friends.

Yours truly
Justus G. Matteson

Camp Bayard, Va
Sunday Mar 1st, '63

Friend Mary,

I will now try and answer your kind letter which I recieved some time ago hopeing that you will excuse my tardiness as I have been on duty for two weeks. we have been on pickett. had a first rate time. foraged all of our provisions of the Rebs. took several prisoners. we had a heavy snow storm when we wer out. it fell some ten or twelve inches deep but it did not last long. Spring is near at hand here for the peach trees begins to bud now.

Well Mary, I was some what surprised to hear that you had gone to the County House to live, but then as I have been there before you I know what for a plase it is. I once lived near by there so that I am well acquainted in those parts.

You speek of its being good sleighing there. I think if I was there I would have as much as one good sleigh ride, but I cant say whether it would come up to the one we had last winter or not when we went up to Cars. what do you think about it. I should like to be up there for a short time.

Oh; Co. M. is here. they have fifty men all told. Orcutt and Peck are with them. I am afraid that they will not find it quite as comfortable living here as at home. I do not. I say Mary, I saw some pretty nice secession girls whilst out on picket. I had some notion to go in for one of them, so as to get a large plantation and negroes etc. now what would you think of that.

My health is as good as it ever was in my life. hopeing that these few lines may find you well. I will close hoping to hear from you soon.

Yours truly
J.G.M.

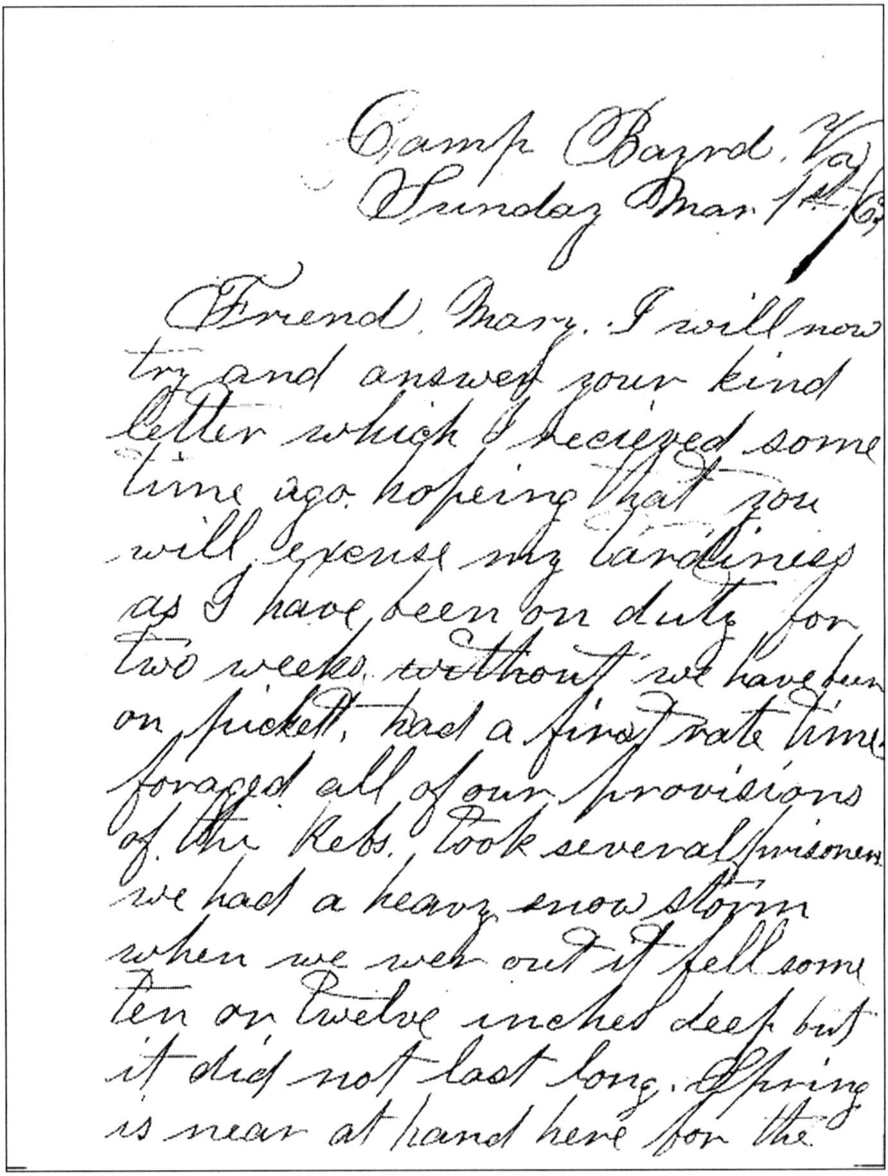

Camp Bayrd, Va
Sunday Mar. 1st /6..

Friend Mary, I will now try and answer your kind letter which I recieved some time ago. hopeing that you will excuse my tardiness as I have been on duty for two weeks. without we have been on pickett, had a first rate time foraged all of our provisions of the Rebs, took several prisoners we had a heavy snow storm when we wer out it fell some ten or twelve inches deep but it did not last long. Spring is near at hand here for the

Figure 2.5 Part of the letter from Justus to Mary, Sunday, March 1st, 1863

Figure 2.6 A Few of the Tenth New York Troopers in January, 1863

Reorganization of the Cavalry Corps

While in winter camp at Camp Bayard Company M joined the 10th New York regiment, as Justus mentioned in his March 1st letter, completing the roster of the third battalion. Partly as a result of the failed Mud March General Burnside was replaced by General Hooker as commander of the Army of the Potomac. Gen. Hooker recognized the worth of the cavalry to the success of the war and reorganized all of the various regiments into a Cavalry Corps. In March 1863 all the cavalry units assigned to the Army of the Potomac were formed into this Cavalry Corps and General Hooker placed Brig. Gen. George Stoneman in charge as the Corps commander. The organization of the Cavalry Corps became as follows [4]:

CAVALRY CORPS
Brig. Gen. George Stoneman

FIRST DIVISION - Brig. Gen. Alfred Pleasonton

First Brigade - Colonel Benjamin F. Davis:
Eighth Illinois, Colonel David R. Clendenin
Third Indiana, Colonel George H. Chapman
Eighth New York, Lieutenant-Colonel Charles R. Babbit
Ninth New York, Colonel William Sackett

Second Brigade - Colonel Thomas C. Devin:
First Michigan, Company L, Lieutenant John K. Truax
Sixth New York, Lt. Col. Duncan McVicar, Capt. William E. Beardsley
Eighth Pennsylvania, Major Pennock Huey
Seventeenth Pennsylvania, Colonel Josiah H. Kellogg

Artillery - New York Light, Sixth Battery, Lieutenant Joseph W. Martin

SECOND DIVISION - Brig. Gen. William W. Averell

First Brigade - Colonel Horace B. Sargent:
First Massachusetts, Lieutenant Colonel Greely S. Curtis
Fourth New York, Colonel Louis P. Di Cesnola
Sixth Ohio, Major Benjamin C. Stanhope
First Rhode Island, Lieutenant-Colonel John L. Thompson

Second Brigade - Colonel John B. McIntosh:
Third Pennsylvania, Lieutenant-Colonel Edward S. Jones
Fourth Pennsylvania, Lieutenant-Colonel William E. Doster
Sixteenth Pennsylvania, Lieutenant-Colonel Lorenzo D. Rogers

Artillery - Second United States, Battery A, Captain John C. Tidball

THIRD DIVISION - Brig. Gen. David McM. Gregg

First Brigade - Colonel Judson Kilpatrick:
First Maine, Colonel Calvin S. Douty
Second New York, Lieutenant Colonel Henry E. Davies, Jr.
Tenth New York, Lieutenant Colonel William Irvine

Second Brigade - Colonel Percy Wyndham:
Twelfth Illinois, Lieutenant Colonel Hasbrouck Davis
First Maryland, Lieutenant-Colonel James M. Deems
First New Jersey, Lieutenant Colonel Virgil Broderick
First Pennsylvania, Colonel John P. Taylor

Regular Reserve Cavalry Brigade - Brig. Gen. John Buford:
Sixth Pennsylvania, Major Robert Morris, Jr.
First United States, Captain R. S. C. Lord
Second United States, Major Charles J. Whiting
Fifth United States, Captain James E. Harrison
Sixth United States, Captain George C. Cram

Artillery - Captain James M. Robertson:
Second United States, Batteries B and L, Lieutenant Albert O. Vincent
Second United States, Battery M, Lieutenant Robert Clarke
Fourth United States, Battery E, Lieutenant Samuel S. Elder

Of the foregoing commands the Second and Third Divisions, including the 10th NY, First Brigade of the First Division, and the Regular Reserve Brigade with Robertson's and Tidball's batteries were on the Stoneman Raid, April 13th to May 8th.

The following was the organization of the 10th New York on March 1, 1863. Note that Col. Lemmon was not in this position long- he was replaced by Lt. Col. Irvine a short time later. Unfortunately, Irvine was captured at Brandy Station in June, 1863 and was replaced by Maj. Avery.

FIELD AND STAFF

Colonel, John C. Lemmon
Lieutenant-Colonel, William Irvine
Major M. Henry Avery   Major John H. Kemper
Major Alvah D. Waters [3rd Battalion commander, incl. Co. L]

George W. Kennedy, Adjutant   William E. Graves, Quartermaster
Roger W. Pease, Surgeon   Noble D. Preston, Commissary
Henry K. Clarke, Assistant Surgeon   Rev. Robert Day, Chaplain

COMPANY OFFICERS
COMPANY A
Captain, Henry S. Pratt
1st Lieutenant, William C. Potter 2d Lieutenant, Theodore H. Weed

COMPANY B
Captain, Henry Field
1st Lieutenant, John C. Hart   2d Lieutenant, Thomas Jones

COMPANY C
Captain, John Ordner
1st Lieutenant, L.L. Barney   2d Lieutenant, John Werrick

COMPANY D
Captain, Aaron T. Bliss
1st Lieutenant, William J. Robb 2d Lieutenant, Joseph A. Hatry

COMPANY E
Captain, Layton S. Baldwin
1st Lieutenant, William A. Snyder 2d Lieutenant, Nelson P. Layton

COMPANY F
Captain, Wilkinson W. Paige
1st Lieutenant, Henry L. Barker   2d Lieutenant, Edward S. Hawes

COMPANY G
Captain, Delos Carpenter
1st Lieutenant, John T. McKevitt   2d Lieutenant, John B. King

COMPANY H
Captain, William Peck
1st Lieutenant, Francis G. Wynkoop   2d Lieutenant, Charles E. Pratt

COMPANY I
Captain, David Getman, Jr.
1st Lieutenant, Stephen Dennie   2d Lieutenant, Horatio H. Boyd

COMPANY K
Captain, Wheaton Loomis
1st Lieutenant, Benj. F. Lownsbury   2d Lieutenant, L.D. Burdick

COMPANY L
Captain, George Vanderbilt
1st Lieutenant, Burton B. Porter   2d Lieutenant, Marshall R. Woodruff

COMPANY M
Captain, John G. Pierce
1st Lieutenant, Thomas W. Johnson   2d Lieutenant, James Matthews

Battle at Kelly's Ford

Kelly's Ford (#5 on Maps 2.2 and 2.3) was one of the early larger-scale cavalry fights in Virginia that set the stage for Brandy Station and cavalry actions of the Gettysburg Campaign. Twenty five hundred troopers of Brig. Gen. William W. Averell's 2d cavalry division crossed the Rappahannock River on March 17, 1863 to attack the Confederate cavalry. Brig. Gen. Fitzhugh Lee of the Confederate cavalry counterattacked with a brigade of about 800 men. The action at Kelly's Ford was a victory for the Union cavalry which gave them the confidence they needed for future battles. The Brandy Station map in the next chapter (Map 3.1) shows some of the geography in the Kelly's ford area. A 2006 photo of the

Rappahannock River at Kelly's Ford, taken by the author, is shown in Figure 2.7.

Figure 2.7 The Rappahannock River at Kelly's Ford (2006)

Although the 10th New York was not involved in this battle at Kelly's Ford, since they were in the Third Division at this time, the battle prepared the Cavalry Corps for an even more significant one. On June 9 Stuart's Confederate cavalry fought against Stoneman's Union cavalry in the Battle of Brandy Station in the same area.

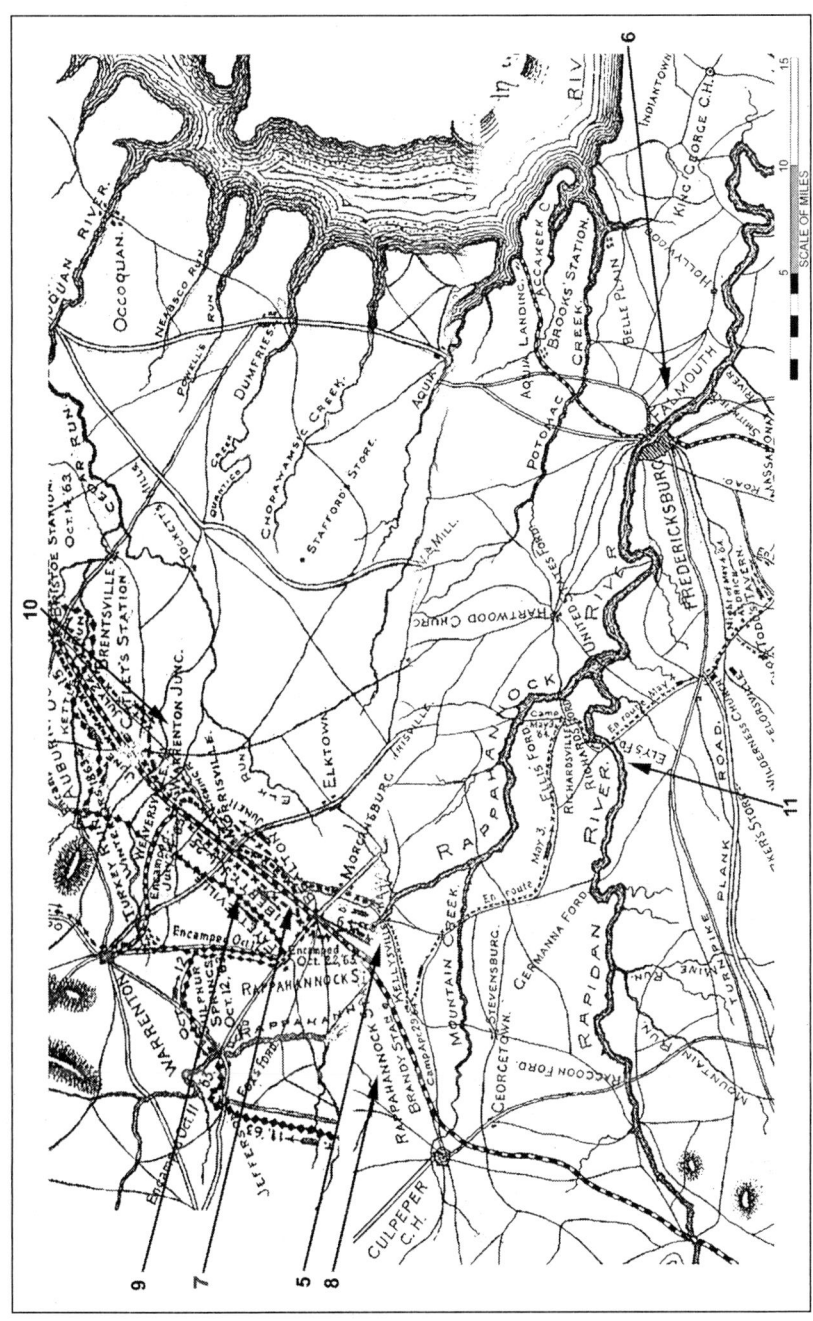

Map 2.2 Along the Rappahannock, Kelly's Ford to Falmouth

The home shown in Figure 2.8 was built in 1787 and was used as a hospital during the Battle of Kelly's Ford. In fact the present occupants claim that there are still bloodstains on stairs used by wounded soldiers going to the second floor. A sign in front of the house states that "George, Tom, Abe and Ulysses slept here."

Figure 2.8 Revolutionary War home used as a hospital during the battle of Kelly's Ford (2006 photo by the author)

This was "the first purely cavalry fight east of the Mississippi River" of any appreciable size. The battle was the first opportunity for the Union cavalry to amass a significant force, because the horsemen had been concentrated into a corps only a few weeks earlier. Perhaps the most important loss to the Confederates in this battle was the death of Major John Pelham, the premier artillerist in the Confederate cavalry. He was struck by a fragment of an artillery shell, ironically, and died shortly after. General Jeb Stuart, commander of the Confederate Cavalry, referred to him as "the Gallant Pelham." A photo by the author of the monument at the battle location is shown in Figure 2.9.

Jeb Stuart, Confederate Cavalry commander, wrote a letter to his wife, March 19, 1863 after the battle of Kelly's Ford, in which he says [5]:

"The noble Pelham … killed. You know how his death distresses me." And Stuart thinks ahead and sees his own death: "I wish an assurance on your part in the event of your surviving me - that [Stuart's emphasis] *you will make the land for which I have given my life your home and keep my offspring on Southern soil.*" And, later, "Poor Pelham's death has created a sensation all over the country. He was noble in every sense of the word. I want Jemmie [his young son] to be just like him."

His order to the cavalry division has in it a great grief and a great pride:

"The noble, the chivalric, the gallant, Pelham is no more. How much he was beloved, appreciated and admired, let the tears of agony we here shed, and the gloom of mourning throughout my command, bear witness. His loss is irreparable. The memory of the 'gallant Pelham,' his many virtues, his noble nature and purity of character, is enshrined as a sacred legacy in the hearts of all who knew him. His record has been bright and spotless, his career brilliant and successful. He fell, the noblest of sacrifices, on the altar of his country, to whose glorious service he had dedicated his life from the beginning of the war."

Figure 2.9 Major John Pelham's monument near Kelly's Ford (2006)

Another interchange of letters was shared between Mary and Justus just prior to more activities that kept the 10th New York very busy for a while.

.

March 23rd 1863

Cortland

Friend Jut

once more I take my pen to write to you. I am well except a hard cold which I have had three weeks or more. it is a hard time for colds. we are having our sleighing. I have been to church today but it was all mud. I suppose that the roads are all dusty where you are. there has been some shugar made in the plaice but I have not had any. Delia [Clarissa Adelia, Justus' sister] was in here this week. I had not seen her before this winter. she has hired out in Freetown for this summer to one of my _____ plaice to work.

Tuesday has come and this letter is not finished so I will finish it in the school room _____ . you know that it is a beautiful place to write. I like the school very well. The school in Cortland closed two weeks ago and commenced yesterday. They had our exaebition the last of the school. Meg Hunter is agoing to teach in Freetown [East Freetown is 3 miles south of Solon, N. Y.] this summer.

The weather is milder this week. it seems more like spring. we have had very cold weather for this month untill this week. I am glad to have it come warm. we have had cold weather enough for one winter.

Jut why do not you come home for a few days? there are a great many that has come home and more that are coming. they stay ten days. I know that is not long but is better than nothing to your friends. I guess that your folks would be glad to see you even if it was for a short time. What are you doing south? I think it is time they done something so they can get through and let the boys come home. it makes rather dull time here.

Jut write when you have an opportunity and excuse this paper and miserable writing.

Believe me your friend
Matie.

Camp Bayard
Near Pratts Landing
Sun, Mar. 29th 1863

Dear Friend,

again I will try and pen to thee a few lines in answer to your kind note that I recieved last night. I was vary happy to hear that you have a good school, and that you are enjoying yourself as well as you can under the present sircumstances. i would like to call in to your school some day and see you. for there is no place which seems more like home to me than the school room. you spoke about furloughs. they have played out intirely.

there has been two in our company that wint home but by order of Gen Hooker there is to be no more given out. I should liked to have come up there and seen my old friends vary well and got some warm shugar to eat. Oh; wouldent I made it suffer. but there is no use of talking for I am here and I cant come untill Uncle Sam gets ready to let me and that will be in about two and a half years probably [That was a pretty good guess- Justus was discharged on July 19, 1865].

I was over to the 157th Reg a while ago. saw Ike Waler. he appears to like the buisness vary well. The most of the boys was wishing themseves in the Cav and I dont blame them for it. would kill me off to have to carry the knapsack as they do.

You may talk about its being mudy there and dry and dusty here. but I never saw the mud half so deep there as it now is here. it is a vary backward spring here, so says the old setlers.

We have been out on picket since I wrote last and stayed ten days. we had two or three chases after some Rebs, but did not get them. Our Co has gone out again this morning. I did not go for my horse was not able, and we have to learn some to take care of the camp.

It is a vary cold windy day. my tent shakes so that it is most impossible to write.

I think that we shal have to brake camp in a few days. the infantry have been sending off all of thier extra clotheing to Washington for the summer. they had orders to move forward yesterday, but it was countermanded. It is so cold that I shal have to give up writing.

Pleas answer as soon as convenient and excuse mistakes and poor writing and except this from your humble servant.

J. G. Matteson
P.S. in the directions in place of Vanderbilt put Lt. B. B. Porter.

Review by President Lincoln

On April 6, 1863 the Third Cavalry Division under Brigadier General David McM. Gregg, including the 10th New York, marched to Falmouth (#6 on Map 2.2). There the entire Army of the Potomac was reviewed by General Hooker and President Lincoln.

Two-Week March Prior to the Stoneman Raid

On April 13 they started on a two-week march which seems kind of pointless: they visited Bealton (#7 on Map 2.2), marched to Kelly's Ford (#5 on Map 2.2), went back to Bealton, visited Waterloo (#9 on Map 2.2), Warrenton Junction (#10 on Map 2.2), and finally crossed the Rappahannock at Kelly's Ford (#5 on Map 2.2) for the start of Stoneman's Raid on Richmond. Preston describes the march in more detail [6]:

> Gregg's division bade adieu to Camp Bayard [#1 on Map 2.1] after a stay of nearly four months. The time passed there and on the Northern Neck, if not always pleasant, had been varied. The hours of yawning and yearning, waiting and wishing, fretting and freezing, had been sandwiched with others full of fun and frolic, shouting and scouting, picket and poker, so that, taken together, the boys of the Tenth no doubt felt something of regret at the parting with the old and familiar scenes.
>
> The Regiment was formed in line on the morning of April 13th preparatory to leaving the camp. When the order came that set the command in motion there was many a glance toward the rough old camp, the little log-cabins and the oft-trodden paths. If not audible, there nevertheless was felt in the hearts of many the sad "good-by," a faint echo of that farewell that had moistened the eye and loosened the tension of the heart-strings when they saw the dear old homes they had left away up North growing fainter in the distance months before. They knew the spring campaign was about to open, and they would return no more to Camp Bayard.
>
> At about 8 A.M. the Regiment, under command of Lieutenant Colonel Irvine, broke into column of fours, preceded by the other regiments of the brigade, and after a march of about twenty miles went into camp. Next day, the 14th, it reached Bealton, and thence to the Rappahannock, with the apparent design of crossing; but,

71

after "demonstrating," a portion of the First Maine Cavalry effected a crossing, driving off a force of rebels who were guarding the bridge, and recrossed to the north side during the afternoon. It rained hard the latter part of the day. The boys had more gloom than glory as they settled down in a heavy rain that night.

Again the men were in the saddle at eight o'clock the next morning, the rain still falling. After changing base several times, the Regiment finally went into camp in the woods. The night was, if possible; more dreary than the last, cold and raw, and the rain continuing.

The river had now become a mad torrent; crossing was impossible. Meantime, like the fabled general who marched his army up the hill and then marched it down again, the cavalry corps was kept moving, breaking camp in the morning, marching a little, and going into camp again. ...

Foraging parties brought in considerable corn on the 17th [of April, 1863]. A light mist hung over the camp on the 18th, when the Regiment was ordered out. Some cannonading occurred at the river. After marching a short distance, the Regiment went into camp near Bealton. Field report on the 19th showed five hundred and ninety-three effective men and horses. [This was less than 50% of authorized strength; but more attrition during the next two years would make this figure even lower.]

Moving out in a rain-storm which set in the night before, the Regiment marched at 8 A.M. on the 20th, and passing through the village of Liberty, struck the road leading to Waterloo, south of Warrenton, and encamped at 5:30 P.M. Here Lieutenant Preston [author of *The History of the Tenth New York*] was detailed as acting brigade commissary by Colonel Kilpatrick.

Breaking camp at 11 A.M. on the 22d, the Regiment marched to Warrenton Junction and settled down in a cold rain, which continued during the night and most of next day. On the 24th it rained hard all day, and the boys were compelled to move the camp to higher ground. ...

There was some rain on the 28th, but it cleared up in the afternoon. The entire command marched at 6 P.M. and bivouacked near Kelly's Ford about nine o'clock. ...

Stoneman's Raid April 28-May 8, 1863

The crossing of the Rappahannock was the first move of the entire Cavalry Corps in making the raid around Richmond referred to as the Stoneman Raid:

> At 11 A.M. on the 29th of April the cavalry commenced crossing the Rappahannock at Kelly's Ford [#5 on Maps 2.2 and 2.3] on a pontoon bridge [see Figure 2.10], the boats of which were composed of canvas. After crossing, the Tenth bivouacked about two miles from the river at 6 P.M. Some skirmishing after crossing, but the Tenth did not participate.

> And now the start has been made on what has been gilded on the pages of history as the Stoneman Raid. The delay in crossing his troops on the day of arrival at the place of crossing, when the river might have been easily forded, has caused General Stoneman to be severely criticized. His opportunity was lost by one day's delay. General Hooker, under date of April 15, 1863, sent him a dispatch, urging promptness in making the movement, in which he says:

>> "As you stated in your communication of yesterday that you would be over the river with your command at daylight this morning, it was so communicated to Washington, and it was hoped the crossing had been made in advance of the rise of the river." ...

Many American political leaders have been accused of direction of military field operations that is too tight (micro-management). President Lincoln was no exception. In fact he seems to be a good example of the process. In the following letter to General Hooker Lincoln strongly urges Hooker to get the show on the road with respect to the Stoneman Raid. He sends the following to Hooker on April 15, as related by Preston:

Figure 2.10 Pontoon bridge

"Major-General Hooker: It is now 10:15 P.M. An hour ago I received your letter of this morning, and a few moments later your dispatch of this evening. The letter gives me considerable uneasiness. The rain and mud, of course, were to be calculated upon. General S. [Stoneman] is not moving rapidly enough to make the expedition come to anything. He has now been out three days, two of which were unusually fair weather, and all three without hindrance from the enemy, and yet he is not twenty-five miles from where he started. To reach his point he still has sixty to go, another river [the Rapidan] to cross, and will be hindered by the enemy. By arithmetic, how many days will it take him to do it? I do not know that any better can be done, but I greatly fear it is another failure already. Write me often; I am very anxious. Yours truly, A. Lincoln." ...

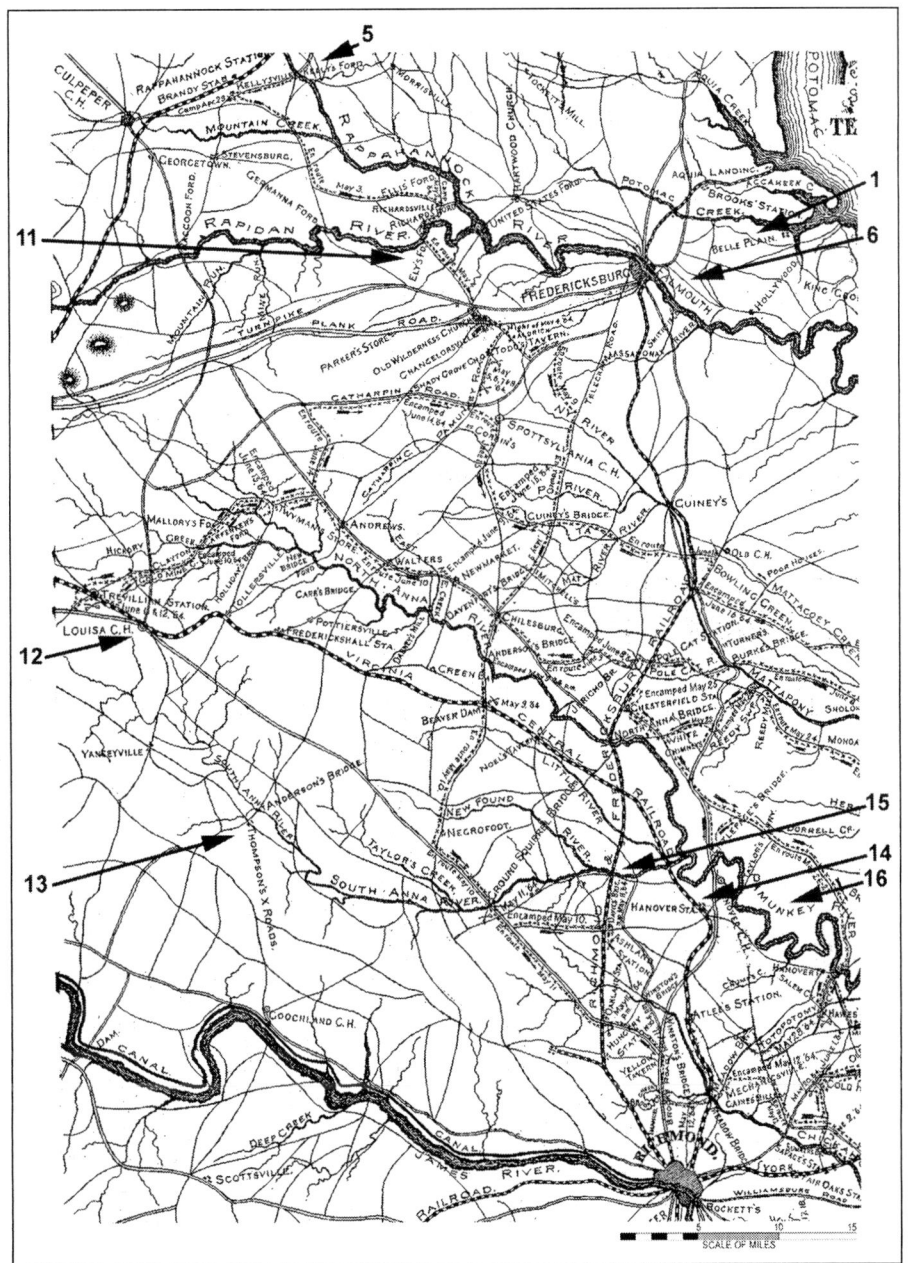

Map 2.3 The Stoneman Raid, May 18, 1863

The route of Stoneman's Raid can be followed by referring to Map 2.3, and is described by Preston:

> By the long-enforced delay in crossing and the maneuvering of the corps in the vicinity of the upper fords of the Rappahannock, the enemy were given timely notice of an intended movement, but were evidently deceived as to the point of General Stoneman's crossing. The bivouac on the night of the 29th was without fires. A few hard-tack and a moiety of salt Jewish abomination [a small portion of salt pork] was all the boys received to quiet their stomachs' demands.
>
> The morning of the 30th the command moved silently away from its camp on the east bank of the Rapidan at six o'clock. The wagons, extra and sick horses, mules, etc., were sent from here to United States Ford under command of Commissary Preston and Lieutenant M.R. Woodruff.
>
> After crossing the Rapidan [#11 on Maps 2.2 and 2.3], the Tenth marched in the direction of Louisa Court-House [#12 on Map 2.3], going into camp at 9 P.M.
>
> A very early start was made on the morning of Friday, May 1st, the same general direction being pursued. Some skirmishing occurred, but nothing sufficiently serious to impede the onward march. Reaching the vicinity of Louisa Court-House at night, the railroad was destroyed each side, and at 4 A.M. on the 2d the Tenth charged through the town. A considerable force of the enemy was encountered. Some brisk fighting took place for a time, the Regiment losing three men wounded and three taken prisoners. Some Government supplies fell into the hands of the Regiment.
>
> The Tenth left Louisa Court-House at 5 P.M., the rear of the column, and arrived at Thompson's Cross roads [#13 on Map 2.3] at 10 P.M., the men pretty well worn out.
>
> In his report, dated May 15, 1863, covering the operations of the Third Cavalry Division on the Stoneman raid, General D. McM. Gregg says:
>
>> "Leaving Orange Springs at 6 P.M. (May 1st), the division arrived within three fourths of a mile of the Court House at 3 A.M. on the following day. At once placing

the two sections of artillery under command of Captain J.M. Robertson, Second Artillery, in a commanding position, and forming Colonel Wyndham's brigade as supports, I directed Colonel Kilpatrick to form his brigade into three columns of attack- one to strike the town, one the railroad one mile above, the third the railroad one mile below the town. These parties, commanded respectively by Colonel Kilpatrick, Lieutenant-Colonel Irvine, and Major Avery, Tenth New York, did the work handsomely."

The command broke camp and the Sabbath at 3 A.M., May 3d, and moving eastward encamped at 5 P.M. near Hanover [#14 on Map 2.3], to which place a detail of one hundred and ten men from the Tenth was sent to destroy the railroad bridge. The bridge was a strong one and the force of rebels guarding it still stronger, so the boys tore up the railroad track and burned some warehouses and retired.

Thompson's Cross-roads was the objective on the 4th [May]. A half-hour's halt for rest was made near a brick church at about 1:30 A.M. Here the detachment sent from the Regiment the day before to destroy the bridge at Hanover joined the command. The march was resumed at 5 A.M., and the Tenth bivouacked at Thompson's Crossroads at 3 P.M. The forced marches and lack of sleep were beginning to tell on the men. They slept in the saddles while on the march. ...

At 2 P.M. of the 5th [May] the Regiment left camp, and crossed the South Anna River [#15 on Map 2.3] at 4:30 P.M. and the Pamunkey [#16 on Map 2.3] at 11 P.M. The marching was continued all night in the rain. It was intensely dark, and in some places the surroundings and soil were in perfect harmony, being dressed in deep mourning. Halts were made from time to time, and during these short stops the men would fall asleep, the horses, with heads down, joining in the effort to relieve overburdened Nature. At such times the quiet that prevailed would have made a Shaker meeting seem like a pandemonium, until some luckless fellow would lose his equipoise and fall to the ground, the rattling of saber and accoutrements waking those about, causing a general tender of choice adjectives, gilded with sulphur, as the only assistance to the unfortunate comrade. Or, perchance, some poor, exhausted fellow would give audible expression to his peaceful slumbers by snoring, when his fellows would hurl at him such choice epithets as "Put a nose-bag on him!" "Buck and gag him!" etc.

Wednesday, the 6th, the march and sleep was continued. A brief halt was made at 9 A.M., on the 7th [May], the first since leaving camp the morning before, and, crossing the Rapidan [#11 on Map 2.3], reached Kelly's Ford [#5 on Map 2.3] and encamped at 9 P.M. in a drenching rain.

It would, no doubt, have been considered impossible to cross the Rappahannock in its swollen condition, had the command been on the north side, but the troops were now in a position that admitted of no argument. They must cross, and they did. On the morning of the 8th [May] the jaded animals were urged into the rushing torrent by their riders and compelled to swim, reaching the opposite shore wherever they could secure a foothold, the current carrying them swiftly down-stream. Although attended with great danger, the crossing was made with the loss of only one man in the Tenth, that of Private Tittsworth, of Company H. ...

Thus the daring and challenging raid by Stoneman's Cavalry Corps came to a conclusion. Preston continues:

The exhausted condition of the command, the two or three days preceding the crossing of the Rappahannock on the return march, was such as to invite attack from an enterprising enemy; but Stuart, the spirit of the Confederate cavalry, had been called to the command of General Jackson's corps, on the wounding of that officer at the battle of Chancellorsville, on the 2d of May, and the *esprit de corps* of the rebel horse appeared at this time somewhat broken. ...

The Stoneman Raid will be remembered by those who participated in it, for the test of endurance it entailed rather than for any great damage inflicted on the enemy. It was one of the many hard strokes which followed rapidly the organization of the corps that finally made the homogeneous mass a solid, compact body, and gave it power and endurance.

Stoneman's Raid destroyed millions of dollars' worth of Confederate property. It also cut Lee's communications system for a while and gave the Union cavalry a much-needed boost in their self-esteem. An unfortunate consequence of the raid, however, is that it deprived Hooker of the use of his cavalry at the battle of Chancellorsville. This battle was considered a major Union defeat, and if the eyes of the cavalry had been available, the defeat might have been avoided.

Picketing around Bealton Station

The Regiment encamped at Bealton Station [#7 on Map 2.2], and took on various picketing assignments through early June, as described by Preston [7]:

> The Regiment continued on picket around Liberty, Fayetteville [#2 on Map 2.2], and on the Sulphur Springs road until Friday, May 29th, when it was relieved by the First Maryland Cavalry. The following day it marched to Warrenton Junction [#10 on Map 2.2] and went on picket. Frequent alarms kept the boys wide awake. It grew quite monotonous if they were not called out at least once every day to meet some threatened attack or to intercept some imaginary raiding party. On being relieved from picket by the First Maine Cavalry on the 2d of June, the Regiment returned to camp.

About this time Justus receives another letter from Mary.

Absent but remembered friend

You will think that I have entirely forgotten you but it is not so. far from it. if I had written to you every time that I have thought about it, it would have been many times. but I must tell you the reason for this long delay. when I received your kind letter I was to Mr. Benjamins but was sick, so that I could not get up but a few moments at a time. I received it friday eve. monday I was carried home and have remained there most of the time since. I could not sit up for a number of weeks and when I could write my paper and finely every thing was to Mr. B. and I could not remember all of the adress. last week I went up to Mr. B.'s so I take this eveing to write to you. it has been a long time since I have heard from you. it seems like an age to me but I am getting quite smart now so that I begin to work some. I have followed your regiment in the papers as far as possible. I have looked over the names of the list but have been happy to find none of our Solon boys in them. that you all may keep in good health and return to your home is the prair of many hearts. It has been quite healthy around here this spring but you know that death loves a shining mark and he took Wats Davis boy away. he was burried last sunday. he was a pretty boy of six years old. their girl is very sick. the disease is Diptheria. Dr. Boles docters the girl. Smith from Freetown doctered the boy. I am afraid that It will go through this place as it has through others. I must close for to night.

Tuesday eve. We are having some rain this week and considerable of wind. the rain we need for we have not had any for a long time. the wind I think we could get along without, but the evening is a beautiful one. how I wish that you was here. I am shure that I should enjoy it far better than I do writing or scribling on this paper. your people are all smart. I saw Delia to meeting last sunday. I guess that she has made up her mind that it is plesanter to stay at home for she does not intend to work out any more this summer. Patience Walker workes to Mr. Carsons. Julie Graves to McGrawville, Jerome and Minerva live to Mr. Whites. they have seperate rooms. I have called to see Clarisa. she appears to enjoy herself ver well.

Ed Graves went west in the Spring. he likes it very well and writes for his folks to come out. I guess that he got the metten [?] so he thought that he would go west. I think it is a very good plan. I guess that I have give you all of the news unless I tell you that Phil Hays is married. he married his lady in Syracuse. he is keeping house on his fathers farm. there is one consilation that William is not married.

80

Jut, I must close this for I have a chance to send it. you must write just as soon as you get this, direct to McGrawville. I think that I shall be here most of the summer.

I remain your friend
Matie L. H.

[Matie, Mate, and Molly were all names that Mary Hatch used for referring to herself.]

The next chapter describes the Battle of Brandy Station, and the beginning of the "Gettysburg Campaign".

References

[1] Preston, Noble D., *History of the Tenth Regiment New York Volunteer Cavalry*, New York, NY: D. Appleton and Company, 1892; reprinted by Higginson Book Company, Salem, MA in 1998; p. 58.

[2] Ibid, 60-64.

[3] Ambrose, Kevin, Dan Henry, and Andy Weiss, *Washington Weather*, Fairfax, VA: Historical Centerpieces, 2002; ISBN 0963950249.

[4] Preston, *History of the Tenth New York*, pp. 64-67.

[5] Thomason, John W., Jr., *Jeb Stuart*, University of Nebraska Press, 1994; pp. 360-361.

[6] Preston, *History of the Tenth New York*, pp. 67-73.

[7] Ibid, 81.

Figure 2.11 Hat insignia for Tenth Cavalry

CHAPTER 3

Start of the Gettysburg Campaign
June-July 1863

"I never saw a dead cavalryman." Gen. Hooker

General Lee Moves North

Coincidentally, both the Union and the Confederate armies decided to be more proactive in mid-1863. Lee planned to start a fast, secret march north into Pennsylvania; and Hooker sent his cavalry corps towards Culpeper in an effort to wipe out the Confederate cavalry, which had been causing considerable havoc to Union plans. Lee had moved his army to Culpeper, and Stuart had his cavalry nearby at Brandy Station. Lee's plan was to use Stuart to shield his movements from Union observers. This meant keeping the union cavalry east of the Shenandoah Valley while Lee moved his infantry north in the Valley to Maryland and into Pennsylvania.

Somehow Hooker, commander of the Army of the Potomac, had discovered that Stuart was in the Culpeper-Brandy Station area and sent his newly-appointed cavalry commander, General Pleasonton, in that direction to do damage. (General Pleasonton had been promoted from commander of the First Division. Also, General Gregg was transferred from commanding the Third Division to command of the Second Division.) Gen. Stuart, in a rare lapse of concentration, decided to have a "grand review" of his cavalry by Gen. Lee and his staff and had no idea that Union cavalry was headed his way. Lee was asked to come over from Culpeper and the review was planned for an area outside of Brandy Station on June 9, 1863.

The events leading up to the Battle of Gettysburg are summarized in Table 3.1. These events are now referred to as part of the Gettysburg Campaign, although no one knew at the time that they would end up there.

General Gregg starts to hear rumors of the huge Confederate movements towards the north, as stated in the following official report to his Third Division counterpart:

HEADQUARTERS THIRD DIVISION,
CAVALRY CORPS
May 23, 1863
Colonel J. H. TAYLOR, *Chief of Staff, Cavalry Corps*

COLONEL: I have the honor to report that nothing of unusual interest has occurred along this line. The depredations of guerrillas and bushwhackers are continued, notwithstanding daily efforts made to drive them away. Their operations are carried on in such a manner as to defy their arrest. Yesterday I had a private of the Tenth New York Cavalry killed near this place, and it is reported that a commissioned officer and one man were captured near Morrisville. The pickets of the enemy along the river are cavalry. Today there was brought to me a contraband, recently the servant of an officer of the Thirteenth North Carolina Infantry. He says when at a house near the Wilderness, and at which his master lay wounded, he saw four regiments of cavalry pass; that a lieutenant of one of the regiments called to see his master, and in his presence stated that these regiments were going to join the other cavalry regiments near Culpeper; that they were going to make a great raid through Maryland. A deserter from the First North Carolina Cavalry confirms the report of the assembling of the cavalry near Culpeper, but knows nothing of the projected raid. I am just sending a command in pursuit of a party of South Carolina cavalry who were sent over to drive in my pickets that they might ascertain our force. I have no doubt that the rebels contemplate making a raid, and of course am interested in knowing what force of cavalry is at Warrenton Junction or thereabouts, as a strong force there would be to them a very serious obstacle.

I am very respectfully your obedient servant,
D.McM. GREGG
Brigadier-General of Volunteers, Commanding 2d Division

Figure 3.1 The Cavalry is on the march (from Preston)

Map #	Events	Dates - 1863
	Battle of Brandy Station	June 9
1	Culpeper	
2	Brandy Station	
3	Beverly's Ford	
4	Kelly's Ford	
5	Fleetwood Hill	
6	Stevensburg	
7	Rappahannock RR Bridge	
	Gettysburg Campaign	
8	Aldie, VA	June 17, 22
9	Middleburg, VA	June 18, 20
10	Upperville, VA	June 19
11	Ashby Gap	June 21
12	Goose Creek	June 22
13	Leesburg	June 24
14	Edwards Ferry	June 26
15	Frederick, MD	June 28
16	Westminster, MD	June 30
17	Hanover Junction, PA	July 1
18	Gettysburg, PA	July 2

Table 3.1 Start of Gettysburg Campaign in 1863

The Battle of Brandy Station June 9, 1863

When Major General Joseph Hooker formed the Cavalry Corps and appointed General George Stoneman as its commander in February, 1863 he did a good thing. Stoneman drilled the men relentlessly that winter and spring, and this laid the foundations for the success to come.

The Battle of Brandy Station was the next big event to come in the life of the 10th New York, L Company and Justus Matteson. The Battle of Brandy Station (sometimes referred to as the Battle of Beverly's Ford) was the largest cavalry engagement of the Civil War. It is also referred to as the start of the "Gettysburg Campaign", leading up to the Battle of Gettysburg (discussed in the next chapter). A map of the area around Culpeper and Brandy Station is shown in Map 3.1. Key points in the Battle of Brandy Station are shown in Map 3.2.

This battle was a major turning point in the role of the Union cavalry in the Civil War. Partly due to Stoneman's rigorous training program, the cavalry became a major fighting force and a major distraction for the Confederate cavalry, which hitherto had been given free reign over many of the War's areas.

Dissatisfaction with the results of the cavalry operations in the rear of the Confederate army (Stoneman's Raid on Richmond) caused the removal of General Stoneman from the command of the corps and the substitution of General Alfred Pleasonton in his stead. The Union debacle at Chancellorsville, when Hooker felt that Stoneman's cavalry could have been of more use than the raid on Richmond, undoubtedly contributed to the decision to replace Stoneman.

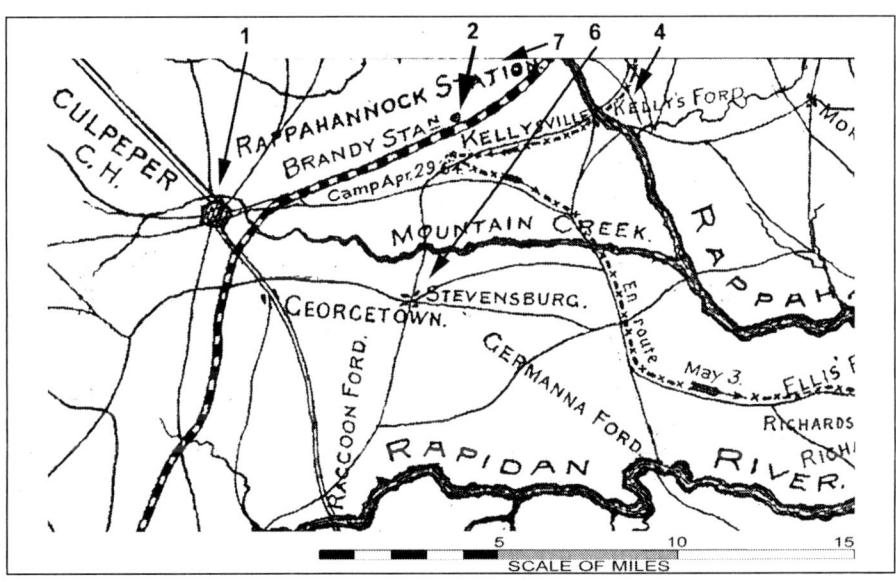

Map 3.1 Area including Culpeper, Stevensburg, Brandy Station etc.

In the reorganization of the cavalry under Gen. Pleasonton, and for the march on Brandy Station, the cavalry consisted of two "wings". The Right Wing consisted of the 1st Cavalry Division, as follows:

> 1st Cavalry Division under Brig. Gen. Buford
> > 1st Brigade, Col. Davis
> > 4 cavalry regiments plus part of the 3rd (West) VA
>
> > 2nd Brigade, Col. Devin
> > 2 cavalry regiments
>
> > Reserve Brigade, Maj. Whiting
> > 4 cavalry regiments
>
> > US Horse Artillery, Capt. Robertson
> > 3 artillery units with 4 batteries each

The Right Wing crossed the Rappahannock at Beverly's Ford (#3 on Map 3.2) on June 9, 1863. As the battle developed, some changes occurred. One battery of artillery was added to the 2nd Brigade, three regiments of cavalry and one battery of artillery were added to the Reserve Brigade, and Brig. Gen. Ames' infantry brigade was added to the Wing.

The Left Wing of the cavalry comprised the other two cavalry divisions, the total Left Wing under the command of Brig. Gen. David McM. Gregg:

> 2nd Cavalry Division under Col. Duffie
> > 1st Brigade, Col. DiCesnola
> > 3 cavalry regiments
>
> > 2nd Brigade, Col. J. Irvin Gregg
> > 3 cavalry regiments
> > 1 artillery battery

3rd Cavalry Division under Brig. Gen. David McM. Gregg
    1st Brigade, Col. Kilpatrick
    3 cavalry regiments, including the 10th NY
    1 company of DC volunteers

    2nd Brigade, Col. Wyndham
    3 cavalry regiments
    1 artillery battery

    Infantry Brigade, Gen. Russell
    5 infantry regiments

    1 artillery battery

Company L of the 10th NY was left at Kelly's Ford (#4 on Map 3.2) with Russell's Infantry Brigade. They crossed to the south side of the river to serve as pickets for Gen. Russell; more later on this dangerous assignment.

The Left Wing crossed the Rappahannock River at Kelly's Ford and moved northwest to link up with the Right Wing.

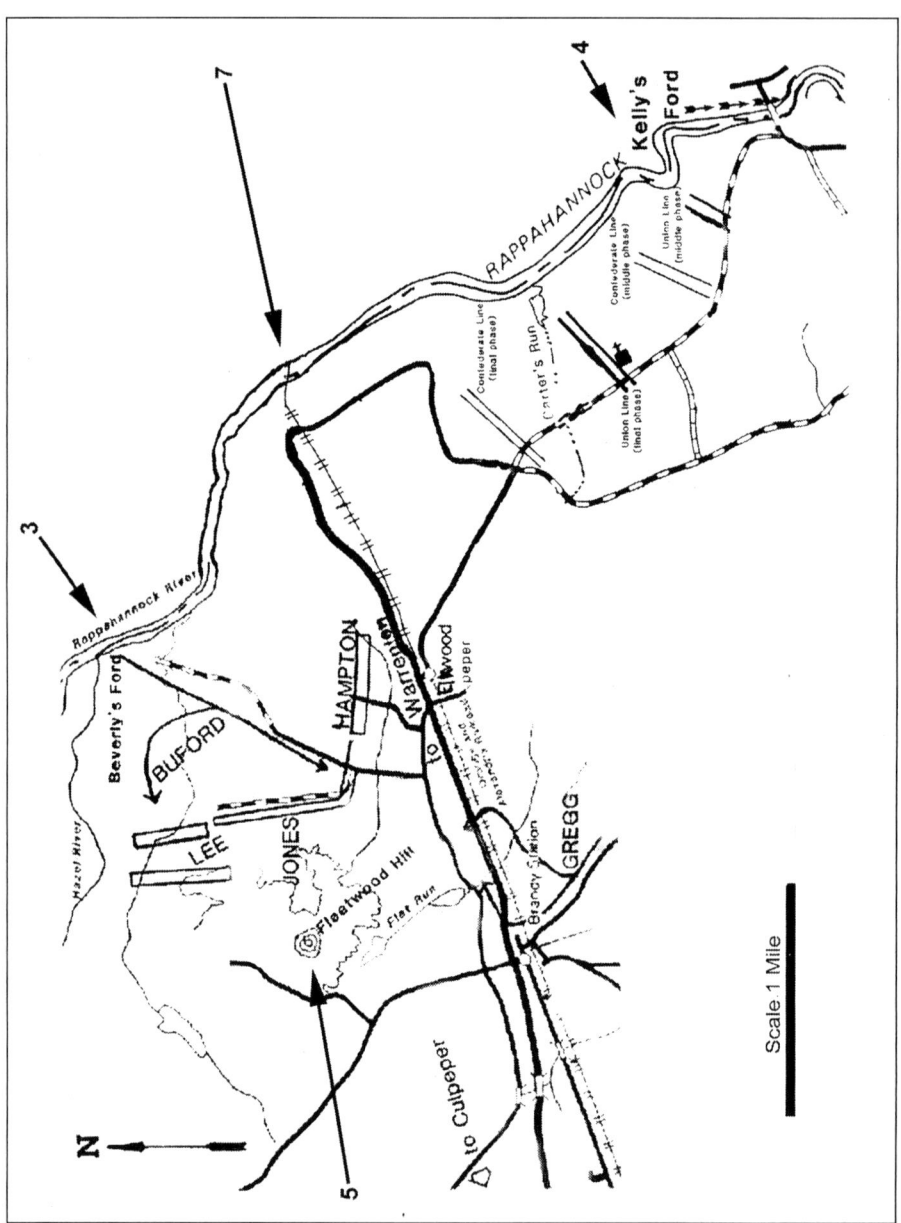

Map 3.2 Area where the Battle of Brandy Station occurred

**Figure 3.2 Barbour House used by Lee and Stuart as HQ
During Brandy Station (2006 photo by author)**

Prior to the move to Brandy Station the regiment was in camp at Bealton Station, about midway between Warrenton Junction and Brandy Station. The troops were on picket duty for most of the time rather than being in camp, until the time came for them to move out. Preston describes the development of the battle as follows [1]:

Colonel Kilpatrick returned and took command of his brigade on Sunday, June 7th. [He had left the rest of the cavalry to take off towards Richmond and ended up at Gloucester Point, VA, at the mouth of the James River, across from Yorktown, with a few rebel prisoners. The 10th New York was not involved in this excursion.] The same evening a number of officers of the brigade assembled at his headquarters and enjoyed a few hours' social intercourse, recounting the scenes and incidents of the raid. It was late when Colonel Kilpatrick remarked, in a jocular way, that the "boys" had better turn in early, and get as much rest and sleep as possible, as the Cavalry Corps would beard the lion in his den, by crossing the Rappahannock the next day, and give battle to the enemy at Brandy Station. This announcement was greeted with expressions of satisfaction, and a desire to meet the Confederate horsemen in an open field fight. The following day was one of busy preparation for battle. ...

General Hooker, having received information that the Confederate army was withdrawing from his front, and massing in the vicinity of Culpeper [#1 on Map 3.1], ordered General Pleasonton to cross the [Rappahannock] river with the Cavalry Corps, and attack whatever force he might encounter, with the view of ascertaining, as far as possible, the numbers and purposes of the enemy. With the impression that no considerable force of Confederates were near the river, General Pleasonton's plan was to cross one division at Beverly Ford and two at Kelly's Ford at the same time, and uniting south of the river, advance until the enemy was encountered. But [unbeknown to Gen. Pleasonton] Stuart had moved his corps near the upper fords, preparatory to crossing the same day [in the opposite direction!], to clear the way and guard the flank of the main army, which was to follow, on an invasion of Maryland and Pennsylvania. There was, therefore, a surprise in store for the Union as well as the Confederate cavalry, when the latter were encountered as soon as Buford's troops gained the southern shore of the Rappahannock, on the morning of the 9th of June. [This was an unusual lack of concentration on the part of Stuart, not to know that a large force of Union cavalry was approaching the Rappahannock, and in fact planning to cross over.]

Camps were broken in Gregg's division [3rd Division, including Kilpatrick's 1st Brigade and the 10th New York] at 2 P.M. on the 8th of June, and the march taken up toward the Rappahannock. The day was very warm and the rising dust almost stifling. Reaching Kelly's Ford in the evening, the troops went into bivouac on the north side. No fires were permitted. The men had neither coffee nor comfort that night, but the loss of these did not chill their ardor. They exhibited an enthusiasm and a desire to measure blades with the Southern horsemen that gave promise of success.

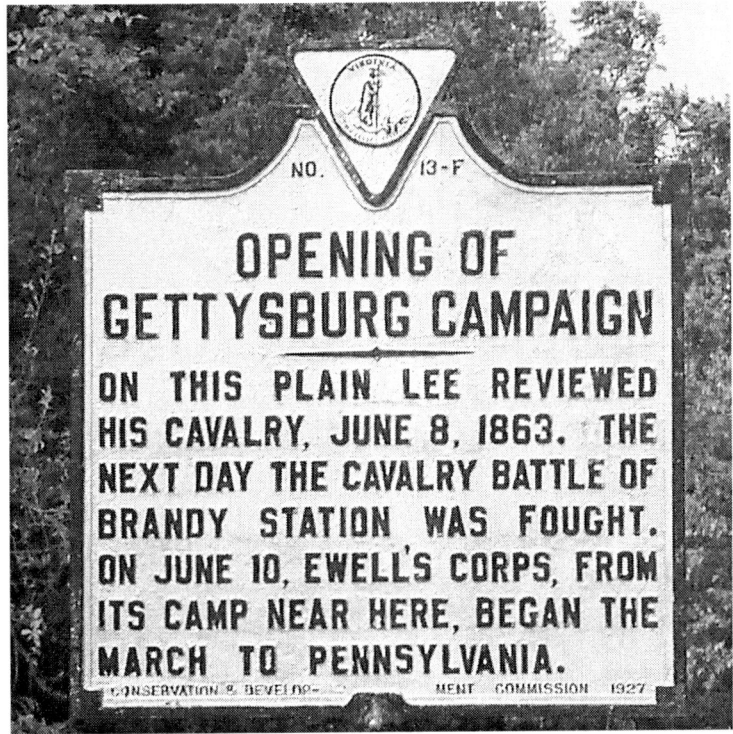

Figure 3.3 Current road marker for Brandy Station battle location (2006 photo by author)

Longstreet's corps of the Confederate army was assembled at Culpeper Court-House on the evening of June 7th, preparatory to crossing the Rappahannock and moving north for the invasion of the loyal states. The Confederate cavalry corps, numbering at least ten thousand men, was reviewed on the open field between Brandy Station and Culpeper Court-House by Generals Lee and Stuart on the day the Federal troops were moved to the vicinity of the fords, preparatory to crossing the next day.

The Comte de Paris relates that Pleasonton's corps numbered scarcely seven thousand five hundred men, and that, to make up for the numerical inferiority, Ames's [infantry] brigade, from the Eleventh, and Russell's [infantry] brigade, from the Sixth Corps, numbering, all told, about three thousand men, were added to Pleasonton's command; but the Comte de Paris adds that, notwithstanding the excellent qualities of these soldiers, "their cooperation interfered with the mobility of the cavalry, and consequently destroyed part of its chances of success."

Early on the morning of the 9th the column under General Gregg crossed at Kelly's Ford unobserved. Buford's division crossed at Beverly Ford, farther up the river, about the same time. General Pleasonton moved with this latter column. General Gregg, leaving the brigade of infantry, under General Russell, at the ford [with Company L of the 10th NY], sent the Second Division, under Colonel Duffie, to Stevensburg [#6 on Map 3.1], while he with his own division, the Third, proceeded direct to Brandy Station. The sound of Buford's guns up the river served to hasten Gregg forward. The unslinging of carbines and snapping of caps along the column before coming in view of the open fields around Fleetwood Hill [#5 on Map 3.2] had an ominous meaning. The arms were closely inspected, the belts tightened, and the ammunition arranged with a view to easy access. Like the gladiator preparing to enter the arena, everything was put in readiness for the conflict.

As the Tenth emerged from the woods, the Second Brigade, under Colonel Wyndham, was already engaged away to the left. The scene was most inspiriting, and called forth many expressions in the Regiment of a desire to participate in the fight. The men had but a moment to wait. Colonel Kilpatrick formed his [First] brigade for attack [with the 10th NY, but without Company L as mentioned above], and with his usual impetuosity led his troops in the charge.

The Comte de Paris says [2]:

> "Wyndham, pressed by superior forces, has fallen back near the station, taking with him his two guns [an artillery battery consists of two guns], together with the three pieces he has captured from the enemy. Gregg, in order to relieve him, orders Kilpatrick's brigade to fall upon the left flank of the Confederates. The latter, strong in numbers, do not yield one inch of ground. Their leaders perform prodigies of valor, for this is a decisive moment. Along all the slopes of Fleetwood Hill and around Brandy Station the hostile lines

are mixed in such a melee as was never before witnessed in America."

Captain Willard Glazier, of the Second New York Cavalry, writes as follows of this trying moment [3]:

"Kilpatrick's battle-flag was seen advancing, followed by the tried squadrons of the Harris Light [2nd NY], the Tenth New York, and the First Maine, in echelon of squadrons. His brigade was quickly formed and he advanced like a storm-cloud upon the rebel cavalry which filled the field before him. The Tenth New York received the first shock of the rebel charge, but was hurled back, though not in confusion."

In this charge a portion of the Second New York Cavalry gave way as the Confederate line was met, and, striking the left flank of the Tenth, threw that part of the Regiment into momentary confusion. The broken nature of the ground over which the command was compelled to pass also contributed to weaken its formation. Nevertheless, the Confederate line was met in a gallant manner by the major part of the Regiment. The First Maine was ordered forward at this opportune moment, and part of the Tenth retired, while another portion continued to engage the enemy at close quarters. The First Maine went gallantly forward, and striking the Confederates in flank, drove them back.

The fact should not be lost sight of that the splendid charge made by the Tenth on this occasion was upon the enemy in superior numbers in front, the Regiment thus meeting more than man for man. Whatever of credit or glory attaches to this particular part of the engagement of the day belongs quite as much to it as to any regiment. It was a memorable charge for the Tenth, one in which it acquitted itself with credit.

In the midst of the struggle [10th NY commanding officer] Colonel Irvine's horse went down with him near the railroad, and he was immediately surrounded and made a prisoner. He fought until overpowered, but was finally forced to surrender. In speaking of his capture afterward, Major Avery [who became Irvine's replacement as 10th NY commanding officer] said: "I never saw so striking an

95

example of devotion to duty. He [Col. Irvine] rode into them slashing with his saber in a measured and determined manner just as he went at everything else, with deliberation and firmness of purpose. I never saw a man so cool under such circumstances."

Gen. Abner Doubleday (incidentally the reputed inventor of baseball) gave a concise overview of the Battle of Brandy Station. Here is part of his report [4]:

"The First Division, under Buford, came upon the enemy between Brandy Station and Beverly Ford. A battle ensued at St. James Church [see Figure 3.4], and, as their whole force confronted him, he was unable to break their line. After fighting some hours he was obliged to turn back with a portion of his command to repel an attempt against his line of retreat. Gregg next appeared upon the scene, and succeeded in getting in Stuart's rear before the rebel general knew he was there. Buford having gone back toward Beverly Ford, as stated, Gregg, in his turn, fought the whole of Stuart's force without the cooperation of either Buford or Duffie. It can hardly be said that Duffie's column took any part in the action, for he did not reach Brandy Station until late in the day; and then, as the rebel infantry was approaching, Pleasonton ordered a retreat."

Preston continues his discussion [5]:

C.W. Wiles, of Company L [10th NY] relates that, at the time of approaching the scene of the conflict in the morning, Captain Vanderbilt was sent to report with his company, L, to General Russell, commanding the brigade of infantry, who ordered him to post pickets [on the south side of the Rappahannock River] to give warning of any movement down the roads in his front. And so it chanced that the Regiment was deprived of the services of this excellent company in its operations around Fleetwood Hill. [Justus and L Co. therefore missed the big fight.] Toward evening the cessation of firing at Brandy Station caused Captain Vanderbilt to feel that the battle must have ended, and he looked anxiously for orders from General Russell to withdraw his pickets; but none came.

It was after sunset when the pickets reported large numbers of horsemen in their front. It was impossible to determine the color of their

**Figure 3.4 Location of St. James Church,
landmark in the Battle of Brandy Station (2006)**

uniforms, and Elias Wright and Fred Tillinghast were sent forward to observe and report. They were immediately fired upon, and as they retired they were pursued by quite a number of the enemy. Captain Vanderbilt rightly conjectured that our troops had been withdrawn to the north side of the river, and that his little force had been forgotten. He, therefore, hastily called in his pickets, and gave the enemy a volley, and started his company on a run for Rappahannock Bridge [#7 on Map 3.2], some three miles away [three miles northwest of Kelly's Ford, where the Orange and Alexandria railroad crossed the river]. The enemy, recovering from the bold action of the Captain and his squadron, immediately commenced the pursuit. Captain Vanderbilt kept his command well together, as they sped onward as rapidly as spur and voice could urge their horses. Shouting and shooting, the rebels followed, close behind. While the pursued were making every effort to increase the gap between themselves and their pursuers, Andy Ginn's horse stumbled, throwing Andy to the ground. Captain Vanderbilt was not made of the stuff that deserts a man in such an extremity. Calling on a couple of his men to halt, they assisted in getting the horse and man properly adjusted for a continuation of the race, the rest of the men meantime causing the pursuers to check their horses for an instant by a practical display of their marksmanship. Then away they went like the wind again, until their hearts were gladdened by the sight of our troops across the river. Our artillery, mistaking them for Johnnies, sent several shells into altogether too close proximity to be comfortable. The gathering darkness prevented recognition, and the boys were compelled to run the gantlet of the shells until their identity was disclosed to our troops at the river. Then the guns were elevated to suit the requirements of the case, and Company L came into camp under flying colors.

Night settled down on the Regiment, near Bealton Station [#18 on Map 4.4, next chapter], in a broken and rather dejected state. The men, all begrimed and battered, entertained no thought of sleep, but remained grouped together, discussing the great battle, with its many incidents of daring deeds and noble sacrifices. There were many touching allusions to the loss of tent-mates, and the heroic efforts to save companions from death or capture, but all were imbued with the glory of having met and successfully measured sabers with the much-vaunted and by many thought to be invincible rebel cavalry.

The [10th NY] Regiment sustained a severe loss in the capture of Lieutenant Colonel Irvine, Captain Getman [I Co.], and Lieutenant King [G Co.], and the death of Lieutenant Robb [D Co.]. Colonel Irvine, while a good disciplinarian, was by nature kind and sympathetic, and his presence with the Regiment was a guarantee that every interest of the men would be carefully looked after and attended to.

The capture of Captain Getman was a severe loss to the Regiment, and a source of mortification and disappointment to himself. He was an educated military man, a superb horseman, and an accomplished swordsman. Although of a retiring nature, he would most surely have attained to a high position in the service had he not been cut off from all chance of advancement by his long imprisonment.

Lieutenant King, with a shattered arm, was borne away to die in a rebel hospital, after enduring a long and painful imprisonment. Want of the simplest attentions to his wound at the proper time deprived this gallant officer and noble man of his life.

No braver man ever drew saber than Lieutenant Robb. Full of dash, energy, and enterprise, he was an officer calculated to keep an enemy on the alert, and to impress his own character upon those about him.

The gallantry of the Tenth on the field of Brandy Station is well attested by its losses, which are given in the Official Records, vol. xxvii, page 169, as follows:

Officer killed	1
Officers wounded	3
Officer missing	1
Enlisted men killed	2
Enlisted men wounded	15
Enlisted men missing.	60
Total	82

Table 3.2 Casualty list for the 10th New York Cavalry at the Battle of Brandy Station

Or more than twice the loss of the entire brigade outside the Tenth. [Although difficult to prove at this point, the strength's of the Union and Confederate forces were fairly evenly matched, at about ten to twelve thousand horsemen each.]

The lesson of Brandy Station was healthful to our cavalry. It gave them the much-needed confidence in themselves which ever after proved disastrous to their opponents.

Major McClellan, Gen. Stuart's assistant adjutant general, frankly said [6]:

One result of incalculable importance certainly did follow this battle, it made the Federal cavalry. Up to that time confessedly inferior to the Southern horsemen, they gained on this day that confidence in themselves and in their commanders which enabled them to contest so fiercely the subsequent battle-fields of June, July, and October.

Commenting on this defeat of the Confederate cavalry at Brandy Station, the *Richmond Examiner* of that period said:

> The surprise of this occasion was the most complete that has occurred. The Confederate cavalry was carelessly strewn over the country, with the Rappahannock only between it and an enemy who has already proven his enterprise to our cost. It is said that their camp was supposed to be secure because the Rappahannock was not supposed to be fordable at the point where it actually was forded. What! Do the Yankees then know more about this river than our own soldiers, who have done nothing but ride up and down its banks for the past six months?

Conclusions from the Battle of Brandy Station were universally favorable from the Union standpoint, as indicated in this quote from the Civil War Home web site [7]:

> Brandy Station was really the turning-point in the evolution of the Federal cavalry, which had heretofore been dominated by a sense of its own inferiority to Stuart's bold horsemen.

Official Report by Colonel Judson Kilpatrick on Brandy Station

Below is the official report submitted by Col. Kilpatrick immediately after the battle.

OFFICIAL REPORT

Report of Colonel Judson Kilpatrick, Commanding First Brigade, Third Division, Cavalry Corps, at the Battle of Brandy Station, June 9, 1863.

HEADQUARTERS FIRST BRIGADE, THIRD DIVISION,
CAVALRY CORPS, *June 10, 1863*
    CAPTAIN: I have the honor to submit the following report of
the part taken by my brigade in the cavalry action yesterday:

After receiving orders from General Gregg to move to the
right of Colonel Wyndham and engage the enemy, I formed line
of battle in echelons of regiments, with a section of artillery on
the right of the Second Regiment, and moved rapidly forward,
pushing my whole line of skirmishers up to and beyond the
railroad crossing. At this moment the enemy with a large and
superior force drove our forces from the hill on my left so
gallantly taken by Colonel Wyndham. I ordered Colonel Irvine,
of the Tenth New York, who was on the left of my line, to
charge and drive the rebels from the hill and hold it. Colonel
Irvine had scarcely advanced one hundred yards when my whole
line was threatened by a superior force of the enemy. I ordered a
section of artillery to commence firing, and advanced Colonel
Davies, of the Harris Light Cavalry, with one battalion, to
charge the enemy in flank. Before, however, Colonel Irvine or
Colonel Davies had passed the railroad crossing with any
considerable portions of their commands, the enemy in two
heavy columns struck their advance and threw them into
confusion. I sent orders to these two officers to withdraw and
rally their commands, and with the First Maine (Colonel Douty)
swept to the right and charged the enemy in flank. They
outnumbered us three to one, but could not withstand the heavy
saber-blows of the sturdy men of Maine, who rode through them
and over them, gained the hill, captured a battle-flag and many
prisoners, among them the rebel General Stuart's adjutant-
general.*

* Preston writes that "This is an error. Stuart's adjutant-general was
not captured, but one of his aides was."

From this moment the fight was one series of charges, every regiment of the brigade charging, rallying, and again charging until ordered to retire. Each regiment left the field with its organization preserved and in good order.

We captured one stand of colors, upward of one hundred prisoners, and a battery of four guns - two by Colonel Douty and two by Colonel Davies. The guns could not be brought off, but all the horses were killed.

The following is a list of casualties in my brigade:

Harris Light Cavalry: One lieutenant and fourteen enlisted men wounded, and thirty-three enlisted men missing.

The First Maine Cavalry: Three enlisted men wounded, fourteen missing, and seven prisoners.

The Tenth New York Cavalry: Three commissioned officers wounded and missing, two wounded and present; eight enlisted men wounded, and forty-four missing.

Total: Commissioned officers, six wounded; enlisted men, thirty-two wounded and ninety-eight missing.

I regret the loss of Lieutenant-Colonel Irvine, of the Tenth New York Cavalry, who since the fight has been missing. He led his regiment most gallantly in the last charge, and was seen to fall, overpowered by numbers. [Col. Irvine was captured.]

I can not single out individual cases of gallantry. Each regiment rivaled the other in deeds of daring. For the first time we have fought as a brigade. We tried to do our duty like men. I am proud of my brigade, and only hope that in this its first effort it has won the good opinion of our general.

Respectfully submitted,
J. KILPATRICK, *Colonel, Commanding Brigade*
Captain H.C. WEIR, *Assistant Adjutant-General*

Another Reorganization of the Cavalry Corps

The division moved to Warrenton Junction on the 10th of June, and next day the Cavalry Corps was reorganized into two divisions: the First, consisting of three brigades, was commanded by Brigadier General John Buford; and the Second, of the same number of brigades, by Brigadier

General D. McM. Gregg. The Third Brigade of the latter division was made up of the First Maine, **Tenth New York**, and Fourth and Sixteenth Pennsylvania, and was commanded by Colonel John Irvin Gregg of the last-named regiment (cousin of Brigadier General David McM. Gregg).

Figure 3.5 10th New York on the March to Brandy Station

The first brigade of the second division was commanded by Kilpatrick, after a promotion to Brigadier General.

On the March to Gettysburg: Aldie, Middleburg and Upperville

After the Battle of Brandy Station, Lee moved north in the Shenandoah Valley. The Union intelligence must have indicated something about the movements of Lee's army and the Army of the Potomac started moving north also. Jeb Stuart tried to hide Lee's movements with the Confederate cavalry by guarding the passes through the Blue Ridge, but the Union cavalry, on the other hand, tried to find out what was going on. This led to numerous confrontations between the blue and gray cavalries. They battled back and forth over what is now known as Virginia Route 50, the "Mosby Highway", running through Aldie to Middleburg and on to Upperville and Ashby's Gap through the Blue Ridge. [#'s 8, 9, 10, and 11 respectively on Map 3.3].

Just east of Aldie, on the Mosby Highway (Route 50) is the Mt. Zion Church, built in 1851. This church was used by the Confederates as a meeting place for John Singleton Mosby's guerrilla fighters. It was also used as the Union's hospital after a battle between Union cavalry and Mosby's band. This battle came out badly for the Union - a sign on the site indicates over 100 Union cavalry soldiers were killed in the battle. The cemetery used for burying Union dead cavalry men can be seen just to the left of the Church shown in Figure 3.6, a photo taken by the author in 2006. This attack by Mosby occurred later in the war, in 1864.

**Figure 3.6 Mt. Zion Church, east of Aldie on Rt. 50
(2006 photo by author)**

Preston relates some of the actions that occurred after leaving Brandy Station and on the route to Gettysburg [8]:

The Tenth remained in camp near Warrenton Junction until the 15th of June, when the cavalry commenced moving northward. The infantry had been marching in the same direction for several hours before the cavalry broke camp. Reaching Union Mills late at night, the Regiment bivouacked, and next day marched with the brigade to Aldie, where it arrived about 3 P.M. As the Regiment neared the village, the sharp crack of the carbines indicated an engagement. The Tenth was moved to the right of the road just before reaching a bridge over a little creek in the edge of the village.

The First Maine Cavalry had been detached and ordered to report to Kilpatrick, who had been promoted to brigadier-general on the 10th of June and now commanded the First Brigade of the Second Division. They were immediately ordered forward to charge the enemy, who were posted behind stone walls, hay-stacks, etc. The First Maine did noble service here, losing heavily, among their killed being the brave Colonel Douty, who fell pierced by a rebel bullet while gallantly leading his regiment in the charge. The Tenth did not actively participate in this engagement, but portions of the Regiment were on the skirmish-line for a time. It remained near Aldie during the night of the 17th, and the next morning advanced with the brigade on the road to Middleburg, skirmishing sharply with Robertson's and Chambliss's Confederate brigades, steadily driving them back. The Regiment encamped on the pike, midway between Aldie and Middleburg, with pickets near the latter place.

Aldie Mill is shown in Figure 3.7 in a 2006 photo by the author. This mill existed in Civil War days. The Tenth New York and other units pursued Stuart along the Mosby Trail, resulting in battles along the way. Middleburg was the next confrontation. Middleburg presently is a quaint little town with considerable architecture dating from before the Civil War. Figure 3.8 shows a typical building on the main route through the town.

Figure 3.7 The old Aldie Mill (2006)

Figure 3.8 Example of Middleburg pre-Civil War architecture (2006)

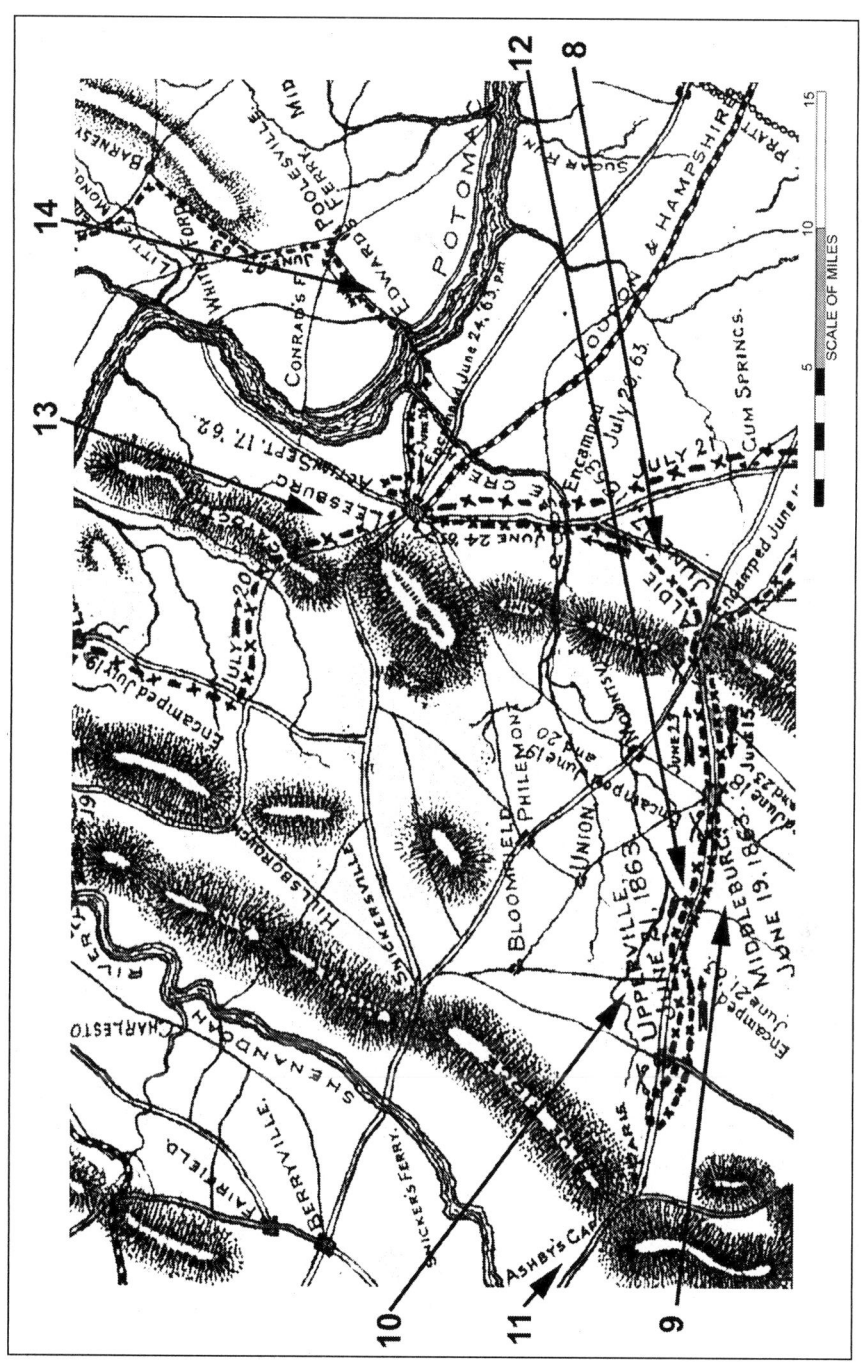

Map 3.3 From Brandy Station to Leesburg

Preston describes the involvement of the 10th New York in the Battle of Middleburg, and continued fighting along the line through Middleburg, Upperville, and back to Aldie [9]:

> Early on the morning of the 19th [June 1863] the advance was taken up, the enemy gradually falling back before the skirmishers. When near the village [Middleburg], the Fourth Pennsylvania charged through the town and for some distance beyond, the Tenth advancing on either side of the road. When about one mile west of the village the enemy made a determined stand. The nature of the country was well suited for defensive operations. The road led through an open timber, with a wheat-field intervening on the right. A heavy stone wall separated the road from the wheat-field, this wall extending the entire distance between our skirmishers and the timber. The road was narrow, making it impossible to charge mounted except in column of fours. The rebels occupied the timber as well as the stone wall. Skirmishing in the wheat-field was quite brisk, while from their protected position behind trees and walls the enemy were delivering a destructive fire into our ranks. General Gregg came upon the ground, and, seeing the necessity of carrying the position, ordered Major Avery to drive the enemy out of the woods. The skirmishers in the wheat-field were advanced, and that portion of the Regiment which was in the road was immediately sent forward to clear the woods. It was exceedingly hot work, but the command sped gallantly to the charge, driving the rebels from cover into the open beyond.

A commemorative sign currently describes the battle, also, as shown in Figure 3.9.

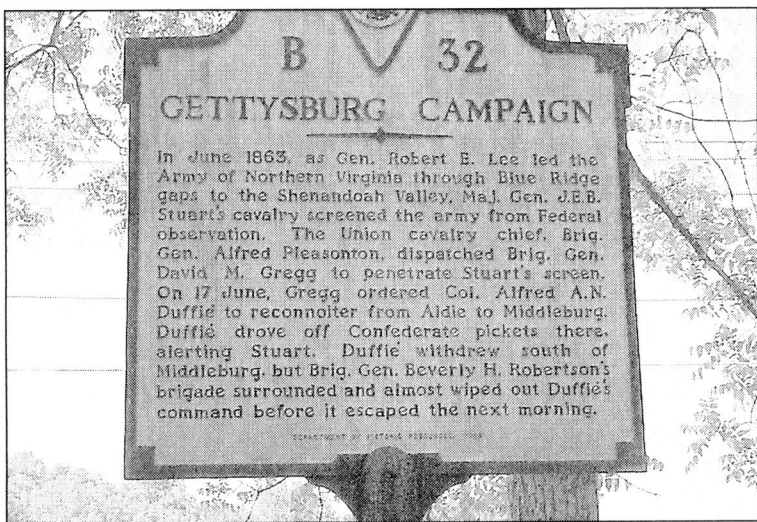

Figure 3.9 Road sign describing the Battle of Middleburg (2006 photo)

In the 1990's the Civil War Sites Advisory Commission (CWSAC) and historians of the National Park Service generated descriptions of what they considered the 384 most significant conflicts (out of approximately 10,500 total recorded conflicts) which took place in the Civil War. The battles at Middleburg and Upperville were two of these significant conflicts. Here is their description of the Battle of Middleburg [10]:

> Maj. Gen. J.E.B. Stuart, screening Lee's invasion route, sparred with Pleasonton's cavalry. On the June 17, Col. Alfred Duffie's isolated 1st Rhode Island Cavalry Regiment was attacked by the brigades of Munford and Robertson. The 1st Rhode Island Cavalry was routed, taking about 250 casualties. On June 19, J. Irvin Gregg's brigade [third brigade of the second division, with the Tenth New York] advanced, driving Stuart's cavalry one mile beyond the town. Both sides were reinforced, and mounted and dismounted skirmishing continued. Stuart was gradually levered out of his position but fell back to a second ridge, still covering the approaches to the Blue Ridge gap.

The Battle of Upperville took place on June 21, 1863, and was also described by the CWSAC, as follows [11]:

> On June 21, Union cavalry made a determined effort to pierce Stuart's cavalry screen. Hampton's and Robertson's brigades made a stand at Goose Creek [#12 on Map 3.3], west of Middleburg, and beat back Gregg's division. Buford's column detoured to attack the Confederate left flank near Upperville but encountered William E. "Grumble" Jones's and John R. Chambliss's brigades while J. I. Gregg's and Kilpatrick's brigades advanced on Upperville from the east along the Little River Turnpike. After furious mounted fighting, Stuart withdrew to take a strong defensive position in Ashby Gap [#11 on Map 3.3], even as Confederate infantry crossed the Potomac into Maryland. As cavalry skirmishing diminished, Stuart made the fateful decision to strike east and make a circuit of the Union army as it marched toward Gettysburg.

The reason that the CWSAC referred to Stuart's decision as "fateful" is the following: Lee lost contact with Stuart until Stuart finally reappeared at the Battle of Gettysburg after it had started. The Union cavalry did a good job of keeping Stuart isolated to their east, preventing him from rejoining Lee's main force. Stuart's cavalry had two primary missions - keep the Army of the Potomac from finding out where Lee's army was located and keep it from finding out where Lee was headed. As a result of Stuart's detour, neither Meade's Army of the Potomac nor Lee's Army of Virginia knew exactly where each other was located and where they both were headed. The Battle of Gettysburg therefore happened accidentally as the two armies tried to occupy the same place at the same time.

The road sign shown in Figure 3.10 currently marks the Battle of Upperville. The tranquil look of the countryside shown in Figure 3.11 belies the frantic activity that took place there on June 19, 1863. The architecture in Upperville is similar to Middleburg, as shown by the 2006 photo of one of the buildings there, in Figure 3.12 [photos by author].

Figure 3.10 Road sign marking the Battle of Upperville (2006)

Figure 3.11 Location of Battle of Upperville (2006)

Figure 3.12 Stone structure in Upperville (2006)

Preston continues with his description of the ongoing Gettysburg campaign [12]:

> Fresh from Brandy's well-fought field, the troopers of Buford's and Gregg's divisions gained additional renown by the series of engagements terminating before Longstreet's corps at Ashby's Gap, and the Tenth was authorized to inscribe on its banners the additional name of Middleburg to swell the constellation of its glorious achievements.
>
> The retrograde movement commenced on the morning of the 22d. The Regiment retired to a point near a mill, between Upperville and Middleburg, and formed in line on the east bank of Goose Creek. The rebels, following at a safe distance, brought a battery to play on it, and the boys were compelled to remain stationary while the shells whizzed over their heads in uncomfortable proximity, or struck in the ground about them, until, just about as their patience was beginning to give out at being set up as targets for the rebel artillery, an order was received changing location. [A photo of the Goose Creek Bridge near Route 50, taken by the author in 2006, is shown in Figure 3.13. The bridge is no longer in use, but the remnants remain.]

Figure 3.13 Goose Creek Bridge

The Regiment was kept in readiness for action during the night of the 22d, on the road between Upperville and Middleburg. The horses were unsaddled on the 23d, and obtained the much-needed grooming - the first in five days. Having received orders to report to General Slocum, commanding the Twelfth Corps, the Regiment started on the morning of the 24th for Leesburg [#13 on Map 3.3], where they arrived about noon. The men felt ill at ease with the infantry. The life was so unlike that with their own corps, they longed to return, even before they had fairly arrived at their destination. On the 25th Sergeant Landers, with fifteen men, was sent to Aldie to bring up the regimental wagons and mail. ...

During the next month the Tenth New York covered a lot of real estate. From Aldie and Middleburg they went north to Leesburg, then to Frederick, MD, Westminster, MD, Hanover Junction, PA and on to Gettysburg, PA (the last 4 locations are identified as #'s 15, 16, 17, and 18 on Map 3.4) for the Big Battle. After the Battle, the Tenth New York pursued Lee's army back down through Pennsylvania, Maryland, West Virginia, and Virginia, as described in the next chapter.

Preston describes the journey as follows:

> The march northward [from Leesburg] was commenced on Friday the 26th. The Tenth moved out with the Twelfth Corps, leaving the little village, through whose streets some of the boys had charged nearly a year before, in a more quiet and orderly manner than on that occasion. Crossing the Potomac at Edward's Ferry in the afternoon, the Regiment went into camp at Point of Rocks. The march was continued on the 27th, and camp was made in the evening at Keatorsville, Md. The following day, Sunday, June 28th, the Regiment entered Frederick, Md., and encamped on the outskirts of the city, where the boys cooked their suppers over fires made from good, dry loyal rails. The Union troops were swarming in and around Frederick on the arrival of the cavalry, and many familiar forms and faces were met by members of the Regiment. The chief topic of conversation was the change in commanders of the army, which took place on the day of the arrival at Frederick, General Hooker having been relieved, and General Meade appointed in his place.
>
> While here, on the 28th [June, 1863], Stahle's division of cavalry, which had been operating about Washington, was assigned to the Army of the Potomac, as the Third Cavalry Division, and General Kilpatrick placed in command of it.
>
> And here, too, on the same day, the Tenth was reunited with the Cavalry Corps, taking its former place in the Third Brigade of the Second Division, to the great joy and satisfaction of the members of the Regiment.

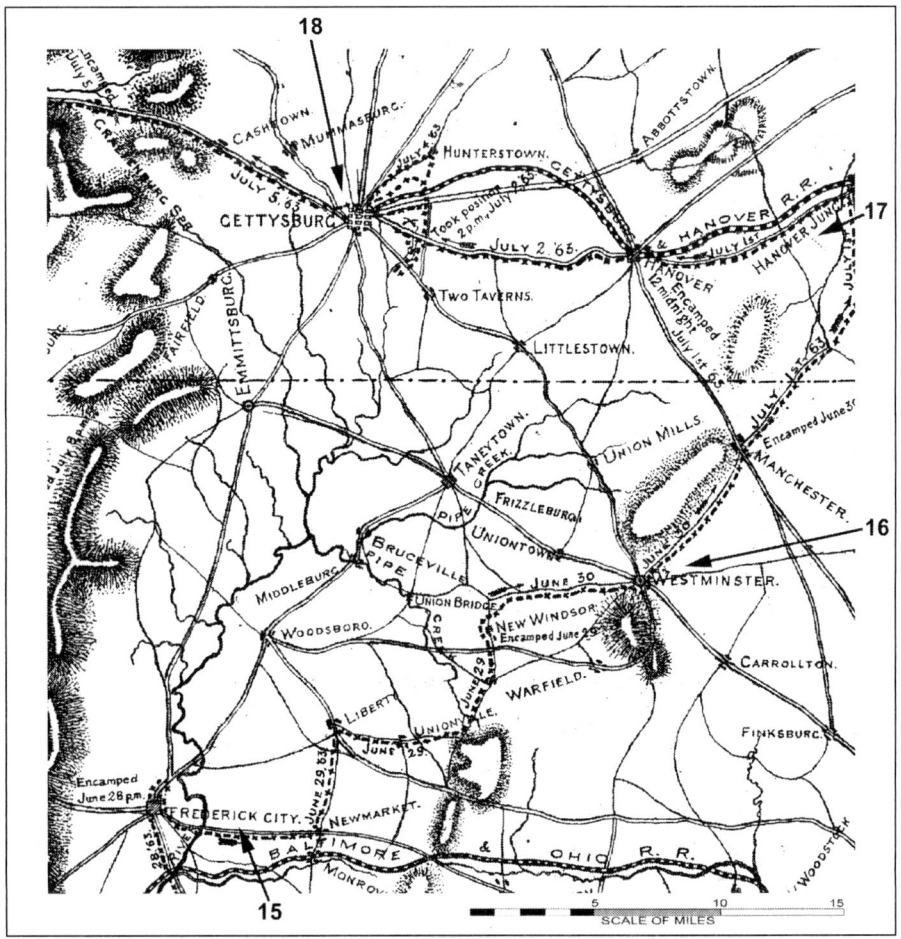

Map 3.4 From Frederick City, MD to Gettysburg, PA

The Army of Northern Virginia had wandered north and got lost. [According to Preston; they knew exactly where they were going. Maybe the Union didn't know where it was; and certainly Stuart was not helping keep Lee informed about the movements of the Union army, as mentioned previously; but Lee was heading for Pennsylvania.] The Federal cavalry was started in search of it. Gregg's division left Frederick, MD on the afternoon of the 28th of June, the Tenth encamping near Newmarket late that night. Then on to New Windsor, where the Regiment bivouacked, after a hot, dusty march. The 30th, Westminster [#16 on Map 3.4] was reached about 10 A.M. Here our First Brigade, under Colonel McIntosh, had driven a small force of Confederate cavalry through the town early in the morning. There yet appeared some evidence of the presence of rebels about the place, and the battery was brought into position in the road above the town, and the Tenth was ordered forward to support it. Before any shooting was done, it was discovered that the enemy had decamped. The boys received a cordial reception from the inhabitants of the beautiful village, numbers of the pretty maidens tendering the hospitalities of their homes, and offering the bronzed and dirt-begrimed veterans such delicacies as they could procure. A detail under command of Sergeant Mitchell secured a good supply of corn, oats, and flour from a mill near the village. After a halt of a couple of hours here, the march was continued.

After a time Major Avery said, "I think we must be in Pennsylvania." The means for ascertaining were at hand. A blooming little miss, from a farmhouse situated away back from the main road, had ventured down to the gate to look at the passing troops.

"Miss, will you please tell us whether we are in Maryland or Pennsylvania?" was asked.

"You are in Maryland yet, but the edge of the woods, just ahead, is the State line," she replied.

"We will cross the line singing John Brown," said Major Avery. Everybody sang, or attempted singing. It was a grand swelling of loyal voices in spontaneous accord - a sublime crossing of the threshold into the grand old Commonwealth whose sons formed so large a part of the command. Reaching Hanover Junction [#17 on Map 3.4], a halt was made about noon on Wednesday, July 1st. Some of the men, fearing that when the march was resumed it would be in the direction of York, started out on the road to Gettysburg, and were gathered in by the provost-guard when the column overtook them later on.

The march was resumed through clouds of dust and the burning rays of a July sun, and the command reached Hanover village at midnight. The inhabitants loyally brought forth such provisions as they had, and gave to the weary soldiers. It was learned from them that Kilpatrick had met Stuart's cavalry the day before, just outside the village, and had a severe fight. This was verified by the leveled fences, dead horses, etc., seen when the Regiment resumed the march early next morning.

Battle of Hanover, PA

This Battle of Hanover (8 miles west of Hanover Junction, towards Gettysburg) was another crucial fight with Jeb Stuart's cavalry, delaying once again his circumlocution of the Union Army and hindering the aid he could have given Lee about the movements of the Union forces. The CWSAC gives the following description of this Battle of Hanover [13]:

> Maj. Gen. J.E.B. Stuart's cavalry, which was riding north to get around the Union army, attacked a Union cavalry regiment, driving it through the streets of Hanover. Brig. Gen. Farnsworth's brigade arrived and counterattacked, routing the Confederate vanguard and nearly capturing Stuart himself. Stuart counterattacked. Reinforced by Brig. Gen. George A. Custer's brigade, Farnsworth held his ground, and a stalemate ensued. Stuart was forced to continue north and east to get around the Union cavalry, further delaying his attempt to rejoin Lee's army which was then concentrating at Cashtown Gap west of Gettysburg.

The following story from Preston's account concerns the surgeon of the Tenth New York. He was working in the Union hospital in Hanover, before the Tenth New York arrived there [14].

> Surgeon Lyman W. Bliss, of the Tenth, was in charge of the field hospital at Hanover at the time the fight between Kilpatrick and Stuart took place. During the engagement the Doctor noticed a regiment or detachment give way, and then he saw that they appeared to be without an officer to lead them, and, turning to a fellow-surgeon, he said: "Those fellows have no officer with them; let's go and lead them," and, discarding all insignia of the medical staff, they each obtained a saber and sailed in, urging the men forward to renew the action, but they appeared somewhat demoralized and refused to stand when another charge was made, but broke, leaving the gallant quinine dispensers in the hands of the enemy. After making the acquaintance of some of the Confederate

117

leaders, who undertook the useless task of drawing some valuable information from them, they were paroled after being retained two or three days. The old adage was peculiarly applicable in this case, " where ignorance is bliss," etc. …

Preston continues with his description of the campaign:

Sleepy and tired the command started toward Gettysburg at 3 A.M., July 2d. Reaching the heights, some three miles east of the village, about noon, the Regiment halted and dismounted on the south side of the Hanover road. [The second day of this huge conflict was underway by this time.] A rail fence on the opposite side of the road was leveled to give free passage for mounted troops. This had an ominous look, and chilled the ardor of some of the men, who were expecting to visit friends in Gettysburg.

The reports of the conflict raging in the direction of the town admonished the impatient ones that it would be necessary to defer the visit to their Gettysburg friends to a more convenient season. The men therefore threw themselves upon the ground under the burning rays of the sun and patiently awaited orders, while they discussed the situation, etc.

John Madole, of Company L, was perhaps the first man from the Regiment to enter Gettysburg. As he was a member of one of the new companies, and therefore not with the command during its stay in the town in 1861-'62, it must have been love of adventure rather than woman that took him there. He was in the town when Buford's cavalry passed through its streets out to Seminary Ridge on the 1st of July. He made a very complete survey of the quaint little village, about which he had heard his comrades say so much. On leaving the borough he was arrested as a spy and taken before General Kilpatrick. The General questioned him closely for a few moments, when, convinced that he was a member of the Tenth, he ordered his release. He gave much valuable information, which the General afterward acknowledged to Major Avery.

The next chapter relates the involvement of the 10th New York and L-Company at the Battle of Gettysburg and the pursuit of Confederate troops after the battle. Additional events occurring in the last half of 1863 will also be discussed.

Justus writes to Mary about Brandy Station and his experience of being stranded on the wrong side of the Rappahannock by General Russel, in a letter to Mary several days after the occurrence. He also writes about being at the Battle of Gettysburg and mentions the surrender of Vicksburg, a major victory for General U.S. Grant in the western fighting.

Figure 3.14 On the march

Middletown, M.D.
July 10th, 1863

Absent but remembered friend,

you may think it strange that I have not answered your kind note before this but in the first place your letter was miscarried. second our mail was delayed. third there has been no chance to send out our mail untill now. therefore I will improve the first oportunity. I am glad to hear that you are recovering your health and hope that you will soon be well if you are not before now.

Mary I have seen some of the hardships of a soldiers life. I last wrote to you I was in the battle of Brandy station. our Co was detailed to support a battery and by a mistake of Gen. Russel we were left in a piece of woods for two hours after the rest of our troops had recrossed the river at rappahannock ford. well the first thing that we realised was the yelling of the rebs. they wer charging upon us with a large forse. well we mounted in a hurry and out and gave them a volley and then wheeled and skedadled for the river which was three miles distant. the rebs wer within ten rods of us yelling like so many demons and the balls ahumming about us like fun. we made good our retreat without the loss of a man.

Our next fight was at Middleburg & Uppervill. from here we crossed the potomac at Edwards Ferry. it seemed as though we wer liberated from prison as soon as we got into Maryland. the people wer so different, so much like home. we had a tedious march to Gettysburg. I was not in the fight at that place but close by it. I should have been but my horse played out so I was dismounted and had to go behind with the mule train. I will [not] give an account of this battle for you can get it in the papers more correct perhapse for I could not see much of it.

P.S. your letter was miscarried, on the account of your leaving off the Cav in the directions.

We are now at Midletown [MD] about ten miles from Frederick city waiting for some new horses.

we have official dispatches of the surrender of Vicksburg to day. the news created quite an excitement. and now if we can capture Lees army here I think the rebellion would go down.
I am in good health. you must excuse mistakes etc.

120

Mat I must close for it is supper time. I have just drawn my rations. they are the first that I have got in two weeks. we have had to beg or buy them for that time as our trains could not come up to us. Mat write as soon as convenient and oblige.

your friend
J. G. Matteson

Figure3.15 Fording the river

References

[1] Preston, Noble D., *History of the Tenth Regiment New York Volunteer Cavalry*, New York, NY: D. Appleton and Company, 1892; reprinted by Higginson Book Company, Salem, MA in 1998; pp. 82-85.

[2] Comte de Paris, *The Battle of Gettysburg*, Digital Scanning, 2000; ISBN 1582180660.

[3] *Three Years in the Federal Cavalry*, Capt. Willard Glazier.

[4] Doubleday, Abner, *Campaigns of the Civil War*, Da Capo Press; Reprint edition (April 1994); ISBN: 0306805499.

[5] Preston, *History of the Tenth New York*, pp. 89-92.

[6] McClellan, Henry B., *The Campaigns of Stuart's Cavalry* (reprint, Blue & Grey Press, Secaucus, New Jersey, 1993), p. 294.

[7] "Photographic History of the Civil War", Volume 2, Article by Charles D. Rhodes, Captain, General Staff; United States Army; on the Web at http://www.civilwarhome.com/cavalrybattles.htm, Brandy Station, from "Civil War Cavalry Battles and Charges", p. 2.

[8] Preston, *History of the Tenth New York*, pp. 93-94.

[9] Ibid, 94-95.

[10] National Park Service, Civil War Sites Advisory Commission (CWSAC), http://www.cr.nps.gov/hps/abpp/battles/va037.htm, Battle of Middleburg.

[11] National Park Service, Civil War Sites Advisory Commission (CWSAC), http://www.cr.nps.gov/hps/abpp/battles/va038.htm, Battle of Upperville.

[12] Preston, *History of the Tenth New York*, pp. 101-104.

[13] National Park Service, Civil War Sites Advisory Commission (CWSAC), http://www.cr.nps.gov/hps/abpp/battles/PA001.htm, Battle of Hanover.

[14] Preston, *History of the Tenth New York*, pp. 104-105.

CHAPTER 4
Gettysburg and the Chase
July-August 1863

"The brave men living and dead who struggled here will not soon be forgotten," A. Lincoln, Gettysburg Address

A Very Active Summer

The 10th New York cavalry entered into a very active summer, starting with the historic battle at Gettysburg. The following table lists their travels in July and August 1863. Men and horses were tired and hungry by the end of this period. They were engaged in several major and minor battles, and the constant travel was wearing them thin. Horses were used up at a fast rate and the horse facility near Washington became very useful to the 10th New York for replacements. Table 4.1 shows the events for these two months. (Locations are in Virginia unless otherwise noted.)

Return to Gettysburg

The sight of Gettysburg on the morning of July 2, 1863 brought back many memories for the 10th New York's companies A through H, where they had their recruit training after the initial formation of the Regiment. To find out more about these early days at Gettysburg read the interesting book by George Rummel III [1]. Companies of the 3rd battalion were not recruited until later and had their training in Elmira. For Justus and the other members of the 3rd battalion, therefore, this would be new scenery. Preston describes some of the impressions of the 1st and 2nd battalions who returned to the scene [2]:

> The intervening timber veiled the regimental parade-grounds of 1861-'62 from view, as it also screened the maneuvering of the Confederate cavalry, when preparing for the movement to the Union right flank on the succeeding day [July 2]. But the men of the First and Second Battalions of the Tenth were confident that just over the hill and beyond the wood lay the parade-grounds where verdant officers had endeavored to manoeuvre the Regiment of verdant soldiers many months

123

before. The efforts to "form close column on fifth squadron" generally resulted in forming close columns of confusion, to get out of which the men were compelled to "pass defile to the rear."

The grounds were now inside the enemy's lines. It seemed almost like a dream to the boys that they should find

Map #	Events	Dates - 1863
1	**Gettysburg, PA**	**July 2-3, 1863**
	Chasing Lee-	**July 5-23**
2	Cashtown, PA	July 5
3	Graefenburg, PA	July 6
4	Chambersburg, PA	July 6
5	Quincy, PA	July 7
6	Waynesboro, PA	July 8
7	Middletown, MD	July 9
8	Boonsboro, MD	July 11-12
9	Harpers Ferry, WV	July 14, 17
10	Shepherdstown, WV (Engagement)	July 15-16
11	Lovettsville	July 19
12	Leesburg	July 20
13	Goose Creek	July 20
14	Bull Run	July 21
15	Manassas/Broad Run	July 22
16	Catlett's Station	July 23, Aug. 15
17	Warrenton Junction	July 24
18	Bealton Station (picketing)	July 25
19	Near Warrenton	July 29
	Amissville	July 30
	"Little" Washington	Aug. 3
20	Sulphur Springs camp	Aug. 7-15
	Jeffersonton and Oak Shade	Aug. 24

Table 4.1 Actions in July and August, 1863

themselves back again near the old parade-grounds after an absence of eighteen months, replete with hard service. When the Tenth halted and dismounted, as already stated, it was on the south side of the Hanover road, near the Reever house [See Map 4.1; Map 4.2 shows an expanded view of part of Map 4.1]. Major Avery and the regimental staff availed themselves of the very economical shade afforded by a superannuated peach-tree. Here they lay upon the ground speculating on the possibilities of meeting old acquaintances in the village, who were "so near and yet so far," and also of meeting other friends [?] who had come so far and were quite too near. ...

The Tenth New York Starts Fighting at the Battle of Gettysburg on July 2

After rushing to Gettysburg, there was no time for sight-seeing. A squadron consisting of Companies H and L (including Justus Matteson) was pressed into duty skirmishing on the ridges from which the Confederate troops were advancing. Preston continues his narration of the early events at Gettysburg:

> Soon after the arrival of the command near the Reever house the squadron composed of Companies H and L were ordered forward to relieve the Union infantry line of skirmishers on Brinkerhoff's Ridge. During the afternoon this force, together with a mounted squadron in the road, under command of Major Kemper, were driven back, and two more squadrons were advanced on the right and the balance of the Regiment on the left of the Hanover road. ...

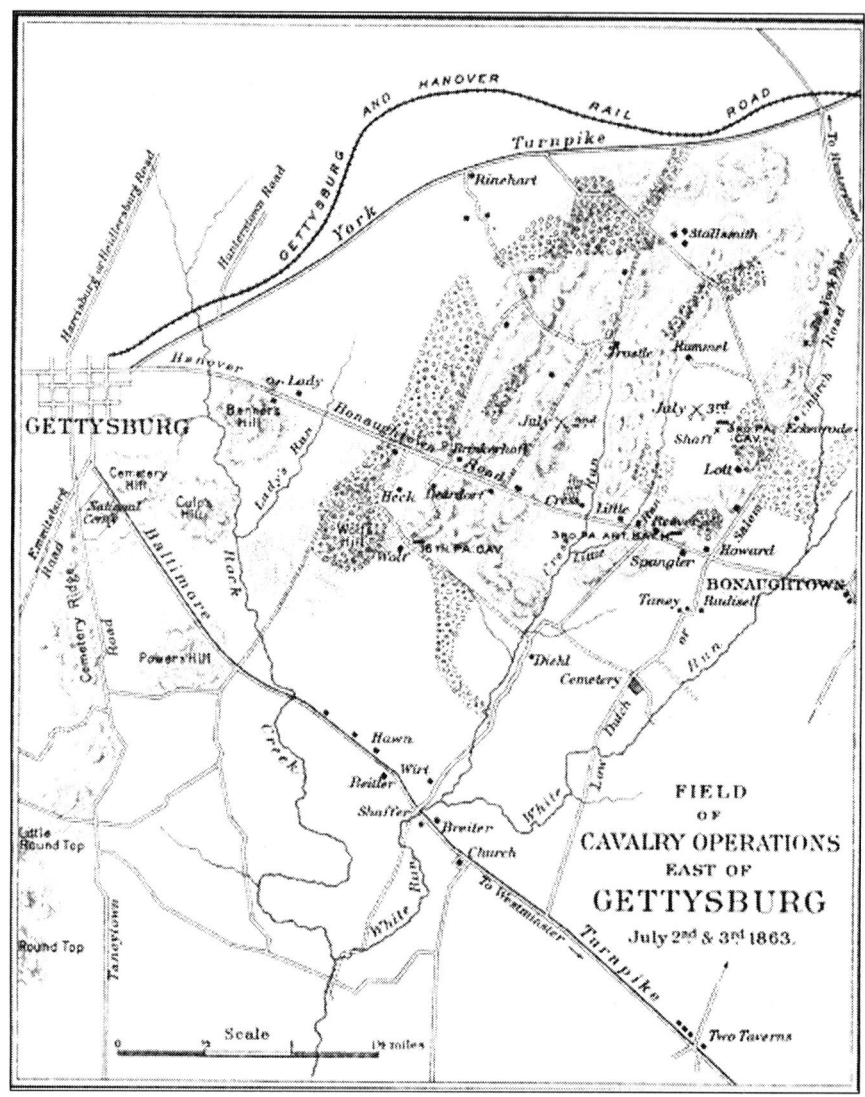

Map 4.1 Tenth New York field of cavalry operations east of Gettysburg

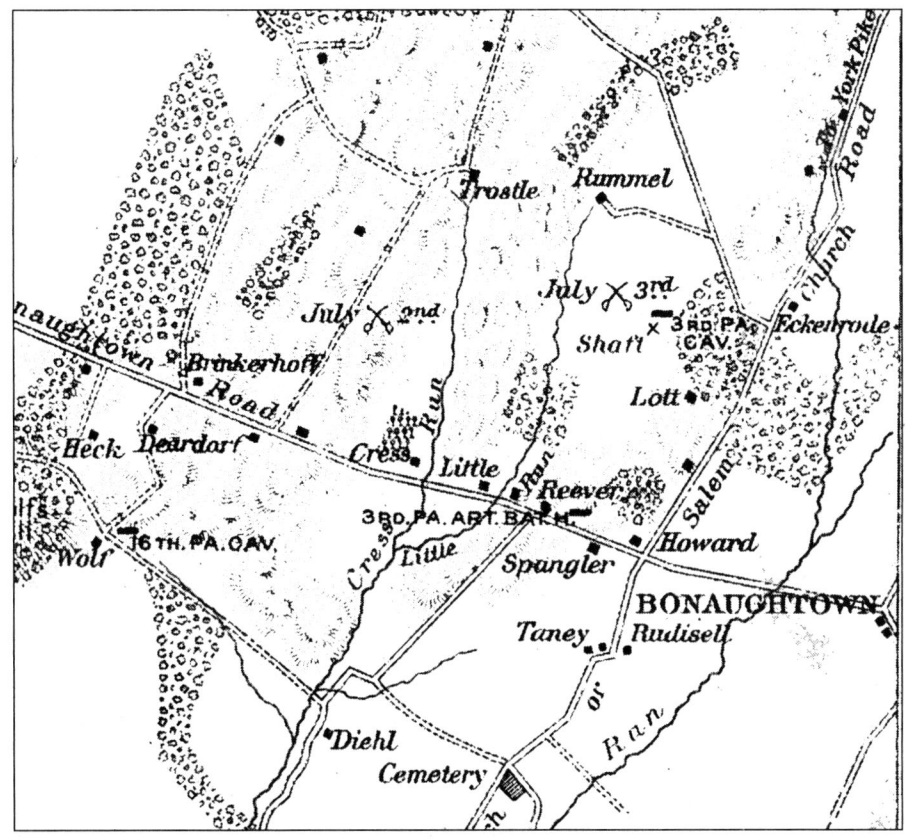

Map 4.2 Expansion of area of interest for the Tenth New York

Colonel William Brooke-Rawle, formerly of the Third Pennsylvania, states that the section of Rank's battery, which did such excellent service on this occasion, joined General Gregg's command on the 29th of June. …

The Tenth was the first regiment from the Second Cavalry Division to engage the enemy on the right flank at Gettysburg.

The Tenth deployed as skirmishers along Brinkerhoff Ridge, and with the help of Rank's guns, they were able to hold off repeated attacks by Confederate infantry forces and the enemy eventually retired to a piece of woods about 200 yards away.

The fire of Rank's guns had delayed the enemy's advance for a sufficient length of time to enable the Tenth to get to the ridge first and give a withering reception to the enemy infantry with their breech-loading carbines. About ten o'clock in the evening of July 2 the line was withdrawn, and Gregg's two brigades moved over to the Baltimore Turnpike near White Run and there went into bivouac. Preston continues his narration of the Gettysburg events [3]:

> The troops confronting the skirmishers of the Tenth on Brinkerhoff's Ridge were from the celebrated Stonewall Brigade (Stonewall Jackson's old command), constituting the left flank of Johnson's division of Ewell's corps, which was making preparations for the assault on the position held by the [Union] Twelfth Corps, and the result of the sharp skirmishing on the part of our cavalry compelled [CSA] General Johnson to move to the assault without the assistance of this veteran [Stonewall] brigade. In his report, General Johnson says, in reference to the movement against the Twelfth Corps:
>
> > "General Walker was directed to follow, but, reporting to me that the enemy were advancing upon him from their right, he was ordered to repulse them and follow on as soon as possible. The opposing force was larger and the time consumed longer than was anticipated, in consequence of which General Walker did not arrive in time to participate in the assault that night."...
>
> The monument [shown in Figure 4.1] erected by the State of New York to mark the site of the engagement of the Tenth New York Cavalry on the right flank, on the 2d of July, 1863, is located on Brinkerhoff's Ridge, on the north side of and near the Hanover road. ...
>
> The monument is nine feet high, made of Gettysburg granite, Quincy granite, and has the cavalry corps badge on the front and rear. State coat-of-arms in bronze also appears on the front and rear of the monument.

Amid the whizzing and banging of shell and the sharp rattle of carbines and muskets, a portion of the Regiment spent the night of the 2d on the skirmish-line, the balance remaining on reserve at a large barn on a hill farther toward the Baltimore pike. ...

Figure 4.1 Tenth New York monument at Gettysburg

More Fighting on July 3 at Gettysburg

The morning of the 3d Gregg's troopers were again in the saddle and moving back to the position vacated the night before on the Hanover Road, where General Custer's brigade, of the Third Cavalry Division, was found disposed along the Hanover and Low Dutch Roads. General Gregg placed his First Brigade, under Colonel John B. McIntosh, on General Custer's left, and the Third Brigade [including the 10th New York], under Colonel J. Irvin Gregg, still farther to the left along the Hanover Road. The Sixteenth Pennsylvania Cavalry, of the Third Brigade, was advanced dismounted as skirmishers in the direction of Gettysburg, encountering the Confederate infantry, whom they drove back, and succeeded in establishing connection with the Twelfth Corps near the base of Wolf's Hill and extending the line on the right to the Hanover road.

About noon General Gregg was apprised of Stuart's movements [Jeb Stuart, commanding general of the Confederate cavalry forces] by a dispatch from General Howard to General Meade, saying that from his (Howard's) position on Cemetery Hill he had observed the movement of a large body of cavalry toward our right. This dispatch was forwarded by General Pleasonton to General Gregg. Except for the many lines of fences, the country occupied by the forces under General Gregg was well adapted for an engagement between mounted troops. The Low Dutch road crossing the Hanover road at right angles near the Howard house, and running north to the York turnpike, distant about two miles, traverses a slight ridge for some distance. The same road running south intersects the Baltimore pike about two and a half miles from the Howard house. About a half mile west of the point where the Low Dutch road crosses the Hanover road is another road starting southward near the Reever house - the point where the Tenth dismounted on its arrival from Hanover, the 2d of July.

Stuart, screening his movements by the woods to the south of the York road, upon which he advances, seeks to gain the Baltimore pike by following along the base of Cress's Ridge to the rear of the Army of the Potomac, where he hopes to create a panic and thus make a diversion in favor of Pickett, who will soon launch his division against the Union left center in one of the most heroic [and ill-fated] charges of the war. ...

If, as has been frequently asserted, the Confederate cavalry leader hoped to gain the rear of the Army of the Potomac unobserved, by moving along the base of this ridge, his actions at this time appear strange, as Stuart pushed one of Griffin's guns to the edge of the woods and fired a number of random shots in different directions. ...

All was quiet when, about noon, Colonel McIntosh moved his brigade upon the ground to relieve Custer's command, but there were evidences of trouble brewing, as the enemy were reported in considerable force in the woods beyond the Rummel buildings. Colonel McIntosh, believing the most effective way of knocking the chip off the other fellow's shoulder was to hit him in the nose, promptly took the initiative. About two o'clock the First New Jersey, under Major Beaumont, was sent forward mounted, and a strong skirmish-line was at once deployed from the Rummel buildings to meet them. The Jerseymen dismounted and took position behind a fence, while two squadrons of the Third Pennsylvania, under Captains Rogers and Treichel, were deployed dismounted to their left, and the squadrons of Captains Miller and Walsh advanced mounted, on the right. Pennington's battery now opened with damaging effect on the enemy. [The artillery barrage knocked out the Confederate artillery, making things a lot easier for the Union cavalry.]

At the time that McIntosh moved to the relief of Custer, who was about to rejoin the Third Division, in compliance with General Kilpatrick's orders, General Gregg was with Irvin Gregg's brigade, on the Hanover road, near Cress's Run. At the first sound of conflict he hastened forward, and meeting Custer, turns him back to the assistance of the First Brigade, until the Third Brigade can be brought up. With the instinct of a true soldier, Custer responds with alacrity, and, moving his tried battalions back, disposed them in support of McIntosh's troops, now actively engaged. Colonel Gregg, leaving the Sixteenth Pennsylvania on the skirmish-line from the base of Wolf's Hill to the Hanover road, as already stated, moved with the balance of the Third Brigade to the south side of the Hanover road, near the Spangler house. Here the brigade remained in reserve during the engagement between the opposing cavalry forces, in momentary expectation of being brought into the action. Custer's brigade had become so far enlisted in the battle, however, by the time of the arrival of Irvin Gregg's regiments, that it could not be withdrawn, even if it had been deemed advisable to do so. Thus the Tenth escaped the hand-to-hand fighting of that day. It becomes no part of the history of the Regiment to record the details of that brilliant encounter, but, as constituting a part of the Second Division of Cavalry, the members of the Tenth take a just pride in having contributed to the general results of the operations of that division on the right flank at Gettysburg, which gave additional luster to its already well-earned reputation for gallantry and reliability. The Tenth suffered the loss of some men wounded by the enemy's shells, while lying in reserve.

The final result of the battle was the withdrawal of Stuart's forces to the woods from which they issued at the beginning of the conflict. The Rummel farm-buildings, originally in the possession of the enemy, were inside Gregg's lines at the close of the fight.

With the retirement of the Confederate horsemen to the cover of the woods, the action of the day practically ended. Pickett's assault on the Union lines west of Cemetery Hill, made almost simultaneously with this engagement, had failed, and darkness settled down upon the dreadful scene of carnage. Desultory picket-firing continued well into the night.

The force under General Gregg in this engagement consisted of the First and Third Brigades of the Second Cavalry Division, commanded respectively by Colonels John B. McIntosh and J. Irvin Gregg, and the Second Brigade of the Third Cavalry Division, known as the Michigan Brigade, commanded by Brigadier-General George A. Custer, numbering, all told, about five thousand men, only about three thousand of whom were actively engaged, Colonel Gregg's brigade remaining on reserve, as already stated. Opposed to this force was the entire

Confederate Cavalry Corps, commanded by General Stuart in person, numbering between six and seven thousand men. ...

[The 10th New York lost 9 troopers killed, wounded, missing, and captured, in the actions on July 2 and 3, 1863. The total losses for Gregg's Cavalry Division were listed in the official records as 55.]

General Stuart reported his losses on July 3d at one hundred and eighty-one, exclusive of the losses in Jenkins's brigade, and his horse artillery. ...

Surely the cavalry is entitled to honorable mention in connection with the great battle of Gettysburg. It was Buford's gallant troopers who received and withstood the first fierce onslaught of the Confederates on the 1st of July; it was Gregg's and Custer's tried squadrons that struck the final blow and administered the last chastisement to the audacious and confident enemy on the evening of the day of Lee's humiliation.

But as the report of musket and carbine was blended along those hills in the determined effort for the mastery, so may the songs of praise and rejoicings of a loyal people ever be to the glory of the Union soldier, without distinction as to the arm of service to which he was attached.

On the evening of the 3d, immediately following the closing of the conflict, the Tenth was sent to picket the section of country in the immediate front of the Confederate cavalry. Sergeant Hayes, in charge of a detachment from the Regiment, was sent to picket the woods through which the Low Dutch Road runs. ...

To summarize, the Union Cavalry Corps helped win the Battle of Gettysburg in three major ways:

Buford's 1st Division stopped the confederacy on the outskirts of Gettysburg for a day on July 1, preventing them from commanding the high ground in the subsequent fighting.

General D. McM. Gregg's 2nd Division foiled Jeb Stuart's attack on the Union right. Stuart's attack was designed to divert Union resources away from the area of Pickett's charge, but was prevented from doing so by the 2nd Division.

Finally, Farnsworth's regiment in Kilpatrick's 3rd Cavalry Division attacked Confederate troops from the Union left, engaging Confederate forces that would have been helping Pickett.

In addition, as described in the next section, J. Irvin Gregg's 3rd Brigade, including the 10th New York, gave hot pursuit to Lee's retreating army for the next 17 days, back through Pennsylvania, Maryland, West Virginia and Virginia.

General Meade and President Lincoln did not agree on the results of the Gettysburg Battle. Meade felt that it had been a great victory - he had protected Washington, DC, and had driven the Confederate Army from Pennsylvania, Maryland, and DC. Lincoln was at first elated over the victory, but as the days wore on after the Battle he felt more and more disappointed - "Meade had an opportunity to defeat the Confederate Army, and didn't take it." He thought that Meade should have pursued Lee with great vigor after the Battle, corner him, and crush him before he crossed back over the Potomac into West Virginia. Lincoln wrote a letter of rebuke to Meade in his disappointment, but never sent it on to him. He had enough respect for Meade and his capabilities that he feared that Meade would resign after receiving such a letter from the Commander-In-Chief.

Lee finally had a face-off against Meade, his back to the Potomac River, on July 12-13. He was delayed in crossing by high water, but his engineers built some bridges and he made it safely across by July 14.

Lincoln came to Gettysburg on November 19, 1863, to give his famous Gettysburg Address to dedicate the new cemetery on the battlefield grounds.

The Pursuit of Lee by the 10th New York Starts on July 4

The Regiment remained on picket until near noon the next day, July 4, when the Third Brigade was started in pursuit of the retreating rebel army, the first organized body of Union troops that passed through Gettysburg after the battle.

Preston continues [4]:

The night of the 3d of July the Confederates were gloomy and crestfallen. Every effort to break the Union lines or turn the flanks had been unsuccessful. Their losses were enormous; their ammunition and supplies well-nigh exhausted. The Union-loving people of the village noted their dejection and were not slow in guessing the reason. The spirit of the Confederate army was broken; that the contest would not be renewed on their part was plainly evident. It was not, therefore, a great surprise to the observing, intelligent citizens to find the village comparatively deserted by Confederates on the morning of Independence Day. It was desirable that General Meade should be informed of the situation of affairs, and Mr. David Gendle-hart, who had left home early in the morning with his sons, John L. and J. William, aged twelve and nine respectively, on a tour of observation, decided to seek the commander of the Union army after having satisfied himself that the Confederate army had really fallen back. ...

General Meade gave the gentlemen immediate audience, and exhibited great surprise and pleasure when informed that the Confederate army had certainly fallen back, thanking them again and again. It was the first definite information he had received of the important event.

Passing through the village, the Third Brigade marched out upon the Chambersburg road, passing over the battle-field of July 1st, strewn with the dead Union soldiers. The road was littered with broken and abandoned wagons, caissons, muskets, clothing, etc. War's devastation was more clearly shown on this route than any upon which the Tenth had ever marched. Squads of Confederate soldiers were met with, plodding dejectedly along toward the place where their valiant conduct had challenged the admiration and respect of their adversaries. Some were under guard, others marched without. They were, generally speaking, a surly, uncommunicative lot. Every building that would afford shelter from the storm or protection from the burning rays of the sun was filled with Confederate wounded and stragglers. Late at night the Tenth went into camp at Graefenburg Springs [#3 on Map 4.3, 12 miles west of Gettysburg]. The greater part of the Regiment had been sent back to Gettysburg during the day as guards to rebel prisoners. [Map 4.3 shows locations of the first part of their journey from Gettysburg back to the Warrenton area.] …

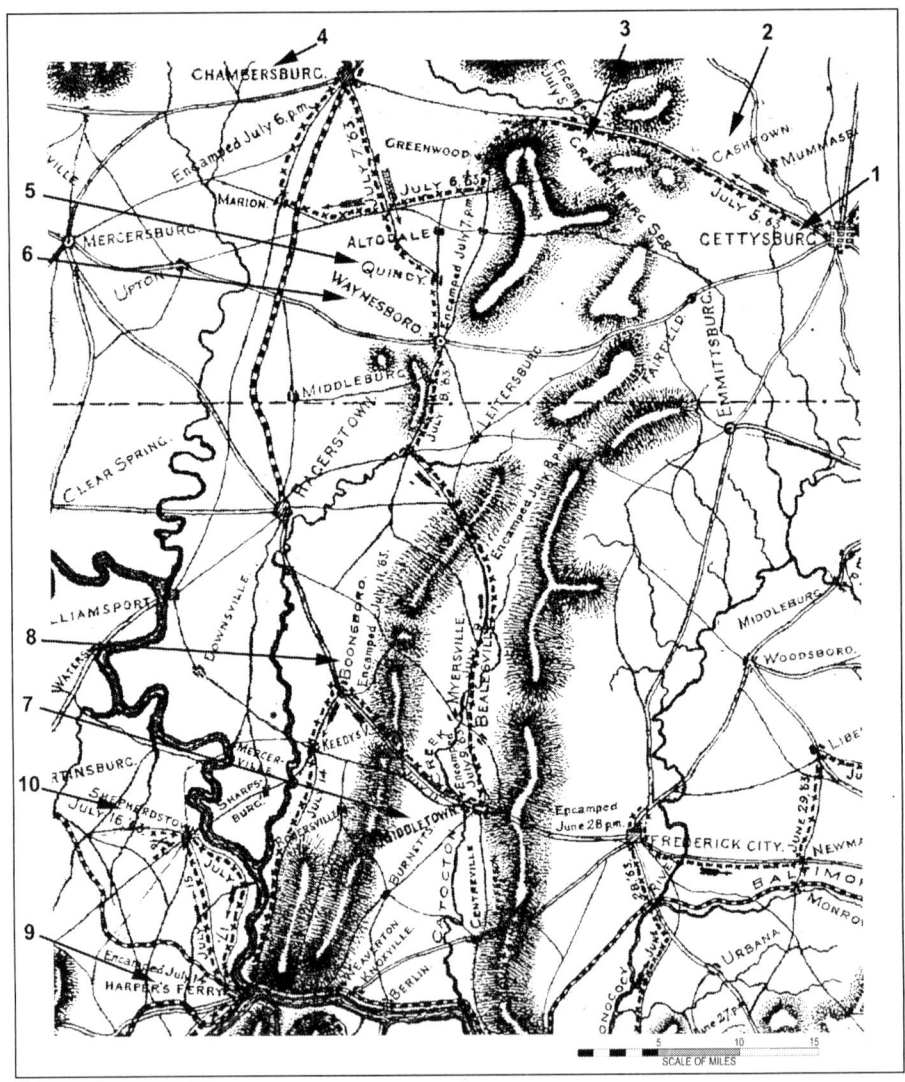

Map 4.3 From Gettysburg to Harper's Ferry

Of this day's march Lieutenant B.B. Porter says

"Our advance-guard commenced bringing in rebel prisoners as soon as we reached Seminary Ridge. With every squad of fifty prisoners two men were sent back as guards. When the Regiment reached Cashtown [#2 on Map 4.3], I think Avery, Graves, Preston, and myself were the only commissioned officers with the Regiment. I had the management of the prisoners. I think over three thousand were sent back under guards furnished from the Tenth. At Cashtown I was kept busy for a long time searching rebel prisoners. I had quite a stock of knives, pistols, revolvers, etc. As soon as the men sent as guards rejoined the Regiment we followed after, and soon came up with the rest of the brigade."

The suffering from hunger was probably never greater in the Regiment than while on this march. Men ate corn from the ear, birch-bark, anything that would appease the gnawings of hunger. ...

Reaching Chambersburg [#4 on Map 4.3] on the evening of the 6th [of July], the Regiment was marched through the town and into a meadow of clover and encamped. ...

Resuming the march on the 7th, Quincy [PA, #5 on Map 4.3] was reached in the evening, where the Regiment went into camp during a hard rain-storm, which prevailed all night; then again on the 8th to Waynesboro [PA, #6 on Map 4.3], going into camp in the mountains at 8 P.M., and to Middletown [MD, #7 on Map 4.3] on the 9th, encamping late in the evening. Here the Regiment remained, doing picket duty until the 11th, when it was again set in motion at noon, and settled down at Boonesboro [MD, #8 on Map 4.3] the same night. The severe strain and lack of forage to which the animals had been subjected in the forced marches over the mountains told seriously on them. A large number were condemned in the Tenth on the 12th.

Rain fell again from the 12th to the 14th in sufficient quantities to make the roads soft and pliable. On the latter date the brigade broke camp at Boonesboro and marched to Harper's Ferry [WV, #9 on Map 4.3], where it crossed at 5 P.M. on a pontoon bridge and established camp on Bolivar Heights, the first troops from the Army of the Potomac to reach Virginia soil after the battle of Gettysburg.

Harper's Ferry

Although Preston refers to Harper's Ferry as Virginia soil, it had just within the last three weeks achieved statehood as the State of West Virginia on June 20, 1863. Residents of Virginia supported the Confederate views, but many in West Virginia favored the North, hence the move to make it the 35th state of the United States.

The "fort" used by John Brown's group in his raid of October 16, 1859 on Harper's Ferry is shown in Figure 4.2. This building is still there, as shown by this photo taken by the author. The old railroad bridge across the Potomac is shown in Figure 4.3.

Figure 4.2 John Brown's Fort at Harper's Ferry (2006)

Engagement at Shepherdstown

After a couple of days in Harper's Ferry, the regiment went up to Shepherdstown [WV, #10 on Map 4.3]. On the morning of July 16 at Shepherdstown, one battalion under the command of Major Waters was formed. The battalion consisted of companies H, L, C and G, and was sent out as pickets, as described by Preston [5]:

Figure 4.3 Old railroad bridge at Harper's Ferry (2006)

Companies H and L, under Captains Peck and Vanderbilt, and C and G, under Lieutenants Sceva and McKevitt, respectively, were sent to picket the Winchester Pike. At the same time Captain Pierce, with Companies K and M, was sent to picket the Dam No. 4 road; the balance of the Regiment, under Major Avery, picketing the Martinsburg road.

About noon the squadron under Captain Peck was furiously attacked, his outposts driven in, and the reserve thrown into confusion. Fortunately, the First Maine Cavalry, under Lieutenant-Colonel Smith, were just coming up, on their way out to obtain forage. Colonel Smith instantly took in the situation, and so disposed his regiment as to give the rebels a reminder of Brandy Station, Aldie, and Gettysburg. Lieutenant

Sceva's post was first attacked, but the enemy were temporarily checked by his squadron, when he retired without loss. Captain Peck's squadron was then charged by an overwhelming force just as the First Maine came upon the scene, as stated. ...

After this [still in Shepherdstown] the companies all joined their Regiment [10th New York], and were directed to take position on the right of the line as dismounted skirmishers. The stone walls afforded good works, from behind which the skirmishers kept up a brisk fire. From the position occupied by the Regiment long lines of troops were plainly visible behind the woods, which screened them from view from our troops in the center and on the left. The fighting was continued until late at night, when the Regiment was withdrawn from the right and placed in a grove in rear of the right center of our line. Here the men, although supposed to be "standing to horse," sank down upon the ground exhausted. The rebels appeared to have an especial spite against the location, sending shells with much rapidity and accuracy; but the men slept soundly while the shells tore through the trees and crashed and shrieked around them. Before daylight on the 17th, the men were quietly awakened, and as quietly stole away and joined the brigade in the streets of the village on its retrograde movement.

On the next morning, the Tenth New York marched back to Harper's Ferry.

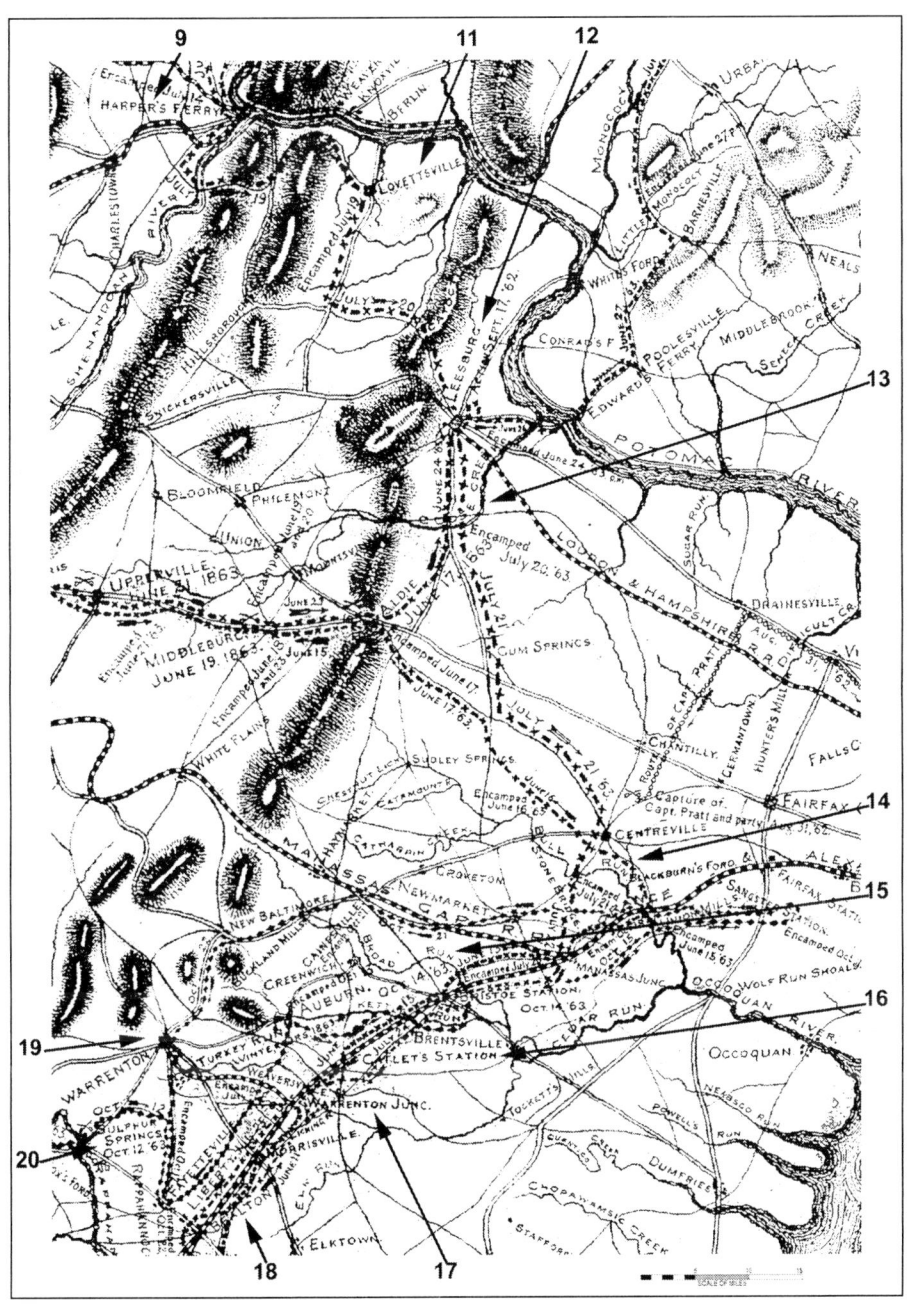

Map 4.4 From Harper's Ferry to Warrenton

The Official Report of Major Avery on the Engagement at Shepherdstown

Report of Major M. Henry Avery, Tenth New York Cavalry:

NEAR JEFFERSON, VA
August 13, 1863

SIR: I have the honor to submit the following report of the part taken by my Regiment in the operations of the Third Brigade, Second Cavalry Division, subsequent to the battle of Gettysburg and up to the arrival of the same at Warrenton, Va. [July 5-29, 1863].

On the morning of July 5th I left bivouac about one and a half miles east of Gettysburg, passing through the village on the Chambersburg pike. The Tenth New York on that day having the right of the brigade, nearly the whole of the Regiment was disposed as flankers for the purpose of thoroughly scouring the country and arresting the numerous stragglers of the enemy, who singly and in squads were endeavoring to make their way into the mountains.

Owing to the wholesale capture of prisoners and the necessity of the column following as rapidly as possible the rear of the enemy, I am unable to make any accurate estimate of the number taken. Each detachment under my command, on accumulating as large a number as could be safely guarded, proceeded to Gettysburg and turned them over to the provost marshal. Encamped that night at Graefenburg Springs.

Next day marched via New Franklin to Chambersburg; encamped at that point.

July 7th, commenced march for Middletown, passing through Quincy, Fayetteville, and Waynesborough, arriving there July 10th.

July 11th, marched to Boonsborough, rejoining the division at that point. July 13th, marched to Harper's Ferry.

July 15th, the Second Cavalry Division marched on reconnaissance to Shepherdstown, the Third Brigade having the advance. A few pickets and a small supporting force of the enemy were encountered at this point and easily captured or dispersed by our advance. This Regiment on that day, being the third in column, took no part in the engagement. Encamped that night at Shepherdstown.

Next morning two squadrons, consisting of Companies H and L under command of Captains Peck and Vanderbilt, and Companies C and G, under command of Lieutenants Sceva and McKevitt - the battalion being under command of Major A.D. Waters - were placed on picket on the Winchester pike. One squadron, under Captain Peirce, on the Dam No. 4 road, and the remaining three squadrons, under my command, were ordered to picket the Martinsburg road.

No force of the enemy was visible until about 2 P.M., when the vedettes from the battalion on the Winchester road were rapidly driven in by the advance guard of a heavy force, since ascertained to be under the command of General Stuart. Major Waters at this time, feeling seriously indisposed, retired, leaving Captain Peck in command. Lieutenant Sceva's squadron, being at the outer post, succeeded in momentarily checking the charge of the enemy, and then retired on the reserve, without losing a prisoner, although the attack had been fierce, impetuous, and by an overwhelming force. At this reserve, Captain Peck succeeded in temporarily repulsing their advance, with a loss of seven men, missing and wounded, three of which latter have since died in hospital, and Lieutenant John T. McKevitt, of Company G, a brave and gallant officer, severely wounded through the lung.

The enemy having brought forward a strong reinforcement, Captain Peck was compelled to retire until reenforced by the First Maine, when the enemy was held in check until the remainder of the brigade came up. Soon after Captain Peck was withdrawn and sent to strengthen the line picketed by my command, and which, by the nature of the attack, had become a line of skirmishers, covering the extreme right of the division.

During the remainder of the engagement this regiment

remained comparatively idle and without any loss on our part, annoying the opposing skirmishers of the enemy, and driving back any force which appeared. On the cessation of the firing, my line remained the same as at the commencement of the attack, and was held as a line of pickets until midnight, when we were withdrawn and marched for Harper's Ferry, arriving there soon after daylight [July 17].

July 19th, marched for Warrenton, via Leesburg [#12 on Map 4.4], encamping respectively at Goose Creek [#13 on Map 4.4], Manassas [#14 on Map 4.4], Broad Run [#15 on Map 4.4], Warrenton Junction [#17 on Map 4.4], and Bealton [#18 on Map 4.4], until July 29th. During the period from the 22nd ultimo to that date we were engaged in picketing the line of the Orange and Alexandria Railroad. July 29th, marched for Amissville [13 miles west of Warrenton], encamping that night about two miles from Warrenton [#19 on Map 4.4].

I have the honor to remain, very respectfully,
Your obedient servant,
M. HENRY AVERY,
Major Commanding Tenth New York Cavalry

A Digression on the History of Shepherdstown

Shepherdstown, WV was located too close to the battlefields of South Mountain and Antietam.

Even though the following record is out of context with the current time-line of this chapter, it is an interesting and terrible illustration of the horrors of the Civil War. After the battles of South Mountain and Antietam the Confederate army crossed the nearby Potomac River at Pack Horse Ford and delivered many of their casualties to the Village of Shepherdstown. One estimate was 5,000-8,000 casualties. A lower estimate is given in the following record, written by one of the residents:

In September, 1862, after the Maryland battles of South Mountain and Antietam, Shepardstown became a scene of indescribable suffering. "The whole town was a hospital," wrote resident Mary Bedinger Mitchell. "There was scarcely a building in town that could not with truth seek protection under that plea."

The wounded Confederates streaming into Shepherdstown after the South Mountain actions of September 14 became a flood totaling 2,000-3,000 by the 18th, the day after Antietam. Soon, even places normally deemed unfit for human habitation were turned into hospitals. They included the old abandoned tobacco warehouse at the north end of Princess Street and the incomplete town hall, now Shepherd University's McMurran Hall. Mary Mitchell wrote, "The unfinished Town Hall had stood in naked ugliness for many a long day. Somebody threw a few rough boards across the beams, placed piles of straw over them, laid down single planks to walk upon, and lo it was a hospital at once."

Shepherdstown experienced the passing of the armies for another two and a half years, but the events of the 1862 Maryland Campaign proved the most traumatic for the residents.

"The wounded continued to arrive until the town was quite unable to hold all the disabled and suffering. They filled every building and overflowed into the country round, into farm-houses, barns, corn-cribs, cabins - wherever four walls and roof were found together. ... There were six churches, and they were all full; the Odd Fellows' Hall, the Freemasons', the little Town Council Room, the barn-like place known as the Drill Room, all the private houses after their capacity, the shops and empty buildings, the school houses, - every inch of space and yet the cry was for more room."

-Mary Bedinger Mitchell

An example of current Shepherdstown architecture is shown in Figure 4.4, possibly typical of what existed in Civil War years.

Figure 4.4 Example of Shepherdstown architecture
(2006 photo by author)

After the duty at Harper's Ferry and Shepherdstown, the Regiment camped near Warrenton, VA in August, 1863. For the next couple of months they engaged in details, scouting, picketing etc. around the area. Preston describes some of this duty, including a serious engagement by one of the squadrons near "Little" Washington, VA (22 miles west of Warrenton) [6]:

> On one of these expeditions made by a squadron under the command of Lieutenant Sceva, on Monday, the 3d of August, a force of Confederate cavalry was encountered near Little Washington and driven through the village. As the little force under Lieutenant Sceva reached the top of a hill, commanding a view of the country for some distance ahead, with Little Washington in the distance, the sharp crack of several carbines was followed by the singing of bullets by their ears. The rebels had dismounted and taken position behind a high, winding stone wall that ran along the road, and could not be seen.

Lieutenant Sceva immediately deployed a portion of his little command as skirmishers in the open field to the right, but before the formation had been completed the position of the enemy had been discovered and the skirmishers were called in. Lieutenant Sceva gave the command, "Draw sabers!" and then followed a bold and successful saber charge. The rebels broke from cover, mounted their horses, and sought safety in flight, our boys in close pursuit, down across a bridge, through the village, and out on the Sperryville Road, making both the rebels and the dust fly. Finally, the boys came back with four prisoners as the result of the charge, and the command returned to the camp at Amissville in the evening. The number of the enemy was fully as great as Lieutenant Sceva's force. Our loss was none. This little adventure appeared to awaken the latent fire in the Lieutenant's bosom, and next day, the 4th, he led three companies to the same place, without encountering or observing any rebels. On the return, however, when a short distance from Little Washington, he found himself confronted by a force of rebel cavalry that had gained his rear and had torn up a bridge over the creek and stood ready to dispute his further progress. But the detachment was at once put in readiness for another charge and went forward with a cheer. Again the rebels broke and fled and were pursued for some distance. In this encounter we lost one man taken prisoner.

George Hines, of Company A, had a queer experience in this skirmish. He encountered a Confederate in a personal struggle, each firing all the cartridges from his revolver, when they grasped each other in a rough-and-tumble fight, at the termination of which Hines mounted his antagonist's horse and rode off, trading horses without guaranty. The command reached camp about 4 P.M.

Surgeon H.K. Clarke mentions the skirmishes in these words:

> "On the 3d of August, 1863, Lieutenant Sceva was sent to Little Washington on a scouting expedition. Sceva was a gallant fellow. His great desire was to charge into Richmond with saber only. He disdained the

revolver; did not want one in the command. When near Little Washington his command was fired upon. Sceva gave the command to draw saber, and away he flew down the road, his long hair streaming back. He was closely followed by his little command with sabers gleaming in the sunlight. The enemy broke from concealment, mounted, and started toward the mountains. In the scrub race that followed we gathered in some prisoners, among the number one of those who fired the first shots, whose saber and spurs I took and still retain. Next day Sceva went out again. Captain Blynn and I went out on the road for a distance after he had gone. We saw a detachment of rebs that had barricaded the road and were awaiting Sceva's return. Sceva gave them a good fight, losing, however, one man taken prisoner, Charles Clifford, of Company E."

The Fourth Pennsylvania Cavalry relieved the Tenth from picket on the 5th, and the latter returned to camp at Amissville [13 miles west of Warrenton]. Then on the 7th the division left for Sulphur Springs [#20 on Map 4.4], where it encamped until the 15th. While here on the 13th of August, the brigade designation was changed from the Third to the Second, and the Second and Eighth Pennsylvania Cavalry Regiments were added to it. The same day a detachment of one hundred and fifty men from the Regiment went on a reconnaissance to Gaines Crossroads encountering none of the enemy.

Crossing the Rappahannock at 9 A.M. on the 15th, the division marched to Catlett's Station [#16 on Map 4.4]. ... The Tenth did picket duty in this vicinity for several days. ... The Regiment broke camp and marched with the division to the vicinity of Jeffersonton [8 miles southwest of Warrenton] and Oak Shade on the 24th, and went on picket along the Hazel River.

Next the Regiment participated in the Bristoe and Mine Run Campaigns, as discussed in the next chapter. Justus and Mary exchanged letters in August, shown in the next couple of pages.

August 9, 1863
Homer, Cortland Co.

Friend Jut,

It has been a long long time since I have taken the pen to write to you and you do not know how I have missed your letters. soon after I wrote to you I went to Homer to sew and left word with Smiths to send my letters to Homer, but he neglected it so I only got your letter a few days ago.

I am quite well, like sewing here very well. think that I shall stay all summer. I have been here seven weeks. have not been home yet. but think that I shall go next week. they are having quite a time in Solon with the diphtheria. Mr Grant has lost two children. Mrs. Gardner two, Helen and Albert. Aaron and George had had it but are getting better. Mr. Brown has lost one. Three of Mrs. Adkins' boys were sick and others in the place. the last that I heard it was raging in Freetown very hard, There is a number died. we do not get much more news now. how I do wish that it would come to a close, but I guess that I do not wish so any more than you boys do, for you have the hardest of it. I do not believe that I could ever stay away from home as long as you have.

After the battle at Gettysburg there was a number of buddies back here in Homer. Dr. Green and the baptist minister went down and fetched home some of the wounded and dead. Your aunt Katy-Ann works here. I have seen her once. We have had a flood here. It took off most of the bridges in McGrawville. It done more damage than it did here. it took one house in the road. the fences are all gone. the grass and grain is flat on the ground and is full of mud and stick. it has done a great deal of damage. we have very hard showers.

I wish that you were here today to go to church. they have built a new Presbetarian church. it is perfectly splendid. it was dedicated a few weeks ago. I have been there a number of times but go mostly to the Methodist.

Jut, I am looking forward to the time when this writing will be closed and you will come home and we can sit down and have a good long chat, and not have to scribble on paper. it will seem like old times. or if you make up your mind to take a cesesh[1] girl for your wife and live down there and never come home then I shall not write for she would be jealous, but I should come down and make you a good long visit and stay two or three years.

Write as soon as convenient. direct to Homer and I will try to do better next time. remember me as your friend,

Matie

Mr. Salsberg is to be hung the 14th of this month. he has made no confession yet, but says that he never poisened his wife.

Matie L. Hatch

1. "Cesesh" is short for secessionist.

**Figure 4.5 Soldier writing a letter home
(sketch by Kevin Crandall)**

Camp near Jefferson Va
Aug 29th 1863

Friend Mary, as I have some leisure time to day I will improve it by writing a few lines to you in answer to your welcomed letter that I recieved some time ago.

I was glad to learn that you wer well and enjoying yourself as usual.

My health is good at present except I am lame. while on picket the other day I got a pretty hard kick from a horse, so that I have been excused from duty for a few days.

We are having pretty good times here now. not much to do and a plenty to eat. fruit is getting ripe and corn big enough to boil, so the boys helps themselves to that they like best.

We have stirring news from the south now. fort sumpter is battered down and Admerald Dahlgrene is bombarding Charleston and there is no doubt but we shal soon hear of its downfall. after that probably there will be something done here. now we can only act on the defensive for a large amount of the troops have gone south. when they return we can go on in these parts.

You said you wished the war was over but thought you did not more than we do. you wer rite there, but most of the boys are bound to fight as long as there is any rebs to be found. Mary, it is now one year minus a week since I inlisted. you think it a long time but I can say that seemingly it has passed away in a short time.

You speaking of going to church puts me in mind that I have not been to church since I left Cortland. we have a chaplain in our Regt but he has not preached but one sermon since I came here.

Mary, I hope the time will come (and that soon) when we can sit down and have a good chit-chat and not have to be under the necessity of writing.

Ha, ha, you spoke of my taking a secession gal for a wife. I cant see the point for the looks of one is enough for me, without coming any nearer, so I dont think you will have to come here to see me.

I have seen a list of the drafted in Cortland Co. I find a good many that I know. as this sheat is full I shall have to bid thee good by.

Write soon and oblige your Friend
J. G. Matteson

References

[1] *72 Days at Gettysburg: Organization of the 10th Regiment, New York Volunteer Cavalry*, by George A. Rummel III; White Mane Publishing Co., Inc. 1997; ISBN 1-57249-086-1.

[2] Preston, Noble D., *History of the Tenth Regiment New York Volunteer Cavalry*, New York, NY: D. Appleton and Company, 1892; reprinted by Higginson Book Company, Salem, MA in 1998; selected excerpts from pp. 106-107.

[3] Ibid, 114-122.

[4] Ibid, 128-131.

[5] Ibid, 134-135.

[6] Ibid, 138-139.

CHAPTER 5
Bristoe and Mine Run Campaigns
September-December 1863

"Stand firm and give it to 'em!", Capt. Charles E. Pratt, Tenth New York

Last Quarter of 1863

The last quarter of 1863 was busy, but not quite as intense as the third quarter. The "Bristoe Campaign" included battles at Sulphur Springs, Auburn (first and second), Bristoe Station, Buckland Mills and Rappahannock Station. There were also many skirmishes at various places; lots of picketing activity; and the other major campaign of Mine Run. A list of some of the activities is shown in Table 5.1.

The Bristoe Campaign

The "Bristoe Campaign" consisted of engagements at Auburn (I and II), Bristoe Station, Buckland Mills and Rappahannock Station.

The regiment camped near Warrenton (#8 on Map 5.1) in August and September. Warrenton was the home of Major John Mosby, the infamous leader of the Confederate band referred to as Mosby's Raiders. A recent photo of his home by the author is shown in Figure 5.1. Current plans are to open this as a Civil War museum in Warrenton in the near future.

A major problem in the cavalry was the availability of an adequate supply of healthy mounts. The Confederate troopers were handicapped - their sources of supply of fresh mounts were limited. The Union forces eventually were well-organized for the resupply of mounts. Preston records this and other activities referred to as the Bristoe Campaign, in October and November of 1863 [1]:

> A detail of eighty men was made from the Regiment on the 4th of September to proceed [from the Warrenton area] to Washington for horses. This detachment, which was under command of Major Weed, returned to camp on the 10th, with fifteen hundred horses, which were distributed among the various regiments of the division.

Map #	Events	Dates - 1863
1	Warrenton Junction	Sep. 13
2	Culpeper C. H.	Sep. 18
3	Brandy Station	Sep. 24
4	Fayetteville	Oct. 1
5	Bealton	Oct. 2
	Bristoe Campaign	**Oct. 9-22**
6	Rixeyville	Oct. 11
7	Jefferson	Oct. 11
8	Warrenton	Oct. 11
9	Washington, VA	Oct. 12
10	White Sulphur Springs Battle	Oct. 12
11	Auburn Battle	Oct. 13-14
12	Brentsville	Oct. 14
13	St. Stephen's Church	Oct. 14
14	Bristoe Station skirmish	Oct.15
15	Catlett's station	Oct. 16
16	Bull Run	Oct. 16
17	Fairfax Court House	Oct. 17
18	Buckland Mills	Oct. 18-19
19	Gainesville	Oct. 21
20	Rappahannock Station	Oct. 24
21	Morrisville	Nov. 7
22	**Mine Run Campaign:**	**Nov. 24-Dec. 2**
23	Grove Church engagement	Nov. 19
24	White Hall	Nov. 26
25	New Hope Church engagement	Nov. 27
26	Parker's Store engagement	Nov. 29
27	Stevensburg	Dec. 7
28	Expedition, Bealton to Luray	Dec. 21-23
29	Turkey Run winter camp	Dec.-Spring '64

Table 5.1 List of activities in the last quarter of 1863

Figure 5.1 The John Mosby Home in Warrenton, VA (2006)

The command marched to the vicinity of Warrenton Junction [#1 on Map 5.1], and went into camp on the 13th [September, 1863]. It rained, as usual, when it approached Warrenton Junction. There were about eight hundred of the horses brought from Washington by the detachment under Major Weed, and on the 18th the command, encumbered with these, marched to Culpeper [#2 on Map 5.1], crossing the [Rappahannock] river at Rappahannock Station [#20 on Map 5.1] on a pontoon bridge. Next day a detail of one hundred and fifty men from the Regiment went to Catlett's Station [#15 on Map 5.1] for beeves. The Tenth was encamped south of Culpeper from the 21st to the 24th. While here an issue of wormy hard-tack and rusty pork was made to the Regiment. The men busied themselves in taking a census of the inhabitants of their hard-tack, and investigating the oxidized pork, during the time that could be spared from eliminating the timothy-seeds from their nether garments. Then on the afternoon of the 24th they were again in the saddle and moving northward, encamping at night at Brandy Station [#3 on Map 5.1], where they remained until the 1st of October, when they marched to Fayetteville [#4 on Map 5.1], and did picket duty along the Rappahannock River [see author's photo, Figure 5.2].

Figure 5.2 Rappahannock River near Kelly's Ford (May, 2006)

Relieved by an infantry force on the 2d [of October 1863], the Regiment marched to Bealton [#5 on Map 5.1] in a heavy storm. Here it picketed the surrounding country until the 9th, when a scouting expedition was ordered to Warrenton. A few rebels were seen, but they retired rapidly before the invading host. On the return of the detachment to camp it was dispatched on another reconnaissance beyond Warrenton and Sulphur Springs [#10 on Map 5.1], returning late at night, having encountered nothing of a hostile nature. Early on the 10th the division was on the move, going over well-trodden and familiar paths, to a point below Culpeper Court-House. Next day the Second Division marched through Culpeper and halted on the hills to the west, from where Kilpatrick's troopers could be seen to the south of the town, falling back. The entire [Confederate] army had abandoned their camps and were moving northward.

Our signal officers on Pony Mountain [2 miles south of

Culpeper] had made out from the enemy's signals General Lee's purpose of making an immediate march around the right flank of the Union army. General Meade, instead of disposing his army to meet this intended movement and give battle, at once began a retrograde march northward. ...

Resuming the march from Culpeper, the Second Cavalry Division crossed the Hazel River at Rixeyville [#6 on Map 5.1], and passing through Jeffersonton, reached its old camps at Sulphur Springs at dusk, the Tenth settling down in the quarters vacated by it but a few days before. [The village of Jeffersonton is sometimes referred to as "Jefferson" in Preston's *History of the Tenth New York*; and in fact shows up as "Jefferson" on a lot of the maps of that period, as shown in Map 5.1. Jefferson is about 8 miles southwest of Warrenton (shown by #7 on Map 5.1). Here, all unconscious of the proximity of the enemy, a good night's rest was enjoyed. General Gregg had sent scouting parties in various directions, however, none of whom were heard from on the 11th [October 1863].

**Figure 5.3 Civil War artillery piece on display
at the New York State Military Museum**

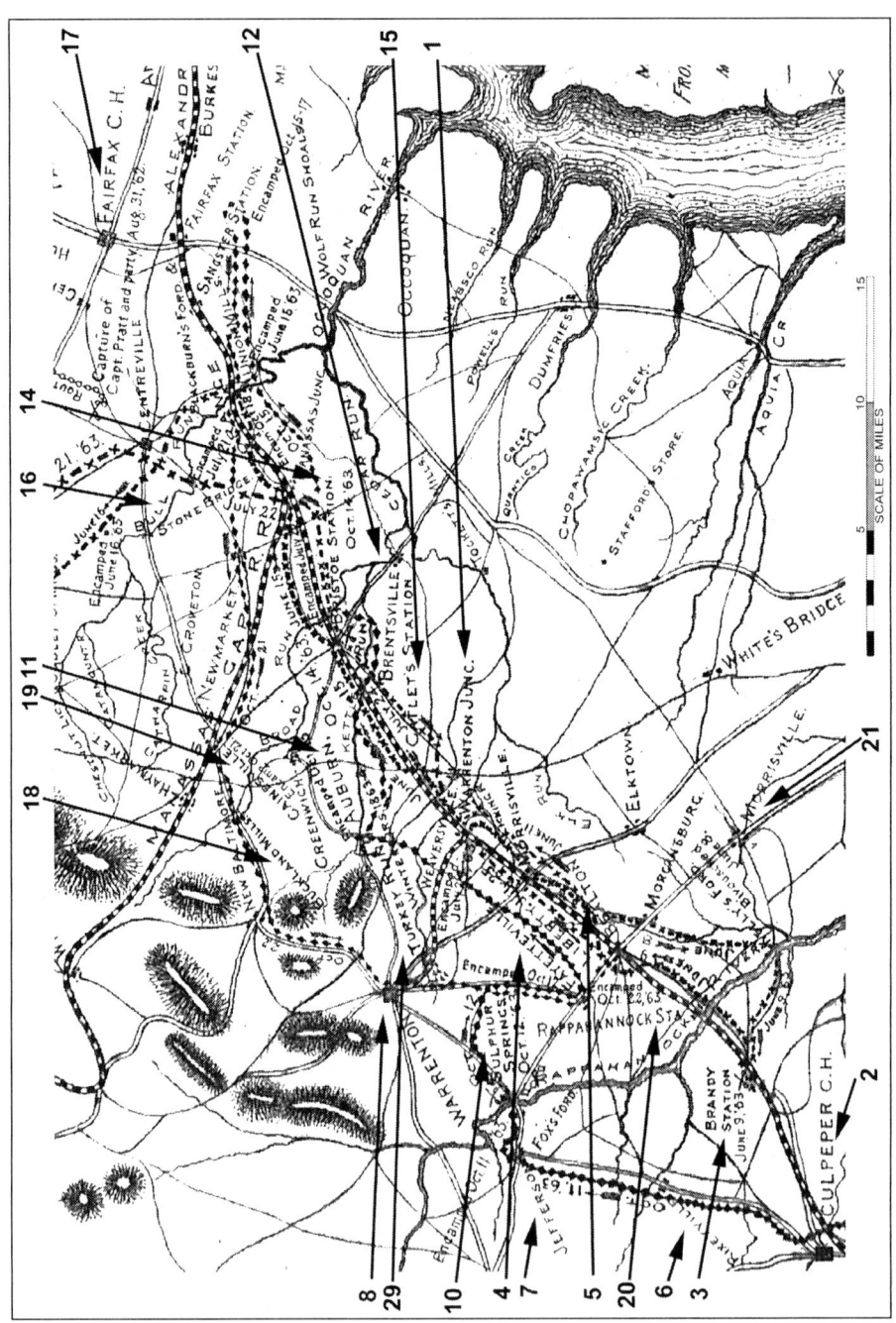

Map 5.1 Bristoe Campaign and Sulphur Springs

The First Maine Cavalry, for example, had been sent to "Little" Washington [Washington, VA, shown as #9 on Map 5.3] on a reconnaissance early on October 12, and on their return late at night, found parts of the rebel army encamped and in their way of march. This regiment had to find an indirect route, and after a two-day march full of hardships and adventure, they finally found the Army of the Potomac near Bristoe Station [#14 on Map 5.1].

Washington, VA is another historic Virginia village with many remembrances of Civil War days. Figure 5.4 is the author's photo of the monument to Robert E. Lee in the village.

Figure 5.4 Lee's monument in "Little" Washington, VA (2006)

Sulphur Springs Engagement

In the following from Preston's book he has the regiment crossing over to the east side of the Rappahannock River [2]:

> At an early hour [on October 12, 1863] the command was moved across to the east side of the river, leaving the Fourth and Thirteenth Pennsylvania Cavalry Regiments on picket in the direction of Jeffersonton. The Tenth halted about half a mile from the ford, on the south side of the road leading to Warrenton, and went into camp. Colonel Taylor's brigade had been sent to Warrenton before the Second Brigade had crossed the river. While the men were busy making preparations for future comfort, the sharp crack of carbines was heard across the river, and then the bugle summoned them to horse. The Regiment was quickly mounted and moved to the support of the battery posted near the ford. While this movement was being made, the Fourth and Thirteenth Pennsylvania Cavalry, which had stubbornly resisted the advance of the enemy, made by infantry and cavalry in overwhelming numbers, were seen to break from the woods, and the Tenth was ordered to their assistance. While the rear of the Regiment was coming into line behind the battery, the right broke by fours and moved to the ford.
>
> After crossing [to the west side of the Rappahannock River again], Major Avery deployed a part of the Regiment as skirmishers, which extended the line so that the right reached beyond the woods in which the two regiments already named were maintaining the unequal contest. From the right of the line a view could be had behind the woods. Infantry in solid columns were in plain view, while the open field swarmed with cavalry and artillery. Those on the east side of the river, who witnessed the advance of the Regiment under a heavy fire on this occasion, spoke of it with great admiration. The alignment was perfect, and was maintained until the wood was entered. From the position here attained the large force in front of the Regiment was partially

disclosed. After a brief resistance the Tenth was compelled to fall back, together with the Fourth and Thirteenth Pennsylvania, as the flanks were overlapped.

The Confederate report on these activities reads as follows [3]:

> The Seventh Virginia Cavalry was sent to the left and the Twelfth Virginia Cavalry to the right, with the intention of penetrating to the enemy's rear and cutting them off from the fords. Colonel Funsten, with the Twelfth Virginia, soon encountered the Tenth New York Cavalry, and after a brief but severe struggle drove them back toward the river. ...
>
> Sending two regiments to cross the Rappahannock higher up, Stuart proceeded to force the passage of the river at Warrenton Springs. Here the ford and bridge were commanded by rifle-pits, into which the enemy had thrown a considerable force of dismounted men.

Resuming Preston's discussion of the Sulphur Springs engagement [4]:

> The organization of the Regiment became broken by its inability to resist the great numbers brought against it, and as the men broke from the timber the rebels followed with their characteristic yell. The right of the Regiment was thus cut off, but most of the men escaped, going directly to the river, and, plunging in, swam across. Meantime the battery was doing excellent service at the ford, and aided by the carbineers along the river's edge, compelled the enemy to retire to the cover of the wood again.
>
> General Gregg caused the dismounted men to be organized and placed along the river's bank during the quiet that followed the falling back of the enemy to the wood, knowing their services would soon be required. A staff-officer called for a report of the number of mounted men in the Regiment. This report showed seventy-eight men [out of a theoretical size of 1200!]. Upon receipt of this, Major Avery was directed to take them to one of the fords up the river to prevent the crossing of the enemy. The command had proceeded about a mile on its

destination when the ominous silence was broken by the simultaneous discharge of several cannon in the wood on the hill opposite the ford. The guns were worked vigorously for a short time, and then loud and clear rang out the yell which invariably accompanied the rebel charge. With the first discharge of the rebel guns the Regiment had halted, and as the tumult of conflict was heard at the ford, Major Avery directed Commissary Preston [the author of the book "History of the Tenth..."] to proceed to that point and ascertain the condition of affairs. It was then just dusk. Passing rapidly through the weeds surrounding the ruins of the large Sulphur Springs House, Lieutenant Preston encountered a line of dismounted troops who were being pursued by mounted men. Supposing the pursuers to be officers and mounted troops trying to rally the dismounted men, the Lieutenant passed some of them.

He suddenly discovered his mistake and found himself inside the enemy's line, and a sharp summons to surrender was made by one of the rebels, who at the same time made an attempt to grasp the bridle of his horse. A quick jerk brought the horse's head around and a vigorous working of the spurs unlimbered his muscles. Over the rough ground the animal bounded with the Lieutenant bending forward on the pommel of the saddle, passing safely through a shower of bullets and reporting to Major Avery that the entire brigade [except for the 10th New York] had retired on the Fayetteville road, with the rebels in possession of the ford and advancing up the Warrenton pike. There was a crossroad leading from the one the Regiment was on to the Warrenton road, a few rods back- that is, toward the advancing enemy. Major Avery's objective point was that road. If the rebels got possession of it, the Regiment would be cut off. Countermarching the command, the march was rapidly taken up and the road gained; but the rebels were already in the dense timber which flanked the road on the right, and they opened a rapid and well-directed fire on the moving column. A little disposition to unsteadiness in the ranks was checked by the prompt action of the Major, who brought the men into line and commenced an action that appeared almost hopeless.

There seemed no way out of the predicament unless the command could gain the Warrenton pike, now so near at hand. Suddenly a dark column appeared on the pike directly across the Regiment's path! But *they* were moving toward the ford; and, sure enough, they were opposing the same force that the Tenth were. "What regiment is that?" sang out one of the flankers. "First Jersey," always a welcome name, never was so welcome as at that moment. The cheer that followed the announcement must have surprised the Jerseymen, who could hardly have expected Union troops from that direction. The Regiment was hastily moved to the pike, which it reached just as the gallant young Colonel Janeway led a squadron of the First New Jersey in a charge down the road. Here was Colonel Taylor's brigade. The Tenth took the position assigned it, and as the regiments broke by fours into the road toward Warrenton, it followed in its turn, taking the gallop as soon as the command had all gained the road. About midway between Sulphur Springs and Warrenton a road led from the Warrenton pike to Fayetteville. Turning upon this road, the march was continued until Fayetteville was reached, about 3 A.M. on the 13th [of October], where the balance of the Regiment and brigade was found in a pretty exhausted condition.

At the time that Major Avery proceeded up the river with the main body of the Regiment, as already narrated, another portion, consisting of about thirty men, was sent down the river some three miles to Fox's Ford, where they were attacked, but stubbornly held their position and kept possession of the ford until a portion of the First Massachusetts Cavalry relieved them, when the detachment from the Tenth retired to Fayetteville [#4 on Map 5.1].

Still another portion, which had lost their horses and had served as dismounted carbineers after the Regiment fell back across the river in the early part of the day, had accompanied the small force under General Gregg, which were forced back from the river to Fayetteville in the final charge of the rebel hosts. These detachments were reunited at Fayetteville on the morning of the 13th of October, where the bronzed and bruised veterans gathered around the camp-fires and recounted the incidents of the previous day's operations and the heroic deeds of fallen comrades.

If Justus was able to receive his mail, he would have received the following letter from Mary about this time.

Figure 5.5 Foraging (Preston book)

September 20, 1863
Homer, Cortland Co.

Friend Jut,

I sit down this eve to answer your kind letter that I received a few days ago. Your letters are allways welcomed ones. I am glad that you are jeneraly well. hope that you have recovered from your accident with your horse before this. but how you keep up such good spirits I do not see. whilst I only look on the dark side of the question I see that you look on the bright side. I am glad that it is so. I should try to encourage instead of discouraging. I will try and do so in the future. We are having quite cold wether for September but I suppose it is warm enough in the sunny South. I wish that I could be there for one week. I think that I could find some that I should know, would not I enjoy it. perhaps you will see me down there one of these days. would you believe your eyes. or would you think that it was a ghost.

My health is very good, better than it has been for a long time. I have been home since I wrote you last- staid one week- it was the week after Clarisa died. I suppose that you have heard of it long before this. it seems hard that one so young and enjoying life so well should be taken away. Larenzo takes her death very hard. I did not see Delia whilst at home to speak to her.

They have very good sunday school to our school house every sunday and preaching once in two weeks. I think it is to bad for you to have a chaplain and no preaching. I do not see but you would be just as well without one. I thought that was what they were sent for. Mr. Bowdish has resined and came home last week. his health is not very good. John Seeber was fetched home two weeks ago to be burried. he was wounded at Gettisburg and suffered all that a person could suffer.

165

Camp meeting was held in East Homer two weeks ago. I did not as much as go once although it was so near. we are very busy in the shop. the fair is this week. I think that I shall go one day. I enjoy myself in Homer very well but my thoughts often wander back to other days. I would that they could return again but they are gone, forever gone. can think of the red schoolhouse and truly say that my happiest days were spent there, and my mates where are they. I can go to the grave yard and point to a number there and the rest are scattered over the earth. but I do believe that they will one day come back again.

The bell is ringing for meeting and I must close. Write soon, keep good care of your health. remember that that is one thing nessessary for happiness and remember me as your true friend,

M. L. Hatch

Perhaps that you will see some of the drafted down there one of these days. I thank you for those verses that you sent. they are very good.

Auburn Engagement

On the 13th of October, the regiment marched to Auburn (#11 on Map 5.1) with the infantry. Companies H and L were sent out to picket the road to Warrenton under the command of Captain Vanderbilt. Preston describes this engagement in the following paragraphs, also referred to as "Catlett's Station" and "St. Stephen's Church" [5]:

> A guide was furnished, and Commissary Preston was sent with the detachment [Vanderbilt's squadron] with instructions to return as soon as the Captain had established his reserve, to acquaint himself with the route traveled in case Major Avery should desire to communicate with the Captain. The guide led the party through the darkness into a ravine, the first part of the march being made amid the wagon train of the Second Corps. The jaded horses and worn-out riders were marched a distance of three or four miles, making a partial circuit of the camp of the Second Cavalry Division, and, trusting to the guide, Captain Vanderbilt supposed he was a long distance from camp; but while establishing his reserve the hum of many voices and driving of stakes was plainly heard, showing the presence of the division encamped, as it proved early next morning, quite nearby. After establishing his reserve, Captain Vanderbilt proceeded out upon the road, through the dense wood, to locate a picket post. Lieutenant Preston accompanied the party. While instructing the picket, the unmistakable presence of a large force of troops in his front was made known by the noise of the men and the commands of the officers. The situation was not a pleasant one for the Captain to contemplate. Lieutenant Preston left to report to Major Avery the condition of affairs, but, getting mixed up in the confused wagon-trains *en route,* he did not reach the regiment until an early hour in the morning, just before the attack was made in force on Captain Vanderbilt's little command.

In a letter to the historian, several years ago, Captain Vanderbilt says, in making mention of this engagement:

"Just before dawn (I need not tell you I did not sleep a wink that night after you left me) I posted my reserves, dismounted, behind the barricade, with Lieutenant Charley Pratt's and Lieutenant Woodruff's assistance, and gave Charley orders to have all the men ready. I started for the outpost, and waited for light. Just at gray dawn I could distinguish the road and fields full of men, a column of mounted men coming down the road. I formed my men obliquely by the side of the road in the woods, so that each man could fire up the road. I then sang out: 'Halt! who comes there!' No reply, but the advance seemed to be mixing up. I suppose the ones ahead wanted to change places with those in the rear. I waited but a moment, and then I shouted, 'Fire!' Eight carbines rang out on the still morning air. After a moment of preparation they charged down upon us, mounted, and we took position behind the barricade. On they came right up to the barricade. Then brave Charley Pratt's voice rang out as he gave the orders to his men to 'stand firm and give it to 'em!'

"Our boys just warmed them up in good style, and the rebels disappeared from our front. Then I received an order from Avery, through you, 'For God's sake, Van, hold them for ten minutes longer, if possible!' He wanted time to get the Regiment together, to come to my help. Then I called for twelve volunteers to charge into the woods. I wanted to break them up before getting formed for another charge. Lieutenant Marsh Woodruff and a dozen men came into line quicker than I am recording it, and, wasting no time in words, I gave the direction and command to charge, and down the road they went, yelling like demons. The rebels broke, and we chased them down the road, through the woods, until we ran up against a barricade, which they had erected with the same benevolent purpose I had built mine. Here we lost nine horses killed out of the twelve, and, strange to relate, not a man hit! Then, as we fell back, we found the

Regiment advancing to our assistance. Major Avery exhibited his sterling qualities as a commander that morning in getting the Regiment, worn out and sleepy as the men were, in line and ready for action in so short a time."

It was unfortunate that the reserve under Captain Vanderbilt was so near the command, as it gave the division but little time for preparation before the rebels, in overwhelming numbers, came down upon him and required the most desperate fighting by his few men to hold them in check. As soon as the Regiment came upon the ground, Major Avery ordered Lieutenant Thomas W. Johnson to charge, mounted, with his squadron. It was necessary that bold, determined action should be taken at once, as the division was not yet prepared for action, nor the batteries in position. Lieutenant Johnson went forward with something of the feeling which must have impelled the gallant Keenan, of the Eighth Pennsylvania Cavalry, as he charged Jackson's victorious corps at Chancellorsville. Johnson well knew the character of the undertaking. He knew, as Captain Vanderbilt had already demonstrated, that the force he was about to charge was infantry, and that their numbers were sufficiently great to give no hope of permanent success. But time was necessary, and it must be had, even at a sacrifice. Drawing his saber, Johnson rose in his stirrups, gave the command to charge, and, plunging the spurs into his horse's flanks, sped onward, closely followed by his gallant command. Men and horses went down before the terrible fire that met them, Johnson being one of the first to fall. Over his prostrate form went the charging column, until its object was attained, when it fell back, leaving its gallant leader in the enemy's hands.

Preston continues his description in the following account [6]:

General Gregg, always apparently coolest in exciting times, had his command well in hand in a few moments. The enemy were held until the trains had safely passed, when Gregg withdrew and followed in rear of the Second Corps.

Major McClellan states [7] that at 4 P.M., on the 13th of October, Stuart arrived with his cavalry at Auburn [#11 on Map 5.1, near St. Stephen's Church], where he left Lomax with his brigade, while he proceeded with the balance of his force toward Catlett's Station [#15 on Map 5.1]. When near the station he suddenly found himself in the presence of the Union wagon-trains and moving columns of infantry and artillery hurrying northward. Stuart sent Major Venable of his staff to inform General Lee of the situation of affairs and suggest an attack; but when Venable reached Auburn he found it in possession of our [Union] troops and was compelled to make a detour to the north to reach Warrenton, first sending Stuart word of the condition of things at Auburn. As evening was coming on, Stuart moved toward Auburn, hoping to force a passage at that point; but he found himself hemmed in on both sides by the columns of our infantry moving northward by parallel routes. He was compelled, therefore, to remain quiet in the fields with but the hills and darkness to conceal his presence from our troops. Posting his guns on the crest of the hill in his front, Stuart with his troopers remained during the night within three hundred rods of the road along which our troops were marching. Major McClellan says:

> "So close were we to the marching columns of the enemy that we could distinctly hear the orders of the officers as they closed up the column. We could even hear the voices of the men in conversation, etc."

He further states that as daylight came on our infantry stacked arms nearby and began straggling in search of water, when, knowing their discovery was inevitable, their batteries were put in readiness, and as "a few shots on the side of the enemy next to Warrenton informed us that some one was about to commence work there, in an instant our seven guns were raining shell and canister upon the enemy." Our infantry moved to the attack, and after a brief engagement Stuart uncovered himself by moving to the rear, thus extricating his command from its perilous position.

Bristoe Station Battle

When the Tenth left the hillside at Auburn skirmishing was briskly going on, our skirmishers being under command of Captain Bliss; but the enemy exhibited no disposition to push further fighting seriously, and Gregg's regiments left with as much order as if going on parade. After passing Cedar Run [a creek which runs near Brentsville, #12 on Map 5.1, near Catlett's Station] the men were compelled to leave the road, which was in possession of the enemy, and march Indian file through the underbrush and timber to its right for some distance.

Just before dark the Regiment issued from the woods south of Bristoe Station [#14 on Map 5.1], and the men beheld a long column of infantry drawn up on the opposite side of the railroad cut, which in the fading light of day were mistaken for Union troops, but, a moment later, a volley directed against the Regiment changed not only their opinion, but the direction of march as well. The First New Jersey, under the gallant Colonel Janeway, were deployed mounted to meet the rebel infantry; but the intervening railway cut prevented their doing effective service, and the whole force finally retired through the woods toward Brentsville and took position on the left of the Second Corps, then in process of retirement by the right flank after the brilliant fight at Bristoe Station, in which they punished the rebels severely and captured several cannon. In the early evening, when attacked by the rebel infantry, the horse of Harry Freeman, of Company A, was shot, and Sergeant Mitchell bravely returned under fire and assisted Freeman to join his company.

At 1 A.M. the Regiment left its position in line near Brentsville, and moving by the right flank followed the rest of the brigade, passing over the battlefield in the woods, where the pitiful cries of the wounded rose on the still night air pleading for water and assistance. The march was continued all day in a hard rain, crossing Broad Run at night and going into camp soon after.

The next day two squadrons were sent to picket along Bull Run [#16 on Map 5.1, another small creek made famous by the major battle held there early in the War], and on the 17th [October 1863] the Regiment marched with the army trains, going into camp about four miles from Fairfax Court-House [#17 on Map 5.1, only 15 miles from Washington]. Rations and forage were obtained from Fairfax Court-House on the 18th, and that afternoon the Regiment marched to Union Mills. On the 19th Company H was ordered to accompany the One Hundred and Seventieth New York Volunteers on picket, returning to the Regiment next day.

Major Avery's Official Report on the engagements of the Tenth New York gives a succinct record of the events at Sulphur springs and Auburn.

Official Report of Major Avery

Report of Major M. Henry Avery, Tenth New York Cavalry, Covering the Sulphur Springs and Auburn Engagements
October 9-22

HEADQUARTERS TENTH NEW YORK CAVALRY, NEAR FAYETTEVILLE, VA
October 23, 1863

SIR: I have the honor to submit to you the following report respecting the movements and operations of this Regiment from the 9th inst.

At this date the Regiment was encamped one mile west of Liberty [#4 on Map 5.1], and picketing the [east side of the Rappahannock] river from Freeman's Ford to Sulphur Springs, and the roads toward Warrenton. On the evening of the 9th instant I received orders to report immediately with my command to brigade headquarters, but owing to unexpected delay in drawing in my pickets I was not prepared to move until daylight the following morning. I proceeded to Bealton, when I found the brigade had marched, taking the road toward Culpeper. I followed on and joined it near Culpeper, where I arrived at 4 P.M. [Oct. 10] and went into camp for the night.

According to directions, my command was prepared to march early the following morning, and at ten o'clock the division moved out with the Second Brigade in the rear. The route of the division on this day was toward Sulphur Springs, proceeding slowly without molestation and covering the left flank and rear of Meade's columns. Arrived at Sulphur Springs about 9 P.M., the Second Brigade bivouacking upon nearly its old camping-grounds near Jefferson.

The next morning the brigade moved across the river and encamped along the Warrenton pike about a mile from the ford. Before arrangements for the camp were completed I received order to be ready to move at brief notice. Thirty minutes after, I moved out in advance of the battery, going down till near the ford, then countermarched a short distance, and, after a short halt in the piece of woods at the right of the road, marched down and was placed in close column at the right and rear of the battery posted on the crest of the hill commanding the crossing and the opposite side of the river. Soon after taking this position the Fourth Pennsylvania, which had been left on picket at Jefferson in the morning and been attacked, was pressed back to within view by the enemy, who was advancing determinedly with a strong force of infantry and cavalry.

The Thirteenth Pennsylvania, which had crossed over and was upon the right, had become engaged sharply, and was being forced into a dangerous position and would require assistance to retire safely. This command was sent to their support and soon gained a position on the slope of the hill in the center, and I immediately deployed one squadron as skirmishers. This engaged the attention of the enemy, and allowed the regiments upon my right and left to retire toward the ford. The fire of the enemy then became principally concentrated upon this Regiment, and after remaining a short time returning his fire as much as possible, I was ordered to fall back across the river. I was now in the rear, and the enemy's numerous skirmishers, with heavy supports pressing upon both flanks and rear, compelled me to fall back hastily, suffering severe loss in men and horses. After crossing the river a larger share of my carbineers were dismounted and posted along the bank of the river about the crossing, and with the remainder of the Regiment, numbering about fifty mounted men, I was directed to move up the river about three fourths of a mile and hold a crossing at this point.

Shortly after arriving here, the enemy's heavy battery opened, which drove our forces from their position at the ford and allowed the enemy's forces to cross. I perceived that they were advancing up the Warrenton pike and driving back our skirmishers. Under these circumstances I thought it advisable to endeavor to gain the road in advance of him, lest I should be cut off from the rest of the command. On reaching the pike I found the advance of the First Brigade moving down to check the enemy's skirmishers, who were advancing rapidly. I formed my men upon the right in the edge of the woods, while the First New Jersey advanced down the road and drove them back nearly to the ford. Heavy skirmishing continued from this time until after dark, the enemy making but little progress. The First New Jersey was principally engaged. The few men I had were maneuvered as far as possible for its support. I lost a few men here in wounded.

Soon after dark the firing ceased, and with the First Brigade I fell back to Fayetteville, where the Second Brigade had halted, and here remained till morning [Oct. 12]. I then collected the available force of my Regiment, which had been considerably reduced by the engagement on the previous day.

The division started at noon, and marched to Auburn via Germantown. Arrived at the former place late in the evening, and this Regiment sent to picket the road toward Warrenton. I established my headquarters about a mile from Auburn, throwing out my pickets to the distance of three fourths of a mile beyond. Everything remained quiet during the night, but as soon as daybreak the next morning the enemy advanced a heavy force of infantry, before which my picket force, consisting of one squadron, in command of Captain Vanderbilt, was obliged to fall back, hotly skirmishing the while.

By the time I could form my men in the field the skirmishers were within three hundred yards, and I immediately sent a squadron to support them. The enemy was then driven back some distance, but, advancing again with increased numbers, Captain Vanderbilt retired again, after a stout resistance, holding the enemy in check for some time. I then withdrew my reserve about one hundred yards farther down the road, and ordered the Fifth Squadron, under Lieutenant Johnson, to charge with the saber. This was gallantly done, and further checked the enemy's advance. I regret to record here the loss of one of my bravest officers, Lieutenant Johnson, who fell while leading this charge, and was unavoidably left in the hands of the enemy supposed to have been killed. After this I fell back slowly till under cover of our guns planted upon the brow of the hill with heavy support. One of my squadrons (Captain Bliss's) was kept on the skirmish-line until I retired with the brigade toward Catlett's Station. My loss during the morning was not serious.

This Regiment took but little part in the skirmishing which continued during the day while the division was moving along the railroad toward Bristoe. The enemy having gained possession of the railroad near this point, attacked us from an ambush with a heavy fire of musketry, and compelled the column to retire in the direction of Brentsville. The division halted here for the night, and started early the next morning and marched to a point three miles from Fairfax Station, and encamped. I remained here till the evening of the 17th, keeping two squadrons picketing on Bull Run. I then moved my command, according to instructions, to Union Mills, having orders to picket from that point to the ford on Bull Run, five miles below.

On the evening of the 19th I received orders to join the brigade at Centreville, and started early the following morning, joining the brigade at noon the same day near Bull Run [#16 on Map 5.1], on the Gainesville road; bivouacked here for the night, and the next day (21st) marched with division to Warrenton and camped one mile south of the town. Marched with brigade next day to Fayetteville, and fell back one mile in the evening and encamped in the woods.

Very respectfully, your obedient servant,
M. HENRY AVERY, Major,
Commanding Tenth New York Cavalry
Per G. W. KENNEDY, *Adjutant*
JOHN B. MAITLAND, *Assistant Adjutant-General*

The CWSAC also discusses these battles in two reports [8], giving the context to the engagements in which the Tenth New York was involved:

First Auburn Engagement October 13, 1863

Other Names: Catlett's Station, St. Stephen's Church

After the retreat from Gettysburg, the Confederate army concentrated behind the Rapidan River in Orange County. The Federals advanced to the Rappahannock River in August, and in mid-September they pushed strong columns forward to confront Lee along the Rapidan. In early September, Lee dispatched two divisions of Longstreet's Corps to reinforce the Confederate army in Georgia; the Federals followed suite, sending the XI and XII Corps to Tennessee by railroad in late September after the Battle of Chickamauga (September 18-20). In early October, Lee began an offensive sweep around Meade's right flank with his remaining two corps, forcing the Federals to withdraw along the line of the Orange & Alexandria Railroad. On October 13, Stuart, with Fitzhugh Lee and Lomax's brigades, skirmished with the rearguard of the Union III Corps near Auburn. Finding himself cut off by retreating Federal columns, Stuart secreted his troopers in a wooded ravine until the unsuspecting Federals moved on.

Second Auburn Engagement October 14, 1863

Other Name: Coffee Hill

As the Federal army withdrew towards Manassas Junction, Owens and Smyth's Union brigades (Warren's II Corps) fought a rearguard action against Stuart's cavalry and infantry of Harry Hays's division near Auburn. Stuart's cavalry boldly bluffed Warren's infantry and escaped disaster. The II Corps pushed on to Catlett Station on the Orange & Alexandria Railroad.

Buckland Mills

Several descriptions of the fighting at and around Buckland Mills (#18 on Map 5.1) on October 18 and 19, 1863 are available. Many are from Confederate sources, since it was a big Confederate victory, and an embarrassment for the Union. The following is part of a description of the battle, in a history of Vermont regiments [9]:

An immediate advance of the division to Warrenton was now ordered and the regiment started, without time to make coffee. Stuart, who was at Buckland with Hampton's cavalry division, retired slowly before Kilpatrick on the Warrenton pike, in order to draw him on till Fitzhugh Lee, who was at Auburn, should get into his rear. Between them they expected to crush him. As they had 7,000 men to Kilpatrick's 3,500, this was not an unreasonable expectation. At Buckland Mills, the passage of Broad Run was forced by Custer's brigade, and after halting for an hour to feed the horses, Kilpatrick pushed on to and beyond New Baltimore after Stuart, with Davies's brigade, leaving Custer at Broad Run. There Custer was found by Fitzhugh Lee, who, advancing from Greenwich with his division, expecting to get unopposed into Kilpatrick's rear, was surprised to find Custer's brigade across his path. Custer had barely time to get into position before he was attacked by a line of dismounted men a mile long, supported by artillery and heavy bodies of mounted men. Custer's left rested on Broad Run, where he placed a section of Pennington's battery, supported by the First Vermont cavalry, his right extended through a piece of woods along a ridge, on which he placed the rest of the battery. At the first sound of Fitzhugh Lee's guns, Stuart turned upon Davies, attacked him in front and on each flank, and drove him back to Buckland with serious loss. His stampede placed Custer in a critical position, and compelled him to get away in a hurry.

Pennington fired till the enemy was within twenty yards of his guns on the right, and then took them across the Run. His left section was protected by two companies of carbineers of the First Vermont, who resisted the enemy's advance till the guns were safely withdrawn. The regiment was pressed on front and flank and was under artillery fire, but withdrew across the Run in good order. Custer then retreated with his own and a portion of Davies's brigade, hotly pursued, till he was met by the advance of Howe's division of the sixth Corps, at Gainesville, where the infantry of the First Vermont brigade relieved his tired troopers from further pursuit and drove back the enemy.

The CWSAC also provides a short description of the Buckland Mills Battle [10]:

> After defeat at Bristoe Station and an aborted advance on Centreville, Stuart's cavalry shielded the withdrawal of Lee's army from the vicinity of Manassas Junction. Union cavalry under Kilpatrick pursued Stuart's cavalry along the Warrenton Turnpike but were lured into an ambush near Chestnut Hill and routed. The Federal troopers were scattered and chased five miles in an affair that came to be known as the "Buckland Races."

The Cultural Landscape Foundation has a paragraph relating to the Buckland Mills Battle [11]:

> During the Civil War, Buckland's mills became a prime military target because of their proximity to the Warrenton Turnpike. Buckland was occupied at different times throughout the war by both Union and Confederate troops. The first shots of the Second Battle of Manassas were fired on Crozet's stone bridge in August, 1862. On October 19, 1863, the Confederate Cavalry enjoyed its final southern victory in Buckland when it rousted the armies of Generals Kirkpatrick and George Armstrong Custer. Referred to as Custer's "First Stand", this was Custer's most serious defeat prior to the Battle at Little Big Horn. After the Confederates recaptured Crozet's Bridge, they sent the Yankees scrambling on a five-mile steeplechase along the Warrenton Turnpike. General J.E.B. Stuart humorously called the victory "The Buckland Races." Later, stating in his official report, "I am justified in declaring the rout of the enemy at Buckland the most single and complete that any cavalry has suffered during the war." The Union Army suffered 230 casualties. Buckland Tavern and the Church were set up as hospitals for the wounded.

Attempting to Keep in Contact with Lee

Lee started moving back towards the Rappahannock in the middle of October. Preston describes the efforts of the Union to try to determine his movements and guess at his objectives [12]:

> The march southward was commenced again on the 21st [October, 1863], General Lee having begun a retrograde move, and the cavalry encamped near Gainesville [#19 on Map 5.1]. From this point a detail from the Tenth was sent to Washington with condemned horses.
>
> On the 22d the Regiment marched with the brigade to Fayetteville, where it continued on picket and scouting duty until the 7th of November, when it was ordered to Morrisville and next day to Kelly's Ford [on the Rappahannock River].

179

Here it went on picket. Returning to Morrisville [#21 on Map 5.1] on the 10th, it was ordered to report to Colonel Huey, of the Eighth Pennsylvania Cavalry, at Grove Church, for picket duty. On the 18th a part of the picket reserve had a slight skirmish with guerrillas.

On the 19th of November, Lieutenant M.R. Woodruff [Company L] with a small force was attacked by largely superior numbers near Grove Church [near Morrisville] and lost five men taken prisoners, and he himself was wounded very severely and left on the field for dead. Warren Irish, of Company D, gives an account of this affair as follows:

> While on picket near Grove Church, a woman who lived outside our lines made a request for eight or ten safeguards. Lieutenant Woodruff, of Company L, was sent out to post them. They had gone but a short distance beyond our picket-line when they were attacked by about twenty-five bushwhackers who were lying in ambush for them. The Lieutenant was shot in the back, and his horse becoming unmanageable, the rebels supposed he was trying to escape and shot him again. He fell from his horse, and feigning death, barely escaped with his life. The rebels proposed to shoot him again, but finally decided that he was dead. All the men were taken prisoners, including W. Brooks, B. Bowman, N. Dimon, S. Leach, J.E. Derrand, and J. Hummel, of Company E.
>
> After the rebels had gone, Lieutenant Woodruff crawled near enough to a small house to have his cries for help heard, and a small boy went to his assistance and aided him to the house, where he remained until an ambulance arrived and took him away.

An unfortunate affair occurred on the morning of the 20th [of November]. The Fourth Pennsylvania Cavalry, returning from a reconnaissance, came upon the pickets of the Tenth, and each supposing the other to be rebels, attacked with vigor. Before serious consequences occurred, however, the mistake was discovered.

Pickets were called in and the Regiment marched to Morrisville and joined the brigade on the 23d of November. Several men were taken from the Tenth this day to serve in Battery A, Fourth United States Artillery, among the number being Robert Trotter and Eli Baird, of Company D.

Judging from the next few letters from Justus Matteson, he missed the Battle of Auburn. He was in the Battle of Sulphur Springs on October 12, 1863, where his horse was shot out from under him. As a result he suffered from a back injury in the fall from his horse, was horseless, and had to walk about 50 miles to Camp Stoneman in Washington, DC. Cavaliers are not used to walking long distances; by the time he got there he was worn out, and suffered from his back injury and the ague (chills, fever and sweating). His back injury plagued him the rest of his life, although he did rejoin the Tenth New York after about two months of recuperation at Camp Stoneman, hence missing the Mine Run Campaign also.

Justus writes the following letters to his father and Mary.

Camp Stoneman
Nov. 25th, 1863

Father, Dear Sir,

As it is some time since I have written to you, I will begin an answer to one that I am daily expecting from you. for it must be that you have heard from me since I came here. I have not heard a word from home in more than two months I think. I suppose though that there is a letter or two at the regt, from you.

I am getting somewhat better than I've been for a few weeks. I shall probably join the Reg't before long. howsomever howbeit I cant say as for that for I thought that I should have left here long before this. The Army is on the move now report says, against ould Lee.

I must get supper now and then go over in the fifteenth Reg't and see some old friends, so good day.

Nov 26th

I will try and write a little more this morning. It was a pretty cold night last, about like our September nights north here it is. Gott to go and water a lot of old horses. That is the way here. One does not know what minute he is agoing to be called upon here. Today is thanksgiving I believe, I hope you all will have a good time. Here tis again- got to go and police up around the officers quarters.

Nov 27th

Sir I was on duty until three in the PM and then I went over to the 15th Cav to see Elie Conklin and James Lucirst. saw both. Elie is fat as a cubb. two of his brothers has been killed in the army- Benjamin and the oldest one. also one or two of uncle Thomasses boys I think he said wer knocked over.

we have good news from Gen Grant's army today. he has taken five or ten thousands prisonors and 52 pieces of artillery. He has routed the Rebbs. He is the man to dig them out if there is any to be found. I am on guard again to day. I have put in for a pass to day to go to Washington tomorrow to see if I can get my pay and get my watch fixed etc.

As it is noon I suppose you are planning to eat your dinner. I think I will have some beef stake, coffee, toast bread, etc. for mine.

182

I wish you could be here and see the boys get them meals. It would be quite a novelty to you I think. I believe if I wer at home I could go to work and get a meal as well as the best of the wimen.

Have you got the house fixed yet? have you had any trouble with it. have you spondulux enough to take you through with it. How much butter have you made this year. How much is it worth per lb. How many apples have you and potatoes and corn. How is the honkers. have you a horse now. a good one or not. Oh, I have heard that Adie Bakers wife and child wer dead. is it so or not. How did Mr. Boys get along about these that wer drafted. Uncle Sam is after them again this winter. I wonder how they will like that. I must quit and get my dinner now so no more for today.

Nov. 28th '63

I have just been relieved from gard. it is raining quite smart. I think that the stormy weather must begin here soon. last year it was awfle here at this time. we have had vary nice weather here so far for moveing an army. the report is this morning that Gen. Meade ocupies the hights of Fredericksberg. it is thought that he has out Geniraled old Lee again. and I sinserially hope that he has. if so we shal winter farther south than we did last. and we shall have a better chance for forageing among the rebs for their poultry, pigs, sheep, and often cattle. have to appease our hunger. perhapes our ma think it rather hard to take stuff in that way but I find it is all in getting use to a thing of that sort.

I am getting well quite fast now. shal be able to join the Reg't in a few days. my back is some lame but it is getting better fast. I begin to think that some of you are sick and dont want to let me know it, or I should have heard from you before this. I hope you will not do this for I should only feel the worse when I should hear of it. is the diphtheria about there now. if any of you begin to feel your throat sore take and gargle some vinegar with cayan pepper and salt in it three or four times a day. it is said that will cure it if taken soon enough. I suppose that they are doing big buisnness in Cortland this season in the line of building.

I hear that Peter is running his shop in big stile. have plenty of work and hands to do it. I have written to them and Hunteys but they do not appear to care about returnnig the favor so I think that I will bid them good by untill they notice my [other sheets missing].

183

Father, I got this sheat dated and then had to leave it without writing any, so I will try again. This day and year of our Lord Dec 3rd eighteen hundred and sixty three.

I am just relieved from gard. they have me on every other day.

We are getting good news from all quarters a most now. Gen Meade is likley to flank Lee and get to Richmond first if old Longstreat from Tennesee does not reinforse Lee. Longstreat has been oblige to save the siege of Knoxville, and retreat before Gen. Burnside and is like to be cut off before he can get through the mountains. Gen. Grant has put the rebel Bragg to flight at Chattenooga. Our men are bummin away at Charleston yet. Our Cav. has been having another tustle with the rebs. our division lost two hundred and fifty in killed and wounded. havent learned whether our regt was in it or not. Our Co Lieftennant has been badly wounded by a guerrilla in ambush.

I have got well now and am fatting up first rate.

I have got tired of waiting for a letter from you so I will finish this sheat and send it on. I have not had but one letter since I've been here and that was from Henry. I shall wait anxiously for a reply to this and if I do not get one in a week or ten days I will try once more and only once. for I do unto them as they do unto me.

I hope that this may find you all well and enjoying yourselves. I suppose that you have sleighing there now while here it is as dry and nise as you ever saw it ther in September. Tell mother that I send her my love, allso Adelia. Tell her to write oftener to me. give my respects to all enquiring friends. no more at present.

Your Son,
J. G. Matteson

Direct-
J. G. Matteson
Co. L 10th N. Y. Cav.
Camp Stoneman, Washington, D. C.

Camp Stoneman
Washington, DC
Dec 3rd "63

Friend Mary, as i am at leisure now I will pen a few lines to you. It has been a long time since I had a letter from you. your last was welcomed I assure you. as a letter from an old school mate and friend who have enjoyed our-selves together in our younger days.

You spoke of my keeping up good courage. in this when our country's and liberty is at stake, if we (the soldiers) did not keep up good cheer I would not answer for the safety of our cause.

We are having good news from the front now as allso from the armies in the different departments else whare.

I am now in the dismounted camp near Washington. I've been here ever since the army fell back to Centerville. I was in the Cav fight at Sulphur Springs. my horse was shot and I had to walk here a distance of fifty miles and was sick with the ague at the time. when I got here I was completely worn out. it was the hardest time that I seen yet and I hope that I may not have to endure it again.

I am well now and ready for duty again. there is some of the boys here now that wer in the hospitals and went home to vote. they say that they had a good time. I think that I shall try and get a furlough home this winter. if I succeed I shall try and make you a call.

Mary, I doubt whether you will get this or not for I know not where you are at present. I suppose you are having sleighrides etc. there now. here it is as pleasant as summer amost.

I shall have to cut this letter short for the sargent has detailed me for fatigue after dinner. so you will have to excuse me for this time.

Mary remember me as your friend and well wisher. and hoping that we may some day meet where this writing may cease etc etc.

Your Friend,
J. G. Matteson

P.S. Direct:
J. G. Matteson
Co.L. 10th N.Y. Vol. Cav
Camp Stoneman, Washington, DC.

Mine Run Campaign Nov. 24-Dec. 2, 1863

The Army of the Potomac infantry and Gregg's cavalry traveled east and west in the corridor formed by the Rapidan River and the Plank Road, running between Fredericksburg and the Mine Run (#22 on Map 5.2). The Campaign is described by Preston as follows [13]:

> Leaving Morrisville [#21 on Map 5.2] at 6 A.M. on the 24th [of November, 1863], the Regiment marched to Ellis Ford, on the Rappahannock, where it crossed and went into camp at Union Church. The day was raw, cold, and rainy. Then on Thursday, the 26th, it marched to Ely's Ford [on the Rapidan River] and crossed, the Second Pennsylvania Cavalry leading. After crossing, the Tenth took the advance in the Second Brigade, which was ahead, and bivouacked late in the night at White Hall. The march was taken up again at daybreak on the 27th, and about noon the plank road running from Germanna Ford to Fredericksburg was struck, when the First Brigade took the advance, and after reaching New Hope Church [near Parker's Store, #26 on Map 5.2] the latter brigade came upon the rebels in force and suffered considerably before assistance could reach them. The Fifth Corps had come upon the road between the two brigades, making it necessary for the cavalry boys to march in single file part of the time in passing them to go to the help of their hard-pressed comrades of the First Brigade, so that by the time the scene of the conflict was reached it had degenerated into a brisk skirmish. There were abundant evidences of the hard struggle as the Regiment came upon the ground. The dead and wounded in great numbers were lying in the shade of the trees surrounding the little church, while nearby the surgeons were busy plying knife and saw upon the unfortunate wounded. The Tenth was at once dismounted and advanced as skirmishers in a dense undergrowth to the left of the road upon which it had advanced. It was next to impossible to preserve alignment or to keep within sight of each other in the rank jungle. Toward evening

186

the infantry took the places of the cavalry, and the latter encamped in the woods in their rear.

The Tenth was assigned to picket duty on the cold, stormy 28th of November. The Second and Sixteenth Pennsylvania Cavalry and the Tenth were the only regiments of the division present, Colonel Taylor's brigade having been sent for the supply-trains. The weather remained cold and disagreeable on the 29th. While a featherweight issue of rations was being made to the Regiment on this day, there suddenly appeared a bareheaded horseman coming into the open from the direction of Parker's store - in our rear - shouting wildly, "Rebs! rebs!" at the top of his voice. In an instant all was commotion. The men scattered for their quarters, the bugles resounded on every side, and for a few moments all was confusion; but General Gregg soon had his command in good condition for receiving visitors. The Tenth was moved down the road whence the alarm came, and a portion of the Regiment dismounted and advanced a strong line of skirmishers on the right of the road in the woods. The enemy were found in force, and a brisk skirmish ensued. A section of the battery came flying down, and taking position in the road, began shelling the enemy vigorously. General Gregg had taken the precaution to have a company of sharpshooters from the Sixth Corps in reserve. The officer commanding the section of artillery complained that rebel sharpshooters were picking off his men and horses.

The captain of the sharpshooters detailed a man to discover the rebel marksman and snap his brittle thread of life. A tall, stooping, ungainly-looking specimen of humanity responded to the Captain's call, and swinging an immense rifle (with a long telescope sight running the entire length of the barrel) over his shoulder, he shambled along under cover of the trees until he passed just beyond the skirmish-line. Stationed behind a large tree, he watched intently a tree near the bridge which crossed the little stream in our front, along which the rebel line extended.

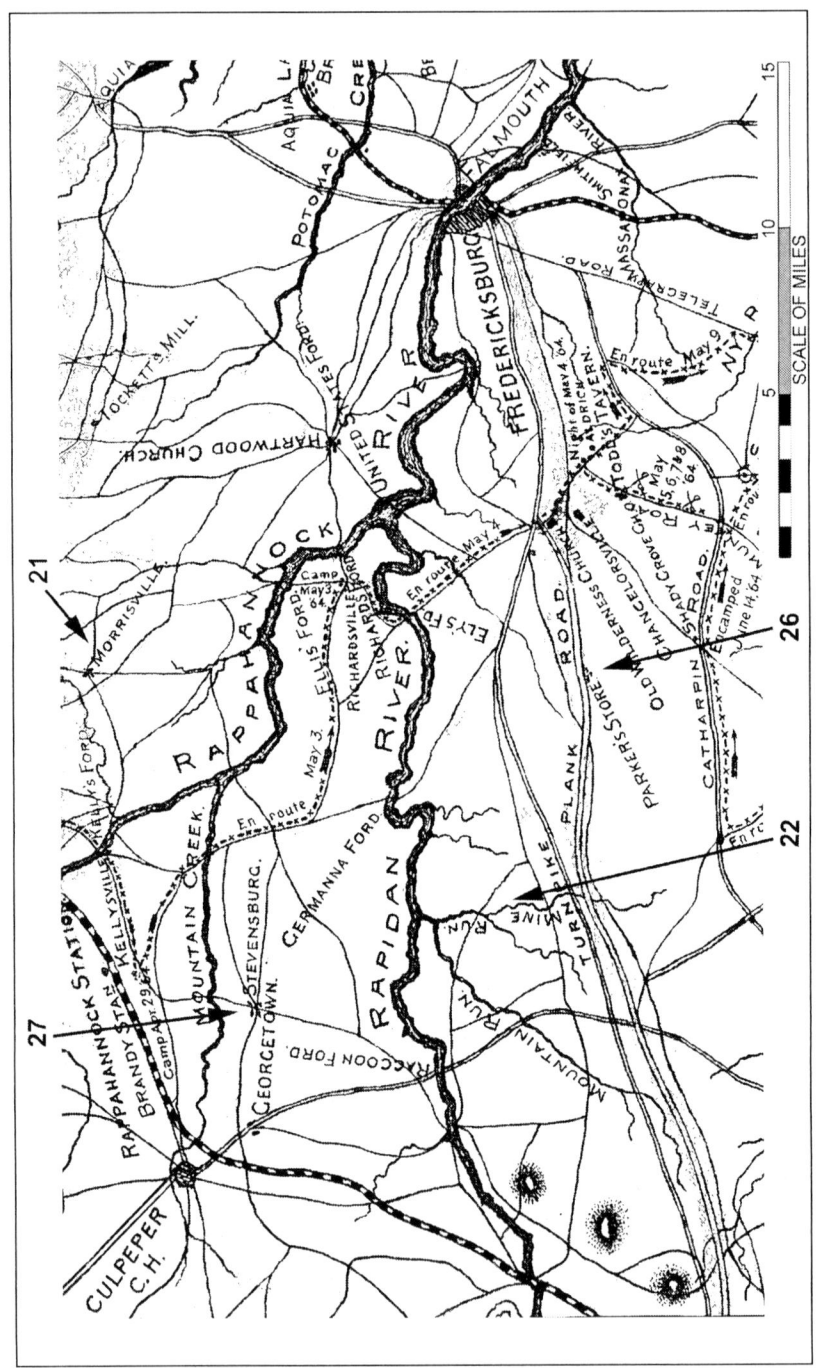

Map 5.2 Map of Mine Run Campaign

Presently he brought the immense rifle to his shoulder, the report of its discharge was blended with those of the carbines on either flank, and those who had been watching the proceedings saw a man fall from the tree on which his attention had been fixed. A few moments later the rebels fell back, and as a part of the Regiment passed the spot in pursuit, the lifeless form of the rebel sharpshooter was seen lying as he had fallen, a victim of the barbarous mode of warfare which he had himself chosen. Major Weed, Assistant Adjutant-General Maitland, Adjutant Kennedy, and Commissary Preston, galloped over the road to Parker's Store [#26 on Map 5.2], following close upon the retreating rebels. The latter officer captured a soldier belonging to the First North Carolina Cavalry.

Preston continues his review of the Mine Run Campaign [14]:

Few of the troopers of Gregg's division were aware, perhaps, how near they came to opposing a heavy movement of infantry at this point, intended for the destruction of the left of the Union army. Major McClellan says [15]:

Hampton occupied the extreme right of the Confederate line. A personal reconnaissance on the 30th [of November] brought him into a position where he was in rear of the Federal left wing, which was fully commanded by his post of observation. Hampton was looking down on the rear of the Federal guns as they stood pointed against the Confederate lines. There seemed to be no reason why a heavy force could not be concentrated at this point, which might attack the Federal lines in reverse, and perhaps reenact some of the scenes of Chancellorsville. This information was quickly communicated to Stuart, who, after himself examining the ground, conducted General R.E. Lee to the same place. A council of war was held at night. The talk among the staff was that General Lee and General Stuart favored an immediate attack, but that Generals Ewell and Hill did not deem it best. General Lee made another personal reconnaissance on the 1st of December. In his report he says: "Anderson's and Wilcox's divisions were withdrawn from the trenches at 3 P.M. on the 2d and moved to our right, with a view to make an attack in that quarter. As soon as it became light enough to distinguish objects it was discovered that the enemy's pickets along our entire line had retired, and our skirmishers were sent forward to ascertain his position; ... preparations were made to attack him on Wednesday morning. This was prevented by his retreat."

The Army of the Potomac commenced falling back from Mine Run on the 1st of December, and Gregg's division was assigned the duty of covering the retreat. It was a bitter cold night, the men becoming thoroughly chilled through while standing to horse, awaiting for the trains and columns of infantry and artillery to pass.

Finally, falling in, the cavalry followed in rear of the last of our troops, urging and aiding stragglers along, and crossed the river on the morning of the 2d, the rebels following to the river and throwing a few shells.

Major Weed writes the official report to headquarters of operations of the Tenth New York Cavalry in the Mine Run Campaign:

Report of Major Theodore H. Weed, Tenth New York Cavalry, covering the Mine Run Campaign, November, 1863.

HEADQUARTERS TENTH NEW YORK CAVALRY,
December 4, 1863

SIR: I have the honor to submit to you the following report of the part taken by this command in the operations and movements of the Second Brigade from the time the same left its camp at Morrisville [#21 on Maps 5.1 and 5.2], November

24th ultimo, up to the date of its arrival at Richardsville [between Ellis' Ford on the Rappahannock River and Ely's Ford on the Rapidan River] on the 2d instant [November 24-December 2, 1863].

I broke camp near Morrisville at daybreak on the morning of the 24th and moved with the brigade, which crossed Ellis's Ford and marched to Richardsville via Ely's Ford road. I bivouacked here for the night, and sent one squadron to picket the roads in the rear of the camp leading to Ely's and Germanna Fords. On the 25th a detail of one hundred and fifty men was made from the Regiment for picket. My camp was not moved on this day.

Early on the 26th I crossed the Rapidan with the brigade, being second in order of march. Shortly after crossing the river this Regiment was put in the advance, which place it held during the remainder of the day's march. No enemy was encountered during the day except a few straggling parties of cavalry, which ran at our approach. Encamped soon after dark near White Hall. Resumed march early the next morning, taking the extreme rear of the column. I arrived at New Hope Church, where the First Brigade had been engaged, about 2 P.M., and was posted upon the left of the plank road, near the railroad grade, and opposite the church. Two squadrons were immediately sent to picket the road leading from the church across the railroad southward. This being a weak point in our line and exposed to sudden attack, the remainder of the command was held, the entire night following, with ranks unbroken, in readiness for immediate action.

The following morning, 28th, the battalion stationed across the railroad the evening previous was driven in a short distance, and remained to picket the roads and neighborhood in that direction. Another battalion was sent up on the plank road after the withdrawal of the infantry, with directions to picket from this road across the grade, joining with the other battalion upon the left. A reserve of one squadron was stationed at the church. No further disposition or change was made during the day till I was relieved by the Eighth Pennsylvania at sundown, when I reported with the Regiment at brigade headquarters, and was directed to go into camp in the field nearby.

At 5 A.M., the 29th, I was notified that my Regiment was detailed to report to the Second Corps. I remained near brigade headquarters awaiting further orders until late in the afternoon, when I was sent down the road toward Parker's Store [#26 on Map 5.2] to support the battery. After the firing had ceased, the Regiment was advanced a half-mile farther, and one battalion sent forward to the store to reconnoiter. This returned soon after dark, capturing three prisoners. The enemy had fallen back and no force was discovered. I remained to picket this road, sending during the night one squadron to communicate with the First Brigade. The next day at 5 A.M., I moved up to headquarters and camped in the woods south of the road, leaving one squadron to picket road toward Parker's Store. At 4 A.M. December 2d, I left camp here and marched with division to Richardsville, via Ely's Ford, encamping at 2 P.M. that day.

I have the honor to be, very respectfully, your obedient servant,
THEO. H. WEED, Major, Commanding
Tenth Regiment New York Cavalry.
Lieut. John B. MAITLAND,
Acting Assistant Adjutant-General

The CWSAC gives the following description of the Mine Run Campaign [16]:

Payne's Farm [approximately 20 miles west of Fredericksburg] and New Hope Church were the first and heaviest clashes of the Mine Run Campaign. In late November 1863, Meade attempted to steal a march through the Wilderness and strike the right flank of the Confederate army south of the Rapidan River. Maj. Gen. Jubal A. Early in command of Ewell's Corps marched east on the Orange Turnpike to meet the advance of William French's III Corps near Payne's Farm. Carr's division (US) attacked twice.

Johnson's division (CS) counterattacked but was scattered by heavy fire and broken terrain. After dark, Lee withdrew to prepared field fortifications along Mine Run [#22 on Map 5.2]. The next day the Union army closed on the Confederate position. Skirmishing was heavy, but a major attack did not materialize. Meade concluded that the Confederate line was too strong to attack and retired during the night of December 1-2, ending the winter campaign.

Preston continues his narration of the 10th New York history which followed the Mine Run Campaign [17]:

> Then came a resumption of picket duty along the Rapidan until the 7th [December 1863], when the Regiment rejoined the brigade near Stevensburg [#27 on Map 5.2]; and back to the Rappahannock, crossing at Kelly's Ford on the 12th, and thence to Bealton. On the 15th it marched through Warrenton Junction and relieved the Sixth Ohio, guarding the railroad, and at 3 P.M. Company H, the advance of the Regiment, settled down at Turkey Run, near Warrenton.

The Tenth New York made one last expedition for the year, from Bealton to Luray (Bealton is #5 and Luray is #28 on Map 5.3). This expedition took place from December 21 to December 23. With the activities of 1863 finally at an end, the 10th New York settled in at Turkey Run (#29 on Map 5.1) for the winter.

Justus and Mary exchanged letters during December, given in the pages following Map 5.3. Justus has returned to his regiment from Camp Stoneman in Washington, DC.

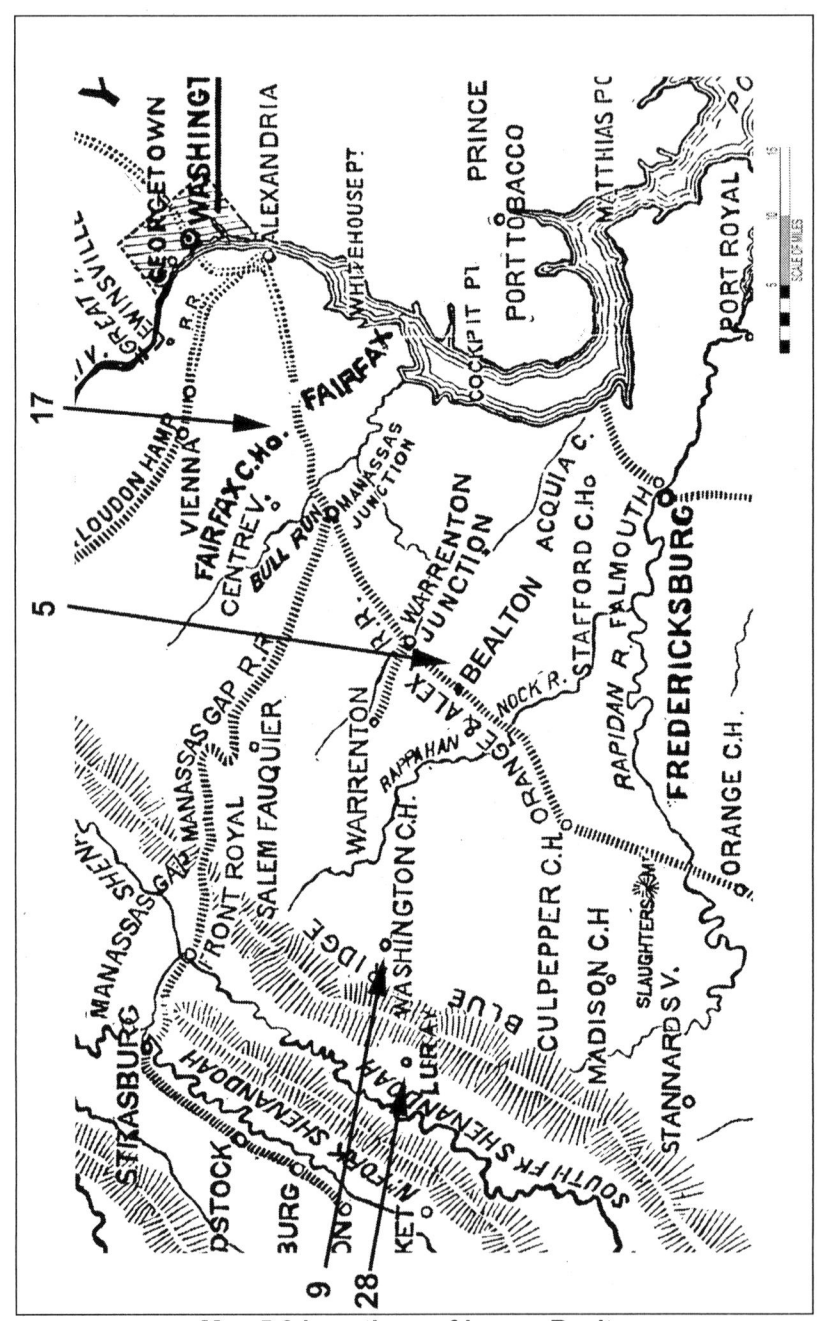

**Map 5.3 Locations of Luray, Bealton,
Fairfax Court House, and Washington, VA**

Friend Jut,

your welcomed letter came in town Dec. 17. right glad was I to hear from you again. I do not think that we have very good postmasters. if we had It would not take the letters so long to come, for your letter was maled Dec. 1 from McGrawville. I think that 16 days is a long time for a letter to come from McG. to Homer and I am in the ofice most every day. But I was agoing to tell you how glad I was to hear from you. I had looked for a letter and looked in vain for none came from you. I thought that I was entirely forgotten or that you were sick. yes I imagined that you was lying in some hovel with no one to care for you like thousands of our young men, but I am happy to learn that you are well. I think that you must have had a nice little walk of fifty miles.

Jut I hope that you will not change your mind about coming home. do try to get a furlough. I am sure you will suceed if you try. I know one that will be glad to see you and I am shure that you know others but if you do come and do not call to see me I shall never forgive you _no never_. Jut I forgot to tell you that I am almost sick. I have one of the hardest colds that I ever had. I have had to stay from church all day. you spoke about sleigh rides. they are _minus_ so far. we have not had any snow to speak of. yesterday I saw a few sleighs in the street for the first time. I dare say that in Solon they have plenty of snow. how I wish that I was there to day. I went home two weeks ago sattirdy. staid untill monday morning which is not half long enough.

they are having a protracted meeting in Solon. they are all getting good. I went one evening. it did not have much effect on me. they were to noisy for me to feel serious.

I enjoy myself here in Homer as well as usual. they are making quite a parade for christmas and New Years. I suppose that I shall remain here untill spring perhaps, longer I cannot tell.

They are talking about another draft to come off the fifth of March. oh but how I dread it. it is hard to have friends enlist but to have them drafted it is harder. I do hope that this cruel war will soon be over and then this waiting will also be over.

I *must close hoping that this will find you well and I must ask you to excuse this poor writing and hoping to hear from you again will close.*

Matie L. Hatch
Homer

Jut- I think it is hard for me to stay away from home so long. I have been here 6 1/2 months and have not been home only three times. do you not think I am old enough to get weaned from home by this time. I am a shamed when I think how long it has been since you have seen your friends.

Dec 25th, 1863

Friend Mary,

Wright glad am I to hear from you again. I recieved your letter last night. I am sory to hear that you have a bad cold, for I know what it is to have one myself. I am well at present and enjoying myself prety well for a soldier.

Mary I presume that you will see some of the old boys at home before long. for a most all of them have reinlisted for three years more, and they are a coming home on a thirty five days furlough. Our Battalion have not been in the service long enough to inlist over.

Mary I am afraid that you will not see me home this winter. for before I got back here to the Co most of the boys had put in for a furlough so that my chance will be slim indeed.

Mary I should think myself well off if I could be home once in two months as you are. but then I think that I am pretty well weaned. if not I shall be by the time that Uncle Sam gives me my time.

It is pretty cold weather here now. it has snowed a little here. the ground is frozen as hard as it was any time last winter. One of the other boys got a letter last night. I saw the directions on it. I think that I can guess who wrote them.

Mary, I wish you a merry christmas and a happy newyear and I wish that I could be there to enjoy them with you as I know we should.

Mary it is getting late so I must hurry so I can get my supper before it is dark.

Ha ha, how you would laugh to see the boys go to work and cook their victuals. for my supper I am going to have some fried meat, fried potatoes, hard-tack and coffee.

The bugles are blowing for roll call. So no more at present. write soon and oblige your faithful friend

J. G. Matteson

P. S. Direct to the Reg't or as you use to. (ie)

Co. L. 10th N. Y. Vol. Cav.

Wahington, D. C.

References

[1] Preston, Noble D., *History of the Tenth New York Volunteer Cavalry*, New York, NY: D. Appleton and Company, 1892; reprinted by Higginson Book Company, Salem, MA in 1998; selected excerpts from pp. 140-141.

[2] Ibid, 141-142.

[3] McClellan, Henry B., *The Campaigns of Stuart's Cavalry* (reprint, Blue & Grey Press, Secaucus, New Jersey, 1993), p. 385.

[4] Preston, *History of the Tenth New York,* pp. 142-144.

[5] Ibid, 146-148.

[6] Ibid, 149-151.

[7] McClellan, *The Campaigns of Stuart's Cavalry,* pp. 387-392.

[8] National Park Service, Civil War Sites Advisory Commission (CWSAC), http://www.cr.nps.gov/hps/abpp/battles/va039.htm, and http://www.cr.nps.gov/hps/abpp/battles/va041.htm. Battles of Auburn, October 13 and 14, 1863.

[9] Vermont in the Civil War web site, Battle at Buckland Mills, October 18, 1863; http://www.vermontcivilwar.org/battles/bucklandmills.php.

[10] National Park Service, Civil War Sites Advisory Commission (CWSAC), http://www.cr.nps.gov/hps/abpp/battles/va042.htm, Battle of Buckland Mills.

[11] The Cultural Landscape Foundation, URL- http://www.tclf.org/landslide/2004/pdf/buckland.pdf

[12] Preston, *History of the Tenth New York,* pp. 151-152.

[13] Ibid, 152-153.

[14] Ibid, 154-155.

[15] McClellan, *The Campaigns of Stuart's Cavalry,* p. 398.

[16] National Park Service, Civil War Sites Advisory Commission (CWSAC), http://www.cr.nps.gov/hps/abpp/battles/va044.htm, Battle of Mine Run.

[17] Preston, History of the Tenth New York, p. 155.

CHAPTER 6
Grant Takes Over, Sheridan's
Raid on Richmond May 1864

"It was good fighting all around on the 11th", N.D. Preston

Early 1864

When the Tenth New York encamped at Turkey Run in mid-December, 1863, near Warrenton, VA, they at first didn't realize that this was going to be their home for the entire winter. Eventually they caught on, though, and made do with some more permanent facilities that they could construct out of the local timber. The major events covered in this chapter are all in Virginia, and are listed in Table 6.1.

Preston writes about camp life, which was boring at times [1]:

> An occasional relief from the *ennui* of camp-life was afforded by an attack on the pickets, or the stampeding of some horses by the enterprising partisans who peopled the surrounding country. Some times the men were unceremoniously hustled into line, fresh from sweet slumbers or an all-absorbing game of cards. …

The flags of the Tenth New York suffered much from wear and tear, as did the flags of most other units. The original flags were given to the Tenth while they were still in training in Gettysburg, as discussed by Preston:

> The Tenth possessed two flags, both of which were received while the Regiment was stationed in Gettysburg, in February, 1862. One was the regular cavalry standard issued by the Government; the other, much the same in size and general appearance, was presented by Miss Elizabeth Porter, of Niagara Falls. One of these flags, reduced to shreds, was forwarded in December to Colonel Lockwood L. Doty, Chief of the Bureau of Military Statistics at Albany, N.Y., for deposit in the military archives of the State. The receipt of the

flag was duly acknowledged by Colonel Doty, but in his official reports no mention was made of it in the list of regimental flags in the archives. The other standard, also worn to tatters, was so far dissipated at this time that but a single star of the former constellation was left. This flag remained in possession of Colonel Irvine. Adjutant Kennedy plucked the single remaining star, still left clinging tenaciously to the field of blue, and sent it to a lady in New York State, accompanied with some appropriate verses by the poet-surgeon of the Regiment, Dr. Clarke. The poem was published in various newspapers in the State, while the star of gold was carefully preserved in a beautiful case especially made for it.

Figure 6.1 shows two soldiers holding flags which also were carried in the War. They are typical of what happened to them as they were carried in battle after battle. Little remained of the flags which could be sent to museums after the War. The New York State Division of Military and Naval Affairs: Military History Department has an ongoing program to salvage and restore military flags dating from the War of 1812 to the present. They are responsible for the care and interpretation of the New York State Battle Flag Collection, a group of over 1,800 military flags.

A descendant of Capt. Kennedy's sent this author the photo in Figure 6.2 showing the last remaining star mentioned above, which is in his possession. The "beautiful case" mentioned by Preston appears to have been lost years ago. Unfortunately, the New York State Military History Department now has no record or evidence of the flag sent to them, as mentioned in Preston's book. Perhaps it was so damaged that they didn't think it was worth keeping.

Map #	Events	Dates
	Wilderness Campaign	**May 4-8, 1864**
1	Chancellorsville	May 4
2	Todd's Tavern	May 5-6
3	Wilderness	May 6-7
2	Todd's Tavern	May 7-8
	Gen. Sheridan's Raid to the James River	**May 9-24**
4	Jarrold's Mills	May 9
5	North Anna River- Anderson's Bridge	May 9
6	South Anna River- Ground Squirrel bridge	May 11
7	Yellow Tavern	May 11
8	Glen Allen Station	May 11
9	Fortifications of Richmond	May 12
10	Bottom Bridge	May 13
11	Haxall's Landing	May 14
12	Jones Bridge	May 18
13	Baltimore Cross-Roads	May 18
14	Hanover Court House	May 19
15	Cold Harbor	May 20
16	Gaines Mills; Meadow Bridge	May 20
17	White House Landing	May 22
18	King William Court House	May 23
19	Aylettsville	May 23
20	White Chimneys	May 24
21	Chesterfield Station	May 25
22	Morrisville	

Table 6.1 Major events in May, 1864

Figure 6.1 Regimental flags which have been through the war (New York State Division of Military and Naval Affairs photo)

Mary, Justus' future wife, writes to him in January, bringing him up to date on things at home. Justus replies and discusses the guerilla problems around Warrenton. They exchange two more letters in February and March.

**Figure 6.2 The last remnant of the
flag of the Tenth New York**

Union Forever (embossed)
January 17th, 1864

Friend Jut-

I sit down to write the first letter in this new year and remember that the first one is to you. I received your letter in due time. I need not tell you that it was welcome for I think that you know it before now. we have beautiful weather now. the New Year come in pretty cold but for a few days it has been quite mild. we have good sleighing. I have enjoyed a few rides and hope that I shall more. I have not been home since I wrote you last. had a letter from Jerome last week. he writes that Mrs. B. Graves is very sick. they do not think that she will ever get well. Ed. Fish'es children have got the Diphtheria. poor Lucy. she will be more lonely if they are taken away from her. she takes his death very hard.

They have talked of having another draft in this place but I think that they will get enough volenteers. they are enlisting every day. some that are only boys are going but it is right that they should go. I would not discourage one from going even if he were a very near friend. I have done it but would not again. The report is that James Atwood is dead.

Jut- I have been to church twice to day. have not I done very well and of corce must go this eve. we have a donation this week. how I wish that you was here to enjoy it. I joined the sons of Temperance last week. think that I shall like it first-rate.

I stood for photography last week but they were not good. if they were I would send one. that puts me in mind that I wish that you would send me one of yours if you have had any taken lately. I should like to see how you look when you are dressed in soldier clothes and have to do your work. it would be fun to come in and take tea with you. I think that I should enjoy it very much.

I do not know about your knowing my hand writing every time that it comes in camp. I shall disguise it the next time. Jut tea is ready so I must close. wishing you health and happiness and a speedy return home. I must bid you once more

Good Bye, Mary
write often.

(Recd this Jan 21, 1864 J. G. Matteson)

Camp near Warrington
Jan 22nd '64

Dear Friend,

I recieved your letter last night and was happy to hear from you once more. I have been a thinking for a day or two of writing to some one but I hardley knew who to. but your letter soon desided it in my opinion for I know of no one that it gives me so much pleasure to write to as you.

This is a lovely day for the time of the year. I am well at present. hope this may find you the same.

Mary, how I wish that I wer there to go riding with you. how I would enjoy it. Hope you will have a good time at the donation. wish I were there. Most of our reg't has reinlisted and gone home except our Battallion. I presume that you will see some of the boys.

I had a letter from Adelia a few days a go. she had just begun to go to school there.

Mary I will send you my picture as soon as I can get one. havent had any taken lately.

We are haveing easy times this winter. not much to do onely to look out for the guerrillaes. there is lots of them about here. there wer a lot of them drawn into ambush the other night. seventeen of them wer killed and two taken prisoners besides some that got a way safe. they goble up our men every chance they can get.

You will please excuse this for it is written in haste, and I will try and do better at another time.

Write as soon as convenient and remember me
a friend that ever thinks of thee

Justus

P.S. Mary, in my hurry I see that I have skipped a page.
HOPE that we may meet again.

February 13th 1864
Homer, Cortland Co. N.Y.

Remembered friend

Your letter of the 22 came in due time and none more welcomed. for what is there in this unfriendly wourld that is so welcomed as a letter from an absent one, from one that is away from friends and home. would not this be a dreary wourld if we did not know the use of pen paper and ink. It would deprive us of half of the enjoyment that we now enjoy.

Well Jut how do you do this eve? are you well? how do you spend your evenings? do you have reading enough? do you have preaching sundays and prair meetings in the tents? will you answer these in your next and a thousand more such questions that I will not ask but wish you to answer in your next. I went down to Marathon two weeks ago to see my sister Mrs. Tompkin. had a very nice time. went to a dance. they have one every friday night. it is the first one that I have been to in a long time. I do not think as much of them as I did a few years ago. last satterday went up to Mr. Benjamins. they are not agoing to stay there onely untill spring. Mr. Gates takes his place. I have not been home since I wrote to you. We have not had much sleighing in Homer. the road is bare now but I dare say that in Solon the snow is piled up over the fences. If I could go there and find the same company there that was there a few years ago I think that I could enjoy myself, but where are they scattered? all over the earth, one is in the silent grave. I cannot make it seem that Clarisa is gone to return no more and that Lorenzo is a widower. but it must be so. yourself and Isac Mel and many more of our company is way down south and Aaron had better be there for I hear that he and his wife do not live very happy together. it is to bad for Aaron was a good boy and deserved a better wife than Fan makes him. I guess that he would willingly take your place. I think that I should prefur it instead of her.

Well Jut I see that this paper is nearly full. I am enjoying myself very well this winter. there is some fun in town every day. I have joined the sons of temperence. they meet every wednesday evening. it is a very good meeting. besides we have lots of fun.

Jut I must close hoping to hear from you again as soon as convenient.

I remain your best friend,
Mary H

206

Camp near Warrington Va

Mar 5th '64

Remembered One

As I was a looking over my diary to day I found that I had not asnwered your last letter. I now therefore take the oportunity to do so. I hope you will excuse me for I supposed that I had answered it before.

Well Mary I am enjoying myself first rate. my health never was better than it has been this winter so far.

I have jest passed through another hard battle this evening. I came out all right only a slight scratch on the wrist. now do not be scart for it was only a sham fight if you may call it such. Only a lot of us got to throwing tin cans, chips, grease at each other. I was taken prisoner in the hotest of the fight but soon escaped.

Well we are a having it rather hard since the Regt went away. we have to be on picket one third of the time so we lose one nights sleep out of three. but I hope that it wont be so long for me. expect the Regt here now every day. they are now at Washington I understand.

We have cheering news from all sources and we are in hopes that this thing may close before long, not more so I suppose than you are.

Now then Mary I will try and answer some of those thousand questions.

First, I was well that evening that you wrote to me.

Second, as for reading, I read the papers and what books I can get a hold of. [I would] read a great deal more if I had it as I have time.

Third, preaching or prair meetings is a stranger here. our chaplain has not been with the Reg't since last winter. I am sorry to say that the sabboth is not respected here no more than a week day. generaly we have more to do that day, inspections come off then of our arms, quarters, horses etc.

You spoke of the company[1] that we use to meet in Solon. never shall we behold them as in these times, yet I hope to find some of them there, in case I get out of this war with my life spared.

I feel sorry for Aaron if it is as you say about him and Fanny.

Well Mary it is getting late and as I do not think of any more to write at present- only beg of you to write soon.

Remember me, my friend,
When far a way
I'll think of thee, my fairest,

Both night and day.
May slumbers soft and light
Be with thee, friend,- good Night.

I remain as ever yours truly,
Justus G. Matteson

PS. Mar 6th
Our Reg't has just arived. they are a feeling first rate.
JGM

1. "company" refers to the circle of friends with which they were associated.

Grant Reorganizes the Army of the Potomac

Preston continues with his discussion of the events of the period [2]:

> General Grant, who had been made lieutenant-general, assumed command of the armies of the United States on the 12th of March [1864] and on the 19th left Nashville for the Army of the Potomac, where headquarters were announced to be. On the 24th orders were issued from the adjutant-general's office consolidating the Infantry Corps of the Army of the Potomac into three, to be known as the Second, Fifth, and Sixth, and numerous changes in commanders of corps, divisions, and brigades were announced. General Pleasonton was relieved from the command of the Cavalry Corps, and was succeeded by Major-General P.H. Sheridan, who had commanded a division of infantry in the West. General Kilpatrick was transferred to General Sherman's army, Brigadier-General A.T.A. Torbert was assigned to the command of the First Division [of Cavalry], Brigadier-General D.McM. Gregg remained in command of the Second, and Brigadier-General J.H. Wilson took command of the Third. The following became the new composition of the Cavalry Corps [3]:

CAVALRY CORPS
Major-General PHILIP H. SHERIDAN
Escort- Sixth United States, Captain Ira W. Claflin
FIRST DIVISION Brigadier-General ALFRED T.A. TORBERT

First Brigade	*Second Brigade*
Brigadier-General GEORGE A. CUSTER	Colonel THOMAS C. DEVIN
First Michigan, Lt. Col. Peter Stagg	Fourth New York,* Lt. Col. William R. Parnell
Fifth Michigan, Col. Russell A. Alger	Sixth New York, Lt. Col. William H. Crocker
Sixth Michigan, Maj. James H. Kidd	Ninth New York, Col. William Sackett
Seventh Michigan, Maj. Henry W. Granger	Seventeenth Pennsylvania, Lt. Col. James Q. Anderson

Reserve Brigade
Brigadier-General WESLEY MERRITT
Nineteenth New York (First Dragoons), Col. Alfred Gibbs
Sixth Pennsylvania, Maj. James Starr
First United States, Capt. Nelson B. Sweitzer
Second United States, Capt. Theophilus F. Rodenbough
Fifth United States,** Capt. Abraham K. Arnold

*The Fourth New York was detached guarding trains.

** Companies B, F, and K of the Fifth US, under Captain Julius W. Mason, were detached as escort to Lieutenant-General U.S. Grant.

SECOND DIVISION Brig. Gen. DAVID McMURTRIE GREGG*

First Brigade	Second Brigade
Brigadier-General HENRY E. DAVIES, Jr.	Colonel J. IRVIN GREGG.
First Massachusetts, Maj. Lucius M. Sargent	First Maine, Col. Charles H. Smith
First New Jersey, Lt. Col. John W. Kester	Tenth New York, Maj. M. Henry Avery **
Sixth Ohio, Col. William Stedman	Second Pennsylvania, Lt. Col. Joseph P. Brinton
First Pennsylvania, Col. John P. Taylor	Fourth Pennsylvania, Lt. Col. George H. Covode
	Eighth Pennsylvania, Lt. Col. Samuel Wilson
	Sixteenth Pennsylvania, Lt. Col. John K. Robison

* Gregg was promoted to Major General in August, 1864.

** The Tenth New York would be transferred to the First Brigade on May 17.

THIRD DIVISION Brigadier-General JAMES H. WILSON
Escort Eighth Illinois (detachment), Lieutenant William W. Long

First Brigade	Second Brigade
Colonel TIMOTHY M. BRYAN, Jr.	Colonel GEORGE H. CHAPMAN
Colonel JOHN B. MCINTOSH *	
First Connecticut, Maj. Erastus Blakeslee	Third Indiana, Maj. William Patton
Second New York, Col. Otto Harhaus	Eighth New York, Lt. Col. William H. Benjamin
Fifth New York, Lt. Col. John Hammond	First Vermont, Lt. Col. Addison W. Preston
Eighteenth Pennsylvania, Lt. Col. William P. Brinton	

The following batteries, constituting the First Brigade of the artillery of the army, were assigned to the Cavalry Corps, all under the command of Captain James M. Robertson:

New York Light, Sixth Battery, Capt. Joseph W. Martin
Second United States, Batteries B and L, Lt. Edward Heaton
Second United States, Battery D, Lt. Edward B. Williston
Second United States, Battery M, Lt. Alexander C. M. Pennington
Fourth United States, Battery A, Lt. Rufus King, Jr.
Fourth United States, Batteries C and E, Lt. Charles L. Fitzhugh

Justus received letters from his sister Adelia and Mary, and replies to Mary with letters from himself. A page from his sister's letter is also shown in her own handwriting. Note that in Justus's letter of April 21, 1864 he mentions being in Morrisville for the previous two weeks or so. Three hundred of the regiment were sent down there (#22 on Map 5.1) to scout for guerillas.

*Assigned May 5.

212

At Home, McGrawville March the 28th

Dear Brother

As this is the first opportunity I have had to write you in a long while. We are well as usual. I came home yesterday and must say that I am glad to get back to old Solon again. I did not like villedge life very well. for a hired girl can enjoy a very great abundance of the current events that is going on. I got a letter from you for Father as I came home, and sorry to hear that you had a hard cold. am in hopes you are better ere this. also was sorry that you were to break camp as soon and go perhaps to battle or I know not where. but am in hopes this will find you well and still enjoying the few pleasures and many tasks that you encounter.

Johney Stevens, Jake Stevens son that went into the Army last summer died in one of the rebel hospitals a short time ago. he was in the Army only about two weeks before he was taken prisoner. Oh a thousand times rather to battle than to fall a prisoner to the Rebs.

It had been a long time since I had heard from you. but I was not alarmed of it as we could not get the mail on account of the flood. I have not received the letter that you sent me the same time that you wrote Father. I presume that it is at Cortland. I received a letter from Andrew Reynolds two or three weeks ago. he stated that you were writing to our folks, and that you had just received your box. So you see I hear from you sometimes when you dont write me. I havent answered his letter yet, but yours before others always.

The money that you sent home came all right, and I presume was very acceptable. I was going to write you last evening but was sick and could not.

Lara's wife was up here twice to see me to day. she said that if I had'nt come home she would come after me for I had no buisiness out there at all. there was nobody in the neighborhood when I was gone.

Oh you stated in your letter that you did not wish the package of letters[1] that you sent home to be opened. but as the package came before the letter, how should Father know it. so I think he is exicusable in opening it. he opened the package and counted the letters, opened one and saw who they were from and laid them away. and when I came home, I laid the letters away in your trunk and they have not been read and are in safe keeping. But you know our folks are down on the Hatch-line. as for one they always appear verry distant and I dont know much about them.

Lucindia was here once this winter but I was not at home. she came to enter a complaint about Johns wife. John and his wife has had another quarrel or I dont know as I can say another for they quarrel and fight all of the while.

Juliett got mad and went home and John sold 4 of the cows and so she bought one of her Father's and brought home. and John made her drive it back home. That is the way the money goes.

Pa is going to work for All Mathers in Jim Martins sugar bush. he is going to work half of a month for $18.

We are making sugar. we have made 28 lbs and are going to sugar off 10 lbs tomorrow. oh dear our folks has gone to bed and I am yawning but must finish this tonight. we have got three cows that give milk. Ma and I are going to tend to the sugar bush and dairy while Pa works out. we have had an awfle flood. it has done milions of dolars damage to this county. bridges and roads are pretty much gone up. the county house bridge is left but it took off the small stone bridges by it, and there was twenty men at work to save the bridge of Midges Mills one day. one end jacked considerable but it didnt go off. the dam above it gave way and the flood wood came against it. the Port Watson bridge has gone off, and the large railroad bridge up above the villedge, and the track is all washed to pieces. the cars has not been able to get through yet or wont in some time yet. I cannot write anymore now but will write again soon. you must write as soon as you can conveniently.

From your affectionate sister
Adelia Matteson

Father sent a letter a day or two ago and some poetry on Jimmies death- I think they was very good and am in hopes you will get them. 4 men is drafted in this town. Uncle Whiting and Jake Atkins is two of them. I believe they are agoing to pay $1,000 for substitutes. I hope they will both have to go. it will be good for what ails them.

1. Apparently a package of letters was sent home by Justus, that he had received from Mary Hatch.

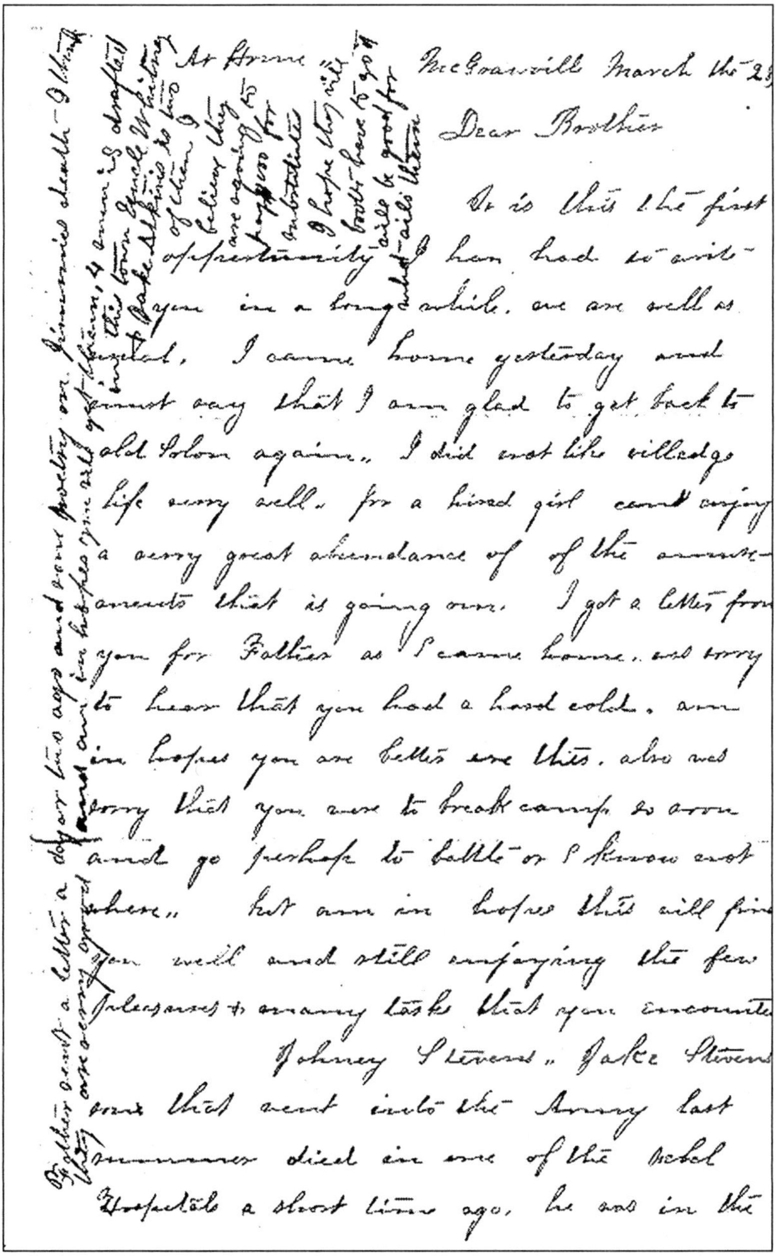

At Home

McGranville March the 2[?]

Dear Brother

It is this the first opportunity I have had to write you in a long while. we are well as usual. I came home yesterday and must say that I am glad to get back to old Solon again.. I did not like villadge life very well. for a hired girl can't enjoy a very great abundance of of the amusements that is going on. I got a letter from you for Father as I came home. was sorry to hear that you had a hard cold. am in hopes you are better ere this. also was sorry that you were to break camp so soon and go perhaps to battle or I know not where,, but am in hopes this will find you well and still enjoying the few pleasures & many tasks that you encounter.

Johney Stevens.. Jake Stevens one that went into the Army last summer died in one of the rebel Hospitals a short time ago, he was in the

Figure 6.3 A page of the letter from Adelia to Justus

March 27th 1864
Homer Cortland Co. N.Y.

Friend Jut

Your kind note came in due time and I was very glad to hear from you and to know that you were well. I am sorry that you have been in such a hard battle. I could not help laughing as I perused it- I should think that you would have fight enough without sham fights. I wish that they could all be such and no need of harder battles. I have been quite well since I wrote last allthough it has been very sickly in Homer. I have not been home this winter. think that I shall go in a few weeks to stay a number of days. now is the time to go to get warm shugar. I have not had any warm yet. shugar is 0.25 a pound. I do not think that there will be much made this spring. We are having nice going. the mud is as deep as you find it down South. I have got a new boarding place and a good one. the first house above the depot, so if you come home (Oh! how I wish that you would) you will know where to find me. I see some home from the 76th but no one that I know. last week there was a soldier thrown from a wagon in Marathon and instantly killed. there was no paper or any thing about his person to identify him by. he is supposed to be a deserter. he had citizens clothes over his. he was burried in Marathon.

I was up to Mr. Benjamins one eve last week. they moove to McGrawvile this week. Mr. Gates takes his place but I do not believe that he can ever fill it. Jut when you come home you will not have to go to Cortland to school for they are agoing to commence the school there next summer. the people of McGrawville have bought the buildings. they are to be repaired before the school commences. I shall wish to go back there to live after the school commences.

I have been to church this afternoon. we have got one of the best Baptist ministers in the world. to know him is to love him. if there were more such men I should wish that you could have just such an one in your regiment, but we could not spare him here. you will see that that is a selfish thought.

I am sorry that you do not have preaching. It is to bad. the saboth would be a long day to me if I could not go to church.

Jut it is eve. I must close hoping that the time is not far distant when this writing will close and you will come home with all of the other friends. will it not be a happy meeting. this war cannot allways continue. it must close and friends will meet again.

Jut excuse this poor writing for I have a very poor pen. Write soon, I remain your best friend,

Mary

Friend Mary,

your kind letter arrived in camp a few days ago. I should of written before but I was out of stamps. I was glad to learn that you were well. I am allso enjoying good health at present.

Romanso Phillipps of Homer one of our company died a few days since. disease scarlett fever. His death is lamented by the whole company.

It has been very bad weather here of late, a great deal of rain and more mud. To day it is quite pleasant. It will soon be time for the army to move again. I understand that all of the organized malitia that is now in the north are to be sent to the field for six months. if so I like it. I think that the ball will open a little diferent his spring from what it did last.

I had a letter from home at the same time that I recieved yourn. Jerry H has sold his farm to Jef Robey. my folks wer well when Father wrote. This is my second letter to day. I wrote one to an old school mate of McLean, one Thomas Darby. Mary how did you mean, that the people of McGrawville had bought the old Colledge or the Acadamy at Cortland?

Mary it is now hoped that we may get out of this this fall. judge Duel of Cortland is a going to try and get us out. if he succeeds I shall be at home next winter. so it will not be but a few months before we may see each other and then I think I could talk with you and enjoy myself much better than I can by writing. It takes to long to express ones thoughts this way. You must excuse my writing more this time for I could send it by this mail. write soon and except this from your friend

J. G. Matteson

Camp at Morrisville, Va.
Apr. 21st '64

Dear Friend,

Mary, once more I will try and write a few lines to you and inform you that I am well as usual.

You will see by the heading that we have changed camp since I wrote last, or a part of the Regt. there is three hundred of the Reg't here. the rest are in the old camp yet. we are scouting the region about here for guerrillaes. we have been here twelve or fifteen days. in that time we have had five wounded and one killed. they sneak up and fire on our pickets night or day. a man is not safe out side of camp. it is vary thickly covered about here with pines and in these they lay in ambush for our men. they fire then run into the woods and you mint as well look for a needle in a hay-mow. but enough of this.

This is a vary drole day. for a short time it will rain & snow. then the sun will shine out warm and pleasant. I think it has changed so six or eight times to day. The peach & chery trees are in full bloom. citisans are puting in their crops.

Mary, the report is here that sending letters from the army of the potomac is to be stopped. now isent that provokeing. it is to me at any rate. I dont know what I should do if I cannot spend a part of my time by writing to my friends. if there is any thing that can make me down hearted it is this. I have- Ho: there is watter call. I have not learned yet whether mail will be allowed to come here or not but I presume it will.

Mary inclosed with in this you will find an ambrotype. if you can make out who the original of it is you will do well. If you see fit to keep it do so. if not throw it a way and I will try and send you a better one. that is if I can get it.

It is getting late. therefore I will close hopeing to hear from you as often as you find it convenient to write.

Except this from your Friend
J. G. Matteson

Co. L. 10th N.Y. Cav.
Washington DC.

Friend Jut.

I received your kind note in due tme and was very glad to hear from you again. I had rather receive letters than to write them, if I did not know that my correspondances would be few if the letters were not answered. We are having beautifull weather for this time of the year. the ground is quite green . the time to make shugar is past and I have not had any warm. I think it is to bad. I have not had been home yet but I keep thinking that there will be a time when I can go for a few days. I went to the new church this afternoon. it is a very nice church. after church went up to the new Cemetry. It will be a splendid place when finished. this eve went to M. E. church. Mr. Burr preached. you must know him. he preached to McGrawville a few years ago. he and his wife have parted. Well Jut it has been 4 long long months since I have seen home. I shall have to go before long or I shall be homesick. I enjoy myself very well here. have lots of fun. had a very good boarding place but I want to see Solon once in a while. I understand that J Greenman and Ed have moved to Buffalo. you know that Brown is there. we shall miss them. they were such good company.

The funeral sermon for Mr. R. Phillipps was preached two weeks ago to day by Mr. Brigham, the baptist minister. he was spoken very highly of as a young man. they know nothing of him as a soldier, but we know that a good man makes a good soldier. I did not see any of the 76th boys from Solon or Freetown. I suppose that they have all returned before this. You wished to know about the school. it is the old Colledge that they have bought. they are to have a school this summer.

Jut you talk about coming home. may that plan prove sucessfull. I hope that it may but I am afraid that that is more than Duel can do. but we will look at the bright side and think that you may come.

I must close hoping to hear from you again. I will bid thee Good night.

Mary

Sheridan Energizes the Cavalry

Preston describes the events shaping up after the assumption of command of the Cavalry Corps by General Sheridan [4]:

> Scouting parties were sent in every direction for guerrillas. The feeling against the citizens of the surrounding country was very bitter. It was generally believed that they were privy to the frequent murders of Union soldiers, if they were not the actual perpetrators of the crimes. None of the scouting parties succeeded in finding any of the supposed guerrillas.
>
> Monday, April 18th [1864], was the day set apart for a review of Gregg's division by the new corps commander, General Sheridan. [Justus must have missed this review, since he wrote on April 21 that he had been in Morrisville for a couple of weeks.] The stirring bugle-blasts brought the men into line, and the march was taken up to the broad fields to the west of Warrenton, where the Second Division was fast assembling. After all preparations had been perfected, the troops were marched past the little General who was to lead them in the campaign now near at hand. All eyes were turned on the Major-General commanding, who was evidently well pleased with the troopers of the Second Cavalry Division. After passing the reviewing stand, instead of marching back to the camps at Turkey Run, the First Maine, Sixteenth Pennsylvania, and the Tenth, were marched rapidly to Sulphur Springs, where it was reported a considerable force of rebel cavalry were assembled. No enemy was found there, and the regiments all returned to their camps, tired and hungry, about 8 P.M.
>
> Three prisoners were brought in by a scouting party from the Regiment on the 22d.
>
> Major Weed, commanding a detachment of one hundred and fifty men at Morrisville [#22 on Map 6.1], received instructions from General Sheridan on the 23d to proceed with his command to Grove Church to strengthen the force there, as it was thought a concentration of rebel cavalry was going on at Fredericksburg for the purpose of capturing the force of two

hundred Union troops at Grove Church [near Morrisville]. Major Weed reported with his detachment to Colonel Harhaus, Second New York Cavalry, in command at Grove Church, the next day.

Captain Snyder with fifty men made a reconnaissance to United States Ford on the morning of the 25th, and returned in the evening with four prisoners.

The detachment under Major Weed, numbering three hundred and four men, was relieved by the Second Pennsylvania Cavalry on the 26th and returned to Morrisville, and thence to camp at Turkey Run the following day.

Friday, April 29th, the Second Division broke camp at Turkey Run and marched out, never to return. At 4 P.M. the Tenth crossed the Rappahannock at Kelly's Ford, and a little later encamped at Paoli Mills, near Brandy Station. An inspection of the Regiment, numbering five hundred and twenty-four men, took place on the last day of April. The division was encamped in the midst of the army, the white tents covering the territory as far as the eye could reach to the south.
…

"Boots and Saddles" resounded through the camps on the morning of the 3d [May 1864], and at 9 A.M. the march was taken up and Richardsville reached a little after noon. It was a chilly night, but no fires were permitted; the men were compelled to shiver, with only hard-tack to appease their hunger. A copy of General Meade's address to the army was placed in Major Avery's hands just as his folding bed had been prepared for service. The address set at rest all doubts as to why the boys were shivering near the Rapidan that night - the Union army had its baggage checked for Richmond.

Leaving Richardsville at 2 A.M., the Second Brigade moved in the following order: Second Pennsylvania, Tenth New York, Battery, First Maine, Fourth, Sixteenth and Eighth Pennsylvania. The First Brigade had the advance. The Second Brigade crossed at Ely's Ford [on the Rapidan River] at 7 A.M. and moved out on the road to Chancellorsville [#1 on

Map 6.1], where it arrived at 8 A.M. A further march of three or four miles brought the command to Aldrich's Cross-roads. Here the advance had some skirmishing and preparations were made for action, but beyond a few picket shots nothing of a warlike nature occurred, and the Regiment remained all night in readiness for action.

The Battle of Todd's Tavern

"To horse!" at 4 A.M. of the 5th [May 1864], was caused by a few picket shots. At early dawn the cannonading commenced on the infantry line. About noon General Sheridan passed along the front of the Regiment on his way to army headquarters, and a little later the Third Cavalry Division, under General Wilson, became heavily engaged on the Catharpin road, beyond Todd's Tavern [#2 on Map 6.1]. General Gregg hastened with the Second Division to Wilson's relief at 1 P.M. Although the day was warm, the horses were urged to the gallop, and as the command neared the scene of conflict it became evident that General Wilson's command was having a hard struggle. A regiment was immediately sent down the road through the woods beyond Todd's Tavern on a mounted charge; while others, including the Tenth, were hastily dismounted and sent into the woods on either side of the road.

The arrival of Gregg's division was most opportune, as Wilson's men were hemmed in on every side, and fighting desperately to extricate themselves from their unpleasant position. The road was opened by General Gregg's prompt action and General Wilson's division relieved. Later the Tenth was withdrawn from the line, mounted, and sent back a short distance to guard the approaches to the rear of the division from the left. While moving up a road through the woods, a voice in the immediate front suddenly called out: "Look out there, Yanks; you'll get hit!" followed by the sharp crack of several carbines. It was unnecessary to repeat the admonition. The Regiment was hastily dismounted, the horses sent back, and skirmishing commenced. So near were the two lines that the men bantered each other between shots for some time. Finally, some of General Custer's brigade came upon them from the rear and the enemy beat a hasty retreat. The Regiment remounted and joined the brigade near Todd's Tavern in the afternoon. Picket firing continued during the night along the front.

At night, on this the first day's engagement under the new cavalry commander, he [Sheridan] sent a dispatch to General Meade recounting the attack on Wilson, and says, "General Gregg attacked the enemy and drove them back to Beech Grove, distance about four miles." In this dispatch he evinces that restlessness of spirit which soon made him a terror to his foes. Guarding wagons he evidently considered as much the province of infantry as cavalry, for he says, "Why can not infantry be sent to guard the trains, and let me take the offensive?"

Figure 6.4 Rifle stacks and flag at reenactment in Ontario Center 2006

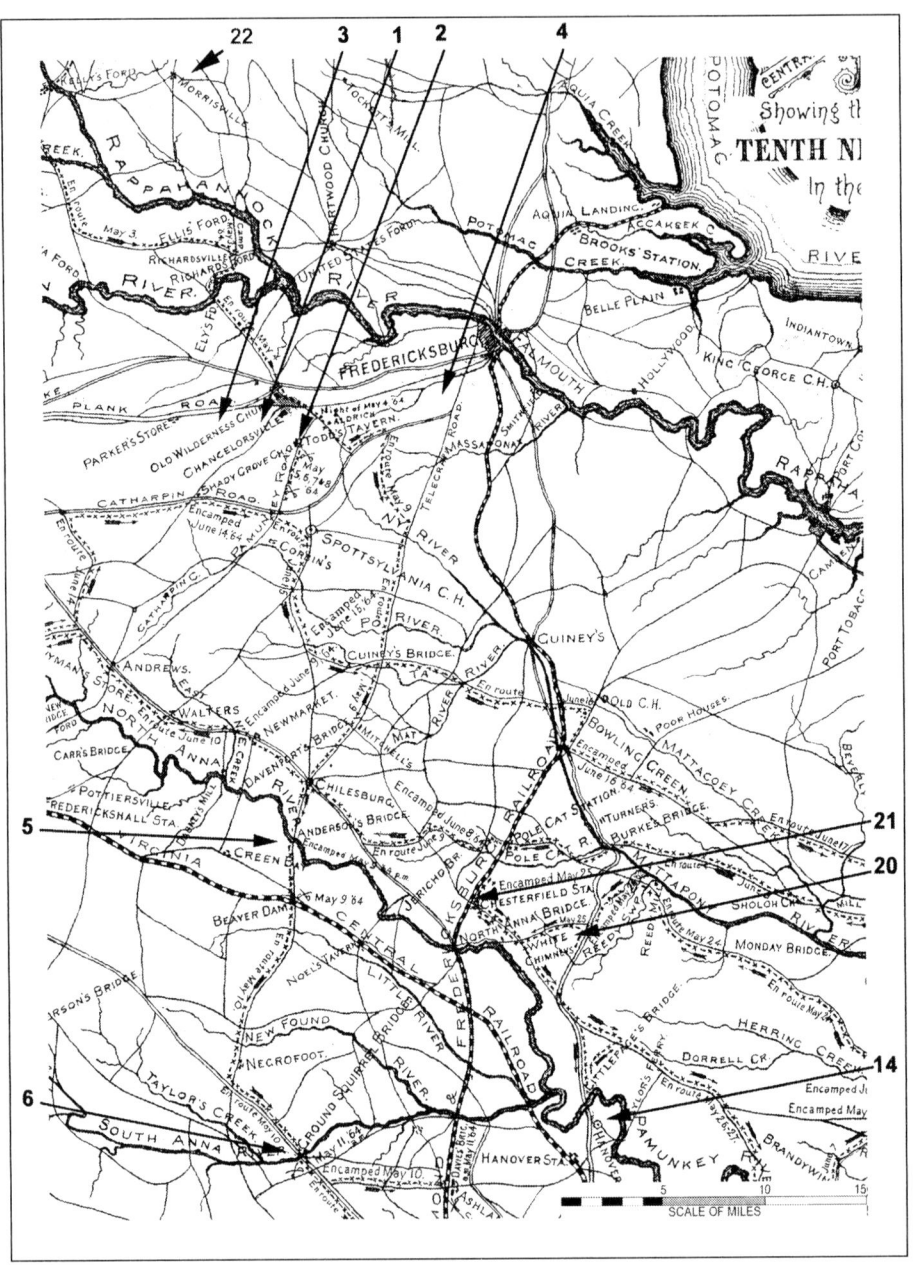

Map 6.1 Location of Events Occurring in May 1864

Battle of the Wilderness

While the Cavalry was having its skirmishes, major warfare was taking place on the Infantry front. The Battle of the Wilderness (#3 on Map 6.1) was in full swing. The CWSAC describes the infantry Battle of the Wilderness as follows [5]:

> The opening battle of Grant's sustained offensive against the Confederate Army of Northern Virginia, known as the Overland Campaign, was fought at the Wilderness, May 5-7. On the morning of May 5, 1864, the Union V Corps attacked Ewell's Corps on the Orange Turnpike, while A.P. Hill's Corps during the afternoon encountered Getty's Division (VI Corps) and Hancock's II Corps on the Plank Road. Fighting was fierce but inconclusive as both sides attempted to maneuver in the dense woods. Darkness halted the fighting, and both sides rushed forward reinforcements. At dawn on May 6, Hancock attacked along the Plank Road, driving Hill's Corps back in confusion. Longstreet's Corps arrived in time to prevent the collapse of the Confederate right flank. At noon, a devastating Confederate flank attack in Hamilton's Thicket sputtered out when Lt. Gen. James Longstreet was wounded by his own men. The IX Corps (Burnside) moved against the Confederate center, but was repulsed. Union generals James S. Wadsworth and Alexander Hays were killed. Confederate generals John M. Jones, Micah Jenkins, and Leroy A. Stafford were killed. The battle was a tactical draw. Grant, however, did not retreat as had the other Union generals before him. On May 7, the Federals advanced by the left flank toward the crossroads of Spotsylvania Courthouse [5 miles north of Todd's Tavern, #2 on Map 6.1].

Returning to Preston's discussion of the actions of the 10th New York during these days [6]:

> At daybreak on the 6th cannonading was resumed on the infantry line to the right. The day opened clear and warm, the woods burning in every direction. The fighting commenced in

Gregg's front at an early hour, and was continued briskly until about 9 A.M. The enemy were driven through the woods to the east of Todd's Tavern. The fighting was kept up during the day, the Second and Eighth Pennsylvania and Tenth New York being most actively engaged. General Humphreys, chief of staff of the Army of the Potomac, says, "Gregg met Fitzhugh Lee's division at Todd's Tavern, repulsing the enemy's attacks handsomely." At about 4 P.M. the Regiment fell back beyond Piney Branch Church and encamped. At the same time the trains, which had been parked near Chancellorsville, were moved back to Ely's Ford. Rations were issued to the Regiment after dark, and the men sought rest for the night in a field of mud.

As soon as the fog had risen on the morning of the 7th, the Tenth advanced a line of skirmishers and encountered the enemy at Todd's Tavern behind barricades, from which they were driven after a brief resistance. Continuing, they [the rebels] yielded the ground of the preceding day's conflict and retired into the second piece of wood east of Todd's Tavern. Here a heavy force was encountered, and the fighting became very severe. Finally, as our line began to waver, Colonel Gregg appeared, urging the men to remain firm, and by his words and example succeeded in holding the line. About 3 P.M. the brigade fell back to Todd's Tavern, and the Tenth dismounted and took position behind light breastworks. The rebels in heavy force charged on the line at five o'clock and were handsomely repulsed.

As they came on with the familiar yell, filling a deep cut where the road entered the opposite woods from Gregg's position, a section of our battery opened on them at short range, and the concentrated fire of the carbines of the brigade added to the discomfiture of the enemy, who halted, and being pressed in the narrow defile by their comrades in the rear, presented more the appearance of a mob than a body of soldiers. Their officers, however, displayed great heroism as they vainly urged the men forward. The charging force retired to the cover of the wood as soon as they could extricate themselves from the gorge in the road, and the opposing lines settled down to the use of the carbine, the firing across the open space being continued late into the night. The Tenth bivouacked on the battle-field with the rest of the brigade.

Then on the 8th [May 1864] the brigade again assumed the offensive, advancing to the opposite wood in the morning and driving the enemy gradually back until a place was reached where the road forked. Here General Gregg, after taking a careful survey of the ground, proceeded with the Tenth New York and the Eighth Pennsylvania up the left-hand or what appeared to be the main road, leaving Colonel Gregg with the balance of the Second Brigade at the junction of the two roads. The Tenth led the way on the road through the wood, which was hedged in by dense underbrush part of the way. As the advance-guard rounded a turn in the road, a little cannon loaded with grape and canister was discharged, point-blank, in their faces, the missiles whistling through the trees like hail, and although the discharge was made within five or six rods of them, strangely enough neither man nor horse was injured. The little gun went whirling up the road and out of sight instantly. On reaching the open, a few rods farther on, a beautiful panorama was spread out before the troops. In front was a valley, and on the opposite slope a few soldiers and some baggage-wagons, looking much like a bait for drawing the Union troops on. A little break in the woods away off on the right disclosed a column of mounted men moving toward our rear. General Gregg directed the skirmishers to be called in, and the command was hastily marched back to the junction of the roads, which was reached just in time to assist in repulsing the rebel force already mentioned. In the severe engagement which ensued, Private Coleman, of Company G, was killed, Lieutenant Gait slightly, and Sergeant Stebbins and Private Main, of the same company, severely wounded, the latter being taken prisoner. Private Drown, of Company E, was also severely wounded.

Lieutenant (afterward Captain) Van Tuyl writes as follows regarding this day's operations:

At Todd's Tavern, on the 8th of May, 1864, Lieutenant Charley Pratt with one battalion was on the left of the road, and I had charge of the one on the right. We advanced through the woods for a mile, driving the rebel skirmishers before us, but finally came to an open space, and a few rods from the woods was a steep descent. As we came out of the woods a whole brigade rose up and gave us a volley. They fired high and but few men were hit. I remember that but two of mine were shot - both tall men. One was a fellow named Coleman, who was six feet six inches in height; the other one's name I do not recall. We returned somewhat faster than we went. Charley Pratt said afterward there were ten rebels reaching for his coat-tail for more than a mile. ...

The brigade fell back, contesting the ground to the position from which the advance was made in the morning, the rebels following and occupying the edge of the timber across the open space. The commands of the Confederate officers could be plainly heard in making dispositions of their troops. The Tenth occupied a position on the left or south side of the road. The boys began a hasty collection of such material as would answer for breastworks, while a band on the rebel line struck up, playing the Bonnie Blue Flag and other Southern airs. When the band ceased playing our boys cheered. Presently one of the bands on the Union line, away to the left, began playing. About eight o'clock an aide came along the line with orders for the officers to move their commands back to Todd's Tavern. A few rods in rear of the position the men had just vacated a heavy line of earthworks had been thrown up by the infantry. Passing through these the Regiment soon reached Todd's Tavern, the men were mounted, and commenced a movement to the rear. The roads were blocked with the ambulance trains bearing the wounded from the front and the woods were on fire, so that the march was attended with some inconveniences, marching sometimes single file through the tangled underbrush by the roadside; but the boys had got used to all these things and took them quite philosophically. Finally, Aldrich's was reached and the command bivouacked late at night.

During the day Quartermaster Graves went to the front from near Ely's Ford with twenty wagons to assist in removing the wounded to Fredericksburg.

General Sheridan's Raid on Richmond

The hope of a short respite as the Regiment settled down at Aldrich's [close to Todd's Tavern] was dispelled by orders issued to the proper officers to draw and issue rations and forage the same night [i.e. get their provisions together for a march the next day].

Monday, May 9th, [1864], came all too soon to the tired troopers of the Cavalry Corps. The rising sun looked like a ball of fire through the smoky atmosphere. The drowsy veterans were aroused from their slumbers by the bugles' blare; staff officers were early astir, galloping hither and yon; the troopers were busily engaged in preparation to respond to the next call of the bugle - "Boots and Saddles!" When the Tenth moved out into the broad, open field, an inspiring sight was presented. Many of the regiments had already arrived and taken position, while others were fast assembling.

Ten thousand horsemen in solid columns were marshaled on the plain, their tattered and torn battle-flags hanging lazily from the staffs in the quiet morning air, telling the silent story of long and hard service by those who marched beneath their folds. Supply trains and ambulances had been reduced to the least possible number for the requirements of the movement about to take place; a rigid inspection had relegated to the rear all men and horses of questionable physical ability. Every regiment of the Cavalry Corps was numbered in the solid mass; every individual was looking anxiously toward the Fredericksburg Road, where a knot of officers and orderlies were assembled. These were General Sheridan with his staff and escort. Speculation as to the destination and purpose of the corps was freely indulged in, but few indeed judged either correctly.

Presently a movement of the troops on the right begins; the great mass of cavalry begins to spin out in column of fours on the road to Fredericksburg, and gradually the grand pageant dissolves into a long line of moving horsemen, enveloped in the tale-bearing dust, by which the enemy later in the day are apprised of the movement.

The First Division, under General Merritt, had the advance, followed by the Third, commanded by General Wilson; the Second, under General Gregg, being last in the order of march.

Marching toward Fredericksburg a few miles, the column changed direction to the south, crossing the river, and moved on the old Telegraph Road across the flank of the rebel army. [The Telegraph Road ran north and south, and could be reached from Todd's Tavern by going about 8 miles east.]

As the sound of the cannonading between the opposing armies grew more and more to the right and rear, the inspiration suddenly seized the men that they were on a raid. Then the Confederate cavalry, guided by the clouds of rising dust, sped to the attack. Wickham's [Confederate] brigade, being nearest, was precipitated upon the moving column, striking the Sixth Ohio Cavalry [2nd Division, 1st Brigade] in flank near Jarrold's Mills [#4 on Map 6.1]. The attack was gallantly made, but was as gallantly met by the Buckeye boys.

Major McClellan says [7]:

> The Sixth Ohio was now reinforced by the First New Jersey, and the rear-guard, thus strengthened, made a determined stand near Mitchell's shop [near Jarrold's Mills]. Wickham attacked promptly, but made no impression.

Reaching Jarrold's Mills, the grain and flour stored in the mill were destroyed. At 9 P.M. the Regiment bivouacked at Hamilton's Crossing [#5 on Map 6.1; called "Anderson's Bridge" on the map], on the North Anna River. Custer's brigade, of the First Division, was sent to Beaver Dam [going

3 miles south of Hamilton's Crossing, to the Virginia Central Railroad] during the afternoon. There they captured two trains of cars with locomotives, and recaptured two hundred and seventy-eight Union soldiers *en route* to Richmond as prisoners of war. A million and a half rations also fell into the hands of General Custer, which were burned, the flames lighting up the country for miles around.

The morning of the 10th the men were rudely awakened by the sharp report of artillery near by and the screeching and bursting of shells in their midst. The enterprising enemy had brought a battery close upon the bivouac during the night, and taking position in the timber on the hills to the rear, opened a brisk fire on the camp at daybreak. The boys mounted and resumed the "on to Richmond" without breakfast or even waiting to perform their toilets. Fording the North Anna at Hamilton's Crossing, the Regiment took its place in the line of march and commenced the second day's tramp through the stifling dust. Skirmishing was kept up on the flanks during the greater part of the day. About three o'clock the Tenth was ordered out upon the right flank to do picket duty until the column had passed, with instructions to join the brigade at Ground Squirrel Bridge [on the South Anna River, #6 on Map 6.2]. ...

After crossing the South Anna at Ground Squirrel Bridge the men cooked supper, groomed their horses, and enjoyed a good night's rest. The reliable First Maine was picketing along the river, and a feeling of perfect security pervaded the command. ...

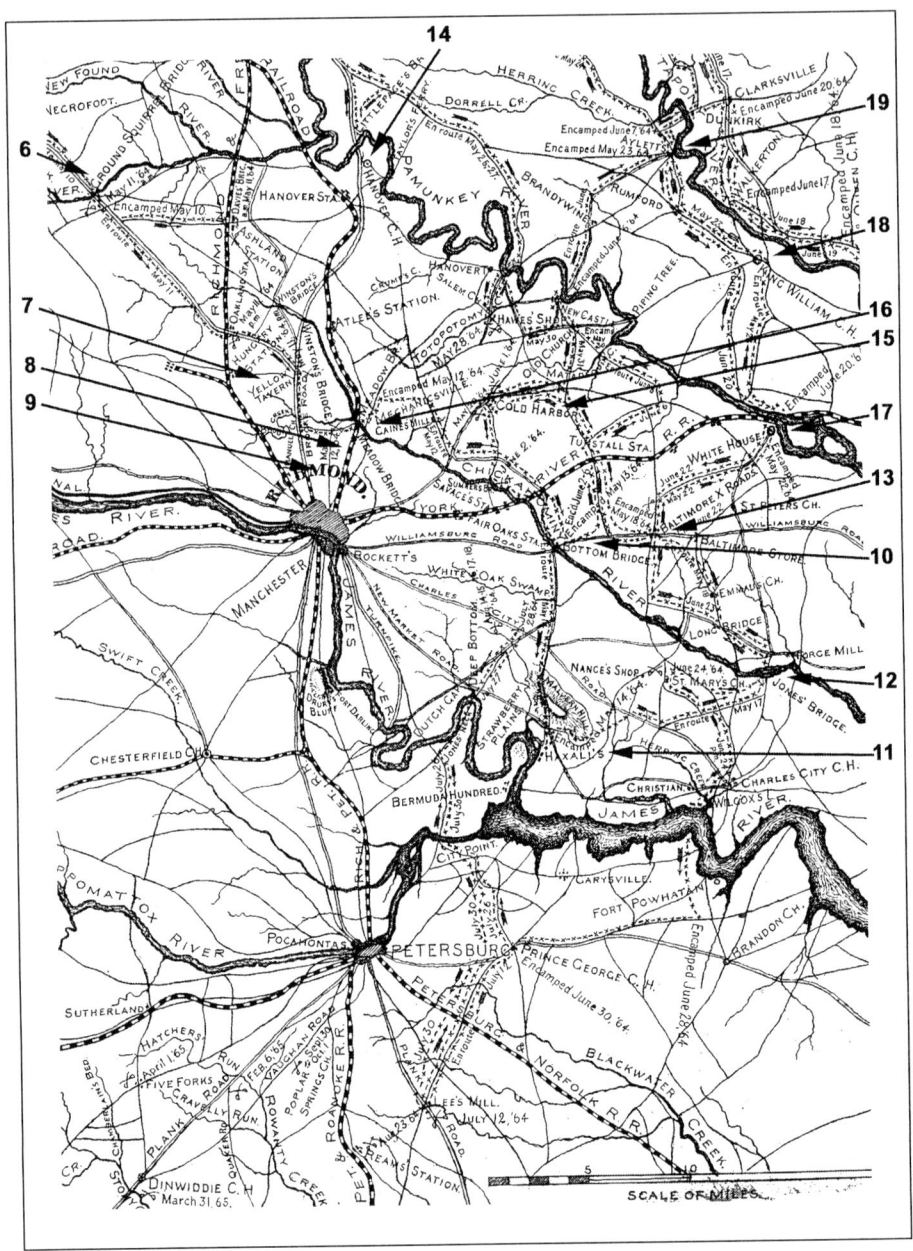

Map 6.2 Locations of events occurring after May 9, 1864

Ground Squirrel Bridge

The Cavalry had about all the action they wanted on May 11. The Tenth New York and the rest of Irvin Gregg's brigade were attacked at Ground Squirrel Bridge, before they even started on the day's march.

The boys were astir early on the morning of the 11th. Horses were groomed, breakfast hastily prepared and eaten, and the march was about to be resumed, when rapid firing and the familiar yell from the rear was followed by a sudden breaking in upon our camp and regiment of a torrent of wild horsemen. In an instant the Tenth, too, was thrown into confusion and carried along with the bewildered mass. It was so sudden, so unexpected, that no one was prepared for resistance. The Tenth had been ordered to the support of the First Maine, and was just preparing to move forward when the cyclone came. None of the boys appear to have retained a very clear recollection of just how the thing occurred or where the Regiment was "when last seen"; but all are agreed that the Regiment as a unit did not remain there long. They stood not "upon the order of going." In point of fact there was not much order to stand upon. Some went via the wood-road, while others sought the freedom of the broad fields to the right. For a few moments it was every man for himself and the rebels take the hindermost. The wood-road became blocked; but a few of the men still remained cool in this bewildering rush and were doing good service with their carbines. In the midst of the surging mass the tall form of the gallant Colonel Gregg towered like a spire above a city as he vainly sought to stop the panic-stricken crowd.

The men of the different regiments were blended in the rush. It was one of those unaccountable panics which sometimes seize bodies of men without cause. These were all excellent men, needing but a show of resistance to bring them to their senses and duty. A small clearing by the roadside gave opportunity for the formation of troops, and reining out his horse, Commissary Preston called for volunteers for a charge. A handful of men had responded to the call, and among others, Captain Charles Treichel, the

233

division mustering officer, swung into line. Declining the command, which his rank entitled him to, he urged prompt action, and away went the party down the road with sabers drawn, meeting the rebels in a hand-to-hand fight. It was a brilliant and determined little charge, and caused a halt in the rebel advance that gave sufficient opportunity for the return of reason to the bewildered troops.

Sergeant (afterward Captain) John P. White, writing of this affair, says

"Our squadron, A and L [Justus was in L Company], were, I think, about in the center of the Regiment, and preserved their formation quite well until the companies in the rear rushed through it. It soon got very hot, and about a dozen of us were engaged in a hand-to-hand fight. John R. Maybury, of Company L, was one of our number. A rebel thrust his saber through Maybury, puncturing his belt and clothing and striking his spine. Another reb was sabering one of our boys, when Ed Stark rode up, and placing his carbine against his back, pressed the trigger and reduced the effective fighting force of the enemy one. While we were riding about and banging away at every rebel we could see, I noticed Joel Frey, of Company L, take deliberate aim at me and fire. I was so close to him the powder almost burned my face. After the fight I asked him, in no very pleasant mood, what he shot at me for, and he replied that he shot a reb just behind me who had his saber ready to strike. Of course, I knew nothing of it at the time. Well, our battery came down the road and fired a blank cartridge as a warning for our men to clear the road, and we gave way to the right and left and fell back while the guns sent the grape and canister into the rebs. As the enemy came up we gave them all the lead we could from our carbines and revolvers. It was about this time that a charge was made and came up to where we were. I didn't notice who led it, but we retired with them. Sergeant Brown, of

Company L, was knocked from his horse, and caught the tail of a passing horse and was dragged out of the melee. Sergeant L. P. Norton, of the same company, received a severe saber-cut on the back of the head. The horse of Henry Bodfish, of Company A, was shot, and Bodfish deliberately commenced taking off the saddle and bridle under fire. He was told to get out quick (with the usual emphasis in such cases), which he did."

Lieutenant Preston was slightly wounded in the charge which he led. Joe McCreary, of Company H, was taken prisoner, and his comrades believed it was he who told his captors the Munchausen stories of the vast numbers that were approaching their capital, an account of which was published in the Richmond papers the next day. It was good fighting all around on the 11th. ...

Preston adds later on in his book the following information about the fight at Ground Squirrel Bridge:

The force with which Gregg's brigade had fought in the morning was Gordon's brigade, of Fitzhugh Lee's division, numbering about four thousand men. The commander of the brigade, General James B. Gordon, was killed in this fight.

Ashland

While Gregg's brigade was fighting Gordon's force at Ground Squirrel Bridge, the First brigade, under General Davies, was fighting a different rebel unit at Ashland, about 7 miles east of Ground Squirrel Bridge, where it had gone early in the morning.

Yellow Tavern

Preston continues his discussion of all the simultaneous fights that were going on this day [8]:

Custer's brigade, of the First division, was doing a smashing business at Yellow Tavern [#7 on Map 6.2], nearer Richmond. Here General Stuart met his death, while rallying his men in a final stand against the impetuous Custer. The first information received in the Tenth of the wounding of General Stuart was from an old negro woman, who informed Sergeant Joyner, of Company A, that "General Stuart had been shot frew de bowels" that evening. This, if true, meant that he was mortally wounded, which was found to be the case next day, he having died in Richmond, whither he was conveyed in an ambulance.

General Stuart, by his knightly valor, his intrepid dash, and bold adventures, had won and maintained the respect of the Union cavalrymen as no other Confederate cavalry leader had. Various accounts as to how this gallant *sabreur* met his death have been given. The particular manner in which he received his death-wound is not of so much consequence; it was the lofty spirit of heroism which found him valiantly defending the passage to the Confederate capital, even to the sacrificing of his own life in the personal endeavor to stay the victorious march of our cavalry that challenged the admiration of all.

Major McClellan, of his staff, who would be quite as likely to know the truth of the circumstances of General Stuart's death as any one, says that about eighty men had collected on the Telegraph Road, where Captain Dorsey, of the First Virginia Cavalry, had been stationed, and

> "… among these the General threw himself, and by his personal example held them steady, while the enemy charged entirely past their position. With these men he fired into their flank and rear as they passed him, in advancing and retreating, for they were met by a mounted charge of the First Virginia Cavalry and driven back some distance. As they retired, one man, who had been dismounted in the charge, and was running out on foot, turned as he passed the General, and, discharging his pistol, inflicted the fatal wound." [7]

The dying chief was removed in an ambulance to Richmond, being compelled to go by a circuitous route, as our cavalry were in possession of the Brooke road between him and the city. After reaching the city Major McClellan paid a hurried visit to his bedside. The spirit of chivalry, always prominent, was manifested in the dying moments of the General, in the following messages, which he delivered to his devoted aide [7]:

> "You will find in my hat a small Confederate flag, which a lady of Columbia, South Carolina, sent me, with a request that I would wear it upon my horse in a battle and return it to her. Send it to her."

And also:
> "My spurs which I have always worn in battle I promised to give to Mrs. Lilly Lee, of Shepherdstown, [West] Virginia. My sword I leave to my son."

Stuart's loss was greatly mourned by General Lee, who prized him highly, both as a skillful soldier of splendid courage and energy, and a hearty, joyous, loving friend [9].

The CWSAC describes the battle at Yellow Tavern as follows [10]:

As the battle between Grant and Lee raged at Spotsylvania Court House, the Union cavalry corps under Maj. Gen. Philip Sheridan embarked on a cavalry raid against Richmond. After disrupting Lee's road and rail communications, Sheridan's cavalry expedition climaxed with the battle of Yellow Tavern on May 11. The outnumbered Confederate cavalry was defeated, and Maj. Gen. J.E.B. Stuart was mortally wounded. Sheridan continued south to threaten the Richmond defenses before joining Butler's command at Bermuda Hundred. After refitting, Sheridan rejoined the Army of the Potomac on May 25 for the march to the southeast and the crossing of the Pamunkey.

Resumption of the March on Richmond and another Fight, this Time at Glen Allen Station

Preston describes the last few events in Sheridan's raid on Richmond [11]:

> After the establishment of a line in rear, Gregg's brigade resumed the march toward Richmond in clouds of dust. It was oppressively warm, and before reaching the railroad at Glen Allen [#8 on Map 6.2] a thunder storm came up. The destruction of the railroad was commenced late in the afternoon, and while engaged in this work Gordon's [Confederate] brigade again assumed the offensive and the Tenth retired to a ridge south of the railroad. On another ridge back of the one occupied by the Regiment the battery went into position, with the Sixteenth Pennsylvania as support, the balance of the brigade being disposed on either flank. While in this position darkness and rain settled down upon the troops. Vivid flashes of lightning lit up the gloom, while peals of thunder rolled away in the distance, to be lost in fresh reverberations near by, each one seeming to increase the fall of rain. Mingled with all this was the continued crack of the carbine, for we were too near the rebel capital to permit its defenders to remain passive.
>
> Along the ridge the boys lay with their rubber blankets drawn about them, banging away at the enemy as the lightning's flash would reveal their position. The horses were in charge of the mounted portion of the Regiment in a slight depression between the two ridges. Word was passed along the line near midnight that Custer had met and vanquished the enemy in front, and the cheers that followed the announcement were taken up by other regiments of the brigade on either flank, and, united with the firing of the carbines and the deep-toned thunder, made an impression on the mind that was not readily effaced. The cheering, no doubt, conveyed impressions to the Confederates that the Yankees were meeting with success in front, and hence the necessity of their creating a diversion. For a time the firing was quite rapid along the line; but finally it

languished, the storm abated, the clouds rolled by, and the line was quietly withdrawn, and the march toward the city resumed. A part of the Tenth was moved dismounted until the Brooke turnpike was reached, to be in readiness to repel any charge which might be made.

The morning of Thursday, the 12th of May, 1864, was all that Nature in her most generous mood could bestow. The rain had opened the curling leaves, the fields were resplendent with luxuriant grass, and beautiful gardens by the roadside gave forth a fragrance that was refreshing to the tired and exhausted men of Sheridan's cavalry, who were pressing forward to seize the prize for which the armies had contended so long - the capital of the Confederacy.

The march over the broad and beautiful Brooke road was more like moving out for review than what it proved to be - a day of hard and at times seemingly hopeless fighting. Passing within a line of earthworks that constituted Richmond's outer defenses [#9 on Map 6.2], a few mounted and dismounted rebel troops appeared on the ridge which hid the city from view. Near a small church the column forsook the main road, making a sharp turn to the left, and passed through the wood over a narrow road. A half-mile brought Sheridan's entire force into the open, where a halt of some time was made. Presently there was rapid firing in front: the Second Division was attacked in rear; while the Third Division, occupying the center, was fiercely assailed in flank. Soon after the dismounted line had been sent into the woods on the right - after facing to the rear - the enemy brought a battery from the woods through which the division had just passed and opened fire; but they found Lieutenant King prepared for them with his battery [Battery A] in position.

The Tenth was ordered up to the guns as support. One battalion was on the dismounted line in the wood; the other two battalions sat their horses for moments that seemed like hours, the shot and shell from the rebel guns playing havoc in the ranks. Never did men exhibit more patience or nerve. One of the most trying positions in which troops can be placed - one that demonstrates their steadfastness and reliability - is inaction while under an enemy's fire. This was grandly illustrated by the Regiment here. Although shot and shell from the enemy's battery went crashing through its ranks or plowed the ground beneath the horses' feet, shells burst over and around it in a terrorizing manner, not the least disposition to unsteadiness was manifested. Solid shot striking the ground in front of the Regiment would ricochet over the heads of the men, causing the horses to fairly squat - to use an expressive term - and with extended nostrils tremblingly crowd together awaiting the next visitation.

A solid shot shattered a foreleg of Sergeant Binkley's horse close to the body, and the poor beast continued to move the shoulder to which the leg dangled in the endeavor to place the foot. One of the artillerymen was holding four horses belonging to the battery when a shot passed through them all.

Twice did Lieutenant King silence the rebel guns, when the men pluckily returned to the place with other pieces. Finally, after exchanging a section of his rifled pieces with Captain Martin for a section of Napoleons, he put the rebel battery to sleep for good. In the meantime, Gracie's and Bartlett's brigades of infantry had been brought from the city and united with their cavalry against the Second Division. Not an inch of ground was yielded on Gregg's line. The rapid discharge of the seven-shooters in the woods to the right gave evidence of hot work there, while the booming of cannon on every side and the ceaseless rattle of small-arms told plainly the desperate nature of the conflict. It was indeed a gloomy outlook; hemmed in on all sides - an impassable stream in front, a heavy line of earthworks on our right, and a force of cavalry and infantry superior in numbers but not in valor to our own on the left flank and rear. None of the troops under Sheridan's command that day behaved better than the Second Division. Their steadiness and gallantry were largely due to the assurance and confident bearing of their commander, whose presence at different points along the line was productive of good cheer and a firm determination to succeed.

Retiring Across the Chickahominy

As the gallant men yielded up their lives on the line, their forms were taken back to the open space some distance to the right of the battery and interred with much care, the graves being made on a line, with rude head-boards put up to each. About 3 P.M. the dismounted line repulsed the last attempt made by the rebels to force the position, and Merritt's men having repaired the bridge over the Chickahominy and drawn off the force on the opposite side, the begrimed and tired troopers retired and, mounting their horses, followed the First and Third Divisions across the Chickahominy at Meadow Bridge [#16 on Map 6.2]. The citizens of Richmond and the government officials were no doubt much alarmed by Sheridan's near approach, notwithstanding there were about four thousand troops inside the works in addition to those actively engaged with the Union cavalry outside. The *Richmond Enquirer* of that date said:

> "It is unknown how long the enemy may be around the city, or at what part they may attempt to enter. Their cavalry, yesterday defeated by Stuart, may today rally, and reinforced, turn the tide of victory, and seek to gallop into the city, and through it to their army at Bermuda Hundred [On the James river, about 15 miles southeast of Richmond]."

Upon reaching the north side of the river it commenced raining. The Tenth was assigned to picket duty, a most unwelcome order, for the men were worn out and hungry. But the line was established in the gloom and rain two or three miles north of Mechanicsville [near Meadow Bridge].

Moving out at 8 A.M. on the 13th, the Tenth became the rear-guard of the entire command. About noon it passed the other troops of the corps and resumed its place with the Second Brigade, and encamped near Bottom Bridge [#10 on Map 6.2] at 5 P.M.

241

Camp was broken at 7:30 A.M. on the 14th, and the line of march taken up again for the James River; Haxall's Landing [#11 on Map 6.2] was reached at 4 P.M. and the entire command went into camp on the hills back from the river. When passing over Malvern Hill [to the immediate north of Haxall's] the officers on the gunboats mistook the column for rebels, and sent some shells of immense size at it. The signal officers attempted communication, but the tars evidently did not understand the code, for they turned their guns on the station and caused them to vacate their position. The signals had been seen, however, by General Butler's officers, and word was sent the enterprising Naval commander to cease firing. Then the begrimed and battered knights went into camp near the river, laundered their long-neglected bodies, drew full-weight rations and forage, and made general preparations for a resumption of hostilities at an early day.

The Tenth was transferred to the First Brigade, General Davies's, on the 17th of May, and about 11 P.M. the entire command was put in motion on the return march to the army. Crossing the Chickahominy at Jones's Bridge [#12 on Map 6.2] early on the morning of the 18th, a halt was made, the horses groomed, fed, and watered, and breakfast prepared and eaten. Then on again to Baltimore Cross-roads [#13 on Map 6.2], which was reached at 6 P.M. when it commenced raining. The 19th was devoted to foraging.

The uncertainty as to the location of the Army of the Potomac at this time caused General Sheridan some uneasiness. Custer's brigade was sent to Hanover Court House [#14 on Map 6.2], while the balance of the corps went on a reconnaissance to Cold Harbor [#15 on Map 6.2]. Breaking camp at 5 A.M. on the 20th, the Second Division, with the Second Brigade leading and the Sixteenth Pennsylvania in advance, moved to Cold Harbor, where it arrived at 2 P.M. driving a small force of the enemy and posting pickets beyond Gaines's Mills [#16 on Map 6.2]. Rations and forage were becoming very scarce, and foraging parties were sent out on the 21st. These met with but indifferent success and a few rebels. A party under Commissary Preston went in the direction of Richmond and secured an abundant supply of flour, sugar, tea, coffee, sweet potatoes, etc., from the residence of one of the F. F.'s. and escaped with the plunder, reaching camp early in the morning on the 22d, most of the men walking, the horses being loaded down with tribute.

Crossing the Pamunkey

Marching at daybreak on the 22d, the Tenth, first in order of march, arrived at White House [on the Pamunkey River, #17 on Map 6.2] about noon. Gunboats and transports had come up from Fortress Monroe, bringing rations and forage. The First Division, under General Merritt, had rebuilt the bridge over the Pamunkey, and were already crossing when the Second Division arrived.

The Tenth crossed at sunrise on the 23d, and with the rest of the command marched to King William Court House [#18 on Map 6.2], where it arrived at 1 P.M.; thence to Aylettsville [or Aylette, #19 on Map 6.2], where the corps went into camp four hours later. From there the Tenth was sent to picket the Hanover road. While posting pickets the men were fired on by the pickets of the Seventh Michigan Cavalry by mistake, but no harm resulted.

Justus writes a letter to Mary from White House Landing telling her about the big raid on Richmond. Coincidentally she writes to him on the same day.

White House Landing Va
May 22nd 1864

Dear Friend,

I recieved your kind and welcome letter a long time a go. should have answered it at the time but we broke camp at about that time and we have been on the move amost every day since. Our Cav. Corps fought the rebs for nine days running. we turned the rebs right after fighting them three or four days. and then our Cav started on a raid. we went straight for Richmond.

we had a number of brushes on the way. in one we had two wounded in our Co. John Maybury had a saber thrust in the back. He would have been run through if it had not been for his saber belt. it struck two thicknesses of that. Sarg't Norton had a saber cut on the head.

We went into the fortifications of Richmond about a mile. went within two and a half miles of the city. Had a fight there all day. I guess we waked them up there some if not more. we had only one man wounded there, John Sargent. think he will have to loose a limb. we went all around the city but on the south side. we have been over all of McLellands old batle fields. we are now on the Panmonkey River. there is a division crossing the river now. I think that we are going back to join the army of the Potomac again. we have done a good deal of damage on this raid.

I have not time to write much this time. you must excuse this writing for I am in a hurry. pleas write as soon as convenient. and oblige your Friend

Justus G. Matteson

244

Absent friend, once more I take my pen to write to you. instead of its being a task it is a pleasure to write to one that is far away from friends and home and also to one that is surrounded by all of the perrils of a warfaring life. I would do all that I can to cheer them and to battle for the right. I should have answered your letter before but when I received it I had just answered your other one and I went home and staid two weeks. I had a very good time. should have enjoyed it better if it had not rained most every day. I see your sister to meeting but did not call there on account of the rain. It seemed good to be at home again but after I had staid at home two weeks I was ready to come back to Homer again. it is rather dull in Solon. there is not any company. I cannot enjoy it as I did a few years ago. They have meetings in the school house every two weeks. Mr. Garry from McGrawville preaches. I have been to church once to day and writen two letters before this so you will excuse this poor writing. We have had vary plesant wether the past week to pay for the two weeks that I were at home. the trees are in full bloom.

Jut, I thank you vary much for your picture. I should have known it if it had been with ten thousand more. I think that it is a very good one. it will not be flatery if I say that I think that you make a vary good looking soldier, for flatery of any kind I do not believe in or approve of.

Jut, I read the war news with much interest now. for I know that many of my friends will be engaged in the present battles. but that they may all come out safe shall be my prair. I know not but that some of them may now be lying on the battle field wounded. oh! the misery that this war one heart cannot tell for there are so many that suffere. If I could help take care of the wounded. I know that I should be a poor hand but if I could do what I could do it would be some consolation. but I am so far north that I can do nothing. Jut, it is time for evening meeting and I must close hoping to hear that you are well soon. I bid thee good night.

Mary Hatch
Homer

245

Preston continues his discussion of the raid [12]:

Marching at 5 A.M. on the 24th, the Regiment bivouacked near White Chimneys [20 miles north of Richmond] at 5 P.M., making a hot, dusty march of about fifteen miles. After going into camp a heavy thunder-shower came up. The rain fell in torrents and the angry bursts of lightning carried terror to many brave hearts. Corporal Bolles and Private Ireland, of Company K, serving in the Pioneer Corps [front-line construction engineers], were both struck, the former being instantly killed. Several men and horses were prostrated. D.T. Fields and Stephen Smith were driving tent-stakes, and both were thrown to the ground by a shock. Jumping to his feet, Smith staggered about and exclaimed in a bewildered way, "Where did that shell come from?" One of the bolts twisted a saber that was leaning against a tree, into the symbolic pruning-hook. The heavy cannonading and musketry-fire in front during the day indicated hard fighting between the two armies. …

Finally, Back with the Army of the Potomac

After the heavy rainfall of the night before, the sun rose bright and warm on the 25th. At 6 A.M. the Regiment led out, and at 1:30 P.M. passed through Chesterfield Station [22 miles north of Richmond], and a half-hour later came up with the infantry, and were greeted by "The boys we left behind us," besides some of the new acquisitions, among the latter being Chaplain Bradley, who wore a sedate expression and a pair of knee-boots as he approached Major Avery and introduced himself. His manner and appearance created a favorable impression on the men, which increased with closer acquaintance. Here Captain Paige reported with forty recruits. An immense mail was in waiting for the boys, which was at once distributed to their great satisfaction. The trains came up, but remained but a short time, Quartermaster Graves having received orders to proceed to Port Royal with his wagons, on the 26th, to bring up supplies.

The raid, replete with incident and excitement, had been severe on the horses and men. But the Yankee cavalry had maintained its supremacy over the Southern horsemen, even when aided by infantry, as was the case in the works of Richmond on the 12th of May. That more property was not destroyed was the fault of the Confederacy in not providing it. We destroyed all we found, and, like Alexander, "sighed for more."

**Figure 6.5 Guidon flag typical of that probably carried
by Company L of the Tenth New York cavalry**

References

[1] Preston, Noble D., *History of the Tenth New York Volunteer Cavalry*, New York, NY: D. Appleton and Company, 1892; reprinted by Higginson Book Company, Salem, MA in 1998; pp. 157-159.

[2] Ibid, 163-165.

[3] Advance Print of Official Records, vol. xxxvi, Part I, p. 207-209.

[4] Preston, *History of the Tenth New York*, pp. 168-171.

[5] National Park Service, Civil War Sites Advisory Commission (CWSAC), http://www.cr.nps.gov/hps/abpp/battles/va046.htm, Wilderness, May 5-7, 1864.

[6] Preston, *History of the Tenth New York*, pp. 171-180.

[7] McClellan, Henry B., *The Campaigns of Stuart's Cavalry* (reprint, Blue & Grey Press, Secaucus, New Jersey, 1993), pp. 409, 410, 413, 416.

[8] Preston, *History of the Tenth New York*, pp. 179-180.

[9] Lieutenant-Colonel C. S. Venable, of General Lee's staff, in Battles and Leaders of the Civil War, Vol. IV, p. 243.

[10] National Park Service, Civil War Sites Commission (CWSAC), http://www.cr.nps.gov/hps/abpp/battles/va052.htm, Yellow tavern, May 11, 1864.

[11] Preston, *History of the Tenth New York*, pp. 180-186.

[12] Ibid, 186-187.

CHAPTER 7
Cold Harbor, Trevillian Raid,
St. Mary's Church - May-June 1864

"... going to fight it out on this line if it took all summer," U.S. Grant

The major events covered in this chapter are listed in Table 7.1, all occurring in Virginia.

Map #	Location	Dates
1	On the Pamunkey River	May 26-28, 1864
2	Totopotomoy Creek	May 27-30
3	Hanoverton	May 27
4	Hawes's Shop	May 28
5	Old Church Tavern	May 30
	Cold Harbor	**May 31-June 6**
6	Cold Harbor	May 31-Jun. 1
7	Sumner's Upper Bridge (Barker's Mills)	June 2
8	Bottom Bridge	June 3
	Gen. Sheridan's Trevillian Raid	**June 7-24**
9	Trevillian Station	June 11-12
10	Kings and Queens Court House	June 18, 20
11	White House Landing	June 21
12	On the Chickahominy River	June 21
16	Baltimore Cross-Roads	June 22
13	St. Mary's Church (Samaria Church)	June 24
14	Charles City C.H.	June 24
15	Wilcox Landing on the James River	June 25

Table 7.1 Major events in late May and June, 1864

The Union Cavalry became much more aggressive under General Sheridan's leadership. They fulfilled their duties of picketing and escorting, as requested by the Infantry, but did so grudgingly. Sheridan wanted to attack the Confederate cavalry, destroy supplies, pick up railroad tracks, and in general do anything to harass and weaken the Confederate cause. Map 7.1 shows the locations of the events at the end of May, 1864 and into the first week of June. Numbered callouts refer to the numbers in Table 7.1.

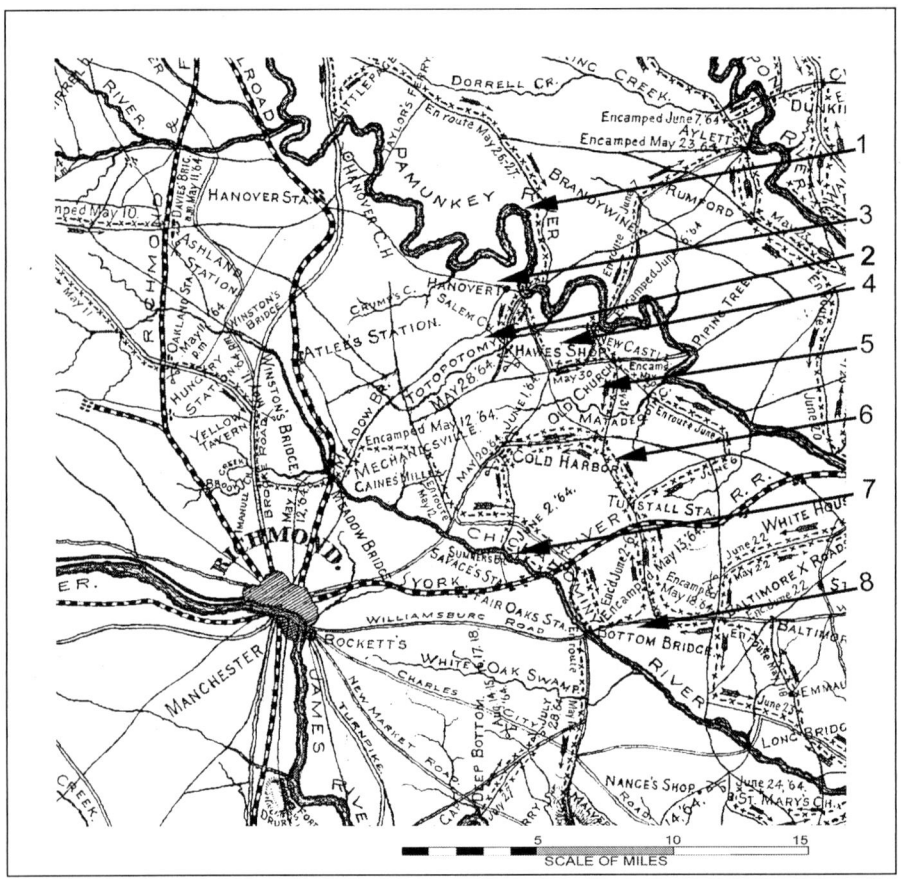

Map 7.1 Events of late May to early June, 1864

Battle of Totopotomoy Creek

The Civil War Sites Advisory Commission (CWSAC) has this description of the battle at Totopotomoy Creek [1]:

Operations along Totopotomoy Creek [#2 on Map 7.1] opened with cavalry combats at the Pamunkey River crossing at Dabney's Ferry (Hanoverton) and at Crump's Creek on May 27. During the cavalry fight at Hawes's Shop [#4 on Map 7.1] on May 28, Union and Confederate infantry arrived in the vicinity. The Confederates entrenched behind Totopotomoy Creek. On the 29th, the Union II, IX, and V Corps probed Lee's position along the creek, while the VI Corps felt its way toward Hanover Court House [about 9 miles northwest of Hanoverton].

The action for the Cavalry at Totopotomoy was fairly light, the Infantry taking over soon after it began. Preston doesn't even mention it. He launches into the Battle of Hawes's Shop in the following [2].

The Battle of Hawes's Shop

On the return to the Army of the Potomac [at Chesterfield Station, 30 miles due north of Richmond between the North Anna and the Mattatopony Rivers] the cavalrymen naturally looked for a short respite, for the purpose of recuperation and reorganization; but the vigor with which General Grant was conducting the war did not permit much time to go to waste. He was going to "fight it out on this line if it took all summer," and all the horses in the army to do it. And the cavalrymen gave a hearty amen to the sentiment, as they gave hearty support to the man. "Boots and Saddles" at 11 A.M., on Thursday, May 26th, gave notice that the services of the cavalry were wanted in front. Marching back on nearly the same route on which they had advanced from White House, the tramp was continued in a drizzling rain until 9 P.M., when a short halt was made; then on, on, through the long, weary night, until the Pamunkey was crossed at Hanover [Hanoverton] at sunrise on the 28th.

Going into bivouac in the open field on the south side, the men cooked breakfasts and fed and watered the animals. At 8 A.M. the Tenth, with Gregg's division, moved out on the

Richmond road. Rations had been issued for four hundred and forty men prior to leaving Chesterfield Station, but the issue included dismounted and train men, sick, etc., so that the probable strength of the Regiment at this time did not exceed three hundred and eighty men present for duty. At ten o'clock the Regiment halted at Hawes's shop [#4 on Map 7.1], and formed on the right of the road.

In its front was a large white house surrounded by trees, under which General Davies established temporary headquarters. Captain Blynn, who had been sent forward with his squadron on a reconnaissance, had halted and sent Lieutenant T.C. White about half a mile farther on, with Company D. White passed beyond the woods with his detachment, and Sergeant Edson had barely posted pickets, when they were driven in and the reserve was viciously attacked by a large force of mounted and dismounted Confederate cavalry. White formed his few men across the road and gave them a warm reception, checking their advance by well-directed and rapid volleys; but the largely superior numbers were too much for continued resistance, and White fell back, closely followed by the mounted force. The stroke of lightning which killed Corporal Bolles, of the Pioneer Corps, on the 24th, deprived his horse of its eyesight. This horse was being ridden by Warren Irish in the race for liberty which Blynn's squadron were making on this occasion. The horse becoming wedged in between a tree and the fence, Irish was forced to take to the fields to escape capture. He made good time, however, and reached the reserve, after passing through a storm of bullets, though pretty badly winded. As the little squad came flying up the road, closely pursued by a force which filled the road and extended a considerable distance back, the First Pennsylvania, with Colonel Taylor at its head, arrived in front of General Davies's headquarters.

The rebel yell found an echo in Colonel Taylor's prompt command to "draw saber!" followed by the "charge!" The rebels suddenly found themselves in a dilemma. Hemmed in on either side by a high rail fence and pressed from the rear by their own comrades, they were mercilessly sabered by the Pennsylvania boys. The First Pennsylvania never wielded the saber with better effect. The Confederates finally extricated themselves, and, falling back, their dismounted troopers began a rapid fire from the woods.

The brigade was ordered forward, the Tenth taking position, mounted, at the edge of the wood, the left resting on the road, near a little church. The battery had taken position a few rods in rear of the Regiment, and was dispensing shot and shell in generous quantities, firing over the Regiment into the woods. A little lull in the action soon after the arrival of the Regiment was followed by a most terrific outburst from the Confederate line, denoting heavy reinforcements. General Davies, who chanced to be near the Tenth at the moment, directed Major Avery to dismount the Regiment and move it into the woods immediately, and connect with the Fourth Pennsylvania on the right and the First Pennsylvania on the left. This was done in perfect order, although it was extremely hot, with no chance of replying until the line was formed in the wood. No sooner had the Tenth taken position, as directed, than they encountered and returned a most galling fire. It was clearly an unequal contest, so far as numbers were concerned, but never did the Regiment display better staying qualities or exhibit more gallantry than on this occasion. While repeated attempts to drive the enemy from their position proved futile, the determined resistance offered rendered the efforts of the enemy to do the same thing with our line ineffectual. As the fight progressed the Confederates appeared to throw in fresh troops, but none came to our assistance. **It was the hardest fight the Regiment was ever engaged in.** An aide from General Gregg came to the line, urging an advance. It was only necessary for the men to know that it was General Gregg's desire that the line should be advanced, for them to attempt it. But that was all they could do, and that they did do with great determination and spirit on several occasions. But it was of no avail. Against such a fire as was brought against them it was impossible to move forward.

Much of the ground occupied by the Regiment was covered with underbrush, while in its front between the two lines was a ravine, across which the murderous missiles flew so thick and fast that it did not appear possible for anyone to survive. Unceasingly the desperate conflict continued until about 4 P.M., when a cheer was heard away to the right. Yes, it was a cheer; a real Yankee cheer! Then the line in our front began to give way; and the cheer was re-echoed as the Tenth went forward, down through the ravine and up the opposite hillside, in close pursuit of the fleeing rebels. Over the open beyond, and clear up to the wood on the opposite side, the pursuit was continued. The ground was strewn with the enemy's dead, but their wounded had been removed. The line was recalled, and then it was learned that Custer had charged on our right with his brigade, dismounted, and turned the enemy's left, and our brigade pressing forward at the same time, the entire Confederate line gave way. The Union victory was complete. It was fairly earned by superior endurance, bravery, and determination. The battle of Hawes's shop has been very properly recorded as the hardest cavalry fight of the war. There was at no time during the engagement the slightest evidence of weakness or disposition to yield an inch of ground on the Union side. The losses in the Tenth were heavy, the number of killed being nearly double that of any other regiment engaged, while the number of wounded was exceeded only by the First New Jersey and Sixteenth Pennsylvania. The Confederate force greatly outnumbered the Union troops in this engagement.

The Civil War Sites Advisory Commission (CWSAC) has this description of the battle at Hawes's Shop [3]:

Gregg's cavalry division, supported by Torbert's division, advanced to cover the Army of the Potomac's crossing of the Pamunkey River and movement toward Totopotomoy Creek. Fitzhugh Lee's and Hampton's cavalry divisions, later reinforced by Butler's South Carolina brigade, met the Federals at Enon Church [Hawes's Shop]. After seven hours of mostly dismounted cavalry fighting, the Federal advance was stopped. Both Confederate and Union infantry began arriving in the vicinity as the cavalry fighting raged.

Returning to Preston's discussion of the fighting at Hawes's Shop:

General Humphreys says [4]:

> On the morning of the 28th General Sheridan was directed to make a demonstration on the road from Hanover Town to Richmond to ascertain where the enemy was posted, and about a mile beyond Hawes's shop Gregg's division encountered the enemy's cavalry dismounted and occupying temporary breastworks of rails. This force, General Sheridan says, appeared to be the Confederate Cavalry Corps and a brigade of South Carolina troops armed with long-range rifles, reported to be four thousand strong and commanded by Colonel Butler.
>
> But I learn from Fitzhugh Lee that the Confederate cavalry force there on the 28th consisted of his own division, of two brigades, Hampton's division, of two brigades, and a brigade under command of Colonel (afterward General) Butler, which had recently arrived from South Carolina. Fitzhugh Lee was on the right of their line, Hampton on the left. A long, hard contest ensued and continued until late in the evening, when Custer's brigade (of Torbert's division) and Gregg's division carried the entrenchments and drove back the enemy.

Major Avery's wish, frequently expressed, that he might receive a slight wound, came near being gratified in the early part of this engagement. A bullet penetrated the right stirrup, opposite the side of his foot, and was deflected, passing through the bottom of the stirrup, directly beneath the hollow of his foot, without touching the boot.

Surgeon Clarke says of the Hawes's shop engagement:

> Hawes's shop was one of the most fiercely contested battles of the war. The wounds of all that came under my observation were very severe. While I was engaged in amputating the leg of Sergeant Reynolds, of our regiment, in a log house, a shell from the enemy's battery knocked the chimney off the house, another took off the leg of an officer standing in front of the building, and still another entered the open door of the house, struck a beam overhead, and rolled down under the operating table. Every face present was ghastly white, expecting the shell would explode, but no one deserted his post. To the fact that the fuse had gone out may be attributed my recording the incident.

Of the Hawes's shop fight General Gregg says:

> In the shortest possible time both of my brigades were hotly engaged. Every available man was put into the fight, which had lasted some hours. Neither party would yield an inch. Through a staff-officer of General Sheridan I sent him word as to how we stood, and stated that with some additional force I could destroy the equilibrium and go forward. Soon General Custer reported with his brigade. This he dismounted and formed on a road leading to the front and through the center of my line. In columns of platoons, with band playing, he advanced. As arranged, when the head of his column reached my line, all went forward with a tremendous yell and the contest was of short duration. We went right over the rebels, who resisted with courage and desperation unsurpassed. Our success cost the Second Division two hundred and fifty-six men and officers, killed and wounded. This fight has always been regarded by the Second Division as one of its severest. ...

The bias of commanders of troops during these eventful days is illustrated by General Lee's report of the Hawes's shop engagement, made at 6 P.M. on the day of the fight, in which he says:

> General Fitzhugh Lee's division of cavalry engaged the enemy's cavalry near Hawes's shop about noon to-day and drove them back upon their infantry, etc.

Preston adds:

> Probably no one would doubt General Lee's sincerity or question his statement of facts, and yet every trooper in Gregg's division knows that not one foot of ground was yielded by them at Hawes's shop, but that, on the contrary, the Confederate cavalry was driven pell-mell for a considerable distance. After driving the Confederates, as related, the line was recalled to Hawes's shop, where the advance of the army [infantry] was found.

> The Regiment remained in camp near the river on the 29th, and on the 30th moved to Old Church Tavern, and commenced skirmishing on the road leading to Cold Harbor. Toward evening the skirmishing became very brisk. The command bivouacked near Old Church Tavern [#5 on Map 7.1] at 8 P.M.

The Cavalry at Cold Harbor

Preston describes the participation of the Tenth New York in the battle at Cold Harbor (see #6 on Map 7.1) in the following [5]:

> The march was taken up again on the Cold Harbor road at 6 P.M. on the 31st [May 1864], and after some standing to horse, and mounting and dismounting, the boys finally planted a few rheumatic seeds by courting a little sleep on the damp ground.
> Up and moving again at daylight on the 1st of June, the Regiment commenced skirmishing. The Confederates were driven to Cold Harbor, the fighting at 9 A.M. being severe.

General Sheridan dismounted in rear of the position held by the Tenth, and walking along the line, encouraged the men to hold the place for a few minutes, saying the infantry was close by and would soon relieve them. This was thought to be a *dernier ressort* to maintain the line. But a half-hour later, sure enough, there appeared over the brow of the hill the standards of the advancing army that was to contend for the possession of this apparently worthless place in one of the bloodiest battles of the war. The dismounted troopers of the Cavalry Corps did excellent service here in holding the rebel infantry until the army came up. General Meade had sent word to General Sheridan to hold the place at all hazards, and he held it, the Tenth contributing its full share in the necessary fighting. General Humphreys says [6]:

> On the morning of the 1st of June Hoke did not become engaged, but took position on the right. Kershaw, however, attacked Sheridan with two of his brigades, one of them his own, but was repulsed by the fire of repeating carbines and artillery. He repeated the attack, with the same result, Colonel Keitt's regiment, the Twentieth South Carolina, giving way, and Colonel Keitt himself being mortally wounded in the effort to rally it. The attack was not renewed, and at nine o'clock General Wright arrived, the head of his column near at hand. As soon as it was up, the cavalry were relieved, and moved toward the Chickahominy, covering the left of the army.

The dancing banners of the Sixth Corps were seen by the boys over the hill-tops, before the infantry appeared in view, and the cheers that followed must have convinced the Confederate infantry that reinforcements had arrived for the Yankees. The fire slackened and the infantry moved down and took the position held by the dismounted cavalrymen, who at about 2 P.M., mounted and moved to the left, and two hours later a part of the Tenth was sent still farther to the left on picket, while the Pioneer Corps was sent out on the road leading to Summer's Upper Bridge to fell trees and barricade the road. This duty kept the pioneers at work till next morning, when, just as they were about to return to camp, they received orders to clear the barricade away as soon as possible, to permit the cavalry to pass. The cannonading and musketry at Cold Harbor continued during the night, and increased with the approaching light of the 2d.

The Civil War Sites Advisory Commission (CWSAC) has this description of the battles at Cold Harbor (Note the mention of "new repeating carbines.") [7]:

On May 31, Sheridan's cavalry seized the vital crossroads of Old Cold Harbor. Early on June 1, relying heavily on their new repeating carbines and shallow entrenchments, Sheridan's troopers threw back an attack by Confederate infantry. Confederate reinforcements arrived from Richmond and from the Totopotomoy Creek lines. Late on June 1, the Union VI and XVIII Corps reached Cold Harbor and assaulted the Confederate works with some success. By June 2, both armies were on the field, forming on a seven-mile front that extended from Bethesda Church to the Chickahominy River. At dawn June 3, the II and XVIII Corps, followed later by the IX Corps, assaulted along the Bethesda Church-Cold Harbor line and were slaughtered at all points. Grant commented in his memoirs that this was the only attack he wished he had never ordered. The armies confronted each other on these lines until the night of June 12, when Grant again advanced by his left flank, marching to James River. On June 14, the II Corps was ferried across the river at Wilcox's Landing by transports. On June 15, the rest of the army began crossing on a 2,200-foot long pontoon bridge at Weyanoke. Abandoning the well-defended approaches to Richmond, Grant sought to shift his army quickly south of the river to threaten Petersburg. [This pontoon bridge was the longest in modern history, and was considered one of the greatest engineering feats of the Civil War.]

The Cold Harbor battlefield location is now under the jurisdiction of the National Park Service. A sign at the entrance is shown in the photo in Figure 7.1.

Figure 7.1 Entrance to Cold Harbor Battlefield Park
(2001 photo by author)

A current signboard at the site has the following information discussing the fearsome infantry battle that took place at Cold Harbor after the cavalry was relieved:

> The night before, Union soldiers write their names on scraps of paper fastened to their clothing, hoping to be identified after the battle. At 4:30 A.M. they are ordered to attack the Confederate earthworks clearly visible across the open field. Most of the dying is over in thirty minutes. Unable to advance or retreat, the surviving Federals use spoons, forks, or bayonets to dig in where they lie, beneath a waist-high ceiling of fire. Afterward the Union Army built the more elaborate entrenchments behind you. Ten days later, in secrecy, Grant abandoned the position to march on Petersburg.

Believe it or not, signs of the earthworks created for the battles can still be seen. Figure 7.2 shows some of the trenches, in a photo taken by the author in February of 2001.

Figure 7.2 Trenches are still visible at Cold Harbor

A cemetery was created near the battle sites to handle all of the casualties of Cold Harbor. Figure 7.3 shows a monument to the New York troops who were killed there. There were several other monuments in the Cemetery, including a monument for Pennsylvania troops, and a monument to 600 Confederate dead from the battles.

**Figure 7.3 Monument to New York soldiers at the
Cold Harbor Cemetery (2001 photo by author)**

Some of the trees in the cemetery have grown large enough to capture the tombstones of some of the graves, as shown in Figure 7.4.

**Figure 7.4 Large tree has grown around
tombstone in the Cold Harbor Cemetery**

Sheridan's Raid on Trevillian Station

The following is Preston's discussion of the activities of the cavalry in actions referred to as the Raid on Trevillian Station [8]:

> At 9 A.M. [on June 1st] the Tenth moved out with the brigade to Summer's Upper Bridge (or Barker's Mills) [#7 on Map 7.1]. The clouds of dust which arose gave notice to the enemy on the opposite side of the wood of the movement, and the batteries in their works rained shot and shell into the open field through which the column was marching. The Regiment was brought into company fronts, and a skirmish-line advanced through the swamp, the men being compelled to jump from bog to log, and, sometimes missing their footing, went floundering into the mire, which would call for the use of a little imported language, kept in stock for such occasions. Reaching the opposite shore, a sandy field with the Confederate breastworks on the higher ground, a little further advanced, was in front of the skirmishers. After exchanging a few shots the Confederate skirmishers fell back behind the works, and our line was ordered to rejoin the Regiment, which

remained in the field before mentioned, where they had been subjected to a brisk artillery-fire, the solid shot, shells, etc., plunging into the sand all around and in the very midst of the Regiment, throwing sand in showers over the boys. About 5 P.M. the infantry took the place of the cavalry, and the latter moved to Bottom's Bridge [#8 on Map 7.1], the Tenth going into camp about a mile from the bridge, on the hill. On the afternoon of the 4th the Confederates shelled the camp of the First Brigade from the opposite side of the Chickahominy, distant about three miles. The Whitworth bolts tumbled around among the men and horses rather carelessly, but did no harm. This diversion was repeated on the 6th, with the same result.

The pickets of the Tenth were called in, and at 11 A.M. of the same day the entire command marched to Newcastle, where the Pamunkey was crossed at 5 P.M. and the command bivouacked. Torbert's and Gregg's divisions were present, Wilson's having taken Gregg's place in picketing along the Chickahominy. The march was resumed on the 7th, and at 2:30 P.M., the Tenth encamped two miles west of Aylett's [10 miles northeast of Hawes's shop - #4 on Map 7.1]. An early start was made on the 8th. It was warm and dusty, and the march was already beginning to tell on the horses. ...

The Tenth was sent on picket in the evening of this day.

General Sheridan evidently intended to get as much of the marching in the cool of the day as possible. The Regiment was on the move at 5 A.M. and encamped at 4 P.M., passing through Childsburg in the forenoon. The morning of the 10th was cool and pleasant. The march was continued at 8 A.M., and at 3 P.M. crossed the North Anna at Carpenter's Ford. Soon after reaching the south side of the river a halt was made, and Lieutenant Preston was directed to take a detachment and go into the country in search of food, with instructions to join the Regiment some miles in advance, where they were expected to go into camp. ...

The next morning, the 11th of June, 1864, the Tenth moved out of camp [on the south side of the North Anna River at Carpenter's Ford, 7 miles northeast of Trevillian Station] with the brigade at 6:30 A.M., going in the direction of Louisa Court-House [and Trevillian Station, #9 on Map 7.2], the First Division in advance, Custer's brigade leading. The sound of artillery came from the direction of Trevillian Station about 8:30 A.M., and an hour later the Tenth was assigned to guard the trains. Hardly had the Regiment left the road for the purpose, when Major Avery was directed to hurry forward, and report with it to General Torbert. After passing through the wood where Torbert was expected to be found in the open field beyond, an aide galloped to the head of the Tenth with orders for the Major to take the Regiment to Colonel Gregg [Colonel Irvin Gregg was General David Gregg's cousin; at this time Colonel Gregg was 2nd Brigade commander, and General Gregg was 2nd Division commander] for special service. Leading the way, the command moved to the left through more woods and scrub-oaks. As the Tenth came into the open, Colonel Gregg approached, and, after giving Major Avery instructions as to the part he wanted the Regiment to take in a charge he was about to make, he returned to his brigade, which was in the wood in front.

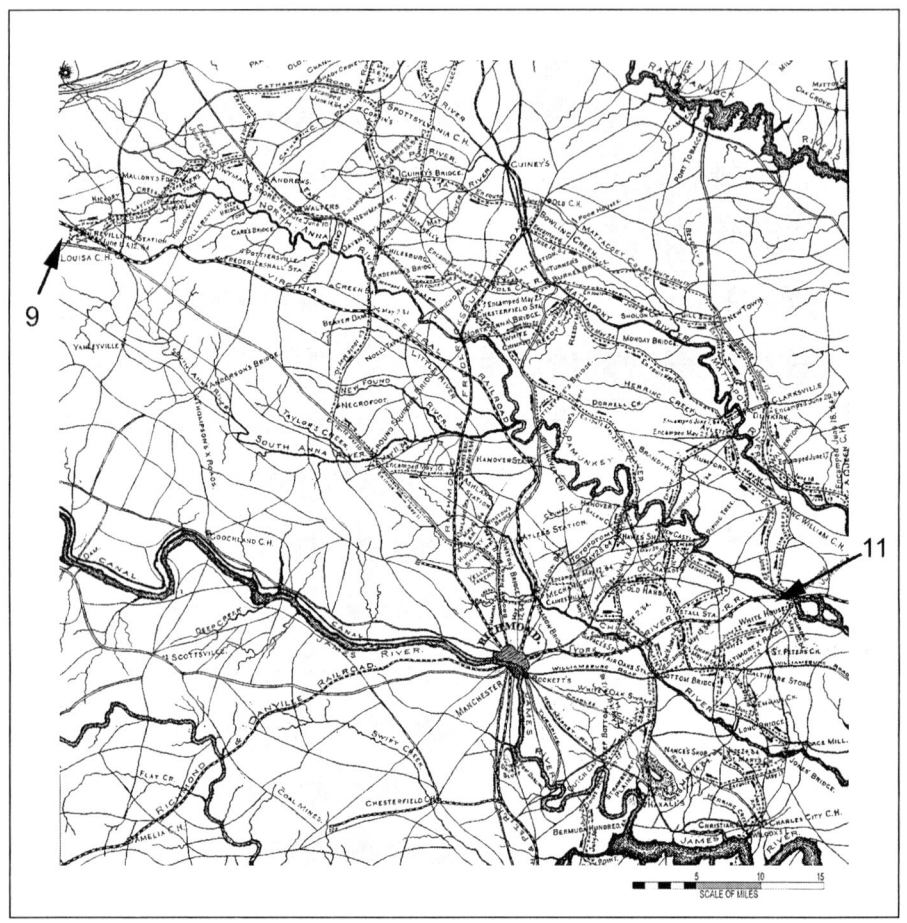

**Map 7.2 End-points of the march from
White House (#11) to Trevillian Station (#9)**

The Tenth was immediately dismounted, and advanced along a fence to the left of and at right angles with the road on which it had moved up. In front of the right of the Regiment and distant about twenty rods [110 yards] were the Confederates in a piece of wood, with plowed ground intervening. In front of the left was a more extended open country. Colonel Gregg's brigade was on the right, with the road intervening. When all was in readiness, the bugles in the Second Brigade sounded the charge. Then followed an incessant rattle of carbines and the cheers of the charging column. The men were hidden from view by the timber and scrub-oaks. After a moment the cheering and firing slackened somewhat. The force of the charge appeared to have been broken. In the mean time the Tenth did not leave its place behind the fence, but kept up a rapid fire on the enemy in its front. Major Avery did not appear to understand that the Tenth was to unite in the charge. Finally, the order was given, however, and the fence was scaled in a gallant manner, and the Confederates driven rapidly from the timber and across the open to the railroad beyond, losing many prisoners. It was **one of the most enterprising and gallant charges ever made by the Regiment,** and called forth warm words of commendation from both the brigade and division commanders, as well as from General Sheridan. Of this action Adjutant Kennedy writes:

When the Tenth was dismounted it was ordered to form on the left of the Second Brigade and to charge with it. In our front was a rail fence, behind which the regiment formed a line. This fence ran nearly the whole length of the brigade. On the other side of the fence was a level field about thirty rods across. After crossing this field we came to the railroad, which here ran through a cut from six to eight feet deep. In this cut the enemy were posted in heavy force. Just back of this cut, on a knoll, was the rebel battery. All this in our immediate front to our right, and in front of the Second Brigade was the station house and several boxcars, and still farther on the right was a cut similar to the one in our front. The enemy was in force all along this line - they retreated down the railroad to our left, and after making the charge we changed front and followed them, moving to the left, and covering a part of the ground over which we had previously charged.

Major Avery was in command, and at this time was on the right of the Regiment. When the bugle sounded the charge, the Second Brigade started, but for some reason unknown to the writer, the old Tenth New York remained stationary. Captain Weir, of General Gregg's staff, came running out of the woods to the right, swinging his saber and shouting for us to charge. We jumped the fence and started. By the time that the Tenth started, the Second Brigade had reached the second fence and dropped down behind it, having drawn the enemy's fire from our front, as well as the fire of the artillery; and as they were now hidden from the enemy, we were receiving a most terrific fire, not only from our front, but from the cut which was filled with Johnnies. As our line reached the second fence, we were forced to take refuge behind it for a short time.

While lying here several of our men were killed, and Lieutenant Van Tuyl called out to me, saying: "For God's sake, Adjutant, what are you going to do? We can't lie here much longer!" I ran down to the right of the line to see what Major Avery was going to do, and meeting Captain Blynn was informed that just as we got over the first fence Lieutenant Preston was either killed or wounded; and that Major Avery had remained with him where he had fallen, to have him carried off the field. Another charge was ordered, and away we went, this time with the Second Brigade. Although we were obliged to cross a plowed field in full view of the enemy, and subject to their murderous fire, the line never faltered, and in a very few moments the Tenth New York Cavalry jumped down in that railroad cut to find that the enemy, not thinking it possible for us to dislodge them, had remained too long to safely retreat, and we reaped a rich harvest in prisoners. The battery meanwhile had limbered up and galloped off the field, taking the road leading down the railroad to our left.

Captain Vanderbilt writes as follows of the Trevillian fight:

The battle of Trevillian Station was in many respects **one of the severest cavalry combats of the war**; but to the Tenth New York not so disastrous as Brandy Station, St. Mary's Church, or Little Auburn. Yet it was a hot fight, so hot indeed for our regiment as to deserve a place in the history of a long line of splendid achievements that made the name of the Tenth New York a synonym for good work on the field. The history of the Trevillian Station fight is not easily told; but here are my views of the engagement:

Shortly after noon, June 11, 1864, our regiment was drawn up behind a piece of wood, in column of squadrons, mounted; soon we were listening to a fight raging on our right front. We rather enjoyed hearing the rattle of carbines and the banging of our battery, being on the reserve out of harm's way. Our enjoyment was of short duration, however; for while our commander, Major Avery, Adjutant Kennedy, and myself were sitting on our horses whiling away our time in conversation, Colonel Gregg approached and ordered Major Avery to dismount his regiment and form it on the left of the line of battle preparatory to a general charge.

The enemy's line of breastworks was on the brow of a small hill in our front. The Major, wheeling his horse, gave the order to dismount, for we were to go in on foot. The Regiment was speedily formed for a charge under cover of woods. The men were told by the Major what was expected of them in a very few choice words. An open plowed field lay before us, say, a distance of three hundred yards, in full view of the enemy's works, which were about five hundred distant. Soon an order came to charge, and we started. We did not attempt to fire a shot, but the way they peppered us was a caution. It was about as severe firing as I ever saw. From the second the charge started, we ran with all our might, stopping such bullets as we could not miss - no man anxious to stop more than one - until we came to the foot of the rise. There we struck a ditch and fence, along which grew a few bushes. This position was about two hundred yards from the enemy's works, which were situated on the crest of a small hill. We halted and reformed, while the fence was being torn down, preparatory to the final charge on the rebel breastworks. Brisk firing was kept up on both sides - they at the bushes, and we at anything that looked like a head above their works.

It was here that Captain John Ordner, of Company A, of my squadron, was killed, and Corporal Kimball Persons, of my Company L, was shot through the body at my side. After he was stricken, he turned to me and said: "Captain, here is my diary; send it to my sister, and tell her that I am not sorry that I enlisted." It was all he said, as he sank down and died. Noble boy. Peter Rourke, also of my Company, was struck down by a ball that hit his belt-plate. In an instant he was up again and said he was all right. Although severely bruised, he went in with the rest of us. Suddenly a cheer started along the line, announcing the renewal of the contest. Onward we pushed, with cheers and yells perfectly demoniacal, as we marched over into their works, which they fought desperately to hold. The tried veterans of Wade Hampton's gallant squadrons were not able to withstand the impetuous charge of the "Bloody Tenth New York."

The combat became hand to hand, and men were clubbed with the butts of carbines, and struck down within arm's length of each other. It was a hot place, and terrible fighting; but they finally gave way and such as could scampered to the rear in wild disorder. It was then "every man for himself," and the Tenth New York take the hindmost. We captured a number of the enemy in their works, and many others while we were chasing them a mile or so, until we came on other works with artillery. Then we halted, and lay down against the face of a slight hill till dark, and afterward fell back. We picketed that night, and next day started on our return march to the White house.

During the charge over the plowed field, Lieutenant Preston [author of *The History of the Tenth New York*] was struck down by a bullet, causing a very dangerous wound. The Surgeon, believing him to be mortally hurt, decided to leave him behind, telling him he could not survive a day's march, but the Lieutenant responded "I had rather die with the boys than live with the rebs." The striking manner in which our boys acquitted themselves was gracefully acknowledged by our brigade commander.

After the Regiment had reached the railroad in the charge at Trevillian, and was under a severe fire from the enemy in front and flank, our battery, away to the rear, with the intent of shelling the enemy over the heads of our men, were firing short and sending the shells into our lines. Major Avery called for a volunteer to go back and advise General Gregg or the commander of the battery to cease firing or to elevate their pieces. It was a perilous undertaking, but Sergeant Farnsworth immediately offered to go. A ridge swept by the Confederate fire intervened, but Farnsworth walked rapidly across the open space to the wood beyond, where he found and mounted his horse and hastened on his errand, and delivered his message to General Gregg. The commander of the battery was notified, and ceased firing. It required great courage to perform such an act - an exposure to the concentrated fire from the enemy's line with none to divide the chances - and the Sergeant was complimented by Major Avery for it, and not long afterward was promoted to a lieutenancy.

The Civil War Sites Advisory Commission (CWSAC) has this description of the battle at Trevillian Station in the following: [9]

To draw off the Confederate cavalry and open the door for a general movement to the James River, Maj. Gen. Philip Sheridan mounted a large-scale cavalry raid into Louisa County, threatening to cut the Virginia Central Railroad. On June 11, Sheridan with the Gregg's and Torbert's divisions attacked Hampton's and Fitzhugh Lee's cavalry divisions at Trevillian Station. Sheridan drove a wedge between the Confederate divisions, throwing them into confusion. On the

12th, fortunes were reversed. Hampton and Lee dismounted their troopers and drew a defensive line across the railroad and the road to Gordonsville. From this advantageous position, they beat back several determined dismounted assaults. Sheridan withdrew after destroying about six miles of the Virginia Central Railroad. Confederate victory at Trevillian prevented Sheridan from reaching Charlottesville and cooperating with Hunter's army in the Valley. This was one of the bloodiest cavalry battles of the war.

Return to White House

Preston records the return march to White House: [10]

General Sheridan commenced the return march on the night of the 12th of June. The Tenth was engaged in tearing up railroad track part of the night. Moving out it took its place in the column of march at 2 A.M. on the 13th, and, after crossing the North Anna, did some foraging. On one of these expeditions some of the members of the band had a skirmish, in which Burt Orser was captured and Thomas L. Townley barely escaped keeping him company. On the 15th the command passed through Spotsylvania Court-House, and over the scenes of the fierce struggles between the two armies the preceding month. The next day Sergeant Nelson Washburn, of Company L, was wounded while on a foraging expedition. Then on the 18th Sergeant Major Farnsworth, with eight men from the Regiment, went out to try and obtain forage, and was attacked by a superior force from the Fourth Virginia Cavalry, and lost five men, two of whom, Clarence Newmire and Orange Egbertson, were killed. Elias Evans, Julius Moak, and Silas Ostrander, were taken prisoners, the latter wounded and afterward recaptured.

Crossing the Mattapony at 7 A.M. on the 20th, the Regiment settled down at White House at four o'clock. All was quiet at the time. In the morning the Confederate cavalry had attacked the immense wagon-train of the army parked there, but had been driven off and kept at bay by the gunboats. [See

Figure 7.5 for an old photo of supply ships at White House Landing during the Civil War.]

**Figure 7.5 Supply Ships at White House
Landing, VA (Library of Congress)**

Moving across the Pamunkey at an early hour, the boys expected to have a brush with the enemy, but finally recrossed the river about 8 A.M.; then, two hours later, passed over the pellucid waters of the Pamunkey again, and succeeded in stirring up a little quarrel with the enemy, but nothing serious resulted. The Regiment was relieved from the skirmish line on the evening of the 22d, and retired to the bluffs, went into camp and drew rations. At two o'clock, again on the road.

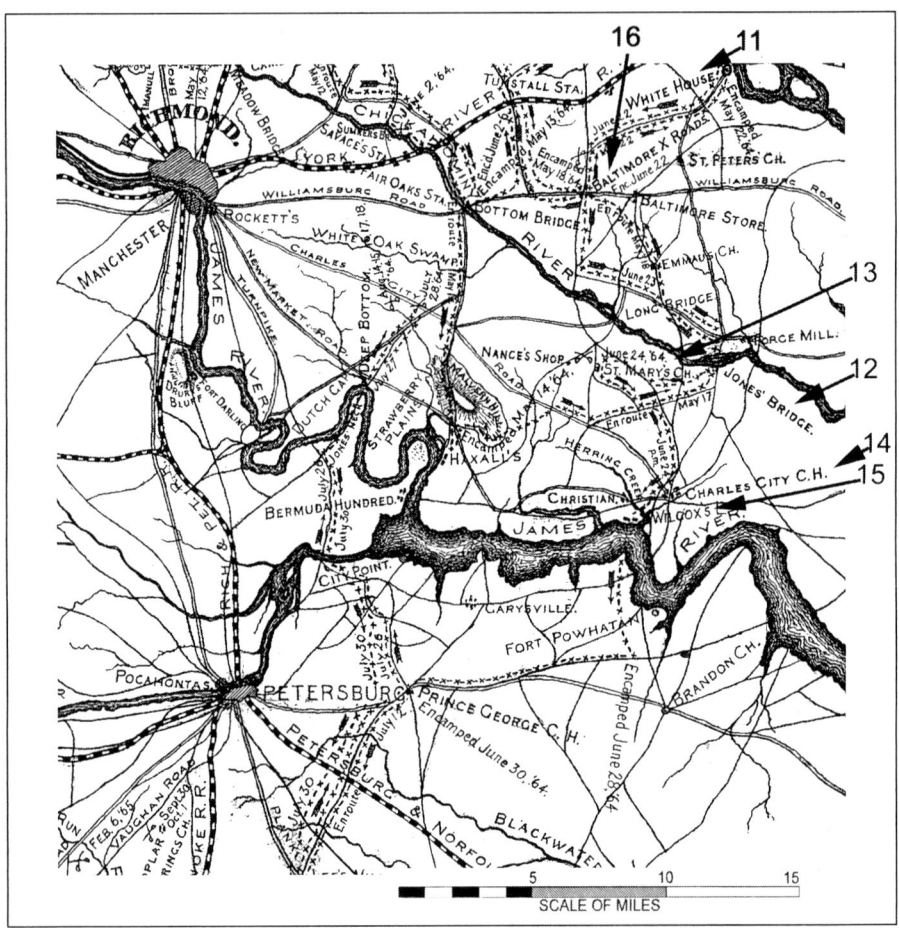

**Map 7.3 Events of the Tenth New York
in the last two weeks of June, 1864**

The Confederates were attacked and driven to Baltimore Cross-roads [#16 on Map 7.3]. They took the aggressive, however, on the morning of the 23d, which ended in slight skirmishing. The Regiment reached Jones Bridge [#12 on Map 7.3], on the Chickahominy, and crossed at 11 A.M. Here the trains passed over in safety, the sharp crack of the carbines on the right, meantime, denoting the presence of the Confederates in force in the woods there. The men were standing to horse when the evening shades came on. ...

Battle of St. Mary's Church

Preston continues describing the movements of the Tenth New York, including the battle at St. Mary's Church [#13 on Map 7.3]:

To the members of the Second Cavalry Division the 24th of June, 1864, will always stand out in bold relief. This was the day on which the battle of St. Mary's Church occurred. The enemy chivalrously allowed time for breakfast, and then the music began. By ten o'clock the skirmishing became quite general and continued until afternoon. About four o'clock the enemy attacked in force with both cavalry and infantry. The Second Division, which had advanced on the Richmond road, to protect the moving trains, bore the shock of the onset alone and unsupported, the First Division having moved on the direct road as escort to the trains. The contest was so unequal - the Confederates outnumbering Gregg three to one - that our line was broken, and in the confusion which followed in the woods and undergrowth, regiments became mixed up and all semblance of organization was lost. It was the first and only time the colors of the Second Division were lowered. But its action saved the trains, which were safely passing along while the engagement was in progress.

Captain George Vanderbilt [Justus Matteson's Company L Commander], provided the following account of the operations of the Regiment from the 20th to the 25th of June. These included the actions at White House Landing, Chickahominy, and St. Mary's Church:

Sheridan, with his First and Second Divisions of Cavalry, returned from the Trevillian raid, reaching White House Landing Monday, June 20, 1864, at 4:30 P.M., where he found some transports and the gunboat *Iola*. Some colored troops were across the

Pamunkey, fighting rebel cavalry, assisted by the gunboat. Tuesday, June 21st, our brigade crossed over at

3 A.M., dismounted, and lay formed on the sand till 10 A.M., then returned across the river. Here we had breakfast, mounted, crossed over again and took a hand in the free fight, and fought till darkness put a stop to it, our Regiment supporting J.I. Gregg's Second Brigade on the extreme right of the line. My squadron, Companies A and L, supported a battery. Stood to horse all night. Wednesday, June 22d, was a dark and cloudy day. We were relieved from the Second Brigade and reported back to our First Brigade, General H.E. Davies, on the left of the line, at 6 A.M. At 2 P.M. moved out to Baltimore Crossroads three miles and camped. The Fourth, Fifth, and Sixth Squadrons, under Major Weed, were ordered on picket half a mile out on the Bottom's Bridge road; they had a very unpleasant time, as there was continuous firing along the line. Thursday, June 23d, was clear and bright. In the early morning five men of Company K, who had been captured during the night, within twenty rods of Captain Snyder's picket reserve, came in, stripped of everything.

We moved out at 8 A.M. to Jones Bridge over the Chickahominy River [#12 on Map 7.3], and saw there an immense wagon-train and realized that we were expected to guard it safely to the James River. Our brigade Band was drawn up beside the pontoon bridge and played inspiring airs as we crossed the famous river. We no sooner reached the opposite side than our brigade with the First Division and some colored troops got into a big fight. We, however, forced the rebs back some distance; by evening all became quiet and we went into camp and unsaddled. It was extremely hot, day and night. We had our frugal supper prepared and just commenced to eat it, when a volley on the line caused a big scramble. "Saddle up and stand to horse," and so we lost our much-needed meal.

Some of the boys were guilty of saying disagreeable things about the Johnnies, for which I did not chide them.

Friday, June 24th, opened clear, hot, and dusty. It was to witness the most desperate fighting ever done by Gregg's gallant Second Division; the First Division and Sheridan himself had gone forward to the James River. We moved out about three miles to St. Mary's Church, halted about noon, dismounted, and ordered to get dinner; had just commenced preparations when the familiar "Boots and Saddles" was blown.

We marched forward say a half-mile, dismounted and formed line of battle; the Second Brigade was already fighting. Our Regiment was posted along the edge of a piece of woods and partly in it. I with my squadron, Company A, commanded by Lieutenant Perry, and my company, L was on the left of the Regiment across an old wood-road leading through the strip of wood say three hundred yards wide, the rebs in plain view beyond the wood. They commenced to advance in earnest about 3 P.M., when Major Avery ordered me to take my squadron to support Captain Porter, who, with his squadron, Companies C and G (Company C commanded by Lieutenant Hinckley), on the right, was being hard pressed by greatly superior numbers. When I arrived he had been forced back out of the woods to the edge of the field, where he had hastily thrown up slight works of fence-rails, etc., about two feet high. I soon found this position untenable, and fell back in good order about four o'clock to a new position about one hundred and fifty yards to the rear behind a fence and ditch; the fence was placed on top of the earth thrown from the ditch, which formed a good breastwork.

The rebs kept up a heavy fire from the woods for a few minutes, then out came a cloud of skirmishers, followed by a heavy line of battle; the skirmishers were soon absorbed by the main line; then with their peculiar yell they charged. We held our fire until they were within fifty feet, then gave them such a terrific fire with carbines and revolvers they could not stand it; they broke and fled pell-mell for the cover of the woods, our men dropping many of them on the way. They opened fire from the woods again in short order, the shells from our battery in our rear bursting in among them. It was a hot spot for us, the shells from both our own and the reb battery screaming over our heads, and the bullets striking the fence-rails and now and again a man.

After some little time they came out of the woods and charged again right up to the fence; but the withering fire our boys gave them compelled them to break for the rear again, notwithstanding the frantic efforts of their officers, who upbraided them with curses. It was of no avail; they kept on to the cover of the woods again. There must have been more dead and helplessly wounded lying on the ground in our front than there were in our whole battalion. Their charging line I calculated was at least fifteen hundred men. A continuous fire was kept up, they at our heads and we at the smoke in the edge of the woods. "Fire low!" was the order constantly given to our men. We were getting short of ammunition, so I sent back for more. None coming, it looked as if we could not hold our position much longer; in fact, it did not seem possible that any one could get up to us from the rear, as they would have to come over an open field a quarter of a mile down a slight incline, in full view of the enemy's lines.

Sergeant L. P. Norton, of my Company L, came to me for more ammunition for his part of the line. I stated the case to him that I did not think any one could get to us alive. He said, "Captain, I know it's risky, but I'll chance it." He soon returned with a supply and distributed it along the line safely. He had a narrow escape; a bullet spoiled his hat (he has the same hat yet), one went through his coat-sleeve and coat between his side and arm; three or four other bullet holes through his clothing, and one through his canteen. The rebels tried their best to kill him, for they could see him with the box, and knew just what he was bringing up. Sergeant Harlan P. Thompson, of Company A, whom I had posted on my extreme left in an important and exposed position, being just at this time shot down severely wounded, I immediately rewarded Sergeant Norton for his gallantry by posting him in Sergeant Thompson's place. By the conformation of the ground it was necessary for a man to stand up behind a gate-post on the left, in order to see the rest of the regimental line. About six o'clock Sergeant Norton reported the Regiment falling back, exposing my left, and I noticed the Regiment on my right falling back closely pursued. At the same time the rebels were advancing with three lines to the charge again. We gave them a volley, as they reached the fence, right in their faces. I then ordered my men to get back as fast as they could, and I set the example (I will state that no one passed me the first three hundred yards or so to the top of the rise, where we came to another strip of wood and a log-house). Colonel Huey, Eighth Pennsylvania, was posted there with a few men behind some rails and logs. He ordered me to halt my men and form with him, saying, "we could hold the enemy." I called his attention to a column passing his right. He said they were our men. I told him they were rebs, and that he was flanked on his left, too. I took my men back. It was the last I saw of Colonel Huey. He and his men were captured in less than five minutes. The country was partly wooded and partly open. The rebs ran their battery right on their skirmish-line. As Lieutenant Perry, commanding

Company A, and I were hurrying along together, still on foot (our led horses had been sent back out of sight)

a cannon-ball took off a man's head a few feet ahead of us. He jumped up about four feet and fell near us. I said to Lieutenant Perry, "Walt, go through his pockets." He replied, "I ain't got time." Some distance farther on we came to a line the staff-officers had formed. We passed through this, say half a mile or so, then formed another line. Soon the line we had passed came running through us; and so the retreat was kept up, running and fighting, till after dark, a distance of about six miles, when the Johnnies stopped chasing us. Our men were completely exhausted and lay down on the ground near the Charles City Court House as fast as they came in. Some died from heat and over-exertion during the night.

I myself was doctored nearly all night. We realized for the first time how it felt to get a good sound thrashing and then be chased for our lives, somewhat as we had served the rebs at Trevillian Station two weeks before. The division lost heavily in killed and wounded, among the number Colonel J. Irvin Gregg, commanding Second Brigade, wounded; Colonel Covode, Fourth Pennsylvania, killed; Captain Phillips, division staff, leg shot off (died); Colonel Huey, Eighth Pennsylvania, taken prisoner. In our regiment, Captain Page, Company M, killed; Captain Porter, Company G, captured; Hospital Steward John E. Cowles, wounded in hand; Sergeant Harlan P. Thompson, Company A, severely wounded; Corporal C.H. Horner, Company L, severely wounded and prisoner (died); Private James M. Bacon, Company L, wounded by grape-shot. Sheridan with the First Division came up during the night. The next morning we marched unmolested to Wilcox's Landing, on the James River [#15 on Map 7.3]. Captain B. B. Porter, of Company G, who commanded the First Squadron in the fight and was captured in the final charge, is with me while I am writing this, and says that the rebel officers told him that Sheridan had sent orders to Gregg to fall back at one o'clock, before the fight commenced, but that they had captured the bearer, thus finding out that Gregg was alone with his two brigades. The request forwarded by General Gregg to General Sheridan for orders was also captured, so they, having eight brigades, told Captain Porter they intended to capture General Gregg and his whole command. Instead of capturing us, they only succeeded in forcing us back after a terrific battle lasting about five hours and only captured eleven officers and one hundred and seven men besides our severely wounded. Their wounded, Captain Porter informs me, was greater in number than the whole of our two brigades opposed to them. He says one of our shells struck down eight men near him, killing four of them instantly.

Preston says that the trains were crossed to the south side of the James River during the 26th and 27th of June, 1864. The Tenth New York, as part of the Second Cavalry Division, crossed on the 28th; and the cavalry was thus reunited to the Army of the Potomac.

Letters were few and far between in the busy months of May and June, 1864. Justus was apparently on his horse more that he was in his tent. Anyway, Mary writes to him about this time, to bring him up to date on what she has been doing at home.

June 26th 1864
Homer, Cortland Co. N.Y.

Remembered friend

Do not think that you are forgotten because I have not answered your letter before. I had just writen to you as I received yours and thought that I would wait a few days. but the few days number many. I was glad to hear that you were well. but of the nine days fight that you wrote about in your last I try to immagine that I were there. I try to see all of the suffering that the soldiers see and suffer, but Jut I do not know anything about it. we read and hear but it is as a story. we do not realize one half of it.

I have not heard from Solon since I wrote to you that I had been home. I dare say that they are making all preparations for the fourth. there is not a very large company, only the younger class. Pa Walker has gone down east to stay with her Aunt through the summer. they expect Isac home this fall if he can get a furlough. Why do not you come home this fall if you can? I wish that you would. They expec Ed Graves home this fall. he is learning the carpenters trade. I heard they were agoing to get their new house done before he came for they expected that he would fetch his lady or wife home with him. I do not know what Patience will do if he does. Jut I read a peice in the paper telling the girls what to write to the soldier boys. it says tell them all that is going on at home, all about the parties and who the boys and girls go with. I think that I do my share of that. I do not know as there is agoing to be any doings here the fourth or not, but there is agoing to be a ride to Glen Haven the 30 of this month which will be next thirsday. it is the division of the sons of temperance. they are most of the division going up. expect to have a nice time. I think that I shall go but have not made up my mind yet so but that it may be changed again before that time. if I do go I will write you more about it. wish that you were here to go. think that you could enjoy it if you were with strangers? I think that we have very good company in Homer. I like it here very much. We are having very warm wether and no rain. every thing is drying up.

I have had some very nice strawberries. do you get any down south or are they all gone before this? I have not been to church to day. it is to warm to go to church. The Academy closed last Thirsday. I did not go to the exebition but have heard that they had a very good one. Mr. Clark the prinsipul leaves. he has been here a long time. they think it is best to try a new one but Mr. Clark was liked by most of the students, but they think that the school has been runing down for a number of years. the Cortland school closes next week. I would like to go down but we are very busy in the shop now and shall be untill after the fourth.

Jut I must ask you once more to forgive me for not answering your letter before for I am very penatant, and do sertanly promise to do so no more if you forgive this time. I wish that I could step in your tent to day or where you are for I do not know as you have tents when you are moving. so often I think that I could say more than I can write. I shall expect to hear from you soon and remember that I remain your friend and wellwisher.

Mary H.

P.S. Have you seen Clifton Wiles lately? I have not heard from him in a long time. thought perhaps that he was sick.

Wine Oak Landing, Va
June 27th, 1864

Dear Friend Mary,

As I have an oportunity now to write I will improve it by penning a few lines to you.

Mary I suppose that you think by this time that I have entirely forgotten you. far from it. there is not a single day passes but my mind wanders back to thee, to the seens of our childhood, and to other times later in life that I have spent in your society. Oh if I could but live those days over again I would be content.

I recieved your letter on the 30th of May and was very glad to hear that you wer well and enjoying yourself. I have had no chance to write but once untill now and then it was only for five or ten minutes and I droped a line to my folks. We have just returned from a raid of over two weeks. I have been in three hard Cav fights since I wrote last, and under shelling five or six times besides. Our Co. has had sixteen killed wounded and missing this season. 4 killed 10 wounded and 2 missing. I have not been touched yet and am well and enjoy myself as well as can be expected in these times & plase. We are now eight or ten miles below Harisons landing on the James R. Our trains are a crossing the river on transports. they will be across in a day or two and then our Cav will cross. nearly all of our forces are on the south side of the river now but the Cav Corps and we will be there soon. then I expect that we will see some more hard times.

Gen. Grant is drawing nigh unto Richmond. there will be some hard fighting there before many days pass by.

It has been vary hot here for two weeks. no rain in that time untill yesterday & to day. it sprinkled yesterday & has just rained a little to day, but not half enough to lay the dust. there is scarcley a day passes but some one of the regt is sun stroke. I came near it several times.

Mary, I would like to be there and spend the fourth of july with you. When peace is declared here again there will be another day for us to hail with joy, in after years, in rememberance of the time when traitors laid down their arms to men who wer more true to their Country.

Mati, please excuse all mistakes and I will try and do better in the future. write soon and you will oblige one who will not forget thee. I remain Your Friend,

284

Justus G. Matteson

P. S. Direct-   *J. G. Matteson*
Co. L, 10th N. Y. *Vol. Cav.*
Washington, D. C.

Figure 7.6 Around the campfire (sketch from Preston book)

References

[1] National Park Service, Civil War Sites Advisory Commission (CWSAC), http://www.cr.nps.gov/hps/abpp/battles/va057.htm, Battle of Totopotomy Creek, May 27, 1864.

[2] Preston, Noble D., *History of the Tenth Regiment New York Volunteer Cavalry*, New York, NY: D. Appleton and Company, 1892; reprinted by Higginson Book Company, Salem, MA in 1998; pp. 188-193.

[3] National Park Service, Civil War Sites Advisory Commission (CWSAC), http://www.cr.nps.gov/hps/abpp/battles/va058.htm, Battle of Haw's Shop, May 28, 1864.

[4] Campaigns of the Civil War, vol. xii, p. 164.

[5] Preston, *History of the Tenth New York*, pp.193-194.

[6] Campaigns of the Civil War, vol. xii, p. 173.

[7] National Park Service, Civil War Sites Advisory Commission (CWSAC), http://www.cr.nps.gov/hps/abpp/battles/va062.htm, Battle of Cold Harbor, May 31, 1864.

[8] Preston, *History of the Tenth New York*, pp.194-204.

[9] National Park Service, Civil War Sites Advisory Commission (CWSAC), http://www.cr.nps.gov/hps/abpp/battles/va099.htm, Battle of Trevillian Station, June 11-12, 1864.

[10] Preston, *History of the Tenth New York*, pp. 211-215.

CHAPTER 8
Before Petersburg July-December 1864

*"Look forth from behind the cloud that is now
before us to the future." Justus G. Matteson*

The events and places discussed in this chapter are listed in Table 8.1, all occurring in Virginia. Maps 8.1, 8.2, and 8.3 have callouts on them showing the location of places, using the numbers shown in the first column of the table.

Much Activity

This chapter summarizes the activity of the Tenth New York in the last half of 1864. Grant would not turn back. Regardless of what the Confederate Army would do, he would not back up. He was stopped before Richmond, so he went around it and went south of Petersburg and put a siege on that city. If he could capture Petersburg, he could cut off all supplies to Richmond and Richmond would have to surrender. This meant lots of work for the Cavalry - shielding the Union Army from Lee, picketing, skirmishing, fighting off the Confederate Cavalry, tearing up railroads, capturing supplies, guarding/destroying bridges, etc.

Looking at Table 8.1, it is seen that the Tenth New York was constantly on the move in the last half of 1864. They started the action by hitting the railroads south of Petersburg with Reams Station as one of the key destinations. Reams Station was on the Petersburg and Roanoke Railroad, commonly called "The Weldon". This was a key railroad for the Confederacy, bringing supplies into Petersburg and on up to Richmond. Lee's Cavalry desperately tried to keep it running, and this effort resulted in several cavalry and infantry battles in the area.

Map #	Location	Dates
	Before Petersburg	**June 26-Dec. 10, 1864**
16	Reams Station	June 30, 1864
	Light House Point	July 1
1	Gaines' Mill	July 2
11	Prince George Court House	July 10, 16
12	Lee's Mills	July 12, 30
7	Point of Rocks, City Point	July 26, …
4	Jones Neck, Deep Bottom	July 27-28
3	Charles City Rd.	July 28
6	Malvern Hill	July 30
8	Fort Powhatan	
9	Brandon Church	
	Demonstration north of James R.	**Aug. 13-20**
	Gravel Hill	Aug. 14
5	Strawberry Plains	Aug. 14-18
13	"Weldon" Railroad (Petersburg and Roanoke Railroad)	Aug. 19-21
16	Reams Station	Aug. 23, 26
	Arthur's Swamp	Aug. 29-30
2	Yellow Tavern	Sep. 2
15	Five Forks	
14	Poplar Spring Church/Vaughn Road	Sep. 29-Oct. 1
15	Five Forks	
21	Boydton Plank Road	Oct. 27-28
10	Blackwater Creek	Nov. 18
17	Stony Creek Station	Dec. 1
20	**Hicksford Raid**	**Dec. 6-12**
19	Three Creeks/ Bellefield	Dec. 9
18	Jarrett's Station	Dec. 10

Table 8.1 Major events in July-December, 1864

Preston describes the action of the Tenth New York at the end of June and into July [1]:

Skirmish at Lee's Mills

After crossing the James River, the Tenth went into camp near Fort Powhatan [#8 on Map 8.2], on the afternoon of June 28th, and later was sent to picket the country below Brandon Church. But the stay there was of short duration, the Second Cavalry Division moving down the Petersburg road next day and night, encamping at daylight on the 30th at Prince George Court-House [#11 on Map 8.2]. …

A skirmish of several hours' duration occurred at Lee's Mills [#12 on Map 8.2], on the 12th [of July], with no serious results. …

"Boots and Saddles" at 1:30 P.M. on the 26th [of July], brought the Regiment out, and after standing to horse until six o'clock, the command started out [moving north] on the City Point road [City Point is #7 on Map 8.2]. Crossing the Appomattox at Point of Rocks [near City Point], it moved to Jones Neck [#4 on Map 8.1], where it arrived, with the rest of the brigade, at daybreak on the 27th, and, crossing the James River at noon, went into bivouac.

Battle on the Charles City Road

Moving out at 9 A.M. the next morning [July 28, 1864], the Tenth came upon the enemy on the Charles City road [#3 on Map 8.1] at ten o'clock, and commenced skirmishing. The enemy presented a strong front, with infantry and cavalry. The fight soon became active and determined, and the brigade was compelled to abandon its position, losing one gun. Captain Blynn, with one squadron, was cut off, but rejoined the Regiment in safety after dark. The Second Corps [infantry] came up, and the cavalry moved back to the place occupied the night before and encamped.

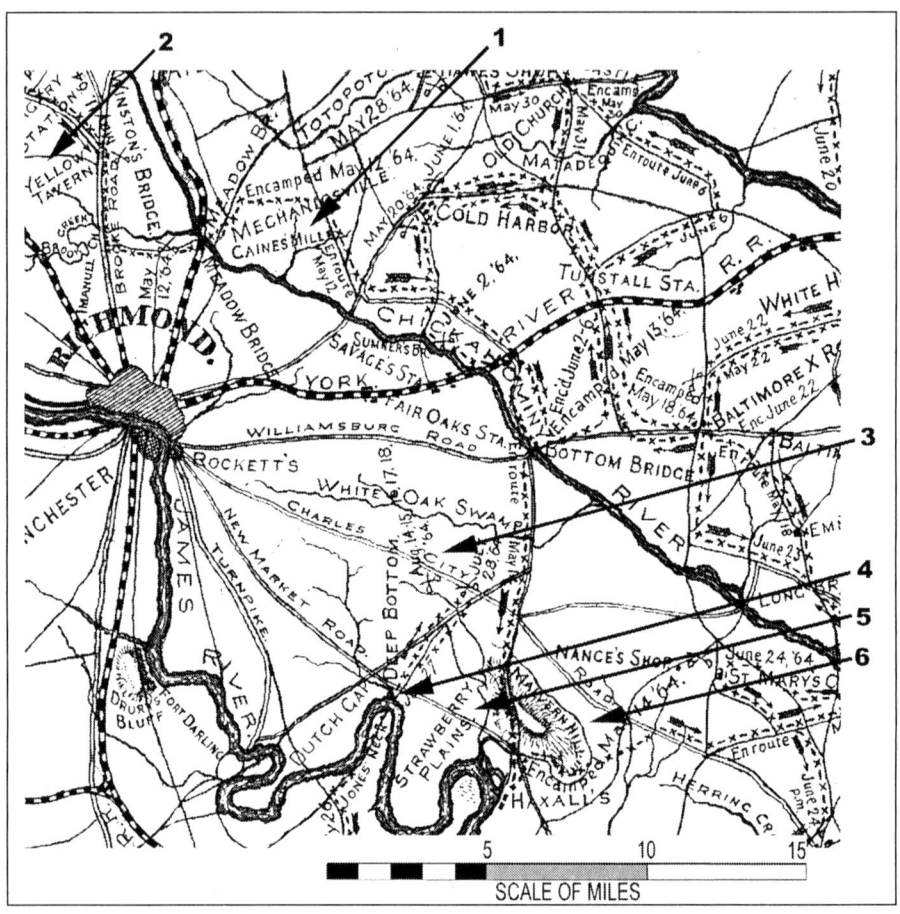

Map 8.1 Area of activity southeast of Richmond, July 1864

A lot of other Union forces were engaged at the same time, and close by. The CWSAC describes more of the global context in the following description, referred to as the First Battle of Deep Bottom, or Deep Bottom I. It was also referred to by other names, such as Darbytown, Strawberry Plains, New Market Road, Gravel Hill; and the battle described above, "Charles City Road" [2]:

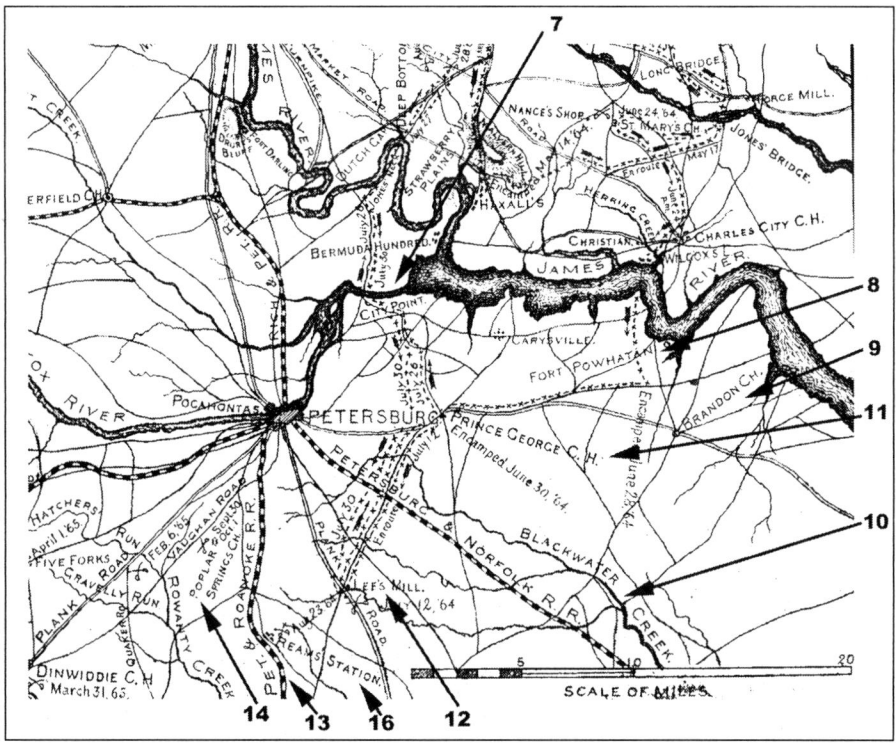

Map 8.2 Area of activity east of Petersburg, 1864

During the night of July 26-27, the Union II Corps and two
divisions of Sheridan's cavalry under command of Maj. Gen.
Winfield Scott Hancock crossed to the north side of the James
River to threaten Richmond. This demonstration diverted
Confederate forces from the impending attack at Petersburg on
July 30. Union efforts to turn the Confederate position at New
Market Heights and Fussell's Mill were abandoned
when the Confederates strongly reinforced their lines and
counterattacked. During the night of July 29, the Federals
recrossed the river leaving a garrison as heretofore to hold the
bridgehead at Deep Bottom.

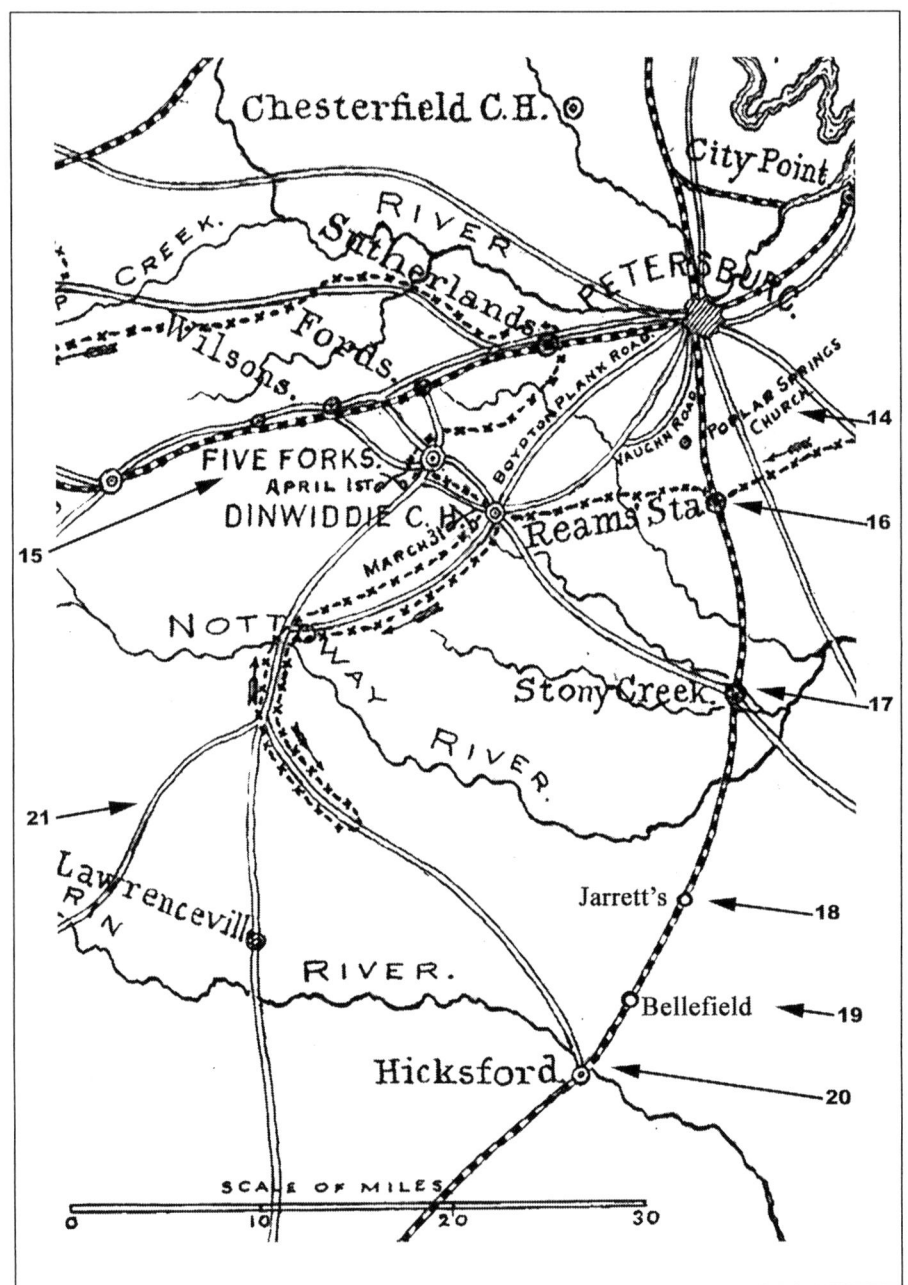

**Map 8.3 Area of activity southwest of Petersburg,
October-December, 1864**

More Fighting at Lee's Mills

Continuing Preston's discussion of the July fighting [3]:

> On the morning of July 29th, the Tenth dismounted and
> prepared to fight on foot [along the Charles City Road]; then,
> moving to the right of the line, took its place as support to the
> battery where it remained a short time. At noon the Second and
> Tenth Corps [infantry] came into position on the left of the
> Second Cavalry Division. The Tenth threw up some light
> breast-works, behind which it remained until midnight, when it
> recrossed the James again, with the Second Cavalry Division,
> moving quite rapidly toward the Appomattox. At sunrise on the
> 30th the command crossed [the Appomattox] at Point of Rocks
> [#7 on Map 8.2], and, marching past General Meade's
> headquarters, arrived at Lee's Mills [#12 on Map 8.2], on the
> Blackwater [#10 on Map 8.2], at 3 P.M., the Tenth in advance.
> Lieutenant Hinckley, of Company C, attacked the enemy at the
> bridge, and in a few moments the entire Regiment was
> engaged. The First Massachusetts Cavalry got on the enemy's
> flank, while the Second Pennsylvania, Sixth Ohio, and Tenth
> charged dismounted, capturing the bridge and taking some
> prisoners. After repairing the bridge the First New Jersey
> charged across, mounted, and took more prisoners.

On Map 8.2, Lee's Mills is not shown as being on Blackwater Creek.
If the map is correct, this fight took place at either Lee's mills, or
Blackwater Creek. Note that the Tenth New York repeatedly crosses the
Appomattox at Point of Rocks, and the James at Jones Neck. They are
major rivers, and must be traversed to go north and south between
Richmond and Petersburg. Rivers, creeks and runs with their bridges
and fords played a major role in the movement of troops and supplies in
the Civil War. The weather, of course, also played a major role. With
rain the larger rivers became impassable. The destruction and rebuilding
of bridges was a major activity of both sides in the war.

About this time Justus receives a letter from Mary:

August 7th, 1864
Homer, Cortland County

Remembered Friend,

I received your kind letter last week and improve the earliest opportunity to reply. it is a plesant _____ day. all is quiet in this vill. what a difference in the place of the _____ the one winter to where all is noise and strife on the saboth day. I have been well since I wrote you last and I must tell you that we have had some rain last week. two or three days it rained most of the time and I do not think that we ever needed rain more than now. but the roads soon dried up and now looks as though it had not rained but it must have done some good. it helped the wells and cisterns fill up _____. It has been quite healthy here until _____ two or three weeks past there has been quite a number of deaths. last friday I saw three children burried in one grave aged 14, 12, 6. they died with diptheria. there are quite a number sick now in town. I sit up last night with a sick lady and chils. therefore have not been to church and feel rather duller than is natural.

I suppose that you have heard before this that they have drafted in this County to fill up the militia. it took most every one in our place under 30 and over 18. I have seen a list of the names and I did not see James Atwood or George Gardners but I heard that every one were drafted but I did not see their names. there were a large number taken from this place but why is it that every one of the (big boys) are found to be ailing- some deaf, others blind just _____ ___ ___ from the draft. I don't understand it - a poor boy must go if he can stand up. I do think that it is wrong. I have not any idea what they are going to do with these men. I guess that they do not know; some think that they are to remain here, others that they will be sent South; but they will find out soon enough.

I have not been to Solon since April but heard from there last week. heard that Johns oldest boy was very sick with the Diptheria but have not heard from there since. Well Jut, I left this, have been up to the cemetry, also to evening meeting. wish that you were here to go. you speak about getting discharged this fall. I am afraid that is only talk.

I do not believe that they will discharge men when they need them so much but I wish that they would do so. The piece of flag that you sent me looks as though it had

294

seen hard times. Jut it is late. I must close _____ this miserable writing for remember that I was up last night.

I remain your best friend
(Mary Hatch)

P.S. I shall be happy to hear from you as often as convenient.

More Skirmishing along the Charles City Road

Preston tells about some of the engagements occurring in August [4]:

> Kautz's cavalry relieved the Tenth on picket on the 12th [August 1864], and next day, at 4 P.M., the Regiment moved out with the brigade to the Appomattox River again, and crossing [going north] at Point of Rocks [#7 on Map 8.2], at 9 P.M., halted for a brief time at Jones Neck [#4 on Map 8.2]. Then crossing the James River before daylight on the 14th, the Regiment advanced on the Charles City road to nearly the same position it had occupied on the 28th of the previous month. The skirmishing became very brisk by 10 A.M., the Second and Tenth Corps coming up on the left of the cavalry. The Regiment was sent on picket at night. …

The CWSAC also describes this fighting along the Charles City Road, referring to it as "Deep Bottom II". It also had other names at various times, such as New Market Road, Fussell's Mill, Bailey's Creek, Charles City Road, and White's Tavern [5]:

> During the night of August 13-14, the Union II Corps, X Corps, and Gregg's cavalry division, all under command of Maj. Gen. Winfield Scott Hancock, crossed James River at Deep Bottom [#4 on Map 8.1] to threaten Richmond, coordinating with a movement against the Weldon Railroad at Petersburg. On August 14, the X Corps closed on New Market Heights while the II Corps extended the Federal line to the right along Bailey's Creek. During the night, the X Corps was moved to the far right flank of the Union line near Fussell's Mill. On August 16, Union assaults near Fussell's Mill were initially successful, but Confederate counterattacks drove the Federals out of a line of captured works. Heavy fighting continued throughout the remainder of the day. …
>
> After continual skirmishing, the Federals returned to the south side of the James on the 20th, maintaining their bridgehead at Deep Bottom.

Preston's description continues:

> Skirmishing commenced promptly with the advent of daylight on the 15th, and increased with the hours. It proved to be a bang-up day for the fighting business. After a time the Regiment was withdrawn to the right and rear of the infantry and a squadron was sent on a reconnaissance. Captain Vanderbilt was detailed, with his squadron, for duty with General Birney, commanding the Tenth Corps. While piloting some of the colored troops through the woods, they fired into troops from the Second Corps, mistaking them for the enemy; the Second Corps men in turn charged the colored boys. Many were killed and wounded on both sides, before the error was discovered. Again the fighting was on with the rising of the sun on the 16th. The Tenth supported a battery in the forenoon, and in the afternoon moved to the left to assist the Second Brigade, which had been heavily engaged, and whose commander, Colonel Gregg, had been wounded during the day.

Preston records an entry from Captain Vanderbilt's diary for August 18 [6]:

> "Showery in morning and heavy rain at noon. Sent to support detachment of Sixth Ohio in the woods. Quiet until 5 P.M., when the rebs signaled our boys with a handkerchief from their battery in the road, on a hill, to look out, which was immediately followed by solid shot and shrapnel. Captain Blynn had just vacated a position behind a pine-tree when a solid shot penetrated it about waist-high. After about half an hour's shelling, the enemy advanced in force through the woods to scare us away. The boys remained behind the rails and light breast-works perfectly cool, while the officers ordered them to hold their fire until the command was given. When the enemy had got near enough the order to "fire!" was given, and such a banging, screeching, yelling, hurrahing, and general hub-bub I never heard; all joined in the familiar chorus of "Give 'em 'ell!" After they got back and found they were not all dead, they came up on a run and cheer again, and we let

them get up a little nearer than before, and then we repeated the same tactics. They appeared to have forgotten something and went back for it in a hurry! They didn't come up again. We were reenforced by the Sixth Ohio, and at dark the Fourth Pennsylvania relieved our Regiment."

Action on the Weldon Railroad and Reams Station

The Weldon Railroad (officially known as the Petersburg and Roanoke Railroad, #13 on Map 8.2) was a key link from the south in the supply of food, supplies, military equipment, etc. to the Confederate facilities in Petersburg and Richmond. The Union made repeated efforts to break this link and keep it broken, and the Confederates tried to keep it open. Toward the end of the War, the line was kept broken, and the Confederates brought supplies the last few miles by wagon train. Preston describes several actions taking place in this area [7].

At 3 A.M. next day [August 21, 1864] the Regiment advanced on the Weldon Railroad toward Reams Station [#16 on Map 8.3], where it arrived with the rest of the Second Division.

The enemy striking our infantry on the left, the brigade, except one battalion of the Tenth, was dismounted and drove the Confederates back. At 2 P.M. the Tenth was ordered to report to Colonel Spear, commanding a brigade in Kautz's cavalry division, and moved with that brigade to Reams Station and burned tanks and other railroad property, after which it returned to its proper command. ...

Then at noon on the 23d of August moved out to Reams Station late in the afternoon, where the cavalry had been attacked. Under direction of Assistant Adjutant-General Weir, Captain Vanderbilt dismounted the Regiment and charged the Confederates in the woods, driving them out and from a strong position on a hill. Captain Vanderbilt led the charge, which called forth compliments from the division commander. ...

In the afternoon the Regiment moved out and commenced skirmishing. Companies H and L charged the Confederate line, but failed to dislodge them.

The CWSAC summarizes some of the action around Reams Station during this time frame, referring to it as "Reams Station II" [8]:

> On August 24, Union II Corps moved south along the Weldon Railroad, tearing up track, preceded by Gregg's cavalry division. On August 25, Maj. Gen. Henry Heth attacked and overran the faulty Union position at Reams Station, capturing 9 guns, 12 colors, and many prisoners. The old II Corps was shattered. Maj. Gen. Winfield Scott Hancock withdrew to the main Union line near the Jerusalem Plank Road, bemoaning the declining combat effectiveness of his troops.

The Battle of Poplar Springs Church/Vaughn Road

In Preston's book he refers to the arrival of the "newly elected" sutler at the encampment on September 15, 1864, bringing along a large selection of goods. The sutler was a civilian who visited Army groups to supply the soldiers with goods that were not standard Army issue. He was the Civil War version of the current Army Post Exchange. Figure 8.1 shows a "sutler" at a recent Civil War reenactment.

Justus writes to Mary about this time:

In Camp Aug 30th 1864

Dear Friend,

I recieved your letter in due time and was vary happy to hear from you. when I recieved your letter I had no paper, and we have been on the move every since untill to day. we have scarcley had the sadles off of our horses in three weeks. we have had two or three fights since I wrote last, have'nt had any hurt in our Co allthough the reg't has lost an number. in the last engagement we charged the enemy, just dark in the woods. they got a cross fire on us, so we had to get up and git. that was at reams station on the weldon R.R. I think that we have got a pretty strong futting on that road.

It has been quite rainy here of late, so much so that our trains could not hardly move, but the roads are getting in prety good condition now.

I have seen a list of the drafted in Cortland Co- I know a great many of them, have heard of some that has got clear[1]. those to that I think were more able to come than many that has to come. Sister writes that Bill Attwood could not get clear. she thinks that his folks will have to go to the County House. I think it is to bad. It is said that Hathaway cleared all of the coperheads[2] by having a coperhead doctor to examine them. I wish he (Hathaway) was oblige to be here.

Sister writes me bad news from your folks, of the deaths of Johns children. It does seem strange that there can be no remady found for that dreadfull disease[3]. I expect to hear that sister has got it every day. I do not know what I should do if she should be taken away. it would seem as though I were left alone in this world. I hear that Ken Attkins is married again, to Pa. Walker.

I have but six days more to serve to make me two years. we have strong belief that we will get out of the service this fall[4]. we shall if justice is done us.

Mary, I am looking forward to a future day when I shall not have to be scribling in this way to when this writing can be stopped, and a more natural way taken up to get at each others ideas. I therefore will close hoping to hear from you as often as convenient.

I remain as ever Your Friend

J. G. Matteson

Co. L, 10th N. Y. Vol. Cav
Washington, DC

1. "Clear" appears to be the process by which a draftee can buy an exemption by paying a sum of money, apparently about $1,000.

2. "Copperhead" was a term used to refer to the northern Peace Democrats political faction.

3. Diphtheria.

4. Justus was not to get out until July 19, 1865.

**Figure 8.1 "Sutler" at Civil War reenactment
in Ontario Center, NY (July, 2006)**

Preston continues with more of his description of the action around
Reams Station and the Weldon [9]:

> Rations were issued to the Tenth on the evening of the 28th
> [of September], and every preparation made for a move. At
> 2 A.M. of the 29th the Second Division marched up the
> Vaughn road [#14 on Map 8.2], halting at 3 A.M. near the
> Perkins house. When near Ream's Station, the Tenth was
> drawn up dismounted, on the left of the Weldon Railroad, and
> advanced about a mile, skirmishing, and then threw up light
> breast-works and made slashings in front. This was about
> 1 P.M. At 5 P.M. the line was advanced, driving the enemy.
> The Second Brigade, on the left of the line, had a sharp
> engagement. At ten o'clock the Regiment fell back to near the
> Wyatt house, where the horses had been left, and bivouacked.
> Captain Vanderbilt was taken very sick, and turned over the
> command of the Regiment to Captain Snyder.

A little skirmishing occurred on the 30th, in which the Tenth as usual bore its share, driving the enemy some distance, and at 11 P.M. bivouacked in the breastworks.

Saturday, October 1st, the Tenth moved to the right and made connection with the infantry, then back to near the Davis house and formed in line. At ten o'clock the order to "prepare to fight on foot" came, and the Regiment advanced skirmishing, and drove the enemy some distance. From this till four o'clock the fight continued, with varying fortune. The attack of the enemy was at first repulsed and they were driven back to their works, in charging which our line was repulsed; then, massing on the right of the Regiment, they charged in heavy force, and compelled a retirement after a hot contest. Following up their success, they charged the line again, driving it from its first position, but were repulsed in the attempt to carry the second. **The men never displayed better fighting qualities than here.** Taking the offensive, the Tenth charged and regained the first line, but afterward voluntarily relinquished it, and took position behind the second line, where they were charged in front and flank by superior numbers, but by stubborn fighting the enemy were again repulsed. A hard rain prevailed during the entire day, and the men were wet, cold, and hungry when they went into bivouac about ten o'clock. In this fight, known as Poplar Springs Church, or Vaughn road, the Regiment lost quite heavily in killed, wounded, and missing. Sergeant Bela Burzette, of Company B, who was acting as sergeant-major at the time, was instantly killed. Captain Snyder, Lieutenant Van Tuyl, and Sergeant N.A. Reynolds were wounded.

Of this engagement, Captain (afterward Major) James M. Reynolds writes:

> The battle of Vaughn's Road, fought September 30 and October 1, 1864, by the First Brigade of Gregg's division, seems to be my pet fight; but in recalling it many others come "front into line," demanding equal recognition.

On September 30th our brigade received orders to proceed to the Jerusalem plank-road and join our troops, which were to advance and form the left of our army at that point. On nearing the locality late in the day we were satisfied from the sound of battle on our right that the army had failed to advance as anticipated. General Davies took position on the border of a belt of timber, flanking the road at right angles, ordering the brigade to throw up a line of works (work we had tired of from lack of use). Just before dusk the General detailed the Tenth New York and a squadron of the Sixth Ohio to accompany him to the plank-road, about two miles distant. The darkness soon became so great the entire escort was obliged to dismount. Proceeding through the dense forest with its obscure little road, guided by the reflected light of camp-fires ahead of us, which from the space illuminated betokened an innumerable host either of friend or foe, our mission was to solve the problem. Which? Arriving at the plank-road we found we were just through the timber, on the outskirt of an army whose camp-fires lit up a vast plain. We were sheltered by a darkness so dense we could only tell each other by our voices and sense of feeling. The picture spread out before us, with the columns of troops marching through the lines of camp-fires was one so weird and striking as never to be forgotten and not often our province to behold. We could hear a large body of mounted troops moving on the plank road toward us. The General ordered the Tenth New York to cover the road on which we had advanced, the Ohio squadron to cover the plank-road. "Halt the advancing column; if the enemy, give them a volley." They were so unsuspecting of our presence, they had no advance-guard out, but were chatting and joking with the prospect of a camp-fire of their own. The captain of the Sixth Ohio halted them with the usual formalities, they answering "Friend!" when he ordered "Dismount one and advance with the countersign," which was obeyed by [the] Captain [adjutant-general on General Granger's staff]. This was percussion to our captain, who made a bodily capture of that particular staff-officer, ordering "Fire!" which was responded to on the instant in such a manner as to send the column flying down the road in one grand mix-up. I can hear the clatter of hoofs and sabers yet in their stampede. It was thrilling to us, but one of the grim jokes of war to them. We were happy to grope our way back, illuminated by the sulphurous atmosphere emanating from our prize captain's conversation.

Next morning [October 1] the brigade made a reconnaissance to our right, when the heavy firing soon told us our army had not reached the plank-road. We returned to our position of the day before. The boys "falling to" without urging soon had (for cavalry) quite a respectable line of works. The General, taking a staff-officer, started out up the road in our front to make a reconnaissance on his own account. Arriving where the road was flanked on either side by marsh, we received a volley that was a full volume of revelation, putting every man on the "ready" behind our works; and none too soon, for immediately they were at us with a savage determination that seemed irresistible. It looked as if by their very numbers they would break through our line and gather us up; but our little brigade was not only full of fire, but rolled one into the enemy with both carbine and pistol that commanded and received respect. On a greater portion of the line the butts of carbines were freely used to cool the ardor of our foes. "It was a glorious sight to him who had no friend or brother there." Soon the field became enveloped in one dense cloud of smoke, and only from the continuous rattle of our arms and the spirit within us could we tell that our little band would prevail.

It was fully an hour before the fierceness of battle ceased, when the enemy withdrew for a renewal. They knew we were isolated and unsupported, so were bent upon our capture. Having made them doubly mad by the usage of the night before and the repulse of their first attack we knew what to expect. In the lull we lined our works with ammunition and planted a "light twelve" in the road on the flank of the old Tenth, which spoke louder than words of the General's estimate of the Regiment. The rain began to pour in torrents, and with it came another storm of shot and shell from two batteries. Under cover of this fire the enemy moved down and formed several lines beyond the marsh-flanked place before mentioned. Their artillery ceased firing, which seemed to be the signal for their advance, as the noise of their guns was immediately replaced by their demoniacal yells, which were calculated to strike terror to our hearts. On they came with a mad rush, one staff-officer leading a charge with such vigor that his horse landed him clear over our works, which proved our salvation, the burning question of the hour being who should have them. The enemy seemed settled in their purpose to preempt the opposite side of them. As we had never had a square fight behind works before, we esteemed them too highly to share with a foe, attesting it by the fiercest fighting I ever saw done by equal numbers. No pen or words can picture it or light up a shadow of the facts. Out of the din and rattle of small-arms, the roaring of cannon, the screaming of shells, out of the fire and smoke, I can still hear the cheering of our men, see our officers riding up and down the line with hat or saber in hand, calling, "Stand firm!" while on the other side pleadings, urgings, and curses were interlaced with their bullets as they tired themselves out charging, rallying, and charging again and again against our solid wall of fire; and thus we won the day. One poor "reb", shot through the head back of the eyes so they both protruded, fell into our works. I saw him sitting by the fire our boys had kindly built for him. His patient despair so impressed me I record the incident. Try as we will we can not shut out these terrible events from memory. At this distance they suggest the question, not if we were brothers, but if we were human.

The *New York Herald* gave a full account of our fight. General Davies issued a general order thanking and complimenting his brigade for their gallant fighting.

Next day, about noon, the Regiment was withdrawn from the works (the enemy having fallen back), and, mounting their horses, moved to the right and relieved the First Maine on picket. In the evening the Second Brigade moved up, and the Tenth returned to near the scene of its day's fighting, and went into bivouac.

Figure 8.2 Campsite at Civil War reenactment, Ontario Center, NY (2006)

Mary and Justus write back and forth in an exchange of three letters.

October 2nd 1864
Homer, Cortland Co. N.Y.

Friend Jut, I sit down this saboth eve to answer your kind letter that was dated Aug 30th which you see was a long time ago. I went home Aug 20th thinking that should not stay but a few days. as they were not very busy they let me stay five weeks. I did not say anything about my letters being sent to me thinking that I should soon go back. But when the five weeks were up I found quite a number awaiting my return. yours was one of the number. I was very glad to hear from you and to learn that you were well. I was glad to get home once more but it does not seem much like home with all of the young people gone. I did not find my folks very well. ma's health is quite poor. she was entirely worn out taking care of the children. they are all well now. I think that they have got along remarkably well if they do not loose but one. he was a pretty boy and it was hard to loose him. I found them all well in the neighborhood. I got home just in time to help pick hops. I helped Mr. White also. picked for Mr. Galpin two days. I saw your sister there. she was well and appeared to enjoy herself very well. I did not have much time to visit but saw most of the girls in the hop yard. it is a place where you can have lots of fun. I wish that you could have stept in some eve and seen me. you would have thought that we were gay. I must say that home is home if it is ever so poor. I always enjoy going to Solon. it is a place that I shall never forget or the happy years that I have spent there. I came back to my work one week ago. I must say that it did come hard to be confined in the house again after having my liberty for five weeks. I enjoy myself very well here in Homer. I find some very good friends and others that I do not wish to class amongst my friends. those we find in every place.

We are having very rainy weather now. last month it rained every sunday and it has rained to day so that I have not been to church.

You spoke of the drafted men. I do not think that the malitia will ever amount to anything. it has not yet. there has been another draft made for the town of Solon to fill up the quota for the 18th regt, but I believe that Mr. Hathaway found enough men to take their place or that was the talk when I left Solon. There was a number that enlisted from Solon, Laren Atkins and Mr. Galpin from our place. they were afraid of the draft. Frank Tompkins my Brother in law went from Marathon allso.

Steve Wood, their familleys moove up to McGrawville. This is coming nearer home than it ever has come before. it seems hard to have Frank go and leave his family, but when I think of the great number that has gone and left

308

home and friends just as dear as his is to him I would not complain but be thankfull that there is one in the family that will go. If I could get a place in a hospital where I could help take care of the sick I should go. I would leave friends and all if I could be of any use to the poor sick ones far from home and friends. I suppose that they are in need of more help but I do not know how to get a situation.

Jut I see that this paper is nearly full and as there is a number more letters that are before me that are not answered I must ask you to still remember me as your friend, one that is looking forward to the time that all of these brave boys will come home for I do think that that time is near at hand when this cruel war will be over.

Hoping to hear from you soon I remain your friend-
Mary L H

Camp in front of Petersburg Va
Oct 9th '64

Dear Friend,

I recieved your letter in due time and was vary happy to hear from you again.

I should have written to you again to day, if I had not got your letter. I had began to think that my letter was miss carried.

I have been quite unwell since I wrote to you last but I am all sound again. hope I shall be hereafter, especally while I am in this service, which I think will not be a vary long time. It looks quite favorable for us to get out of this in a few weeks. if we do not why we shall have to make the best of it we can and stay another year.

We have had some prety lively times since I wrote you. our brigade had a prety hard fight on the first of this month. our reg't had the blunt of it. no casualities in our Co. had to fight three to one. rebs say that we had our whole corps.

The 185th N.Y. Infantry has arived. they are in the fifth Corps. I have not seen them yet. I understand that amost all of the Cortland folks are in it. I have an Uncle in it. I am going over and see it tomorrow if I can get a pass. It has been quite cool here for a few days. the day of the fight it rained vary hard.

Well, Mary, Sister wrote and told me about some of the fun that the hopp girls had trying to sack some fellows. wish it had been me. think would have had quite a job.

Think you must have had quite a play spell while at home. I think that it will be my turn prety soon, but I dont think that I will come back here again if I know myself.

Well, my chum (A. E. Reynolds) says that it is supper time, and I must put this aside. well I will have a good one any way. I will tell you what we drew- some sanitary stuff to day, some sweet potatoes, irish do, onions, and candles.

Mary, I hope that I shall not have to write many more letters, but in stead, be where I can talk to you. I think that I could enjoy myself then.

I have not more time. remember me as your friend and well-wisher

J. G. Matteson
Co.L 10th N.Y. Vol. Cav.
Washington, DC

October 23rd, 1864
Homer, Cortland Co., N. Y.

Jut, sunday has come and mostly passed and I have not writen a letter yet. what shall I do and a number lies before me to be answered. I know of no better way than to sit down and write the remainder of the day. I have been to church all day. it is the first sunday for a number of weeks that it has not rained and it has looked very much like it to day. I received your letter in due time and was very glad to hear from you but sorry to learn that you had been unwell. it is hard to be sick at home but much harder to be sick away from home where no mother or sister is near to cool the heated brow or wet the parched lips. but hope that health may be yours whilst in the land of strangers and on the battle field. I have not been home since I wrote you last but have heard from there. Last week they were all well in the neighberhood but in McGrawville that dreatfull disease Diptheria is raging. there never has been a case of it in the Vill. untill now. last tuesday Ben Greenman's boy was burried, a boy 14 or 15 years old and I understand that there is a number of cases.

I was to a great mass meeting to Cortland tuesday last 18th. there was a great many out and a number of speakers. had two platforms. one of the speakers was Mr. Turner from Texas. others from abroad. they were there from every town. I enjoyed it very much. I see Lyman Galpin one of the 76th boys. his time is out but he said that he thought that he should go back again. he has never been wounded.

You spoke about the nice times that we had picking hops. we did have a very nice time but I was not there the time that you spoke of. I did not stay quite two days but enjoyed it very much and I think that you would had you been there.

Jut, I see that you still think of coming home this fall. I do hope that you will. if you do not I shall not be here when you do for I have made up my mind to go West next spring. I wanted to have gone this last summer but my folks would not hear a word about it but next summer if they are well I shall shurely go. Jut you will excuse this large sheet and a half one at that. I got a letter from Brother Frank last week. he was well then but I have heard since that he and Lorenzo were both in the hospital. but I hope that it is a false report. he likes it very well but would like to see home again. it has been four weeks since he went away. it is a long time to his family. Jut I wish that you could step in the shop some afternoon when we are in a trane. there is four of us girls in a little room. one of them is agoing to Calafornia in a few weeks. then we shall have a new one. hope that they will get one steady one for we need one amongst us. but I will tell you no more but when you come home make us a call, will you not?

As it is nearly time for evening meeting I must close, hoping to see or hear from you soon. I wish that you were here this eve to go to meeting but I suppose that you have them there. I had nearly forgoten to tell you that the teachers institute is being held here now. last week there was quite a number out and I think there will be more this week. there is but a few that I know. I think that the most of them look green. I expect it is because you and I are not teachers.

P. S. Write soon.
Molly H.

Battle of Boydton Plank Road

Preston describes the action on Boydton Plank Road [#21 on Map 8.3] in the following [10]:

> The infantry commenced moving toward the left on the 26th [of October], and at 4 P.M. the Tenth with the rest of the division marched in the same direction and encamped soon after dark. At early dawn the movement around the enemy's right flank via the Boydton plank-road commenced by the Second and Fifth Army Corps and Gregg's cavalry.

General Humphreys says:

> Gregg in the meantime crossed Hatcher's Run, below the infantry, moved along the Vaughn and then the Quaker road, encountering part of Hampton's troops, and united with the infantry on the Boydton road soon after they entered it.

And again he says:

> Gregg's cavalry were sharply engaged. ... The attack on Gregg, General Hancock says, was made by five brigades of Hampton's cavalry and was pressed vigorously until after dark, but that General Gregg held his own. ... General Hancock mentions in high terms the conduct of General Egan, General Mott, General Gregg, and several other oflicers.

The Second Brigade was more seriously engaged than the First, although the Tenth was pretty actively occupied all day. In the evening the Regiment was sent out to open and maintain connection between the two brigades, in the accomplishment of which some brisk skirmishing ensued. It rained nearly all night, but the morning of the 28th was pleasant and warm. A little after midnight the cavalry began falling back, the Tenth bringing up the rear near daylight. Reaching Prince George

Court House [#11 on Map 8.2] the division went into camp, the Tenth on picket.

In addition to the Battle of Boydton Plank Road the CWSAC gives these other names for this battle - Hatcher's Run and Burgess' Mill; and describes the battle as follows [11]:

Directed by Maj. Gen. Winfield Scott Hancock, divisions from three Union corps (II, V, and IX) and Gregg's cavalry division, numbering more than 30,000 men, withdrew from the Petersburg lines and marched west to operate against the Boydton Plank Road and South Side Railroad. The initial Union advance on October 27 gained the Boydton Plank Road, a major campaign objective. But that afternoon, a counterattack near Burgess' Mill spearheaded by Maj. Gen. Henry Heth's division and Maj. Gen. Wade Hampton's cavalry isolated the II Corps and forced a retreat. The Confederates retained control of the Boydton Plank Road for the rest of the winter.

Figure 8.3 Rifle drill at a reenactment in Ontario, NY in 2006

Justus and Mary have another exchange of two letters:

Camp in front of Petersburg, Va.
Nov 4th, 1864

Dear Friend Mary,

I recieved your welcomed letter in due time, and was vary happy to hear from you again. where do you suppose I was when it came to me. well I will tell you. it was Oct 27th when we wer going around on the right of the Rebs. I read it as we road along the rode.

Well we had quite a time that day I can tell you. we did not have as much fighting as we have had at some other times. the infantry had it prety hard on our (the Cav's) right. The Rebs wer allmost clean around us. our Reg't had two men killed, several wounded, and some missing. at night our squadron was on pickett. had several colisions with the enemy in the course of the night. it rained amost all day and night. our forces withdrew before day light. we wer all glad to get out of it as easy as we did. we went over the ground that Wilson was cut up so on last summer. saw the remains of our wounded that wer left in the Johneys hands and died and wer not burrid. It doesent seem possible that <u>men</u> can be so inhuman, does it.

As soon as we got back our Regt was sent out on picket. wer out 5 days. the bushwhackers took one and shot one out of Co. K while we wer out.

I am well except a little cold, which is nuthing here. I have been over to the 185th once sometime a go. I saw your brother Frank & Ren. they wer well then I think. It seemed amost like going home to see so many that I know of my old friends. I am going to try and get a pass to go and visit them again to morrow. I had a letter from Sister a few days since. said my folks wer not vary well. It is getting to be prety changable weather here now. snowed a few flakes the other day. we shall have to go into winter quarters before long. The boys are a having quite a political conversation without. I am hapy to say that there is but a few McClellan men in our Co. or in the army. I sent up a vote for Uncle Abe.

Mati, I suppose that if you go west that you will not quite forget me while in a southern land. but I am in hopes that I shall not be here by the time you start west.

I would like to be there and go to meeting with you. I <u>would like to go to a good meeting</u> once more and see how it would seem. it is so long since I have. we have them here but I do not attend vary often. our Chaplain is not liked vary well. think he drinks to much <u>commissary stubtoe</u>.

Mary as I can not be there to share any of your shop fun, I shall have to close, and go to bed and dream that I wer there haveing a gay old time.

Dear friend, though I am far a way
I often think of thee.
It cheers my heart to think that thou
Dost still remember me.

J. G. Matteson

P. S. *Write as soon as convenient.*

Figure 8.4 Fighting dismounted

November 27th, 1864
Homer, Courtland Co.

Remembered friend,

I sit down this saboth day to write letters to the absent ones as I have a number that are before me unanswered. I have been quite well since I wrote you last and must say that I have enjoyed myself very well, or at least as well as I genely do, for my life is not one of those gay happy lives that know not sorrow. many a day is spent in company where all is gayety and seeming happiness when if my heart was open to all to read they would find onely sorrow there. But why should I weary you with this.

Jut, Winter has come. the ground is covered with snow, but we have not enough for sleighing. I have not been to church to day. I had a very interesting book to read intitled Vernon Grove. perhaps you have read the same. I think it is a very interesting book. I have not heard from home since I wrote to you or have not heard directly from there. I saw your sister up here to a mass meating a few days before Election. I did not see her but a few moments. think that she came from her relatives on the hill. she was looking well and appeared to be enjoying herself. we had a great meeting. one of the best speakers was Pat Corbit from Syracuse. he is quite young but he has tallents. the meeting was in Barbers new hall but it would not hold half of them. they filled both halls. I do think that we have gained a great victory in getting the same presedent and a new goviner. I do not know what more we could ask. now if they will do the best they can I think this wicked war must end. I heard from my cousin Oscar Hatch the other day. he has been in the army nearly four years. last October he was wounded in the right hand and now he has had to have it taken off. he lives in Indiana and is now at home. I have never seen him, but I have learnt to like him by his kind letters that he has writen to us all, but as it is his right hand he cannot write any more untill he has learnt to write with his left one. I hear from brother Frank quite often. he is agoing to leave the regament and join a brass band that they are getting up. he appears to enjoy himself very well but I guess that he often thinks of his family. I have not been down to Marathon since he went away but think that I shall spend New Years with her.

How did you spend Thanksgiving's day? did you have any of the nice things that were sent to the soldiers? I hope that you did. it must remind the absent ones that they are not forgotte at home for surely they are not.

Christmas and New Years are very near. how many friens that were with us one year ago are absent now. Jut you have not been home. why do you not come home this winter, or can not you get a furlough? it cannot be that you will have to stay all winter and not come home. I am sure that we should all be very happy to see you.

Jut you will forgive me for not answering your letter before for I have been very busy. I did sit down a week ago to night to write to you but we had a house full of company from Massachusetts that came to spend a few days. I wrote part of a sheet full but they took it away from me so I had to leave untill to day. I must ask you to excuse this poor writing for the paper is very poor and they have the children where I board and they are always more noissome when they should be still.

P. S. I shall be very happy to hear from you when convenient to write.

Mary Hatch

The Battle of Stony Creek Station

Stony Creek Station [#17 on Map 8.3] was the next station south of Reams Station on the Weldon. As usual, there was a lot of skirmishing going on to determine whether the railroad operated or not. Preston describes the action as follows [12]:

> Stony Creek Station was the objective point of Gregg's cavalry on the first day of December. The men felt in the proper state of mind for a fight at being aroused at two o'clock in the morning and started off without breakfast. There were the usual mumbling and grumbling while the boys packed up and led out, but they were finally lost in the jingle of the sabers and the confusion in getting into line. The march was via Lee's Mills [#12 on Map 8.2] to the Jerusalem plank-road. Passing down this road the Tenth with the First Brigade arrived at Stony Creek Station about noon. The Second Brigade, farther to the left, had already had severe fighting and had captured quite a large number of prisoners. At 1 P.M. the Tenth, crossing the railroad, moved about a mile and established pickets. At 2:30 P.M. it was attacked by a large force, but held its position until the work of destroying the railroad had been accomplished. In this a part of the Regiment participated. While falling back across the railroad the rear of the Regiment was attacked, but the battery opening on the rebels, soon sent them to cover again. The station at Stony Creek with the surrounding buildings was incinerated, together with some Confederate workshops and commissary stores. A few wagons also fell into the hands of the captors.
>
> At three o'clock the return march was taken up, and at sunset the Nottoway River was crossed.

Of the Stony Creek engagement Corporal H.G. Hicks, of Company L, writes:

> In the fight at Stony Creek Station, December 1, 1864, Captain W.R. Perry and his squadron - Companies A and L - took an active part. Perry was sent with his

squadron out on the main road leading to the station from the south, and formed line in a field near where the road forked, and sent out pickets on the road to the right. After a time these pickets were attacked and what seemed to be about a brigade of rebel cavalry came out into the field adjoining the one we occupied, and began forming line of battle. Perry immediately ordered a charge, and away we went straight for that crowd of rebels, with the little bald-headed Captain in the lead. Reaching a high rail fence which separated us from the enemy, the command was dismounted, unslung carbines and were deployed along the fence as skirmishers. We peppered the enemy good. They appeared staggered by Perry's boldness, and could not get men forward to the fence to throw it down while we were there. But another force of rebels, coming in on the road to our left, with the evident intention of cutting us off, compelled a hasty retreat.

I was in the rear, and was caught by the limb of a tree and unhorsed. By the time I was again in the saddle the rebs were close upon me, calling to me to surrender. Of course I declined, and plying the spurs vigorously my horse made a "spurt," that I believe was seldom, if ever, beaten on Virginia war-time roads. We reached the station and found the rest of the Regiment, and with the aid of a couple of field-pieces gave the rebs a warm reception. That was where I came to grief. I had not fired to exceed two shots, when a rebel bullet struck my left arm, crushing the bone, and knocking me out for all time to come. The twenty mile ride back to camp on horseback that night was a terrible one to me. The action of Perry, in engaging several thousand rebels with one small squadron I thought quite strange at the time, but, in thinking of it afterward, concluded that the short delay he caused them doubtless gave the rest of the brigade time to prepare for the action which followed. Captain Walt Perry was a brave officer, whom I would be pleased to have honored as he deserves.

Captain John J. Van Tuyl says of the Stony Creek Station fight:

> Captain T.C. White and I were together at the time he was wounded, at Stony Creek Station. Three squadrons of our Regiment were picketing three roads, while the rest were tearing up track, burning station and buildings, etc., when one of the squadrons was attacked by a heavy force, and the other squadrons were called in. I think I was the ranking officer present. A stand was made at the cross-roads. Finally, the enemy came down upon us in overwhelming numbers; we held our position for some time, but at last were compelled to give way. When the start was made I noticed White reel on his horse, and knew he was wounded. I attempted to hold him on his horse, but my own horse bolted, and reared and plunged, until I found myself surrounded by the rebels, many of whom had passed me in pursuit of our boys. I suppose they considered me a prisoner. I thought I was, anyway; but, when my horse finally settled down, he made a break for the woods, which were filled with a dense undergrowth. I could neither hold nor guide the animal, but clasping my arms about his neck stuck to him like a leech. The limbs and brush nearly tore the clothing off me, but the horse brought me safely out right at General Davies's headquarters. The General remarked that I looked scared. I told him I was.

The Tenth moved back at 3 P.M., crossed the Nottoway River at sunset, and established a line of pickets on nearly the former grounds, on the Lee's Mills road. The following day, at 2 P.M., the Eighth Pennsylvania relieved the Regiment on the picket-line, and it returned to camp.

Justus sends Mary a letter:

Hd. Qrs. 10th N. Y. Cav.
Dec. 4th, 1864

Friend Mary,

I recieved your welcome letter in due time, and I think that I need not say that I was happy to hear from you, for surely I allways am.

I am enjoying myself firs best this winter, allthough it does not look much like winter here at present. for the last week it has been pleasant weather and it bids fair to be so for som time to come. It is a beautiful night and Oh, how I wish you wer here to hear the music. there ar several brass bands playing close by, and it is delightfull to hear them.

All of last week we wer on picket. Nov 8th we wer drawn in and Dec 1st our division went on a requinoisance to Stoney Creek. we started at 4 in the A.M. drove in the reb pickets about day light. we struck the RR at Duvals station, destroyed the station, a steem saw mill, barell factory, stone houses, one train of cars, tore up some distance of the track, got 7 or 8 wagons and trains. allso took 4 pieces of artillery, spiked them, and rolled some of them into a pond. could not get them off for the want of teams. took 187 prisoners in the scrape. our reg't had one man killed, one mortaly wounded, and eight severly. two of the latter wer of our co. one Corporeal John G. Hicks of Cortland. they wer both wounded in the arm. Daniel Ansinger of our Co had his hat shot off. I had a hole through my sleeve.

You wanted to know how I spent Thanksgiving. well I worked all day hard making us a tent. of those good things that wer sent to us, we recieved but little of. I got 1 1/2 apples and half of a turkeys leg. the officers had the first handling of them and took the lions share.

Mary pleas excuse me from writing more for the candle is a most out and I have no more.

Yours truly, G. Matteson

P. S. pleas write as soon as convenient.

Mr. J. G. Matteson
Co. L, 10th Regt N. Y. S. Cav, Washington D. C.

The Hicksford Raid, including the Three Creek and Jarrett's Station Engagements

Preston describes the movement of the Tenth New York farther south to attack the Weldon at the Stony Creek Station (#17 on Map 8.3). The Regiment then went on down as far as Jarrett's Station and the Bellefield Station (#18 and #19 on Map 8.3) [13]:

> Wednesday, December 7th, the Second Cavalry Division started out at an early hour on the Lee's Mills road again, to the plank-road, and thence down to the Nottoway River, which was crossed by the Tenth at Jones Neck, by fording, leaving the plank-road to the left. After crossing, the Regiment halted at 2 P.M., and, then resuming the march, arrived at Sussex Court House [just east of Stony Creek Station, #17 on Map 8.3] at sunset and encamped. The enemy's pickets were driven in during the day at various points. Starting out next morning, at 4 A.M., the Weldon Railroad was reached before noon, and the work of demolition vigorously begun [probably at Stony Creek Station]. Later, the Tenth moved down the railroad with the brigade, to Jarrett's Station, and at 8 P.M., encamped.

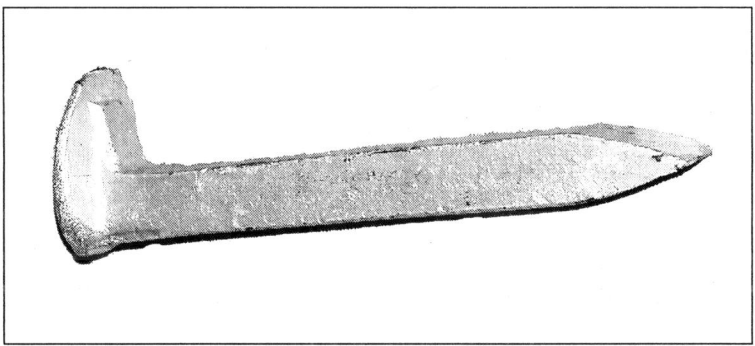

Figure 8.5 Railroad Spike

The Fifth Corps, and Mott's division of the Second Corps [infantry], were associated with Gregg's division of cavalry in this manipulation of railroad stocks, placing the Weldon in the "non-dividend-paying" list.

Again the Regiment moved out before sunrise on the cold, disagreeable 9th of December, and drove the enemy, while the infantry followed, destroying the railroad. The Tenth, finally meeting with a somewhat determined resistance, charged, mounted, down to Three Creeks [near Bellefield], when it was found the enemy had destroyed the bridge. Here it was dismounted, crossed the river, and charged up the hill, and to the line of earthworks held by the Confederates, which, proving too strong to be taken, it fell back. Meantime the enemy had maintained a steady artillery-fire, which had been continued all the afternoon. When the Regiment was about to charge across the river the enemy opened fire from a little Fourth-of-July cannon, which was only about two and a half feet in length. It threw a missile not much larger than a deacon's oath. It was a veritable little son of a gun, but it was as spiteful as a mother-in-law. At dark the Regiment fell back, and the station at Bellefield was burned.

During this engagement, which was known as Three Creeks, Major Sergeant, of the First Massachusetts Cavalry, was killed, while gallantly leading his regiment in a charge. Major Snyder had his horse shot from under him at the head of the Tenth, while making a charge. At 1 P.M. the Regiment went on picket in a storm, the rain freezing as it fell.

At an early hour on the 10th the command moved out, recrossed the Meherrin River [which crosses the Weldon at Hicksford], closely followed by the enemy, who charged about noon, but were repulsed. Then they were charged in turn and driven back.

When the command took up the march, on the morning of the 10th, the slender pine-trees were so heavily laden with sleet and ice that the tops were bent nearly to the ground, and in some places obstructed the road.

The action of this day is known as Jarrett's Station.

C.W. Wiles, of Company L, furnishes the following account of this expedition:

Before daylight on the 7th of December, 1864, the stirring music of "Boots and Saddles" rang through the cold mist and rain, and at four o'clock Gregg's division of cavalry moved out of winter quarters for the extreme left flank of the Union army. The Thirteenth Pennsylvania and Sixth Ohio Cavalry Regiments and one battery of artillery were left in camp. Of the original leaders in the Cavalry Corps General Gregg was the only one remaining- Bayard and Buford were in soldiers' graves; Stoneman, Pleasonton, Averill, and Kilpatrick had gone to other fields; but Gregg retained his old command. His men had followed him through many tedious campaigns and hard-fought battles. He possessed their confidence and affection to the fullest extent. His division followed him out of camp on this occasion with the full consciousness that, whatever the destination or work before them, he would guide them wisely and care for them well.

The attention of the infantry boys was attracted as the column passed by their camps, and the cavalrymen were greeted with such good-natured sallies as, "Don't go out and get into a fight now, for us fellows to settle for you," "Don't go out and stir up the Johnnies in such weather," etc.

We had hardly passed their camps, however, before the drums were calling them out to follow us. Moving south on the Jerusalem plank-road we struck the Nottoway at Freeman's bridge. The bridge was gone, and we crossed the river, which was about three feet deep, by fording, the enemy making a show of disputing the passage. They were quickly driven away, however. Pontoons were in readiness for the infantry to cross next morning early. The cavalry pushed on to Sussex Court-House, five miles farther. Here we found a long building surrounded by a piazza used as a hotel. There were numbers of ladies from Richmond stopping there. There were plenty of fences, and, remembering the orders to "take only the top rails," the boys were soon surrounding cheerful, crackling fires, over which chickens, hams, potatoes, etc., were cooking.

The march was resumed at 4 A.M. on the 8th, the First Brigade leading. The Halifax road was reached near Nottoway Bridge at 9 A.M. The Third Brigade was sent to destroy the bridge. As we turned on the Halifax road an attack was made by the enemy's cavalry, which was handsomely repulsed by the Fourth Pennsylvania Cavalry. About the same time the pickets on the flank were driven in after the passage of the First Brigade, and for a brief period the column severed. The Eighth Pennsylvania Cavalry was sent back and cleared the road in short order. The infantry followed a little later and completed the destruction of the railroad. The cavalry marched slowly along the flanks as a protection to the working parties of the infantry. The destruction of the road for about five miles brought the force to Jarrett's Station, where the depot, etc., was destroyed, and the command bivouacked.

Early on the morning of the 10th the march was resumed, the Tenth in the advance, skirmishing frequently. The weather was cold and the progress slow. Just after noon we reached a small deep stream called Three Creeks. The railroad bridge was burning, the highway bridge, with the exception of one timber, gone, and the fords obstructed by fallen trees. Beyond the stream a force of dismounted cavalry were supporting two field-pieces behind breastworks.

Colonel Avery ordered Major Snyder, with Companies A and L, to charge across the field and cross the stream if possible. Away the boys went, some of them wounded and some horses killed by the fire opened on them as they neared the creek, Major Snyder's horse being killed under him near the railroad bridge. The squadron dismounted and soon after charged across, the balance of the Regiment coming up as they made a dash to get across the creek. Captain Perry, followed by a number of the boys, crossed on the only remaining timber of the railroad bridge. The enemy abandoned their works and ran for the woods, leaving several of their dead and wounded behind. Then the balance of the Regiment came up, followed a little later by the First New Jersey and the First and Third Brigades.

As some of our dismounted boys were passing a house in the edge of the woods they stopped and found several large bottles of whisky. As they came up the stairs they encountered the proprietor, a physician in his office, in dressing gown and slippers. He expressed indignation at the treatment, which turned to violent demonstrations of anger when he saw through the window some of the boys attacking his innocent and defenseless chickens.

The Tenth, acting as support to the First New Jersey, occupied a timber, upon which the enemy concentrated the fire of their artillery, rendering the place quite warm. After dark the Regiment was recalled. Soon after dark a cold rain set in, and before midnight it turned to sleet and ice. There was little sleep obtained by the boys that night. They shivered over the fires through the night, and when morning came men, horses, and saddles were coated with ice.

At break of day on the 10th the Regiment recrossed Three Creeks and started on the return. As the column passed over a hill at sunrise, a most beautiful sight was presented to view. As far as the vision extended the landscape was like shining crystal, suggestive of the home of fairies - in the rear the long column of cavalry and artillery, the brightness of their arms and trappings being reflected by the morning's sun.

On leaving Three Creeks the Third Brigade was attacked in rear by a large force of mounted and dismounted cavalry; but they were finally repulsed, and the march was resumed.

On the return march the Tenth had the advance, with Companies A and L leading. A mounted Confederate in the front fell back as the column advanced. He was finally joined by another, when some of the advance-guard gave chase. On reaching the station they turned to the left. A Confederate officer rode into the highway, took off his hat and made a low bow, and remained there. A few moments later he reeled in his saddle and was assisted to dismount. He had invited and had evidently received a Yankee bullet. As soon as our boys came into sight, the rebels opened with two guns. The first shot from their guns demolished an old chimney just across the road. A colored man, who had taken refuge behind the chimney, scattered in several directions when his tower of refuge came tumbling down.

When near Jarrett's Station [#18 on Map 8.3], the Tenth leading, with Companies A and L, under Captain Perry, as advance-guard, we encountered the rebels, who retired through the woods on a road running at right angles with the railroad. Colonel Avery sent for Captain White to bring up his squadron, Companies E and K. On the Captain's reporting, the Colonel said: "Captain White, I have a mighty fine thing for you. There are a few Johnnies about twenty rods up that road. I want you to charge them with the saber." General Davies with his staff was present. He said to Colonel Avery, "Careful, Colonel." White formed his men, and with sabers drawn led them up the road, the Confederates disappearing around a bend. When the charging squadron reached the bend they were met by a heavy fire from behind logs, etc., on each side of the road, while two cannon in their immediate front contributed to make the visit embarrassing. White fell back and deployed his men on each side of the road, and held the enemy in check until the Regiment got up. The only casualties in Captain White's squadron was the wounding of two men, brothers, belonging to Company K, one being shot in the right and the other in the left arm by the same bullet. Captain Hartwell had been sent with his squadron up another road to get on the enemy's flank, but the underbrush was so dense he found it impossible. The Tenth held the entire rebel force until the column had passed, and then resumed the march. There was a drizzling rain all day.

After leaving Jarrett's Station a horseman, with a United States blanket wrapped about him, rode alongside the column until suspicion was aroused as to his real character. A couple of the boys made a dash for him, when he lit out for the rebel lines. He was a rebel scout. His horse was a good one. To its fleetness he owed his escape.

On the 11th [December 1864] the march was continued. Through Sussex Court House, and crossing the Nottoway in advance of the infantry the column passed, and back to winter quarters at 1 A.M. on the 12th, men and horses nearly frozen.

References

[1] Preston, Noble D., *History of the Tenth Regiment New York Volunteer Cavalry*, New York, NY: D. Appleton and Company, 1892; reprinted by Higginson Book Company, Salem, MA in 1998; pp. 222-223.

[2] National Park Service, Civil War Sites Advisory Commission (CWSAC), http://www.cr.nps.gov/hps/abpp/battles/va069.htm, Battle of Deep Bottom I, July 27-29, 1864.

[3] Preston, *History of the Tenth New York*, p. 223.

[4] Ibid, 223-224

[5] National Park Service, Civil War Sites Advisory Commission (CWSAC), http://www.cr.nps.gov/hps/abpp/battles/va071.htm, Battle of Deep Bottom II, August 13-20, 1864.

[6] Preston, *History of the Tenth New York*, p. 225.

[7] Ibid, 226.

[8] National Park Service, Civil War Sites Advisory Commission (CWSAC), http://www.cr.nps.gov/hps/abpp/battles/va073.htm, Reams Station II, August 25, 1864.

[9] Preston, *History of the Tenth New York*, pp. 227-232.

[10] Ibid, 232.

[11] National Park Service, Civil War Sites Advisory Commission (CWSAC), http://www.cr.nps.gov/hps/abpp/battles/va079.htm, Battle of Boydton Plank Road, October 27-28, 1864.

[12] Preston, *History of the Tenth New York*, pp. 233-235.

[13] Ibid, 235-238.

CHAPTER 9
Appomattox Campaign, Lee's surrender

"Let the thing be pressed," A. Lincoln

The End Game

Most of the war between the North and the South concluded in the first four months of 1865. Grant and Sheridan relentlessly pursued Lee as he tried to escape from Richmond with his army. He couldn't get away, and much of his army was captured between Richmond and Appomattox Court House. He finally surrendered the rest of it on April 9. The following table lists the major actions of Sheridan's cavalry and the Tenth New York.

Map #	Location (all in Virginia)	Dates
	Before Petersburg	**Jan.-April, 1865**
1	Reams Station (on the Weldon RR)	February 5
3	Rowanty Creek, etc.	Feb. 5-8, 1865
	Appomattox Campaign	**March 29-April 9**
2	Dinwiddie Court House	March 30-31
4	Five Forks ("Breakthrough")	April 1
	Confederacy evacuates Richmond	**April 2**
5	Amelia Court House	April 4
6	Jetersville (on the Southside RR)	April 4, 5
7	Burkesville Junction	
8	Paine's Cross Roads	April 5
9	Sailor's Creek/Hillsman Farm	April 6
10	High Bridge	April 7
11	Farmville/Cumberland Church	April 7
15	Prospect Station	April 7
12	Appomattox Station	April 8
12	Appomattox Court House	April 9

Table 9.1 Major engagements in 1865 leading to Lee's surrender

Cutting off the Weldon Railroad

Grant and Sheridan started the final stages by trying again to cut off the delivery of supplies and troops to Richmond via the Weldon Railroad. Preston describes the place of the Tenth New York in this activity [1]:

> The Union lines had been gradually extended south and west, turning the Confederate right, until the South Side Railroad was the only one left by which General Lee could obtain supplies from the South with any degree of reliability. The Shenandoah Valley - the "Valley of Humiliation" - had been gloriously redeemed by General Sheridan. [Confederate General] Early had been sent "whirling up the Valley" while a large portion of his army and material whirled into the possession of the Union army. In the destruction of Early's army, Sheridan's cavalry played a prominent part. They were in at the beginning, and it was they who administered the finishing touches to the remarkably successful campaign that destroyed an army that was by many thought to be invincible, and deprived the Confederates of their richest granary. It is recorded that General Early was in constant dread of the Yankee cavalry getting on his flanks. And they did get on his flanks most effectively. Custer and Merritt and Torbert and Devin were omnipresent. They were constantly feeling the old man Early's pulse. The trembling cry, on the march or in camp, that set the rebels in a panic, was "The Yankee cavalry!" No sleep, no rest, while these dread wielders of the blade were on their path.
>
> Some supplies came to the Army of Northern Virginia by the Weldon Railroad. These were brought to a point as near as it was considered safe, and were transported thence by the precarious use of wagons, to Petersburg. General Grant determined to cut off this source, by a movement of a sufficient force to Dinwiddie Court House [#2 on Map 9.1], to overcome any opposition which might be encountered, to destroy the railroad, capture the trains, and do such other damage to the enemy as was possible. Gregg's cavalry division was selected

for this work, to be supported by the Fifth Corps [infantry] under General Warren. …

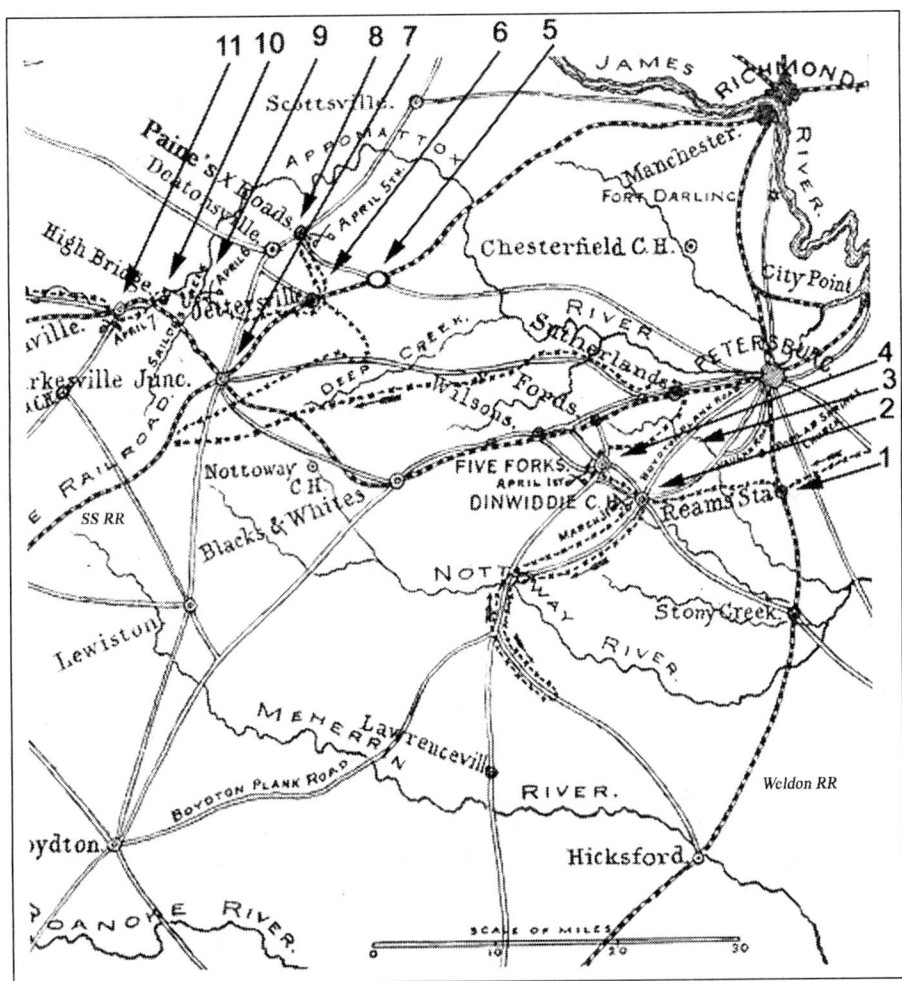

Map 9.1 Actions of the Tenth New York around Petersburg in March-April, 1865

Action at Rowanty Creek

At three o'clock on the morning of the 5th of February the Tenth moved out of camp, and following the Jerusalem plank-road reached Reams Station [#1 on Map 9.1] at 8 A.M.; thence to Dinwiddie Court House [#2 on Map 9.1], passing deserted

Confederate camps *en route,* where the fires, like the Confederacy, were still burning, but very low. Arriving at the Court House at one o'clock, the enemy were surprised, and forty men, including a colonel, together with a number of wagons, were captured. Then returning toward Reams Station, Malone's bridge, over Rowanty Creek was found to have been destroyed by the enemy. Another was built, upon which the cavalry crossed and encamped on the east side. Snow and rain came with the halt- an unsavory admixture and an unwelcome visitation. This day's action by the cavalry has been recorded as Rowanty Creek [#3 on Map 9.1], and by some of the participants has been called the first Dinwiddie fight. During the night connection was made with the infantry on the right.

Hatcher's Run/Vaughn Road Fight

Then followed the Hatcher's Run [#3 on Map 9.1] fight, next day, February 6th. Gregg's division and Warren's Fifth Corps were ordered to the Vaughn road, where the Second and parts of the Sixth and Ninth Corps were in position. The Tenth was reported in readiness to move at 2 A.M., and a few moments later the march was taken up, the Rowanty recrossed, and the march northward resumed, until Hatcher's Run was reached and crossed. Here the Regiment halted for the purpose of preparing breakfast. Hardly had the horses been relieved of their burdens when the pickets in the rear were driven in, and the reserve attacked. The Tenth was speedily formed, dismounted, and followed the Twenty-fourth New York Cavalry skirmishers. The Confederates were driven back, and our troops hastily threw up light breastworks, the fighting continuing meantime. The infantry on the right were heavily engaged and the conflict became desperate along the entire line, the cavalry engaging Pegram's division of Gordon's corps. At 1 P.M. the brigade was relieved by the infantry, and after an hour's respite the cavalrymen in turn relieved the infantry boys, and the fight was continued with increased vigor on both sides. The Tenth made a charge, capturing some prisoners and driving the enemy. About this time General Davies was wounded, and the command of the brigade devolved on Colonel Avery, who dispatched a mounted officer to notify Lieutenant Colonel Tremain to take command of the Regiment.

At 2 P.M., just at the moment when he was about to lead a portion of the Regiment on the skirmish-line, the young Lieutenant Colonel [Tremain] turned to receive the message, and was struck in the hip by a minie-ball. He was at once lifted tenderly up and carried to an ambulance, and thence conveyed to the field hospital [where he died]. Majors Beaumont and Janeway, of the First New Jersey Cavalry, were also wounded in this engagement.

At dusk the Tenth fell back a short distance with the brigade and bivouacked. A cold night, with rain, freezing as it fell, offered little opportunity for comfort or rest to the weary and hungry men.

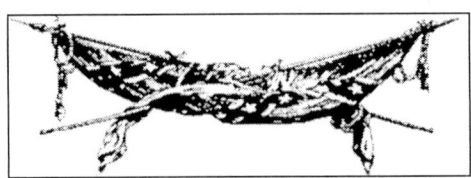

Figure 9.1 Battle flags after battles

Colonel Irvin Gregg replaced General David Gregg (his cousin) as acting Commanding General of the Second Cavalry Division on February 9, 1865. General Gregg had resigned his commission for personal reasons, and left for home on that date. On March 27, when Sheridan returned to the Army of the Potomac, he named General George Crook the Commanding General of the Second Division. Irvin Gregg was promoted to Brigadier General, and resumed his command of the Second Brigade.

**Figure 9.2 Commanding General of the
Army of the Potomac, U.S. Grant**

About this time Mary Hatch sends Justus Matteson a couple of letters, on the following pages. He replies the day before the (second) Battle of Dinwiddie Court House. This letter is shown after Mary's letters. Justus refers to his uncle in this letter, who would be James Matteson, and who served in the 185th Infantry. He was the son of Christopher LeValley

Matteson by his second wife, Lois Huntley. He had two other children with Lois, both girls. His first wife was Anna Grant, a distant cousin of Gen. U.S. Grant, with whom he had 11 children, including Justus Matteson's father Cyrus French Matteson. A page of Mary's letter, in her own handwriting, is also shown in the following.

Figure 9.3 Ladies dress of the period at a 2006 reenactment in Ontario, NY

Feb 12th 1865
Homer Cortland Co. N.Y.

Oh! Jut, if I could only tell you how cold it is here. onely think the cars have not been in onely once in nearly two weeks. They started from Binghampton last tuesday morning, got in here friday night and here they stand. they took a team and carried the ladies and children around the vill where they would keep them. the snow is very deep. I dare not say how deep and it has snowed every day untill to day. they have tried to clear the track every day but when it comes night it blows in all that they have cleared out through the day. Oh! how I should hate to be on the road this cold stormy wether. Jut, I received your kind letter in due time and I must tell you again that it was very welcome. they jeneraly come when I am sad or home sick and they always make me feel better. you will think strange that I ever get home sick when I am so near home, but just think, I have not been home in nearly five months. it is a long time for me and then I am so near home. if I had a father perhaps I should go home oftener, for I think he would think enough of me to come after me. Jut, you do not know how hard it is to think and know that you have no father. I think of it more every day of my life. I hope that you may never know what it is to have no father. I see that I am getting in a sad strain.

Jut, you wish to know where I work. I supposed that I had told you before this. I work for Mr. H. S. Babesch and son. they carry on a large bisness. he has two sons in the front shop and a part of the time a clerk in the back shop. there is a man that sews all of the time and one lady besides myself. her name is Claria Loomis from Groton[1]. there has been three of us untill lately. they have some 20 ladies that sew at home for him. he has work for most of them the whole year. Miss Loomis boards with me, the first house west of the depot. (Now Jut if you will hurry home there may be a chance for you) Miss Loomis is one of my best friends. quite pretty and you could call to see me and get acquainted with her. I guess she is like me in liking all of the soldiers, but if you wait untll next fall it may be to late. she may be gone (forever) from Homer but not to supertend a soldiers home. Jut, take up with my advice and come home.

As for the sleigh riding it is out of the question. we do not have such good long ones as I did in Solon. you knew that Mr. Carr was in the army. I have not been on that hill since we went up there. I do not know as I ever want to go again. as it is late I must cease.

P.S. I shall expect to hear from you soon.
once more Good Bye
Mary

1. About 10 miles west of Cortland.

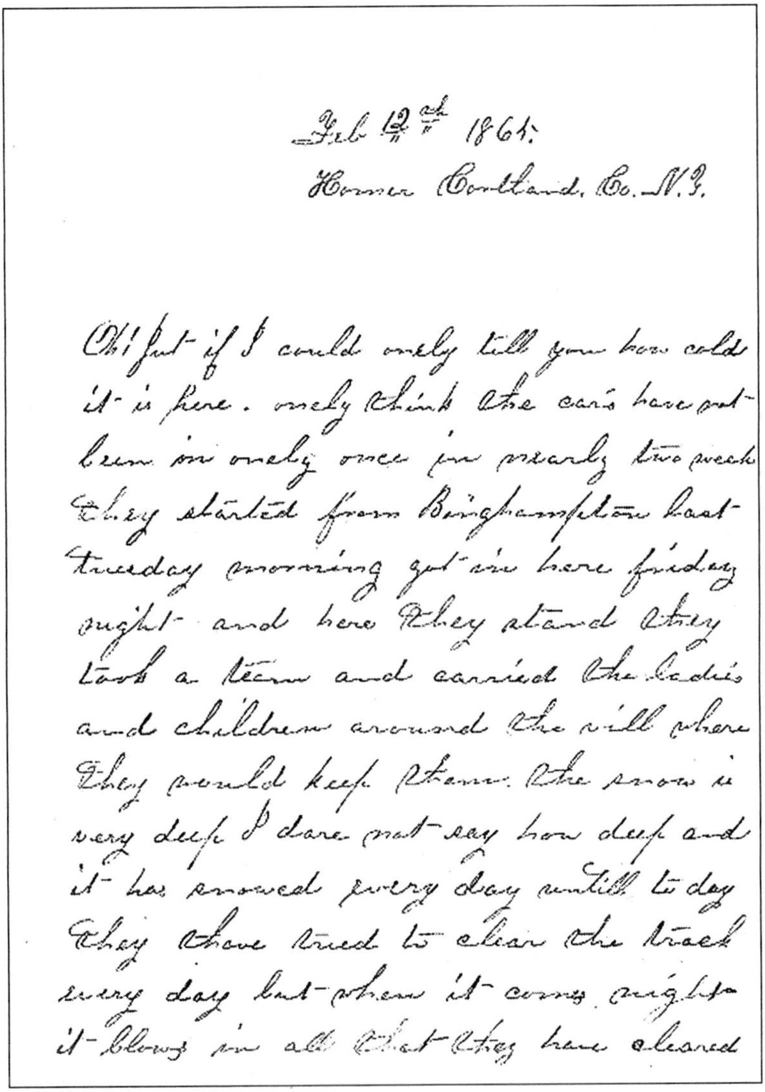

Feb 12th 1865.
Homer Cortland. Co. N.Y.

Oh! but if I could only tell you how cold
it is here. only think the cars have not
been in only once in nearly two week
they started from Binghampton last
tuesday morning got in here friday
night and here they stand they
took a team and carried the ladies
and children around the hill where
they could keep them. the snow is
very deep I dare not say how deep and
it has snowed every day untill to day
they have tried to clear the track
every day but when it comes night
it blows in all that they have cleared

Figure 9.4 First page of the preceding letter from Mary to Justus

A poem, apparently enclosed in one of the letters:

Feb. 20, 1865

Oh; what bosom but must yield,
       When like Pallas you advance
With a thimble for a shield
       And a needle for a lance.

Fairest of the stitching train,
       Ease my passion by your art.
And, in pity for my pain
       Mend the hole that's in my heart.

**Figure 9.5 Monument at Sailor's Creek
(2007 photo by author)**

Remembered friend

I am sure that you will think it is a long time since I recieved your kind and welcomed letter, but I answer it the first oppeortunity. I was to Marathon when your letter and a number of others came in town. My sister Em was very sick. they sent for me to come down. went on the first train. was all day getting 16 miles for the roads were very bad. found her quite sick. staid with her over two weeks. while I was there sent to Homer and got a number of letters. yours was one of the number. I was very glad to hear from you again. I had so much to do for my sister. I did not have much time to write onely as I wrote to Mr. Tompkins, so I had to put it off untill this present time. I left my sister some better. have not heard from her since. Oh Jut, you never heard of such a flood as we have had in Homer and all around here. you know the snow was very deep. last thirsday night it rained very hard. it took off every bridge around here but one. the vill was partly covered with water. I could not get to my work. they went all through main st with a little boat. the cars cannot go. the one below here is in the river. the bridge between here and Cortland is gone. I have heard that the port watson bridge was partly gone and that McGrawville was badly torn up. McLean they say $16,000 will not pay the damage. the cellars were all full. I think it must have injured this vill very much.

Jut, I have been quite well since I wrote you last except a hard cold. it is very bad weather for colds. the last I heard from home they were all sick with bad colds. I have not seen any new shugar but there has been some in town for $.50 a pound. I think there has not been much made yet. how I wish I could have some, and while I was eating it I would not forget you boys down south. just think next spring you will be at home and hope you will be spared to come. then you can make shugar and if you invite me over some day I shall come and help eat it. that will be some help.

You wondered why I wrote as I did about Miss Loomis. she is the lady that boards with me. we both sat at the table a writing. she was writing to her cousin and I to you. she wrote a number of lines to him about me, then read it to me, so I told her it was just as fair for me as it was for her, so I wrote what I first thought off.

You wrote in your last about your Uncle that had just died in the army. which Uncle was it? I did not know as you had an Uncle in that Regt.

It is a very plesant day. it begins to look like summer. the rain took the snow mostly off. how I do hope that you will get discharged before it gets such warm weather. would it not seam good to get home again. I think it would be a happy time to you

341

and your parents and Sister. yes we would all be happy to see you home again. what sweet words Home again.

I have been to church all day and shall go out this eve. this afternoon a gentleman from Ohio preached. he got so far in the cars and cannot go from here.

Jut as I have got my paper nearly full I must close. hoping to hear from you soon. I do not know as you will ever get this for the cars cannot run yet but as I have time thought I would write once more.

Good bye
Mary

Figure 9.6 Cumberland Church today (author 2007 photo)

Camp of the 10<u>th</u> N.Y. Cav.
Va., Mar. 28<u>th</u>, '65

Friend Mary,

I recieved your letter last night and now improve the first oportunity to answer it. for I can not say when I shall have another chance to write. we are now expecting a move every day.

Gen. Sheridan arrived here with his Cav. last night. It is thought that we will join him and then go to meet Gen. Sherman, although there is nothing definite. It is now warm and pleasant here. fruit trees are in bloom, citizans are getting in their cropps as fast as possible.

Last saturday at 4 a.m. the Rebs charged one of our forts just up in front of our camp and took it. they pulled our fellows out of bed. told them that they was giving furlows. they took them (the 14<u>th</u> heavy Artillery) a most all prisonors. now was not that to bad to be routed perhaps from pleasant dreams to find themselves prisoners, But they had to take their turn. The Rebs got through our lines for some ways.

Our men closed up the gap when they came in and cut them off and having a cross fire on them they had to surrender, some 3,500 of them. there was a great many of them (others) killed and wounded. The same day on our extreme left the 5<u>th</u> and 2<u>nd</u> Corps had a fight and took as many more prisoners.

It is the opinion here that this war can not last but a few more months longer. I for one hope it will not. My Uncle that was in the 185th was Fathers half brother. He lived up near the County House. I have not been over to the 185<u>th</u> in a long time.

<u>Mary, Pleas except the Album as a token of esteem and grattitude from me.</u>

I am sorry that I have not a <u>photograph</u> to put in it. <u>I think you have.</u>

Yes, yes, would that I <u>could</u> say <u>Home again.</u> I may not ever have the chance but provided I do I think I'll know how to appreciate them.

Lt. says saddle up for drill.

Well, Mary, just as we got ready to drill there was an order came to get ready to break camp. I presume that we will have to leave these quarters some time tonight. It seems a most like leaving home we have been here so long. Mary do not delay writing on act of our moving. <u>I may</u> not have a chance to write you in some time. I remain as ever your Friend

J. G. Matteson

Appomattox Campaign (Sheridan Returns)

Sheridan returns with the First and Third Cavalry Divisions, and takes command of Grant's Cavalry again on March 27, 1865. Not much had happened in the preceding month, apparently, but Sheridan soon gets things going again for the Cavalry in the Army of the Potomac. Preston describes Grant's concerns, and his next movement [2]:

> On the 27th of March the Cavalry Corps was reunited. General Sheridan, after thoroughly renovating the Shenandoah Valley, took the First and Third Cavalry Divisions and marched overland to the Army of the Potomac. ...
>
> In anticipation of a successful termination of the campaign about to be opened by General Grant, President Lincoln had established himself at City Point, that he might the more readily receive information from the front. [He had come down from Washington on the paddle wheeler *River Queen* to be close to the action when it ended. He took up headquarters on the *Malvern*, a captured blockade runner that Admiral David Porter was using for his flagship.]
>
> General Grant had felt some apprehensions lest General Lee should quietly slip away from his front, and by forced marches unite with General Johnston to try and overcome General Sherman before assistance could reach him. The instructions to General Sheridan were to proceed with the cavalry to Dinwiddie Court House, to be in readiness to strike the enemy in flank and rear, in which he was to be supported by a corps of infantry.

The CWSAC describes the first fight at Dinwiddie Court House as follows, and calls it the fight at Lewis's farm [3]:

> On March 29, in the opening moves of Grant's spring offensive, Sheridan marched with the army's cavalry followed by the V Corps toward Dinwiddie Court House to turn the right flank of Lee's Petersburg defenses. The Union V Corps under Maj. Gen. G.K. Warren crossed Rowanty Creek, moved up the Quaker Road toward the Boydton Plank Road intersection, and

encountered Johnson's Confederate brigades. A sharp firefight forced the Confederates back to their entrenchments on the White Oak Road.

Second Dinwiddie Fight

Preston continues his narration [4]:

The Tenth was in line, and commenced the march with the cavalry at 5 A.M. [on March 29, 1865], going via Reams Station again to Dinwiddie Court-House [#2 on Map 9.1], where it bivouacked.

It rained hard on the evening of the 30th and all day on the 31st, making it impossible to move artillery. In the afternoon of the 30th the Tenth marched toward Hicksford Station, and bivouacked.

General Fitzhugh Lee, with his division, was on the extreme left of the Confederate army on the 28th. He was hurriedly sent by General Lee to meet the threatened movement against his right, with instructions to assume command of all the cavalry, and such infantry supports as would be sent. But on the evening of the 30th General Pickett assumed command of all the troops to move against Sheridan next morning.

General Sheridan was made aware about dark that not only was the entire Confederate cavalry in his front, but that a large force of infantry as well was in position to dispute his further progress. The whole number has been put down at 5,760 cavalry and 6,600 infantry.

The brigade of brevet Brigadier General Charles H. Smith (Colonel of the First Maine Cavalry) occupied the extreme left of General Sheridan's line, and this brigade received the first shock of the Confederates' desperate assault. On the right of Smith was Gregg's brigade [Colonel Irvin Gregg had been recently brevetted a Brigadier General] posted along the low ground, with Davies's brigade joined to their right. The rebels, in greatly superior numbers, swept from the woods and forced General Davies's brigade back toward the right of our line, and then bore down upon Gregg's right flank. But at the same time General Gregg had left his position, and was hastening with his

345

brigade, mounted, to strike the rebels in the rear. After some stubborn fighting Davies's brigade was forced back. The Tenth marched to Dinwiddie Court House at dark, where the led horses were in waiting.

The CWSAC describes the resulting second battle at Dinwiddie Court House in the following description [5]:

On March 29, with the Cavalry Corps and the II and V Corps [infantry], Sheridan undertook a flank march to turn Gen. Robert E. Lee's Petersburg defenses. A steady downpour turned the roads to mud, slowing the advance. On March 31, Maj. Gen. W.H. Fitzhugh Lee's cavalry and Pickett's infantry division met the Union vanguard north and northwest of Dinwiddie Court House and drove it back, temporarily stalling Sheridan's movement. With Union infantry approaching from the east, Pickett withdrew before daybreak to entrench at the vital road junction at Five Forks [#4 on Map 9.1]. Lee ordered Pickett to hold this intersection at all hazard.

Figure 9.7 Dinwiddie Court House photo by author (2007)

Battle at Five Forks

Preston describes the pivotal Battle at Five Forks as follows [6]:

> The morning of April 1st was foggy. General Warren [V Corps] had been ordered to Sheridan's assistance the night before, and was expected to open the ball on the flank and rear of the Confederates. But time passed, and no attack. Meantime Merritt's and Custer's troops were "feeling" the enemy and doing some fighting until evening, when, the Fifth Corps having arrived, it was in conjunction with the cavalry moved against the enemy at Five Forks [#4 on Map 9.1]. The fighting became very heavy and was continued through the night. Prisoners in sufficient numbers to start a fair-sized if not a respectable Confederacy were brought in. Sheridan had evidently struck a soft spot in the rebel line and was pushing things in his characteristic manner.
>
> Ten o'clock, Sunday morning, April 2d, found the Tenth *en route* for the South Side Railroad. The night had been a tumultuous one. The cannonading, at times, fairly shook the earth. General Grant had ordered a general assault of the Confederate lines at 2 A.M., but as some of the commanding officers were not ready, a delay of two hours was granted, during which the artillery were ordered to continue a heavy cannonading.

The CWSAC describes the battle of Five Forks on April 1 in the following description [7]:

> Gen. Robert E. Lee ordered Pickett with his infantry division and Munford's, W.H.F. Lee's, and Rosser's cavalry divisions to hold the vital crossroads of Five Forks at all hazard. On April 1, while Sheridan's cavalry pinned the Confederate force in position, the V Corps under Maj. Gen. G.K. Warren attacked and overwhelmed the Confederate left flank, taking many prisoners. Sheridan personally directed the attack, which extended Lee's Petersburg lines to the breaking point. Loss of Five Forks threatened Lee's last supply line, the South Side

Railroad. The next morning, Lee informed Jefferson Davis that Petersburg and Richmond must be evacuated. Union general Winthrop was killed; "Willie" Pegram, beloved Confederate artillery officer, was mortally wounded. Dissatisfied with his performance at Five Forks, Sheridan relieved Warren of command of the V Corps.

This "breakthrough" of the Confederate lines signaled the nearing of the end of the hostilities between the North and the South. The only hope for Lee was to flee Richmond and join forces in states south of Virginia.

**Figure 9.8 Five Forks today, from
NPS signboard (2007 author photo)**

Destruction of Lee's Trains and Wagons at Paine's Cross Roads

Preston continues his discussion of the current operation [8]:

Then, up and in line again at 4:30 A.M. on the 5th. It was hard work, but the boys responded to every call with alacrity and cheerfulness. This was a star-day for Davies's brigade. It moved out at 6 A.M., and fell upon General Lee's wagon-trains at Paine's Cross-roads [#8 in Map 9.2]. The escort was dispersed, and the dingy vehicles consigned to the flames. Five pieces of artillery and several battle-flags, besides some prisoners, were the substantial rewards of the enterprise and gallantry of General Davies and his followers. [Justus Matteson and the rest of the 10th NY were in Davies' First Brigade of the Second Cavalry Division.] After sending the plunder on the road to Jetersville, the boys were reminded that there was some of the Confederacy still alive, as a vigorous attack was made in their rear. The return march was being made over the same route on which the brigade had advanced. The Tenth, having in charge the captured guns and prisoners, was leading, with Companies A and L, under Captain Perry, in advance. When near Jetersville [#6 in Map 9.2], Captain Perry reported the enemy in great numbers in his front. In the retrograde movement, with the captured property to care for, General Davies had his hands full. The brigades of Gregg and Smith had been sent to his assistance, and they came with ready blades and knightly valor. The First New Jersey was sent forward, and made a gallant charge, in which its brave young commander, already decorated with more than a dozen honorable scars, went down, with a bullet through his brain. And here, too, Major Thomas, of the First Pennsylvania, lost a leg. Rosser's and Munford's divisions of [Confederate] cavalry, under General Fitzhugh Lee, were the troops with which the Second Division was contending. They fought with a determination born of despair.

Amelia Springs

The CWSAC also documents a battle at Amelia Springs, occurring on April 5 [9]:

> On April 5, Confederate cavalry under Fitzhugh Lee and Rosser assaulted Union cavalry under George Crook as they returned from burning Confederate wagons at Painesville. This running fight started north of Amelia Springs and pushed through and beyond Jetersville.

Battle of Sailor's Creek

Preston describes the next fight at Sailor's Creek [10]:

> At daybreak on the 6th the Tenth was on the march with the rest of the division for the enemy's left - if he had any left. The story of this memorable day's action at Sailor's Creek [#9 on Map 9.2, often referred to as "Sayler's Creek"], on the part of the Tenth, is best told in the words of prominent participants.

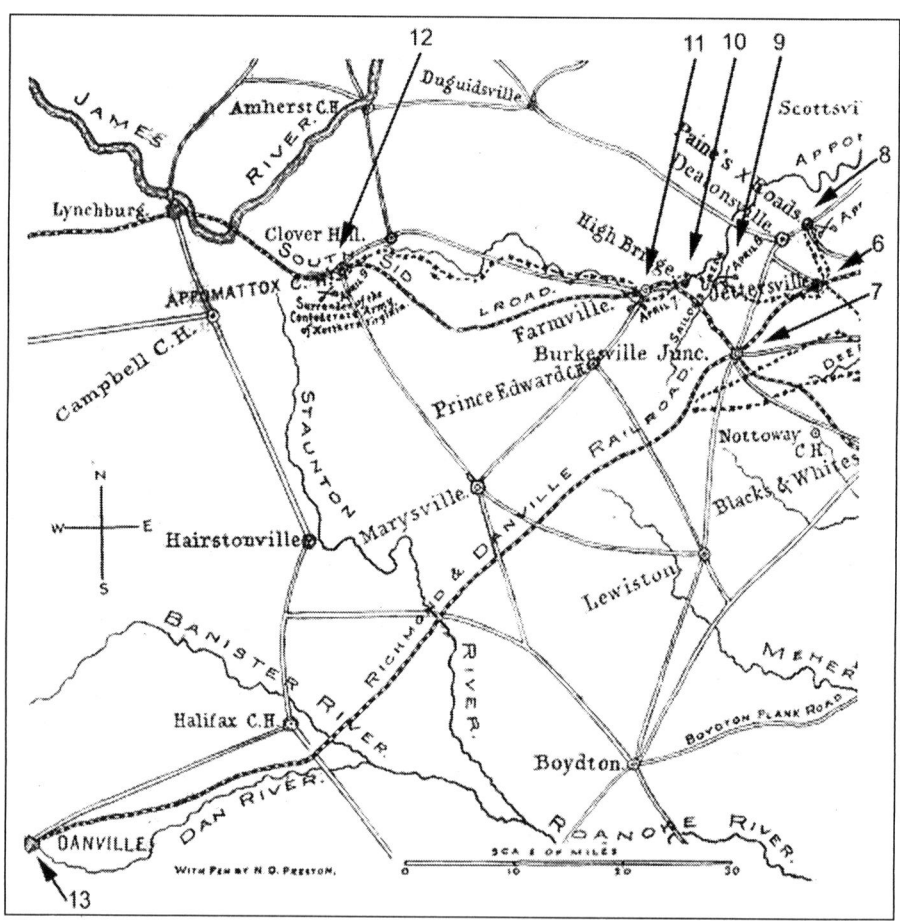

Map 9.2 March/April 1865 Actions of the Tenth New York around Appomattox Court House

Hugo Mulertt, in Company C of the 10th New York, seems to have the most gripping description of this battle, of several that are included in Preston's *History of the Tenth New York* :

> It was the memorable 6th of April, 1865. After several changes in our position, during which we built breastworks and rifle pits, to leave them again when completed, we entered another piece of woods to our right: Here we met a large force of our cavalry preparing for an attack. The enemy had found us out, however, and shelled the woods to such a degree that we were compelled to leave it. Our own battery of four pieces came into action also.

> Before us was a large field. The enemy occupied the woods bordering it on the opposite side, and had breastworks all along the edge of it. About midway between us and the enemy, not much more than a hundred yards from us, was an oak fence. This fence kept us out of sight of the enemy, but it likewise hindered us from making a successful charge on them.

> We dismounted and led our horses into a lower piece of the field, where the latter were out of reach of the bullets. My company was ordered to pull down that fence, and use the rails to barricade a road on the right of us.

> We advanced, crawling on our hands and knees, to the fence, and taking the rails down one by one we passed them along toward the right, where they were used to build the barricade. I was about the third or fourth man from the road. It is hardly necessary to state that we were sharply watched by the enemy, and the least exposure on our part was fatal. In one rail that I was passing, three bullets hit at once while I held it. All this time the charges of eight cannon crossed both ways immediately over our heads.

> Opposite to where we were barricading the road the enemy's infantry prepared for a charge on us. At this moment our bugle called us back.

We had barely reached our horses when Colonel Avery put his case around his pipe, drew his saber, and thundered in his stentorian voice:

"Tenth New York - atten-cho-a-o-n! Draw-sa-ber! Forward-tro-ott!"

Then the bugler sounded the charge. The bands began to play in our rear. Cannon roared and shells screeched all around us. On the spot where the fence had been we encountered the rebel cavalry face to face, horse to horse, in open field - a fair trial! What a terrible mass we were, cutting to right and left against each other and our horses as well! Some took hold of their antagonists with their hands to pull them out of their saddles. Even our horses appeared to make it an individual affair among themselves, for they kicked up in front and bit at each other. How long we were such a solid mass, almost wedged together and pressed against from all sides by the horses that one could almost have broken his legs, I do not know. Riderless horses with bloody saddles became more and more frequent. One man after another disappeared, and the line of battle became so mixed with empty horses that one could not reach his antagonist with the saber, and revolvers and carbines were used.

"Stoop down as much as possible in a saber-fight" was our golden rule; and so, with as little exposure as possible, we got in our work.

There! that bearded fellow who just takes aim; you make a motion to fire at him, but before your carbine is on your cheek he drops his piece, his body falls forward, then to the right, from his horse, which takes fright, turns around and runs away, dragging its helpless rider, whose foot is caught in the stirrup, along on the ground. Somebody else served him before you could. You look now for another target, but, as soon as your shooting "tells," you are served the same way.

Figure 9.9 Battle of New Market reenactment; 2006 photo by author

Reinforcements reached the enemy from the right, coming out of the woods. They made a fierce attack to break our line, but we resisted the strain. Now they wavered; their ranks became weaker. They looked toward the right, then to the left, and at this critical moment our reserve came up. This decided the day. The rebels broke, their bugles sounded the retreat, and we answered it with a hurrah!

We followed them closely, but nearing their breastworks on the edge of the woods we received a volley from the infantry behind it, that, no doubt, injured many in rear of us, but with us there was no stop. We jumped clear over the works, and many of the men behind it were killed by the hoofs of our horses.

Following another road, we met some of the enemy's wagons, broken down and on fire. They were surrounded by several of our men, who hastily searched them and prigged things out of them. We imagined that they were money wagons, and hastened to assist them. But we were agreeably surprised when we discovered that they contained something far more valuable to us then than gold - their contents were potatoes, some already baked. We filled our haversacks with them and went on again.

It was evening, but it was by no means dark yet. Some of the boys directed our attention to the beautiful red sunset. We all looked in that direction, but soon discovered that the red shine over us was not caused by the departing sun. It was the reflex of the numberless wagons, with the supplies of the enemy and the forest, that were on fire. It was terribly beautiful; the firmament in the direction in which the enemy retreated was one immense glow.

We stopped for the night at about eight or nine o'clock. We fed our horses on corn-meal, of which large quantities had fallen into our hands, and soon fell asleep.

About 2 A.M. the bugles awoke us. In such cases we used to touch one another for the purpose of awakening. I took hold of the leg of my neighbor, but oh, horror! It was stiff; he was dead. The next to me, whose head was joining mine from the opposite direction, was asleep yet, too. I touched him; he was also cold and stiff. I jumped to my feet with a spring at this discovery, and stepped to the fire, where I was asked whether I had also slept upon some dead Johnny.

"Not on one, but side by side of two," I replied.

Our Regiment had camped on the battlefield. These bodies we had noticed the night before, but we took them for sleeping soldiers - which, indeed, they were - and were careful not to awaken them in their needed slumber. We had finally laid ourselves beside them for the sake of warmth and company.

At daybreak we passed the headquarters of General Sheridan. Here we saw the Confederate battle flags that we had helped to capture the afternoon before, planted in the ground in a long row in front of his tent. We counted them as we passed; they were twenty-eight in number.

After this we passed a camp containing the prisoners; their number was thousands, including General Ewell himself. In addition we had captured many pieces of artillery, the greater part of Lee's wagon train, and an immense number of mules and horses. The latter came handy for those of our comrades who had lost theirs; they could now be remounted and stay with us. ...

General Sheridan says of the battle of Sailor's Creek:

"The complete isolation of Ewell from Longstreet in his front and Gordon in his rear led to the battle of Sailor's Creek, **one of the severest conflicts of the war**, for the enemy fought with desperation to escape capture, and we, bent on his destruction, were no less eager and determined. The capture of Ewell, with six of his generals and most of his troops, crowned our success, but the fight was so overshadowed by the stirring events of the surrender, three days later, that the battle has never been accorded the prominence it deserves."

And of the action of General Davies's brigade in this fight, General Crook, commander of the Second Cavalry Division, has been pleased to say that it **"made one of the finest charges of the war**, riding over and capturing the works and their defenders. The enemy on the right, who were thus cut off from retreat, surrendered and were taken by different parties."

At the close of this eventful day [April 6, 1865] General Sheridan forwarded General Grant the report, closing with the memorable words, "If the thing is pressed, I think Lee will surrender." This message was transmitted by the Lieutenant-General to the President, who was at City Point, eagerly watching the course of events, and Mr. Lincoln returned the laconic answer, "Let the thing be pressed."

The CWSAC describes the battle of Sailor's Creek as follows [11]:

On April 6 at Sailor's Creek, nearly one fourth of the retreating Confederate army was cut off by Sheridan's Cavalry and elements of the II and VI [Federal infantry] Corps. Most surrendered, including Confederate generals Richard S. Ewell, Barton, Simms, Kershaw, Custis Lee, Dubose, Hunton, and Corse. **This action was considered the death knell of the Confederate army.** Upon seeing the survivors streaming along the road, **Lee exclaimed "My God, has the army dissolved?"**

Figure 9.10 Possibly one of the original double bridges at this Sailor's Creek location (2007 photo by author)

Figure 9.11 Ewell's surrender at Sailor's Creek

Battle of Farmville

Preston describes the Battle of Farmville in the following [12]:

Up and in pursuit again at 6 A.M., on the 7th, Crook's division leading, with the First Brigade [including the 10th New York] in advance. Prisoners, wagons, etc., were constantly being added to the stock on hand during the march. As the column approached Farmville [#11 in Map 9.2], the enemy hastily decamped, after burning the bridge, cars, locomotives, etc. The Tenth charged into the town, to find only hospitals, filled with Confederate wounded. After crossing the Appomattox River, the Second Brigade, under General [Irvin] Gregg, took the advance, and soon after marched into an ambush, and the head of the column was cut off, and General Gregg taken prisoner. General Davies moved his [First] brigade promptly to the assistance of the Second, and the Tenth became engaged with the enemy at close quarters.

Of the fight at Farmville, Captain David Pletcher gives the following account:

> Davies's brigade passed through Farmville on the 7th of April, in hot pursuit of the fleeing Confederates. General Davies halted his command about three miles south of the town, and dismounted the men in the fields to the right of the road. While here, the Second Brigade, with General Irvin Gregg at its head, passed us and took the advance. We were enjoying the rest, lying upon the grass, when the sound of rapid firing came from the direction taken by Gregg's brigade. Our brigade was mounted and marched briskly forward, the First New Jersey in advance. A slight turn in the road revealed a little ravine in front. The Jersey boys had passed this and entered the woods beyond, when they encountered the panic-stricken pack-train of the Second Brigade in full retreat. On they came, striking the Jersey regiment with a vigor that broke their formation, and carried them along with the force of the tide, into an open field, near where the other regiments of the brigade were drawn up in the road. Here the Regiment rallied, and was soon reformed. Our Regiment was just at the turn in the road, waiting for the pack-train to pass. The Regiment came very near

meeting the same fate as the New Jersey regiment, the first squadron being run into and somewhat disorganized. I called upon Captain John P. White, whose squadron was in front of mine, to charge the enemy, who were emerging from the woods in large numbers, and shooting the panic-stricken trainmen. The First Jersey was doing excellent service in the road and to the left of it. I ordered my squadron to draw sabers, and moving to the right of the road, charged the advancing enemy, the officers and men of the broken squadron joining us. General Davies asked Colonel Avery what officer was leading that charge, and, when told, remarked that he would probably get all the fighting he wanted. We captured a large number of prisoners, and had a lively chase after a Confederate stand of colors. The bearer succeeded in crossing a deep ditch, thus saving the colors. Then the Grays replied, and we were compelled to call for help. They came promptly, and again we charged the rebels across the field; then we were in turn driven back across the ravine. Meantime the fight along the road was very hot, the First Jersey and our Regiment being most warmly engaged, the Twenty-fourth New York being in the field to our right. Reinforcements were constantly coming from the woods to the assistance of the rebels in the road, which they made desperate efforts to clear. We took quite a number of prisoners and several colors.

In the charge made by the rebs on the road, quite a number of them were cut off. Lieutenant Reynolds, of Company A, took a prisoner, who, in passing his gun, discharged it full in Reynolds's face, the bullet just grazing his head.

Harris Daniels, of Company F, gave chase to a reb, and when close upon him another comrade came to the assistance of the rebel, and Daniels was compelled to do the flying act. A brother of Daniels came upon the scene and rushed to the rescue. As he was a farrier, he had only a revolver, and that was empty. But he dealt one of the fellows a tremendous blow with it, and threw it at the other one's head as he put spurs to his horse and sped away.

The Regiment lost a number in killed and wounded in this affair.

A Confederate cavalryman, writing of the Farmville affair, says:

"The next morning, April 7th, found us still acting as the rear-guard, and from the High Bridge on to Farmville [about 3 miles] there was a constant skirmish with the enemy's advance. They moved slowly and we were kept in observation. Meanwhile a part of Mahone's division had prepared for their reception at a little church near Farmville, and we retired behind our infantry line there. Just at the point where the road crossed the Farmville road there was a blockade; nearly all the wagons and trains were hopelessly stuck in the mud.

General R. E. Lee was resting quietly at this place, looking over a map, with many officers of high rank grouped around him or dismounted near at hand. As we approached the spot a heavy column of Federal cavalry was seen coming at a charge, evidently bent on capturing the trains. Before they could reach the position, however, a regiment of Rosser's old brigade and a part of Munford's command charged the flank of the Federal column, dispersing the whole force and capturing General Irvin Gregg and bringing him a prisoner before General Lee. Our brigade went on over to the left and picketed that flank all the night. The end was now near. During the night the blockade was relieved and the trains of the army placed on a parallel road."

**Figure 9.12 High Bridge over Appomattox
River 3 miles east of Farmville**

The CWSAC describes the fighting over the High Bridge (#10 in Map 9.2) across the Appomattox River on April 7th in the following [13]:

> On April 6, the Confederate cavalry fought stubbornly to secure the Appomattox River bridges. Confederate general Dearing was mortally wounded. On April 7, elements of the II Corps came up against Longstreet's rear guard attempting to fire the High Bridge and wagon bridge [which runs underneath the railroad bridge]. Union forces were able to save the wagon bridge over which the II Corps crossed in pursuit of Lee's army. Failure to destroy this bridge enabled Union forces to catch up with the Confederates at Farmville.

The CWSAC also describes the fighting at Farmville (#11 in Map 9.2) and Cumberland Church on April 7th in the following [14]:

> Near 2 P.M. on April 7, the advance of the Union II Corps encountered Confederate forces entrenched on high ground near Cumberland Church. The Union forces attacked twice but were repulsed, and darkness halted the conflict. Union general Smythe was mortally wounded nearby, and [Brigadier General] J. I. Gregg was captured north of Farmville.

Preston continues his description of the ending events of the Civil War [15]:

> After the Farmville fight the Regiment recrossed the river, and, marching toward Lynchburg, bivouacked about midnight.
>
> Custer and Merritt moved up the railroad on the morning of the 8th, followed by the Second Division, the Tenth moving out about 8 A.M. Custer's boys captured four trains of cars laden with supplies for Lee's famishing army, besides twenty-five pieces of artillery, a hospital train, and a large number of wagons [at Appomattox Station]. That the already disheartened Confederates might have no rest, General Sheridan directed that skirmishing be kept up during the night.
>
> General Sheridan says in his Memoirs, Vol. ii, p. 190:

> Meanwhile the captured trains had been taken charge of by locomotive engineers, soldiers of the command [Sheridan's], who were delighted, evidently, to get back at their old calling. They amused themselves by running the trains to and fro, creating much confusion, and keeping up such an unearthly screeching with the whistles that I was on the point of ordering the cars burned. They finally wearied of their fun, however, and ran the trains off to the east, toward General Ord's column.

The CWSAC describes action at Appomattox Station (#12 in Map 9.2) on April 8 in the following [16]:

> Custer's division captured a supply train and twenty-five guns, driving off and scattering the Confederate defenders. This unique action pitted artillery without infantry support against cavalry. Custer captured and burned three trains loaded with provisions for Lee's army.

General Davies Official Report of First Brigade Actions from March 28 to April 14, 1865

HEADQUARTERS FIRST BRIGADE, SECOND DIVISION
CAVALRY CORPS, NOTTOWAY COURT-HOUSE, VA
April 14, 1865

Major H.C. WEIR, *Assistant Adjutant-General*
Second Division, Cavalry Corps

MAJOR: I have the honor to forward the following report of the operations of my command from the 28th of March to date: On the morning of the 29th of March the brigade broke camp near Petersburg and marched *via* Nolan's Bridge to Dinwiddie Court-House and encamped for the night on the Boydton Plank Road. On the following day, in the morning, a reconnaissance went out under Major Snyder, Tenth New York Cavalry, and communicated with the left of our infantry forces. On the afternoon of the 30th the brigade moved out on the road leading to Five Forks and reported to Brevet Major-General Merritt, whose forces were engaged at that point. The brigade did not go into action, but stood until dark ready to act, though not called on. That night I encamped near the house of J. Boisseau, on the left of the road, picketing out on my left flank.

On the morning of the 31st of March a reconnaissance was sent out under Captain Craig, First New Jersey Cavalry, which discovered the presence of Johnson's division of the enemy's infantry and W.H.F. Lee's division of cavalry on my left and front. Later in the day I was ordered to move my brigade to the rear and left flank to support General Smith's brigade, heavily engaged with the enemy on the road crossing Chamberlain's Creek. I at once moved in that direction. The road being impassable for mounted troops, I took my men down, dismounted. I rode on in advance, and on reaching General Smith learned that he had succeeded in repulsing the enemy, and was not at that time in need of assistance. I immediately returned to my former position. Countermarching my command as I met it on the road, and hearing the sound of heavy firing on my own picket-line, I directed them to return to their former positions at double quick. I found that my pickets at a bridge over Chamberlain's Creek were attacked by overwhelming forces of the enemy and driven back, and that the enemy had succeeded in crossing a large body of troops, consisting of

362

nearly the whole of Pickett's division of infantry. My brigade, coming up, at once engaged the enemy, but after a severe struggle were driven back, having, however, saved the led horses, which at one time were almost within their grasp. I fell back to the road leading from Dinwiddie Court-House to Five Forks, where I reformed my line, connecting my right with the First Division and endeavoring to open communication on my left with the rest of the Second Division. My men fought bravely, but the overwhelming superiority in numbers of the enemy enabled him to turn my left flank. I then fell back across the country to the Boydton Plank Road. I found there one mounted regiment of the First Division - the Sixth Michigan Cavalry - the commanding officer of which made a vigorous demonstration and checked further pursuit on the Plank Road. I reformed my brigade, and, night coming on and the road being recently picketed by the First Division, which had also fallen back to that point I moved to Dinwiddie Court-House, where my led horses had been sent when the engagement became heavy, and went into camp for the night near that point. In this action I met with a severe loss in killed and wounded, and lost a few prisoners. In view of the large force the enemy brought into the field, I fully believe all that was practicable was done, and that my brigade accomplished all that could have been expected from it.

On the 1st and 2d of April the brigade remained in camp near Dinwiddie Court-House, guarding the trains of the corps. On the night of the 2d I moved from Dinwiddie Court-House, in the rear of the train, to the point where the Claiborne road crosses Hatcher's run, and went into camp. On the 3d of April the brigade moved via Sutherland Station across Namozine Creek to Wilson's plantation. Here the command camped for the night.

On the 4th of April the brigade moved to Jetersville and there took position, expecting an engagement, and encamped for the night at that point. On the morning of the 5th of April I moved out from camp under instructions to make reconnaissance on the enemy's rear and ascertain the position of his trains passing through Amelia Springs. I moved to Painesville, and there learned that General Lee's wagon-trains were passing a point about four miles from that town. I immediately moved down at a trot, sending the First Pennsylvania Veteran Cavalry (my advanced guard) at a gallop, and they succeeded in striking the train just as a piece of artillery had been placed in position to repel my advance. Before the piece could be loaded, my men charged through a deep swamp, were upon them, and at once captured the artillery and the men belonging to the battery, and scattered the train-guard at that point (of about four hundred men) in all directions. I sent two regiments - the First Pennsylvania Veteran Cavalry and Twenty-fourth New York Cavalry - at once to the right along the length of the train, directing them to capture all animals and prisoners and destroy all wagons, as, owing to the condition of the roads and the exhausted state of the teams, I did not deem it practicable to bring off the wagons. The First New Jersey Cavalry I kept near the point where the train was first attacked, to act as a reserve and support and to reconnoiter to the left; and to the Tenth New York Cavalry I gave the charge of the prisoners, guns, etc., captured by the First Pennsylvania Veteran Cavalry, with directions to return with them to Jetersville as soon as they were collected. The commanding officers of these regiments each executed the orders given them with fidelity and zeal, and in a short time I was on my way to Jetersville with five guns, eleven flags, three hundred and twenty white prisoners, an equal number of colored teamsters, and over four hundred animals, captured from the enemy, leaving behind me two hundred blazing ammunition and headquarters wagons, caissons, and ambulances.

Shortly after leaving Painesville on my return, Gary's brigade of rebel cavalry, acting as escort to the train, attacked my rear-guard and kept a running fight with my command as far as Amelia Springs, where I formed my brigade and held them (the enemy) in check until relieved by the Second Brigade of this division. I then rode to the head of my column and found that bolted, and that the enemy had obtained possession of the cross-roads in my front, where the road from Amelia Springs to Jetersville joins that to Amelia Court-House. A regiment of the Third Brigade at that point, with the First Pennsylvania Veteran Cavalry and a part of the Tenth New York Cavalry, handsomely repulsed the enemy and drove him from the cross-roads; and I had the satisfaction of bringing safely into camp the whole of the captured property, not losing one prisoner, animal, or gun, in spite of the desperate efforts made by the enemy to retake them. In the afternoon my brigade again went into action to repel an attempt made by the enemy to reach Jetersville from Amelia Springs, and, though much reduced in strength by the large number of men required to guard prisoners and take charge of the captured property, successfully resisted every attack made by the enemy, and made several mounted charges with great gallantry.

On the 6th of April the brigade moved with the division and took part in the attack made on the enemy's infantry and train at Sailor's Creek. A very splendid and dashing reconnaissance of the position was made by the First New Jersey Cavalry, which was of great assistance in the attack. When the order for attack was given, the Twenty-fourth New York Cavalry, Tenth New York Cavalry, and First New Jersey Cavalry charged in line, mounted, and with great gallantry under a heavy fire, followed by the First Pennsylvania Veteran Cavalry as support. The charging regiments behaved admirably, keeping their line perfectly, and, capturing the breastworks, drove the enemy in confusion, capturing many prisoners. Then, charging right on up the hill, they came upon the enemy's wagon-train, which they followed up for some distance, destroying many wagons and capturing many prisoners. In this engagement, seven hundred and fifty prisoners, two guns, and two flags were captured and turned over to Captain Harper, division provost-marshal. Some three hundred prisoners were inadvertently turned over to another command by the officers in charge; and two guns captured by the Twenty-fourth New York Cavalry, which they were unable to bring off at that time, were taken by some other command. On the 7th of April the brigade moved through Farmville, and, after crossing the Appomattox in the rear of the Second Brigade, formed and checked the enemy advancing. After having driven that command, and night coming on, the brigade was withdrawn from the front and marched to Prospect Station [5 miles west of Farmville], on the Lynchburg Railroad [South Side railroad]. On the 8th the brigade moved to the vicinity of Appomattox Court-House, and there encamped for the night. On the 9th the brigade moved out on a reconnaissance around the enemy's right flank; but while on the road, hearing that the rest of the division had been attacked in heavy force, I made a demonstration in that direction and repulsed a cavalry force moving toward the left and rear of our army. Afterward, having been joined by the Second Brigade, I attacked the enemy's cavalry in my front, and was driving them rapidly, when orders directing a suspension of hostilities were received. ....

The officers of my staff have rendered most valuable service, and are all deserving of highest praise for their courage, zeal, and efficiency. The reports of casualties have been already rendered. I annex a copy of receipt from Captain Harper, provost-marshal, of prisoners, and property turned over to him from this command [shown in Table 9.2].

HEADQUARTERS SECOND DIVISION,
CAVALRY CORPS, ARMY OF THE POTOMAC,
OFFICE OF PROVOST-MARSHAL,
IN THE FIELD, *April 14, 1865*

Received from provost-marshal, First Brigade,
Second Division, Cavalry Corps, during the campaign from
March 29th to April 14, 1865:

April 5th	320 prisoners of war at Jetersville, Va.
	310 colored team drivers
	11 battle-flags
	5 guns and teams
	1 caisson
	310 mules
April 6th	750 prisoners of war at Farmville and Sailor's Creek
	2 battle-flags
	2 guns

Table 9.2 Prisoners and property handed over to Provost Marshall

WILLIAM HARPER,
Captain and Assistant Provost-Marshal,
Second Division, Cavalry Corps
Respectfully submitted:
H.E. DAVIES, JR.,
Brigadier-General Commanding Brigade

Lee's Surrender

Preston describes the day of Lee's surrender [17]:

> April 9, 1865 - the day of deliverance after years of travail - was Sunday. The church-bells throughout the quiet and peaceful hamlets and cities of the far-off homes were calling the people to their devotions, where prayers would ascend for that success to the Union arms which later in the day would be celebrated by the joyful ringing of these same bells. The Tenth moved out at 6 A.M., and with the Second Division, under command of General Davies, and the First Brigade, under command of Colonel Avery [including the 10th NY], marched to the left, and soon began skirmishing. General Sheridan says:
>
> > Crook, who with his own and Mackenzie's divisions was on my extreme left, covering some by-roads, was ordered to hold his ground as long as practicable without sacrificing his men, and, if forced to retire, to contest with obstinacy the enemy's advance.
>
> That at least a portion of Crook's troops did "contest with obstinacy the enemy's advance" can be attested by the members of the Tenth, the Regiment uniting in some spirited charges, and assisting to repel counter-charges. In the last charge made by the Regiment, but a few moments prior to the display of the white flag on the rebel lines, Lieutenant N.A. Reynolds became cut off by the impetuosity with which he charged, and was ordered to surrender, but spurring his horse, he ran the gantlet and reached our lines, with a gunshot-wound in his arm and another in his thumb. ...
>
> The scenes attending the surrender of General Lee have been so frequently told that they are familiar to all. In the culmination of all for which the brave Army of the Potomac had struggled for years, the cavalry did their full share and came in for a large measure of the glory attending that great event; and of that cavalry Davies's brigade was active to the last, the Tenth New York gallantly battling to the end, having a number wounded after the white flag was up.

While the Second Cavalry Division was engaged with the enemy on the extreme left, General Sheridan was disposing Custer's and Devins's divisions for attack. When the formations had been completed, and the command for a sweeping charge over the grassy slope was about to be made, General Sheridan says: "An aide-de-camp galloped up to me with the word from Custer: 'Lee has surrendered, do not charge; the white flag is up!' Orders were given to complete the formation, but not to charge." General Sheridan, while on his way to meet Generals Gordon and Wilcox, of the Confederate army, was fired on by Gary's brigade of South Carolina Cavalry; and when Lieutenant Allen, of Sheridan's staff, reached the contumacious General Gary with orders from General Gordon to cease firing, he replied, with something of a dramatic air, "South Carolinians never surrender!" and immediately made Lieutenant Allen a prisoner. But Custer, having heard the firing, moved out promptly to ascertain its cause; and proceeded to bring the recalcitrant last-ditch General to terms. The flight of Gary's brigade followed. Lieutenant Allen was thus released. The last gun had been fired, and the last charge made on the Virginia campaign.

With the surrender of General Lee and the Army of Northern Virginia the War of the Rebellion was practically ended.

The CWSAC describes the final engagement at Appomattox Court House on April 9th [18]:

Early on April 9, the remnants of John Broun Gordon's corps and Fitzhugh Lee's cavalry formed line of battle at Appomattox Court House. Gen. Robert E. Lee determined to make one last attempt to escape the closing Union pincers and reach his supplies at Lynchburg. At dawn the Confederates advanced, initially gaining ground against Sheridan's cavalry. The arrival of Union infantry, however, stopped the advance in its tracks. Lee's army was now surrounded on three sides. Lee surrendered to Grant on April 9. This was the final engagement of the war in Virginia.

Figure 9.13 McLean home where surrender papers were signed (2007 photo by author)

Figure 9.14 South Side RR Station in Petersburg

References

[1] Preston, Noble D., *History of the Tenth Regiment New York Volunteer Cavalry*, New York, NY: D. Appleton and Company, 1892; reprinted by Higginson Book Company, Salem, MA in 1998; pp. 239-241.

[2] Ibid, 244.

[3] National Park Service, Civil War Sites Advisory Commission, http://www.cr.nps.gov/hps/abpp/battles/va085.htm, Battle of Lewis's farm, March 29, 1865.

[4] Preston, *History of the Tenth New York*, pp. 244-245.

[5] National Park Service, Civil War Sites Advisory Commission, http://www.cr.nps.gov/hps/abpp/battles/va086.htm, Second Battle of Dinwiddie Court House, March 31, 1865.

[6] Preston, *History of the Tenth New York*, p. 247.

[7] National Park Service, Civil War Sites Advisory Commission, http://www.cr.nps.gov/hps/abpp/battles/va088.htm, Battle of Five Forks, April 1, 1865.

[8] Preston, *History of the Tenth New York*, pp. 248-249.

[9] National Park Service, Civil War Sites Advisory Commission, http://www.cr.nps.gov/hps/abpp/battles/va091.htm, Fight at Amelia Springs, April 5, 1865.

[10] Preston, *History of the Tenth New York*, pp. 249-250, 252-256.

[11] National Park Service, Civil War Sites Advisory Commission, http://www.cr.nps.gov/hps/abpp/battles/va093.htm, Battle of Sailor's Creek, April 6, 1865.

[12] Preston, *History of the Tenth New York*, pp. 256-258.

[13] National Park Service, Civil War Sites Advisory Commission, http://www.cr.nps.gov/hps/abpp/battles/va095.htm, Battle of High Bridge, April 7, 1865.

[14] National Park Service, Civil War Sites Advisory Commission, http://www.cr.nps.gov/hps/abpp/battles/va094.htm, Battle of Farmville, April 7, 1865.

[15] Preston, *History of the Tenth New York*, p. 259.

[16] National Park Service, Civil War Sites Advisory Commission, http://www.cr.nps.gov/hps/abpp/battles/va096.htm, Fight at Appomattox Station, April 8, 1865.

[17] Preston, *History of the Tenth New York*, pp. 259-261.

[18] National Park Service, Civil War Sites Advisory Commission, http://www.cr.nps.gov/hps/abpp/battles/va097.htm, Battle at Appomattox Court House, April 9, 1865.

CHAPTER 10
Post-Surrender Events

"It is well that war is so terrible- if it were not,
we would grow too fond of it!" R.E. Lee, Dec. 13, 1862

After the Surrender

The war did not end with Lee's surrender. Sherman was still fighting Johnston in the South, and fighting was continuing in the West and Southwest. Johnston and Sherman met on April 17th to discuss surrender terms. Lincoln's Assassination on April 14th affected all participants greatly, but an agreement was signed. The last forces east of the Mississippi were surrendered on May 4th. Finally, all Confederate forces west of the Mississippi were surrendered on May 26th.

Lincoln couldn't wait for Lee's surrender. Having been in City Point for two weeks, as soon as he heard that Richmond had been evacuated by the Confederacy he went there. It was April 4, and after walking around Richmond for a while he went to the Confederate White House and sat in Jefferson Davis' chair for a moment.

Figure 10.1 Sculpture of Lincoln and son Tadd at Tredegar Iron Works Civil War Center in Richmond (2007 photo by author)

Preston describes anti-climatic action of the Tenth New York after Lee's surrender [1]:

The aimless march back toward Petersburg was commenced by the cavalry the day following the surrender. The Tenth moved out at 8 A.M., and at night encamped at Prospect Station [5 miles west of Farmville]. Pickets were established as usual, but the duty which but a few hours before was fraught with so much danger and importance was now but mere form.

On the 11th the march was resumed and continued to Prince Edward Court House [10 miles southwest of Farmville], stopping at Burkesville Junction [#7 on Map 9.2] on the 12th and Nottoway Court House [12 miles southeast of Burkesville Junction] on the 13th. While at the latter place the sad news of the assassination of President Lincoln was received. At a time when such great and disturbing events were crowding fast upon one another, when denials followed rumors and facts were perverted in the interest sometimes of stock-gambling operators, it is not to be wondered at that the first report of the great calamity should have been received with little credence. Of course, the President hadn't been assassinated; it was too improbable for belief. But the story was repeated until the repetitions finally assumed shape, and the dreadful fact was established that the great and good man had been murdered. What a sudden transition from glory to gloom! Strong men wept; crystal drops, fresh from lacerated hearts, stood trembling on bronzed cheeks as the story of the awful tragedy was repeated. Strange admixture - sadness and anger- yet these were the elements which seemed to struggle for supremacy in the hearts of the brave veterans: sadness that one so wise and good- the nation's father- should have been taken away; anger with the man who had perpetrated the deed and the motive which prompted it.

On the day of Lee's surrender Mary happens to write a letter to Justus; and Justus receives the following three letters from Adelia in April, following the President's assassination.

Friend Jut,

I seat myself this beautiful saboath day to answer your kind and welcomed letter that I received last monday eve. right glad was I to hear from you again. And here allow me to thank you for the albium which you sent. pen and ink cannot express my thanks but I do hope that there will a time come when words and acts of kindness can repay you for your rememberance. I was glad to hear that you were well and do hope this will find you the same. we know that a great many are suffering from wounds just received. wheather our friends are amoung the number we know not but if they are not my friends they are some ones friend and they are suffering. if I could do any thing for them I would willingly leave home and all of the comforts of home. April 3rd was a day of rejoicing here and all around. the news was confirmed of the capture of Richmond. it was good news for the North and I think it was for the soldiers. every kind of goods has gone down with the fall of Richmond which is good news for the poor people and those that have to work for their living. but it is not so good for those that have goods on hand. that day or eve was celebrated by the firing of the canon which made some little noys, the ringing of church bells and bon fires. I thought it was quite a confusion but which I suppose you would not have taken any notice of. I have not heard from Frank in a number of weeks but have seen a list of the names of the 185th that were killed and wounded. do not see any name that I know. I have not heard from home since I wrote you last. I hope you hear from there oftener than I do. my folks think that I am so near home I do not want to hear from there, but I shall live just as long if I do not hear from them. or perhaps they think I do not write to them very often.

We are having a beautifull spring. the ground is dry. I do not know much about how much sugar there has been made but I do know that I have not had any warm sugar. I have been invited out to a few sugar parties but it has always happened that I could not go, so I shall have to wait untill next spring. As it is tea time I must close. hoping to hear from you soon but if you cannnot write soon will you allow me to write before receiving one. I am sure you will not care but I shall be anxsious to hear from you again.

Keep up good cheer for I do think it looks like coming home before long. what a happy day it will be when all soldiers return home, but it will be a sad time when a part come and the rest <u>never</u> come. but we will look on the bright side and think of those that will be happy.

Good Bye, Mary

Central News

Assassination of the President

Abraham Lincoln is dead!- Falling by the hand of an assassin, at the moment when peace had come to his country, the universal rejoicing instantly gave way to overwhelming sorrow at the announcement of his untimely death. Secretary Seward was also headed for the assassin's knife, and, at almost the time instant with the attack upon the President, received grievous wounds, which may yet prove fatal.

The circumstances of these dreadful events were as follows:

On Friday evening, April 14, Mr. Lincoln went to Ford's theater, in Washington, accompanied by Mrs. Lincoln and two friends, to witness a performance. While sitting in his private box, at half past 9 o'clock, he was shot with a pistol by an assassin who entered the box and approached him from behind. The ball took effect in the back of the President's head, penetrating the brain for a distance of three inches, inflicting a mortal wound. The instant after firing the shot, the assassin leaped from the box to the stage of the theater, flourishing a long knife, and, shouting the works "*Sic semper tyrannis*," disappeared behind the scenes, and escaped from the rear of the house, where he mounted a horse and fled. The suddenness of the attack stunned every person who witnessed it, and it was only when the screams of Mrs. Lincoln announced the terrible event that the audience realized what had been done. Loud cries arose for vengeance upon the murderer, but for the moment he was beyond the reach of pursuit.

Figure 10.2 Report of Lincoln's Assassination
(enclosed in Mary's letter)

Sunday evening
Apr the 16th 1865

Dear Brother,

We have just received your letters and had waited long and anxiously to hear from you scaring some accident had befalen you. but now I am happy in thinking you will soon be with us. for it does seam as though this evil war was almost over. We have been having such good news of late about the surrendering of Lee's army. We have now the report that Abraham Lincoln is dead. I cannot believe it can it be that any one could murder a man like that. it dont seam possible. our whole country is dressed in mourning. Jim Reed was brought home and burried last Friday. the taking of Richmond has made many wounded.

How thankfull we should be that you are still spared. Now it seems as though you had passed all dangers. for it does seam I thought the fighting was over. I was glad to receive Gregg's photograph. I think he is a noble looking man. I have got lots of photographs. a regular stack of them and when I get able I will have me a large Album. I have got every little one full. they are all relatives. I have got Jimmies. it was copied from a Ambrotype. if I had another I would send it you. but I wouldent part with this for love or mony Sarahs & Inorahs(?). I wish I could write all I have got but it would take to much time. About the Waverly Magazine. I like it very much and love to read it but I have got about 4 month papers that I havent read. for when I was at Cortland I didant have time to read any thing. Pa sent one up to me. and if I took it up to read in the evenin Peter would say I had better read in the Bible or go to bed. so I brought it home unread and since I have been home I have been verry bussy. as you sent for the Waverly again the first six months had not expired. I believe I should have had 4 more before the time was up but they sent me the receipt and commenced sending the paper. so I got two papers every week just alike. but after the old term expires probbily I will only get one. but there will be 4 or 5 papers that I will not get. that is the last of the last term, the new receipt being dated back. as I dont want to keep two alike I will send you some so that you can have some reading.

I guess I shall go to McGrawville tomorrow. Pa is going down to set some posts for Grandma. So Ma and I are going down. Aunt Hellen is going to start for the West tuesday. Whitney lives at Solomans. I suppose that he and Chatt is happy as skunks. they are riding about as usual. every neighbor between here and McGrawville has turned against her, and all stick up for Hellen. I suppose Whitney & Chatt is proud of their baby. But I never have seen it. Jerry Greenman says some folks wishes Chatt was dead but he dont oh no. not just because she lives with two men. Solomon acts like a fool. he dont sence nothing. he did give Chat a talking to but when she was sick his old love came back for her. Now I cant stick up for any relative if I think they do wrong no sooner than anyone else.

Whitney went off one day just as good natured as ever. said he was going off to find a place. and when he got to Syracuse he wrote a letter to Helen saying she could take one side of the world, he would the other. and she went out to Ponds, some of his relations, and stayed a few days. and then came to McGrawville and Grandmothers folks secreted him and his trunks. and then he went up to Solomans and stayed hid in their parlours. and all of the neighbors wondered and talked about Solomons folks having him in their parlour every day. Well all of this time Hellen was most crazy. she had received the letter and went to McGrawville and was bent uppon going to Syracuse to find him and have him explain. but everyone told her she was a fool, and she would run to Solomans for advise. and then to think that Whitney was hid in Solomans parlour when he could see her all of the time. and she perfectly crazy thinking he had gone to the other side of the world. well before Whitney came back Chatt wrote Whitney a letter and told him he musent let anyone see it and he must come back as she couldent live. well as it happend it was sent back to McGrawville and Hellen took the letter out and read it herself. well he was gone 5 weeks. and Solomon told Grovers folks they must move out of the house or their things would be put in the road. well they couldent get a house any where to live in and Whitney had got tired of staying shut up and Solomon made them move out and they went into Groveses old house. the clapboards was all off, the chamber floor was all out and all of the jresticions(?) so it was just like a barn. and only think, the coldest weather in February. It was pretty hard, when he dident want the house for any thing at all. well the very night after they moved Whit came out. oh for pity sakes I might go on and keep making a bad matter worse. but our folks are snoreing. it was nine oclock when I commenced writing this and I know nothing about the time now. but I do know it is time I went to bed & stop my gabbing and get warm for the fire is all out. Oh I went down to Aunt Helens last week and there was some smith girls there from Lisle and Henry Huntly came up & George Rowley and we played Eucre. and had general nice time.

George has completed his trade and can jerk a tooth or take a picture as good as any one. George Holdren(?) says he likes him the best of any one he ever had sick(?) him, but he never has had the priviledge of taking my jhid(?).

It has been a verry rainy day. Marry Hatch is at home, is going back Monday. I have not seen her. Friends are all well. write me soon and accept this from Adelia.

The Solon Times
A. C. Matteson, Publisher
No. 1 Vo. 6
Friday, Apr the 28th, 1865

Dear Brother,

This is a beautiful day and I will pass a little time in writing. Well ma says it rains, so I am afraid it is not agoing to be such a nice day after all. the sun has shone verry warm this forenoon. the trees begin to leave out and spring flours are in blossome. How nice those old daffadils out in the yard. but I suppose every thing is a great deal earlier down there than here. the grass looks fresh and green this evening. We had some verry hard thunder last night. there was two great lumps of thunder struck on the roof right over my head and rolled down on the roof and tumbled off. it allmost shook me out of bed. Ma hadent gone to bed and she said it shook the muffins off of the table. and I suppose if she hadent held the table it would have tiped over. and oh my how it did sharpen. it sharpened awful light.

I have just been to dinner on cabbage & ham & carates. but I dont eat much. my apettight is verry poor this spring. and people say I grow poor. but I dont see any change. I had the sick head ache tuesday and it has stayed with me ever since. I dont know as I care about entertaining it any longer. I have been reading those books you sent me. they were verry good. only the Lion Killer or Terrible Frank ought to have married the Princess. she hadent ought to have died just then. I could roun up a good story better than that. did you send a book, the title Hall Williams, to Cortland for me? I got one when I was out the other day to Peters. they had taken it out and it was pretty much gone up when I got it. I didnt know who sent it as I didnt see the wrapper. I can tell where anything comes from by the hand writing. I sent you a paper yesterday. the first piece is the Idiott Carl. it is a good piece I think. I guess you will think I did have the sick head ache when I put on that wrapper, and vomited on it and ironed in. but I didnt, oh no, I only accidentaly got on a trifle to much musalage.

Friday evening April the twenty eighth, in the year of our Lord Eighteen hundred and sixty five.

I have been to work in the yard to day making flower beds and tired and sleepy, or lazy, as I believe that is the term generly used. however I will try and get up energy enough to write a little more. Pa has been ploughing the garden to day and planting some potatoes. He bought a half bushel of Prince Albert and a half bu Western seeds, at Cortland to plant and we raised two or three bushels of bhili's (?). he is going to plant those. now its tough to have to eat little old dooryard potatoes and rotten at that, and plant the large good ones. but we live in hopes of having something next year *besides rotten potatoes. We have got two hogs. hogs are very high. Pa gave $3. took them when they was four weeks old. We are going to have 4 cows. I guess we will make our pigs weigh 400 a piece unless they should not happen to grow quite so large. We are raising a calf. havent got but three cows yet. have made one tub of butter. Sold it wednesday for 32 cts lb. has been 35. Our folks has set the old goose . she has been setting over two weeks so I presume by the time I write the second letter after this I will be able to write you the particulars conserning the goslings. It rains. it has thundered amost all of the afternoon. and we have had about a dozen showers and then the sun would shine and be verry pleasant. well it has stoped raining. the showers went only about as long as a string. or may be a little longer. oh the flies are so thick. I have to brush them out from under my hair, and then ma says I brush them on her. they are verry thick to night. the rain drives them in. I cant hardly see them but oh my how I can feel them.*

Mr. Pierce heard that Booth was shot at Chicago but do not know for certain whether it was him or not. but I do know that anyone else would have ben taken before they would have been shot.

I was out to Cortland the day of Lincolns funeral. it was a verry solom place. almost every house was draped. almost all business places closed. Aunt Hellen has gone back to Wilmington. she went over a week ago. her folks stayed here and are going to take care of the little girl that they took. Whitney is to work at Solomons and Aunt Marty. Julia Isaacs don't work there any longer. her folks come and took her away though they had a hard time getting her. they made her leave. Caroline is at home. Uncle Harrys folks are all well. our folks was down there wedensday. Walt Owens and his wife was over here Sunday. Walt has bought the first farm this side of his Fathers. there is a new house & barn. I like his wife verry much. Darius goes to McGrawville to school. Dom Brownell was out the other day. says Lovinia was verry miserable. wanted me to go home with him but I couldent go so far from home. Uncle Edd has gone to Norwich to work. Nancy lives to grandpas. Sait works up to Anningers. Frank takes the old Schwards place of the Salisbury boys. it is where they lived last year. so when you write to her you can ask her how he likes working for Frank. I shouldent be surprised if Sait was married to Tim Rose next fall, as Grandfather is harping her about getting married all of the while and he thinks Tim is a little God Allmighty on sticks and she runs with him. Grand Pa says he will give me a sheep with five dollars & a pig if I will marry this spring, but I shant sell my self for a pig this spring, not as any boddy knows of.

I had my fortune told the other day when I was out to Cortland by an old woman that had never seen or heard of me before. she said she could tell my *disposition if I wanted her to. of course I dident believe she knew anything and told her to tell all she see. she said I hadent much faith in fortune telers she could see, and that I was a strong friend and firm enemy. said was a good friend but folks that I dident like I let entirely alone. told my age. Said was 4 in our family. one was gone away from home but <u>he</u> would return before a great while. said I had had a letter from him within a week and there was a photograph in it, but couldent tell whether it was yours or not. said I had mailed a letter to you in less than a week and that when I went home I would get another, so I did out of the office. said when I got home there would be a man and woman at our house. and the man would wear a black felt hat, was tall, and the woman was <u>short, which was Walt & Wife</u>. now the past was all true every bit, and we will have to wait for time to tell whether the future will be or not. I made several wishes. she said I would get all but one. that was of no consequence. I wished you might come home safe and sound. she said I would get that wish. said I would be married in less that 2 years, and I had never as yet seen the man I was to marry. that he owned lots of land, was a Farmer, and had a trade. was a <u>carpenter</u>, and lots of things to numerous to mention. But I expect some day to verry unexpectadly to meet with the afforsaid carpenter and of coars he wont no me so I shall undoubtadly tell him my name & propose the question. for Matrimony is a nut of every mans digestion, and when the shell is cracked pop goes the question.*

Poor old Jenny cat has got a mouse and is out in the rain crying but she cant come in for she is shedding her feathers.

Thinking of any good fortune which I havent thought of before since I came home, I will stop writing and go to bed to dream of the Carpenter and many acres of land. as I cannot print oftner I shall be obliged to call any paper the semi monthly.

Good night-
Adelia

Thursday evening
May the 4th, 1865

Dear Brother,

I received your letter of the 24th yesterday and as ever was happy to hear that you were, as you call it, all right.

and your letter finds us the same as it left you. I have written you two or three letters that you had not got when you wrote this one, and I have sent two Waverlys that you did not say anything about getting.

I got my Waverly yesterday, and your letter and one from Aunt Hellen, one from Mariam Knapp Picket, one from Erastus Reed, Citty Point. Aunt Hellen arrived all safe. she started half past 6 tuesday evening and got in Wilmington at 11 in the Thursday. Mariam sent me her Photograph. it is a verry good one. her Man is in the Army. her things are over to East Homer but she says she dont relish living alone so she stays over to her Fathers. they live within half of a mile of the depot at Homer.

I havent got any of your Photographs at all to spare. you only left two with us. I had one and Ma had one, and I gave the one I had and one of mine to Hellen a year ago last winter when she was out visiting. the other I keep in my album. oh I dont know what to write for you know we dont know anything when you can come home. but hope you will be here soon, as so many are getting discharged. Yes I hope you will be home to selebrate the 4th of July and go to a Ball. I have got it in my mind long ago how I am going to have you <u>dressed up</u>. when you get home you have got to <u>dress</u> do you understand? its <u>dress</u> that makes the man. but mind, you arent going to be dressed up to have some other gal catch ye, because ye will have a sister to foller ye. You cant have no Mate Hatch hanging to you at all. there is a Ball to night to McGrawville, and poor me has to stay at home. or go with a Bill Atwood or some other <u>Bass-wood</u>. so I choose to stay at home and write to keep from getting crazy and dancing around the chairs or alone. now dont you pitty my love conditions? Delany Thompson that was in the store at Solon comes, and Dan Shuler is in the Hotel at McGrawville. Pa talks of going into or to work for Schuyloer Hunter this summer. he has got a patent for boring into the ground and making wells any where. and if it works well he is going to hire hands to go around making them. he dont know yet. but if it works all right I guess he will give Pa 40 dollars a month and find him. I dont think he will go but Pa thinks that he will go.

380

Sunday evening I have been to the schoolhouse to meeting, and am so tired but must finish this to night so as to take it to the office in the morning as I am going down to the villedge to work for Aunt Adeline. I am going down to clean house for her. she is going to make a genral thing of it all over the house. I think I shall run oposition to old Mrs Lurgy. she goes out all over thevilledge housecleaning but then I must do something to get some <u>cash</u> as I am an ashon (?). I have taken my Bonnet to McGrawville and am going to have it done over. for I think it high time, as I have worn it 3 years this spring. should have got it last week but I wont go after it untill I can pay for it which Providence & weather permiting I will get next saturday.

I went to the Hop after all. as Percival said it was thursday I thought perhaps it might be, although I was invited to go Friday evening. but hearing it was thursday evening I supposed it was, and as I had another invatation to go then I thought it must be. however the Gent came Friday and I went. had a splendid time. lots there. Tim Rose, All Newton. lots from Cortland. but I dident know Tim & All. had the nicest supper I ever saw. but poor me. I only drank a cup of tea, for I had a sick headache and vomited. whew. how I would have enjoyed it if it hadent been for that. I dont know where I'll die, when I go to yet (?).

I never saw a party more united, splendid music. oh yes I got those military registers. and Pa said I could get them framed. so I took them down or he when we went down. George Holden frames lots of them that has been sent home. he has got beautiful moulding, so he put them up with glass, two of them and they are perfectly splendid. they are finished, and I told Pa of it. well he said I might pay for them if I got them, he shouldent such darn foolish things to hang out in a parlour. they are three dollars apiece but are large and a splendid ornament. but I thank my stars I have got hands and can work. I worked out this winter and thought I would get me a nice dress this spring. so when Pa went out to Cortland, I went out. and I told him we needed a carpet for our Parlour so we looked at them and he told them he would take one. and little did I think I would have to pay for it. but when he came to pay for it he said I had got to do it. so I payed all I could which was a considerable over half and never got a dud for myself nor havent yet. now I wouldent for worlds have any one know around here but what Pa bought the carpet. for he might have paid for it just as well as not, and I knew it. it is the first new thing we have had to furnish the new house with. and the other night while I was getting ready to go th the hop, I took my company in the parlour. and mercy on me I wont write what he said. but he says I musent take visitors in the parlour unless there is so many that there isent enough room in the rest of the house. says it shouldent be used only on extra occasions. I am afraid _his_ carpet will get soiled and I'm sure I should feel verry bad.

Hank was to the dance. he is a pretty good dancer. but oh my what a long fellow he is getting to be. with his coat clear down to his heals.

Well I must pick up my duds and go to bed and get some rest for I expect to have to go down to the village on foot in the morning as pa cant afford to carry anyboddys hired girl to their work he says.

our folks went to bed long ago. they have been to meeting this afternoon and are snoreing now. we have got a sheep that is sick. it is the best one we have got. it is all bloated up. Pa says it will be dead in the morning. they are all louzy and any head feals as though dead. Oh dear I dont know any more only Elias & Reubin Underwood laid aside their piety, and went to the dance the other night.

Good night Justus write me soon. Adelia. but dont think Im a fool for writing such a lot of trash, but it was in my mind and I had got to get it out and how could I if I dident write to you. Adelia Sleapy head.

Preston continues his discussion of the final days of the Regiment [2]:

> General Avery [having been recently promoted] was in command of the brigade, which remained encamped near Petersburg until the 10th of May, when it was ordered to Washington overland. Acting Quartermaster Oscar Woodruff was detailed to take the brigade "truck" to Washington by steamer. The Regiment proceeded in a heavy rain the first day, but after an uneventful march reached Alexandria on the 16th at 11 A.M. On the 21st it was ordered across the Potomac to Bladensburg. Soon after starting a rain set in, and the Tenth left Virginia as it had entered it nearly three years before - in a rain-storm. Going into camp near Fort Lincoln, clothing was issued to the men of the Regiment the same night, the work continuing until after midnight, preparatory for the grand review.

General Philip Sheridan missed the Grand Review. Sheridan was sent to the Gulf Department to help coral Kirby Smith, who hadn't recognized the surrender yet. It appears that Justus Matteson did not participate in the review. His letter to Mary on May 25 came from City Point, VA, where he was still serving.

Expedition to Danville

Not mentioned by Preston, but included in other summaries of the actions of the Tenth New York, is an expedition from Burkesville Junction (#7 on Map 9.2) to Danville (#13 on Map 9.2) between April 23 and April 29. Burkesville Junction was a major railroad junction, being at the intersection of the South Side railroad, and the Richmond and Danville railroad. Preston didn't discuss any action that might have occurred along the way, but the war was over so action was probably limited.

Justus receives a letter from Mary, and sends her three more letters before he finally gets home, after thirty four months in the Army without a leave. These letters follow.

Jut, you will see by the heading of my letter that I have left the vill of Homer, but it is onely for a few days. The day that I received your kind letter, I also received one from sister Kate. she was very sick and wished me to come out and take care of her. I took the stage the next morning for Groton. I found her what I call very sick and do not know as she any better now. I have been here over a week but cannot stay with her but a few days longer.

I have also been home since I wrote to you last. went Apr. 14th, onely staid three days. I went home to see ma, but she had gone to Marathon. I was very much disapointed. just think I have not seen her in eight months. I had a very good visit to my sisters. Lu was there. I saw your sister in Cortland. she was well and appeared to enjoy herself very much. I did not get home time enough to get some warm shugar, but had some warmed over, but it was not half as good. I have not been to church to day. staid in the house all day with sister. it is a beautiful day. how I long to be out and enjoy it. if Kate could onely be well and enjoy this splendid day with me.

What sad sad news we have had and yet we can say good news has been with it as we were all rejoicing over Lee's surrender. we were called to mourn in the midst of our rejoicing. How glad I am that Booth can do no more harm and that other traitors are being brought to justice. I hope they will all have to suffer according to their deeds. But I do like our new President[3], for he is agoing to send the soldiers home or some of them. Dont you hope you will be one of that number that are coming home. Mr. Warfield says he shall look for Denis home in a few weeks. hope he will come for he is one good boy. his grand father thinks every thing of him.

It is to bad that Milford Brown is wounded and in his face. how bad he will feel to have a scar on his face.

Jut, you must excuse this short letter for I have no time to write you. there is time but I do not feel like writing when sister is sick. hope she will be better when I stay with her a few more days. please direct to Homer and write when convenient. I shall expect to see you in a few weeks. it will be much plesanter than to write.

I remain as ever, your true friend
Mary H

Remembered Friend,

As I presume that you have written to me long e'ere this and looking for an answer, I will venture to write you. I have not recieved any mail since the first of this month. I have not had any directed to this camp, so it has all gone to the Reg't where I thought I should be before this.

I am well, and am enjoying myself first rate, except it is rather dull laying about camp with nuthing to do to pass off the time. though for a few days past I have whiled away some of the time reading the trial of the assassins.

well Mary, I little thought when I broke camp last spring that the rebellion would be so near closed by this time. there is nuthing of it left but Kirby Smiths army, west of the mississippi. and it is reported & confirmed through reble sources that he has been killed by one of his subordinates and that Magruder has surrendered the army. I do not know it to be so but one thing that makes me think it is so is that the 25 corps (colored) which lays below here, had orders to go to texas the other day. a part of them had got on transports at the Point, but they wer sent back. it is thought that Sheridans Cav wer going also, but I dont know whether that would include our briggade or not. The best thing though if it takes us is that there was an order issued for to discharge all soldiers whose time of service expires prior to the first of Oct next immediatley. now our Co's time of inlistment expires before that time, and our time at muster into the U. S. service expires on the 29 of October, so we are not sertin of getting out on that order[1]. but our discriptive list has been sent for & our names sent in and we are expecting them every day.

I suppose our Regt partook in the grand review at Washington on tuesday.

Mary, I think I've got the start of you getting strawberies & cheries this season for I went out about a week ago and got all I could eat, & I shouldent be surprised if I got home to get some more.

I suppose you are a having jolly times this summer. I would like to be there and partake in some of them with you. you need not answer this untill you hear from me again. for we expect to move to washington every day. and then I will write you again.

I remain as ever your Obt. Servant
J. G. Matteson

1. Justus was discharged on July 19, 1865.

Camp of the 10th N. Y. Cav.
near Alexandria, June 4th, 1865

Dear Friend,

    Allthough it is about ten oclock at night I think I have time to write you a few lines. I recieved your letter a week a go but did not answer it for I had writen you but a few days previous and I thought perhaps that I mint have something of importance to write you. I left City Point one week a go yesterday. we arrived here on monday last. had a splendid time on the boat. we are now at the Reg't in camp about 4 or 5 miles from the city.

    There has been a great deel of excitement here for a few days past about our Battallions being mustered out. was quite shure of being on our way for home at one time before this. it was left to Major Blin, who was in Com'd of the Reg't whether we should be mustered out or not and he decided against us. So I suppose we will have to stay our time out. unless there is an order issued from the war department before that time that will take us out. we did not come under the other orders but as our time was so near out the Secretary of war concluded to let us out. as I said if the Major would concent to let us go. It is thought that there will be another order to muster out all whoes time is out in '65 within ten days. if so it wont be but a short time before we get out. and I shall yet spend the fourth in York State.

    I am well and am in hopes that this will find you the same. am in hopes allso that by return mail to hear of Kates quick recovery.

    I recieved a letter from Sister with yours. said that our folks wer well. said she was going to McGrawville to work for a short time.

    Milfred M. Brown has got his discharge and gone home. The 185th has gone home as I suppose you know. I think that they have made a big thing. got big bounties, came out for one year, get discharged within nine months and go home. and we stay here & serve our time out.

    As it is getting to be late I must abstain from writing much more. I am in hopes that this will be my last letter in the army but I presume that I shall have a chance to write many more. I shall expect an answer from this next friday or saturday so I can answer it sunday. A friend to you as ever. I remain

J. G. Matteson

P. S. Direct as usual:
Co. L 10th N. Y. Cav
Washington, D. C.

Camp of the 10th N. Y. Cav, Va.
June 16th, 1865

Dear Friend,

I recieved your kind and welcomed letter two days a go and was <u>much</u> pleased to hear from you again.

Your letter found me in rather poor condition. and I now am not able scarcely to get around. I was taken with the collic wednesday morning. I could not get off of my bed that day without fainting. I am now so that I can walk around some but I am very weak yet I think I shall soon be all right again.

pleas excuse this writing for I can scarcly hold my pen. my hand trembles so and allso from writing much.

Mary there will be no use of people looking for the tenth to come home before their times are out. we have all given up the idea of it. I suppose that those that have returned home have some big stories to tell of the trials & hardships that they have endured while they wer here. I suppose they have.

I hope by the time you answer this to be able to write something better than this. I must close with the hope of hearing from you soon.

I am as ever your most Humble Servant

J. G. Matteson

[Justus encloses the following poem about Kilpatrick's cavalry brigade at the time the 10th New York was a part of it.]

KILPATRICK'S OLD BRIGADE
AIR- "Louisiana Low Lands."
BY SMOOTH BORE, OF THE FIRST MAINE.

Come listen all you Cavaliers, a song to you I'll sing,
Feeling quite sure that you'll admit 'tis just about the thing.
'Tis of a visit to Secesh by General Stoneman made,
And of the gallant deeds done by *Kilpatrick's Old Brigade*
    In the old Virginia low lands, low lands, low lands,
    In the old Virginia low lands, low.

When Fighting Joseph got his programme well laid out
He set old General Stoneman and Kilpatrick on the route.
As soon as kil had got the key he opened wide th door,
And not only rushed his brigade in, but let in Stoneman's Corps
    Into the old Virginia low lands, low lands, low lands,
    Into the old Virginia low lands, low.

We massed our gallant forces, and depending on our swords,
We crossed the Rappahannock at two, three different fords.
General Averill, at Culpepper, engaged the rebels man to man
While the rest of us "got up and got" across the Rapidan
    Into the old Virginia low lands, low lands, low lands,
    Into the old Virginia low lands, low.

They dealt their choice refreshments out to our *mudsil cavaliers*,
Thinking they were entertaining their own Southern Knights and peers;
But they were not slow in finding out the Yankee trick we played,
They'd been handing out their *apple-jack to Kilpatrick's Old Brigade*
    In the old Virginia low lands, low lands, low lands,
    In the old Virginia low lands, low.

At Gordonsville we punched their ribs for reasons plain to see,
About this time the most of us were in rear of General Lee.
Now that the pot was boiling well from the fire that we made,
We kept on feeding fuel out from *Kilpatrick's Old Brigade*
      In the old Virginia low lands, low lands, low lands,
      In the old Virginia low lands, low.

We destroyed all their railroads and their provisions too.
And from being everywhere at once the Rebels thought we flew.
The chivalry, so frightened got, with one accord, they said
That they rather see the devil than *Kilpatrick's Old Brigade*
      In the old Virginia low lands, low lands, low lands,
      In the old Virginia low lands, low.

We next looked into Richmond to see what might be there,
We created a sensation in the Rebel-*lion's* lair.
They turned out all their jail-birds- armed to resist the raid,
But in face of them *Kilpatrick* took their F. F. V. Brigade
      In the old Virginia low lands, low lands, low lands,
      In the old Virginia low lands, low.

Fitzhugh Lee essayed to nab him, but it did not weigh a hair,
When he put his thumb upon the spot *Kilpatrick* was'nt there.
But lastly, at the terminus of this most successful raid,
He is right-side-up, at Yorktown, with his *famous Old Brigade*
      In the old Virginia low lands, low lands, low lands,
      In the old Virginia low lands, low.

Now all you copperheads, just heed this, my advice,
If you don't do the thing that's right you'll smell a large sized mice;
The orders you'll most likely get will be to make a raid,
Either like Vallandingham or *Kilpatrick's Old Brigade*
      In the old Dixie's low lands, low lands, low lands,
      In the old Dixie's low lands, low.

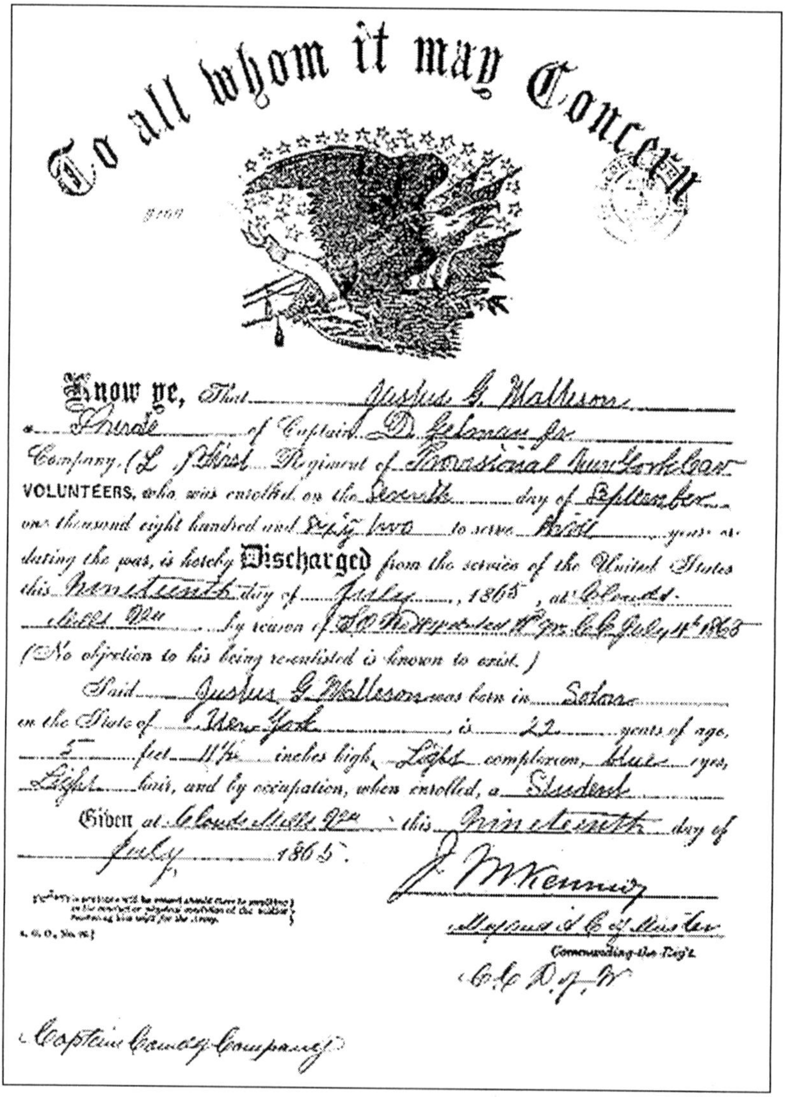
To all whom it may Concern

Know ye, That Justus G. Malleson
a Private of Captain D. [illegible] Jr
Company, (L) First Regiment of Provisional New York Cav
VOLUNTEERS, who was enrolled on the Seventh day of September
one thousand eight hundred and sixty two to serve three years or
during the war, is hereby Discharged from the service of the United States
this Nineteenth day of July, 1865, at Clouds
Mills Va by reason of [illegible] July 14th 1865
(No objection to his being reenlisted is known to exist.)

Said Justus G. Malleson was born in Solon
in the State of New York is 22 years of age,
5 feet 11½ inches high, Light complexion, blue eyes,
Light hair, and by occupation, when enrolled, a Student

Given at Clouds Mills Va this Nineteenth day of
July 1865.

J. McKenney
Major [illegible]
Commanding the Reg't.

Captain Cavalry Company

Figure 10.3 Justus's discharge from the Union Army at Clouds Mills, VA, dated July 19, 1865

Casualties

The 10th New York suffered 537 losses during the War, including killed, wounded, and captured. Company L lost a total of 44. There were 30 members of the Regiment who died in southern prison camps, 22 of whom died in the infamous Andersonville prison camp.

Overall, the Civil War ranks as one of the most disastrous events of American history. There were 970,000 casualties in the Civil War, counting both Union and Confederate sides, and including battle deaths, prison deaths and non-mortal woundings. This is almost as large as the total for our worst war, World War II (1,078,000 casualties), but the population was much smaller during the Civil War - 34 million versus 134 million at the beginning of World War II [3].

Union forces lost 110,000 killed in battle, 249,000 other deaths due to disease, prison deaths, etc., and 275,000 wounded (non-mortal), for total losses of 634,000. Confederate forces lost 75,000 killed in battle, 124,000 other deaths, and 137,000 wounded, for a total of 336,000

The World War II casualties are divided among 292,000 battle deaths, 115,000 other deaths, and 671,000 wounded. Table 10.1 compares the casualties for the five worst American wars in terms of casualties. The Civil War ranks near the top, with World War II being the highest.

War	Battle Deaths	Other Deaths	Wounded	Total
Civil War	185,000	373,000	412,000	970,000
WWI	54,000	63,000	204,000	321,000
WWII	292,000	115,000	671,000	1,078,000
Korea	34,000	21,000	103,000	157,000
Viet Nam	47,000	11,000	153,000	211,000

Table 10.1 Casualties during five major U.S. wars

Conclusion

Justus settled down to a civilian life after the War, probably going back to the farm for a while to help the rest of the family. We know that he lived in Marathon for a while, before moving to Syracuse. Mary also lived in Marathon before they were married, and Justus visited her there from his home in Solon.

Figure 10.4 shows the medal that Justus owned as a member of the Grand Army of the Republic (GAR), an organization of Union veterans who survived the Civil War. The inscription on the medal reads "Grand Army of the Republic 1861-Veteran-1866".

Figure 10.4 Justus Matteson's GAR Medal

Figure 10.5 shows the saber carried by Justus during his tour of duty.

Figure 10.5 Cavalry sword carried in the war by Justus

Figures 10.6 and 10.7 show photos of Justus and Mary when they were each 43 years of age. After the photos are more letters from the post-war period, giving some insight into how people were coping with life at that time. They also show the growing relationship between Justus and Mary, who were married on July 4, 1868.

Figure 10.6 Justus G. Matteson, age 43

Figure 10.7 Mary Hatch Matteson, age 43

(to Mary and Frank Hatch from cousin E.W. McDonald)

Fort Wayne Jan 27th, 1867

Dear Cousins[1];

Yours of "long time ago" has been sadly neglected. utter neglect, nothing more nor less, for I have had plenty of time and spare moments to have written you dozens of letters ere this. therefore I have no excuses to offer. though a certain correspondent of mine says that I always have a full supply of these on hand. be that as it may however, I think I have acquired the name of being uterably punctual with my friends.

Surely you were very unfortunate after you left our house, but variety is the spice of life you know. and had not something of this sort occurred to mar the pleasure of your trip you might possibly forget in the years to come many of the minor specialities of what we can do out West.

I believe that we are proverbial as being a set of pick-pockets. at least the little I have traveled has posted me in the knowledge that however small the station may be along the road, you are sure to see the never failing caution "Beware of Pickpockets!" However, I dispute the truthfulness of any proverb of this kind.

We have been enjoying a regular "down east" winter for about a month. have got the finest kind of sleighing. nice steady weather. none of your ups and downs, but one of the winters that our grandparents used to talk about. Times are awful dull though, scarcely any money afloat. which is the one thing needfull you know to keep body and soul to gether.

I saw Cousin Oscar Hatch the other day. He looks robust and Healthy.

The folks in Scipio were well as usual. No very great change has yet taken place in mothers affairs. Her case has been called in court. Father, contrary to all promises, has come out in opposition to the divorce. Of course he can avail nothing but a prolongation, and delay. this has always been his game in law.

I am still in the Treasurers Office. Burt is in the same old place, where he must remain if it is possible to keep him there, since he loves it so much. Our folks are all well. in fact have enjoyed better health this winter than ever before.

Write soon.
Your Cousin
E. W. McDonald

1. Frank and Mary Hatch (brother and sister)

Friend Mary,

I rec'd your letter last friday evening. on opening it I was somewhat surprised to find from whence it came- surprised I say for I supposed that you had long since forgotten me. I am glad to find that such is not the case.

I am happy to hear from you again, my friend. we have termed each other friends and yet it appears to me that we have not been to each other what friends should be.

I presume you looked for me there to day. if so I am sorry you wer disappointed.

It was not convenient for me to comply with your wish to day. but one week from to day with your permition I will call upon you.

Excuse hast etc.

Yours,
J. G. M.

P.S. Write soon so that I may know whether to come or not.

J. G. M.

November 5th, 1867
Marathon, N. Y.

Friend J.

Your note is at hand. I shall be happy to see you here next sabath at any time that it will be convenient for you to come as I shall be at home all day. Jut I am realy glad that you did not come last week for we had company. I will tell you who when I see you which will be soon.

We are having a plesant day for election. I have been so buisey that I have not had time to write so you will excuse mistakes.

Molly

Fort Wayne
Nov 24th, 1867

Dear Cousin,

There seems to always be a heavy cloud of indebtedness hanging over my head whenever an unanswered letter is "laying around loose." But I can hardly justify myself in thinking "thusly" over your letter. Why? do you ask. Simply because you have treated mine with such <u>profound</u> indifference. However, I will excuse you this time since you have offered sufficient apology & reasons for not complying before. I wish to goodness that I could offer the same excuse and keep you waiting for a <u>short</u> time. May-be, though it would be no very severe punishment after all. But on the other hand I rather anticipate that you would be delighted not to be bored with my dull and prosy offerings quite so often and effectually as you are.

You wish to know if father is still in Ft. Wayne. No. He has gone to dwell in mansions prepared for him above, where reformation is complete and everlasting. He died the 12th of August last, from the effects of an attack of flu brought on no doubt by negligence & want of care in diet & drink. I was with him during his last moments & often during his sickness. What a wreck was there. that an iron constitution broken. What a mind destroyed. What happiness wrecked & all accomplished by that fell destroyer <u>Intemperance</u>!

The property of course is left us but we find it very much encumbered. and in such a way that it keeps my keenest wits at work in order to stay the Sheriffs hammer from it.

We, too, are enjoying most beautiful weather with prospect of rain very soon. which will be very acceptible inasmuch as we have'nt had rain, a heavy one, since last <u>June</u>. If winter should close in on me while we are in the present condition, there would be much suffering, especially among people far from living streams of water. Your visit has lent a pleasant remembrance and we hope it may be soon repeated.

De-Ette is growing quite fast and loves the open air, which is good for health and lungs, you know. Much better in my opinion than too many books & consumption. Burt is "still progressing, still achieving", & no doubt would be <u>very happy</u> to extract that tooth for you.

Mother is still the patient, trustful, good soul, and I the last, the least am first as bad as ever, but am happy to sign myself your cousin etc.

E. W. McDonald.
All send love Solon
Nov 25, 1867

398

Friend Mary,

Ever anxious to correspond with you, I most pleasurably embrace an opportunity which now presents itself of sending you a letter.

To receive a letter from you, ever conveyed the purest feeling of unaffected happiness, to my bosom, when we wer so widely separated, you may, therefore, easily imagine how greatful I should be to hear from you as of old.

I intended to have written to you before this. and as I have no reasonable excuse to make, I shall expect a reprimand in your next.

Mary, I did not get tipped into the river a coming home the other night. I got home about half past one AM. Adelia has been at me ever since to find out where I went that day. do not think she will find out soon.

Our Literary Society has commenced at the old school-house again this winter. had a debate last thursday evening. are to have another this week thursday.

Hiram Rawley is teacher here this winter.

Bordett Peck was brought from Canada and buried here last week.

Mary it is getting late in the evening and I must close. hoping that this may find you as well as it leaves me.

Begging that you will accept my cordial assurances of esteem and respect.

I am,
Yours with the greatest respect,
J. G. Matteson

P. S.
Write as soon as convenient.

(to Justus from Mary)

December 1st, 1867
Marathon, Cortland Co., N.Y.

As I have just finished writing one letter my eyes rest on another one that should be answered this eve. do you ever write letters sundays? I hope not for I do not think it a very good plan, but somehow mine are mostly writen then.

I have just returned from temperance meeting. this eve we had a very good one such that I could tell you all that he sayed, or in other words wish that you had been here. Mr. Gates from Whitney Point spoke to us on temperance.

Jut, how did you spend thanksgiving day? Was not I a good girl to shut up the stove and go to church?

I did not expect that you fell in the river going home for if you had you would have floated down here before this.

I shall not scold you one word for not writing sooner, for it was very exceptable when it did come. I am allways glad to hear from friends whether far or near. it seems like a long road down here to you but it is a very short one to me. the road seems short to me when I am going to see those that are very neer to me. remember it is my home for it is no home here, only a stopping place. I do not love to live here well enough to call it home, allthough it is a good buisness place.

I had heard of the death of our friend Berdett. it is sad to think that he is no more. only a few months ago I met him as well as usual. bade him good bye little thinking that it would be the last. but such is life. how little we know. how soon it will be said of us that we are no more.

Your Literary society - how I wish that I could step in some evening and enjoy it. I think it is a good thing. hope that you will enjoy it very much.

Excuse me for writing such a lengthy note. You will have to sit up all night to read it it is so poorly written.

Did you know that winter had come and that I nearly froze coming from church this evening? are you not sorry?

Jut- How many times have I writen that word, do you know? if so please inform me. I know that I have writen it so many times that have not forgotten how to write it now. but no more at present.

remember me as thy friend and write when convenient
Molly

(continued) Monday morning,

Jut, we have got snow enough to go a sleighing and still it snows. Hope that you will have plesant weather to go to Elmira the 12th and have a good time. you must tell me all about it.

M

Hoping to hear from you soon I remain your friend-
Mary L H

My Friend Mary,

As I have some leisure time, I will write you a few lines.

I rec'd your note as you are well aware. but through neglect and the want of time, have failed to answer it, untill the present time.

I am well, and all of our friends in this place, as far as heard from. may this allso find you enjoying the same. (health)

This is a lonely day for me. and yet, how many there are, that rejoice to see this day, on account of the scarcity of water.

I fear me that we are destined to loose our sleighing, from the appearance of the weather to day, if it is to be so. how are your Holydays.

By the way, Mary, I wish you a merry Christmas.

Oh: I did not hire out to Uncle when I was down there, but he has since sent me word that he wants me this winter and probably next season.

I am going down to see him this week.

We are haveing good times at our Debating schools. I was over East to one last evening. it was their first, and a good one.

Wish you had of been here last week one evening. Adelia had a quilting, and in the evening the young folks turned out en mass.

A few nights after Willard Benjamin had a party. got acquainted with his wife.

I should take her to be a fine woman.

But this will not interest you I think, so I will be brief. J. C. is calling me to supper. Excuse this and remember me as your friend.

J. G. Matteson
Solon Dec 22nd '67

**Figure 10.8 Handwriting of letter from
Justus to Mary, dated December 22, 1867**

December 24th 1867
Homer, Cortland Co. N.Y.

Friend J.,

Your note was fetched to me this evening just as I was starting for the Christmas table to the Baptist church. we have had a very pleasant evening and I have enjoyed it very much to see the children so pleased. the house was full and running over but I guess there would have been some for you if you had come. You wish me Merry Christmas just in time. I will return the Complement and wish you a Happy Happy New Years. It is always a sad thought to think that another year has passed away and how many of our friends pass away with the year.

You speak of the 22nd being a lonely day. I did not know as you ever saw a lonely day or hour. I am glad that there is one besides myself that ever gets lonesome, but I was not lonesome on that day, for I went to church all day and in the evening.

The Debating schools I should like to attend very much, but do not expect to. Oh! I was up home a week ago last sunday. did not get started untill after noon so I did not get down to McGrawville as I expected.

I should like to know how many Uncles you had if you call Mr. Grant Uncle. I call him Uncle Miner but did not know that he allowed everyone to call him so. he is quite sick now so that he does not leave his room. Hope that you will hurry and get down here. perhaps that you will come over this side of the river once a year. shall be happy to see you.

Jut, I shall not make one excuse about this writing, for it is later than I jeneraly sit up to write. When you come down to see Uncle I shall expect a call. Jut, less call him father instead of Uncle. i will try my best if you will. what say you to that. (dont laugh at that.) but go for it.

Molly

Please except this token of remembrance from a friend as a Christmas present.

M

Dear Mary,

As it is so that I cannot call upon you this eve, I am going to try this silent method (by writing) to convey my humble thoughts unto thee.

It seems like an age since I last saw you. and yet, tis but a week. if you stay those three weeks out as you said, I do not know what I shall do, or what will become of me by that time.

my Love, how I wish that you wer here this eve, that I must enjoy your company as heretofore.

Mary, I shall not be able to be with you next sabath unless something more than I know of should turn up. and I pray that something will turn up.

May this find you in good health and enjoying yourself.

my cold isnt much better yet. my arm has got the jumps but-stopp- I know it is Dagert a snoreing, but I thought it was mothers old spinning wheel.

I shall have to hurry up if I get this in the office to night. and another thing is my ink is about played out.

Mary, come to think the thing up, if Uncle goes home saterday I will try and come up. but you must not look for me untill I come. I suppose that I shall find you at G. Whites if I come.

Pleas excuse this for it is written in hast.

Yours truly
JGM

PS. A kiss for thee upon this correspondence.

March 8th 1868
Solon, N.Y.
Sunday morning

My Friend,

Once more I sit down to find a few stray thoughts to thee. the first thing that I shall say is that you are a naughty boy because you have not been up to see me. the next one is that you are not to blame for I know that you would come if you could. how much I would see you can not be put down on this paper, but I am confident that you know that there is none on this wide world that fills such a large shair of my heart as thou hast for years. Jut I received your kind and welcomed letter March 5 and was very glad to hear from you. but so sorry that your cold was no better. mine has nearly left me now, but had not hardly been out of the house since I came here. what cold weather we have had. I never saw the snow deeper. It made me homesick and rather lonesome to see the snow so deep. I did not know as I should ever get back to Marathon again if it kept on snowing. I have enjoyed myself the best that I could and think, on considering the weather, that I have had a very good time. but have not had any warm shugar yet and do not expect to have any this spring fer the woods are full of snow. they had the last debating school over to our school house last Satterday night. they have not had any here for a number of weeks. I have not been over to our part of Solon, and do not think I shall get there this time, for I am going to get back home sometime this week, unless something happens that I do not know of now. I thought that you would be up with Mr. Grant yesterday, but he went past here Friday, so I know that he would stay over Sunday. I should have written before, but know that it would not get to Marathon.

You will excuse this half sheet of paper, for it is all I have got. we had company ysterday and evening Mr. Miller White and wife, Mr. Colell and wife. if you had been here our company would have been complete, but there was one missing, but they all enjoyed themselves first-rate, and they thought I did, so it was just as well. Miller fetched me your letter and they were bound to read it, but did not make out. it is a lovely morning. I have heard the birds singing this morning for the first time, and it reminds me how fast time is passing away. Mr. Peck and I am going to Solon to Laymans this afternoon. I expect that you will be a good boy, as you always are, only when you are plezing me, and go to church. I have not been onely once since I came here but I must close this scribling for it will take you a long time to read it. excuse mistakes and remember me as your best friend,

Molly Hatch

Justus, Mary and Their Descendants

Justus and Mary were married on July 4, 1868, and son Frank Leroy was born on March 22, 1870. Justus and Mary moved to Syracuse, NY after they were married. He was a carpenter and joiner by trade, and among other projects he did much of the wood trim on the interior of the "Yates Castle" building of Syracuse University, working on the ornate staircases in that building. In 1907 he applied for 160 acres of land in the state of Nebraska under the Homestead Act (See Figure 10.9). He never went there, however, raising his son Frank and two daughters Maude and Alta in Syracuse.

Frank married Kittie Sacket, was a grocer in Syracuse, and raised one child, a son Reginald (father of this author). Frank was active in the Masonic Temple, becoming Noble Grand Master in Syracuse in 1907. Reginald practiced as an Osteopathic Physician in Syracuse before retiring in 1972. He was married to Helen Paddock of Ilion, and they had four children - Reginald Jr, Ronald, Bonnie and Mary. Reginald Jr. died in infancy of polio.

Maude Matteson married Austin Burdick, and had one daughter Alta. Alta Burdick married Floyd Goodnough, and had one daughter, Joanne Goodnough Jones. Alta Matteson married Will Harris, and they had no children.

Ronald, Bonnie, Mary and Joanne are the great-grandchildren of Justus and Mary. From there on down things get out of control. I have at least a dozen grandchildren and a couple great-grandchildren. My two sisters each have children and grandchildren. My cousin Joanne, the fourth of the Justus and Mary great-grandchildren, has children and grandchildren, and maybe even great-grandchildren by now. I'm afraid that I have lost count of them.

No one in the Justus and Mary family can list all the descendants, or even come up with an exact number. I can't compute any farther down than Justus' and Mary's great-grandchildren. I may not be able to name you all, but you know who you are. If you have read this book I hope that you have enjoyed learning about your ancestor. In the process I hope that you have also learned some about one of the major periods of American history.

**Figure 10.9 Justus's application for land in
Nebraska under the Homestead Act**

References

[1] Preston, Noble D., *History of the Tenth Regiment New York Volunteer Cavalry*, New York, NY: D. Appleton and Company, 1892; reprinted by Higginson Book Company, Salem, MA in 1998; p. 262.

[2] Ibid, 263.

[3] Louisiana State University, Civil War Center, http://www.cwc.lsu.edu/other/stats/warcost.htm.

APPENDIX
Company L Roster of Privates
as Mustered, October 21, 1862

Avery, Samuel R.	Craft, Jackson	Morse, William P.
Albro, David J.	Dexter, Clark L.	Newcomb, Franklin T.
Albro, Ezra J.	Dexter, Bela A.	Ostrander, Silas
Albro, George W.	Edwards, David, Jr.	Overacker, James S.
Albro, Philan R.	Egbertson, Orange	Parker, Edward M.
Arnold, John	Ellsworth, Edman	Parslow, Uriah
Babcock, Myron	Ellwood, George W.	Patchin, Edward A.
Bacon, James M.	Faritor, John	Pearsons, Kimble
Bacon, Lester	Fougerty, John	Phelps, Cicero C.
Beaumont, George P.	Frye, Joel, E.	Phillips, Romanzo M.
Beaumont, William	Gard, Samuel D.	Reynolds, Andrew E.
Beebe, Mordaunt M.	Ginn, Andrew	Richardson, Jonathan
Bennett, Thomas	Hartman, Robert	Robertson, Charles W.
Bliss, Alonzo O.	Hicks, Horatio G.	Robertson, Solomon
Brown, Asa L.	Hinman, John W.	Rockwell, Garrett P.
Brown, Daniel.	Homer, Cortland H.	Rourke, Peter
Brown, James B.	Kinney, Chester E.	Rudd, George W.
Brown. Milford M.	Lane, Samuel M.	Sergent, John
Chileott, Lewis	Madole, John J.	Sessions, Charles C.
Clark, George W.	Mathews, Joseph F.	Thurston, Henry C.
Cobb, William	Matteson, Justus G.	Tillinghast, Frederick
Colburn, Eugene A.	Morell, Samuel D.	Van Brocklin, Eric O.
Cowlan, Edward	Morgan, John	Wanzo, Henry
Warfield, Dennis B.	Washburn, Nelson	Wolcutt, John
Warner, Daniel	Watson, Robert	Wood, Neville P.
Warner, Joseph B.	Wiles, Clifton W.	Wright, Elias

BIBLIOGRAPHY

Books

1. Bonnell, Jr., John C., *Sabres in the Shenandoah, The 21st New York Cavalry*, Shippensburg, PA: Burd Street Press, 1996.

2. Calkins, Chris M., *The Appomattox Campaign*, PA: Combined Books, 1997 (237 pgs.).

3. Catton, Bruce, *Never Call Retreat*, Garden City, NY: Doubleday & Co., Inc., 1965.

4. Chamberlain, Joshua Lawrence, *The Passing of the Armies*, reprinted in NY: Bantam Books, 1993.

5. Martin, Samuel J., *The Life of Union General Hugh Judson Kilpatrick*, Mechanicsburg, PA: Stackpole Books, 2000 (325 pgs.).

6. Dickson, Keith D., *The Civil War for Dummies*, Indianapolis, IN: Wiley Publishing, Inc., 2001 (384 pgs.).

7. Phisterer, Frederick, *New York in the war of the Rebellion, 1861-1865*, 3rd Ed., 5 volumes + index (Albany, NY: J.B. Lyon Company, 1912).

8. Preston, Noble D., *History of the Tenth New York Volunteer Cavalry*, New York, NY: D. Appleton and Company, 1892; reprinted by Higginson Book Company, Salem, MA in 1998 (710 pgs.).

9. Preston, Noble D., "Historical Sketch of the 10th Cavalry", in *Final Report on the Battlefield of Gettysburg (New York at Gettysburg)* by the New York Monuments Commission for the Battlefields of Gettysburg and Chattanooga. Albany, NY: J.B. Lyon Company, 1902.

10. Rummel III, George A., *72 Days at Gettysburg, Organization of the 10th Regiment, New York Volunteer Cavalry*, Shippensburg, PA: White Mane Publishing Co., Inc., 1997 (254 pgs.).

11. Tenth New York Cavalry, *Dedication of Battle Monument and Annual Reunion of the Tenth New York Cavalry Veterans Association (Porter Guard Cavalry), at Gettysburg, Pennsylvania, October 9 and 10, 1888*. Cortland, NY: 1889.

12. Thomason, John W., Jr., *Jeb Stuart*, Originally published in 1939; Bison Book Edition, 1994 (513 pgs.).

13. Walter, John F., *"Tenth New York Cavalry"*, ©April, 1988, Rev. May, 1996, Middle Village, NY.

Web Sites

1. 10th NY Cavalry Regiment during the Civil War- NY Museum and Veterans Research Center,
http://www.dmna.state.ny.us/historic/reghist/civil/cavalry/10thCav/10thCavMain.htm

2. 10th New York Volunteer Cavalry,
http://www.ggw.org/users/nycav/index.htm
(Created by the author of this book.)

3. Conserving New York State Battle flags - NY Museum and Veterans Research Center,
http://www.dmna.state.ny.us/historic/btlflags/conservation/conservationIndex.htm

4. Alfred Pleasonton's report of the Battle of Brandy Station (Fleetwood)
http://www.swcivilwar.com/PleasantonReportBrandyStation.html

5. The American Civil War Home Page,
http://www.civilwarhome.com/

6. The Civil War Archive, History - New York Cavalry,
http://www.civilwararchive.com/unreghst/unnycav2.htm#10th

7. The Civil War Archives Home Page,
http://www.civilwararchive.com/

8. Civil War Battles,
http://www.civilwarhome.com/cwinfo2.htm#battles

9. Civil War Battles and Charges,
http://www.civilwarhome.com/cavalrybattles.htm

10. Civil War Cavalry (Evolution and Influence)
http://www.civilwarhome.com/civilwarcavalry.htm

11. Civil War Home Page,
http://www.civil-war.net/

12. Civil War Research at the NY Museum and
Veterans Research Center,
http://www.dmna.state.ny.us/historic/research/civilResearch.htm

13. Cyndi's List- U.S. - Civil War/War for Southern Independence,
http://www.cyndislist.com/cw.htm

14. Gen. David McMurtrie Gregg,
http://www.geocities.com/Heartland/Hills/7117/GenGregg.html

15. Index of Civil War Information available on the Internet,
http://www.civilwarhome.com/indexcivilwarinfo.htm

16. Historical Sketch, 10th US Cavalry during the Civil War,
http://www.dmna.state.ny.us/historic/reghist/civil/cavalry/10thCav/
10thCavHistSketch.htm

17. LSU Libraries Special Collections -
The United States Civil War Center, http://www.cwc.lsu.edu/

18. National Park Service- Civil War by Campaign,
http://www.cr.nps.gov/hps/abpp/battles/bycampgn.htm

19. New York State and the Civil War,
http://library.morrisville.edu/local_history/sites/

20. White Oak Museum,
http://mywebpage.netscape.com/whiteoakmuseum/Main.html

ABOUT THE AUTHOR

Ron Matteson started his technical education by enrolling in the engineering program at Syracuse University at the age of 16, intending to major in Chemical Engineering. After one year, however, he enlisted in the Navy near the end of WWII. He went through the Navy AETM (Aviation Electronics Technician Mate) program, serving at the Pt. Mugu missile testing center in California. After returning to SU he majored in electrical engineering due to his electronics training in the Navy. In his last two years at SU he was in the Army ROTC program, receiving a reserve commission as a second lieutenant in the Army Signal Corps. After a year working as an engineer on television studio systems he was called on active duty in the Army to serve during the Korean War. After serving for almost two years in the Army demonstrating the applications of tactical television to various Army organizations, the Korean War ended, and he was released from active duty. He spent the next 17 years at General Dynamics Electronics Division doing research, design, and management of military data communications projects. During this period he received the MSEE degree from the University of Rochester, and a PhD in electrical engineering from Syracuse University.

He then worked at Xerox for 17 years on document processing systems, doing research and development on various areas of document scanning. After an early retirement from Xerox, he became a professor in the Computer Engineering Department at Rochester Institute of Technology, teaching data communications, document image processing, computer architecture and mathematics for 10 years to undergraduate and graduate students.

Dr. Matteson wrote a textbook on document image processing, and a practical book about scanning for the small office and home office. He has also published two editions of his book "Justus in the Civil War" containing letters between his great-grandfather and his great-grandfather's fiancé written during the Civil War. The letters in those books have been included in this book.

To summarize, he has been a student, sailor, soldier, engineer, researcher, inventor, teacher and author. He is a licensed Professional Engineer in the State of New York and has been chairman of a local

Rochester computer users group, a non-profit computer organization for the education of the public in computer operation and application. He also founded the special interest group on digital photography and scanning. He is a Senior Life member of the Institute of Electrical and Electronic Engineers and an active member of the Browncroft Community Church in Penfield, NY.

INDEX

Waters, Alvah, 7, 139, 143
Waynesboro, PA, 137
Weaponry, 43
Weed, Theodore, 220
Weldon Railroad, 287, 296, 298, 302, 319, 323, 332
Westminster, MD, 113
White Chimneys, 246
White Hall, 186, 191
White House, 243, 251, 270, 272, 273
White House Landing, 243, 275
White Oak Church, 32

White Oak Civil War Museum, 42, 44
White Oak Road, 345
Wilcox's Landing, 280
Wilderness, 84, 225
Wilson, James, 209, 212, 222
Winchester Turnpike, 143
Winter Camp, 40, 47
Wolf's Hill, 130, 131
Wyndham, Percy, 94, 101
Yellow Tavern, 236, 237
York Turnpike, 130
Yorktown, 91